A Kiss of Rocking Horses

A Directory of British

Rocking Horse Makers

(Pre 1950)

[signature: David Kiss]

by

David Kiss

To Noreen

First published 2008 by The Rocking Horse Workshop
1, Drayton Road, Hodnet. Shropshire, TF9 3NF

ISBN 978 0 9560326 0 7

Printed by Livesey Ltd. Shrewsbury.

Contents.

Abbott, Bonner & Co.   - 1899 -

Address: 320, Euston Road, London, NW.

See also: Pegram, Henry.   Bonner, George.

The company ' Abbot, Bonner & Co.', appears to continue on from the previous association of 'Pegram, Bonner & Co.' where Abbott seems to have taken the place of Pegram in a partnership of the ongoing business at around 1899.

There are two directory entries for 1899 as **Rocking Horse Makers** and also life size model horse makers.

Abbott, Bonner & Co. Rocking horse makers, 320 Euston Rd. NW

Abbott, Bonner & Co. (late H. Pegram) estd. 50 years, 320 Euston Rd life size model horses.

The name Abbott is only found listed in 1899 , no further mention of Abbott, or the other associated names, Bonner, Pegram have been found beyond 1899.

'Life size model horses' were typically used by saddlers to display samples of their wares such as saddles, bridles etc.

Adams. Edward Goovaerts   1910

Address: 106, Shaftsbury Avenue. London. W.C.

Patent: No. 14,513 (1910)   Accepted 27th April 1911

Trade name: 'Adams Tally-Ho Horses.'

Affiliation: G&J Lines Ltd, London.

As an invention of a jockey, the 'Adam's Tally -Ho Horses' were not
only designed to be fun for the user, but more importantly to teach the
child the use of reins when driving either a pair or a team of four
horses. The frame supporting the horses was joined to a push rod, this
being attached to the child's waist by means of a strong strap. Fig.AS01
shows the drawing that accompanied the Patent specification.

Adams' Drawing 1910 Patent 14,513   Fig.AS01

Adams' Tally-Ho Horses appeared in Gamages 1913 catalogue, but also more importantly in G&J Lines Ltd List No.53 of 1914. Headed as the 'Novelty of the Season' *Fig.AS02*, they were undoubtedly manufactured by G&J Lines Ltd alongside the huge range of their own designs.

THE NOVELTY OF THE SEASON.

PROVISIONAL PATENT № 14513/10.

As above **36 –** each.

From G&J Lines Ltd 1914 Catalogue   Fig.AS02

The horses were described as *"splendidly finished in dapple grey or chestnut, and nicely harnessed in calf leather. Rubber-tyred wheels are fitted, and a strong strap is placed ready for attaching the propeller-crossbar to the child's waist"*.

They were available either per pair or team of four. A few examples are known to have survived, a testament to the manufacturers skill and efforts.

Ajoy Ltd.

Showroom: 24, Silk Street, Whitecross St. London. EC
Works: Keen's Yard, St Pauls Rd, Highbury. London. N1
Registered Office: 28, Budge Row, Cannon St, London. EC4

The company 'Ajoy Ltd' was registered on January 23rd 1920, however, an advert from January 1920, states that they were 'Re-constructed and Re-organised' *Fig.AJ01* implying their existence prior to becoming a registered company. Their products were displayed at showrooms via an agent, W Barker, at 24 Silk Street London and they also displayed their goods at the 1920 British Industries Fair. An excerpt from a description of their stand at the trade fair states, *'Conspicuous amongst the many kinds of wooden toys on this firm's stand was a big new **Rocking Horse**, the first to leave their factory.'* Various advertisements appeared throughout 1920, but the company was wound up in February 1922.

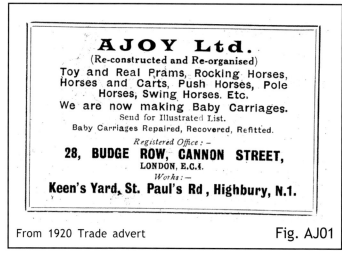

From 1920 Trade advert   Fig. AJ01

An article in a 1920 trade journal gave the following account of their products.

'All of the Toys are made from thoroughly seasoned wood, and the finish is of that quality which one usually associates with the best toys of this kind. Among the various lines is an excellent range of shaped horses. These are made by fully experienced craftsmen, and many leading buyers, have favourably commented upon their excellent finish. Another good line is a range of horses and carts, consisting of eight numbers. The horses are well made, the carts are constructed from the best quality elm, and the wheels are fitted with rubber tyres. Pole and push horses are other good lines which are offered in five sizes. We are pleased to note that Messrs. Ajoy, Ltd,. are

making a big feature of the old fashioned rocking horses. The safety rocking horses are also being made by this firm, and in both types it is notable the shapes of the horses bear the hall-mark of the best workmanship.'

Also incorporated within the article was an illustration of a swing-stand rocking horse *Fig.AJ02* which is believed to be representative of the make as this illustration has not appeared in connection with any other manufacturer.

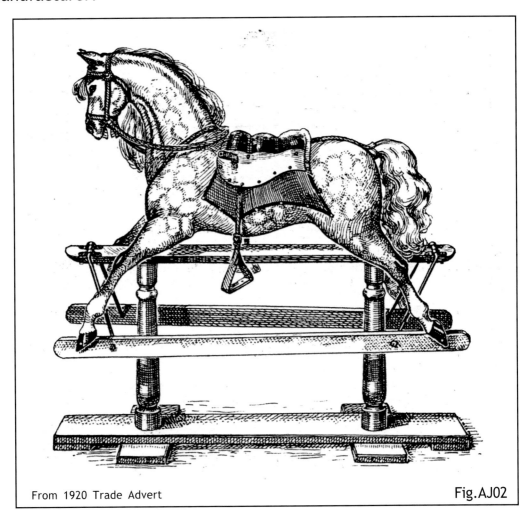

From 1920 Trade Advert   Fig.AJ02

The illustration shows a few distinctive points that may help to identify an Ajoy horse. Notably the top bar of the stand has 'sharp' ends and the posts are turned in a specific style. The saddle blanket is of an unusual design and the saddle has pommels. However, as an illustration, one should be aware of 'artistic licence' and as such, should not be taken too literally. Unfortunately, we do not have an illustration of the 'old fashioned' rocking horse, but this would refer to a **Bow Rocker**. Fig.AJ03 and Fig.AJ04 show two different swing stand horses that are thought to have been manufactured by Ajoy.

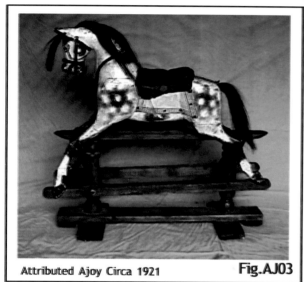

Attributed Ajoy Circa 1921   Fig.AJ03

Although there are a certain amount of differences between the two horses illustrated, Fig.AJ03 & AJ04, they have been made by the same manufacturer. Similarities in their general profile, head shape, and other aspects would confirm this. As with all makers, their horses would have differed from one to another, different craftsmen, change of raw materials, on going workshop efficiency or not,

would all play there part in the production of 'individual' horses from the same family. Besides toy horses, Ajoy produced many other items during their short life. Some of these include, toy and real prams, express carts, sand carts, sack barrows and cricket bats.

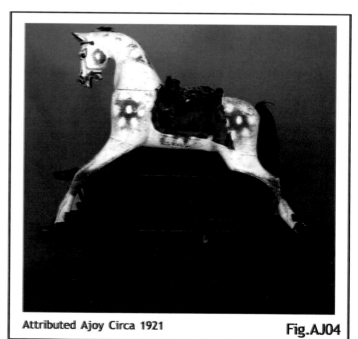

Attributed Ajoy Circa 1921   Fig.AJ04

Fig.AJ05

A visit to Keens Yard *Fig.AJ05* in 2007 revealed that all traces of the old workshops have sadly been long eradicated.

Allen, Charles & George.   1856 - 1886

Address: 4 Hackney Road, London.

See also: Allen & Co., John.   Lines, G & J.

Charles, b 1836 and George, b.1827 were the second generation of
Rocking Horse makers, children of John Allen senior. After the death
of their father in 1856, the boys, who were then 20 & 29, and already
well versed, took over the firm and were known as 'C & G Allen'. They
continued to produce rocking horses and also perambulators.

A London post office directory listed them;

1862 Charles & George Allen. Rocking Horse Makers, 4 Hackney Rd.

However, the following was reported in the London Gazette January 31
1862:
> *"Notice is hereby given, that the Copartnership hitherto
> existing between Charles Allen and George Allen, trading under the
> style or firm of C. and G. Allen, at No. 4 Hackney-road, in the parish of
> St. Leonard, Shoreditch, in the county of Middlesex, as Rocking Horse
> and Perambulator Manufacturers, is this day dissolved by mutual
> consent; and the same stands dissolved accordingly. As witness each of
> our hands hereto this 25th day of January, 1862.*
> *Charles Allen, George Allen."*

It was thought that the break up was to do with a feud over the
purchase of a family grave. Whatever the reason, Charles continued
running the firm and is listed in various London directories;

1871	Allen, Charles. Rocking Horse Maker 27 Hackney Rd.
1882	Allen, Charles. Rocking Horse Maker 27 Hackney Rd.
1884	Allen, Charles. Rocking Horse Maker 27 Hackney Rd.

Before Charles' death in 1886, his firm had become a subsidiary of

G & J Lines, who were also amongst other things, rocking horse and perambulator makers. At the time of the purchase, the firm was referred to as 'James Allen's Firm'.

Work continued at the Hackney road site up until a fire broke out, this started in the adjoining saw mill and spread to Allen's premises and was completely destroyed.

It was reported that some of the Lines children, certainly Walter, were taught how to make prams around 1896 at Allen & Co.,

Walter Lines later recounted that when he was a young lad at Allen's, they held a very large stock of wooden pram wheels fitted with iron tyres and that the wheels were beautifully made with hickory spokes. Alas these too were destroyed by the fire. At one time only wooden wheels were available for all applications and it was only later that steel-spoked wheels with rubber tyres were introduced by the firm G.H.Hughes Wheel Works of Birmingham.

By now Allens had probably become the longest and oldest established maker of perambulators, and with the association to G & J Lines, carried on to 1931. It was 114 years since John Allen set up in business in 1817 to when G &J Lines Ltd. closed down following the death of Joseph Lines on 31st December 1931.

Unfortunately, no products of the Allen's has yet been identified.

Allen & Co., John.   1817 - 1856

Address: 3, Clarence Place, Hackney Road. London.

See also: Allen, Charles & George.

John Allen was born in Lincoln around 1799, and set up in business around 1817, making him one of the earliest professional **Rocking Horse Makers** in the UK. He was also a varnish maker and children's carriage and coach maker. There are a number of London directory entries for John Allen as follows;

1839 Allen & Co, rocking-horse makrs. 3, Clarence Place, Hackney Rd.

1841 Allen John, rocking horse, &c maker.   Hackney Road.

1841 Allen John, rocking horse & child carriage ma. Hackney Road.

1852 Allen John, rocking horse ma. 3&6, Clarence Pl. Hackney Rd.

1856 Allen John, rocking horse maker. 4, Hackney Rd.

An old draft handwritten family letter by Alice Allen, (John's great grand daughter) circa 1910 states:

"John Allen was a Coach builder and Varnish manufacturer established in the year 1817. He had the honour to make the carriage for Princess Victoria, afterwards our late Queen. A copy of the carriage was printed in Lloyds Newspaper of September 20th 1896. The Duchess of Kent presented my mother's grandfather (John Allen) with a Coat of Arms, painted in oil colours and displayed on the parapet of premises known in the year 1817 as 4 Wades Place, now 27 Hackney Rd."

The story, recounted by a descendant of John Allen, is that after John's death this plaque was displayed above a furniture shop of a family relative Russell's, however, the plaque was subsequently removed after it was suggested that they were not officially entitled to display it. Further research has provided no other reference to the 'Coat of Arms', but as with all stories there is probably some element of truth. Certainly, John Allen & Co. became a well known and long established firm.

John Snr was married to Mary and they had three sons, John Jnr. George and Charles. They also had a daughter Elizabeth. Charles and George went into their father's business, John Jnr. and Elizabeth both married and went their separate ways.

By 1852 the business had expanded, as an additional address of 6 Clarence Place appears in a trade directory. John Snr died in 1856 and the two sons carried on the business as 'C & G Allen', (which is dealt with in a separate chapter).

Below is an illustration *Fig.AL01* from Lloyd's Weekly Newspaper, Sept 20th 1896, as referred to in Alice Allen's letter,showing the Princess Victoria on an outing to Kensington Park, 23rd Aug 1822.

AN EARLY OUTING OF PRINCESS VICTORIA.

From 1896 Lloyd's Weekly

Fig.AL01

Allison, John.   - 1824 - 1828 -

Address: Chalcroft Terrace, Gt Charlotte St, Blackfriars Rd, London.

Very little is known about John Allison, except that as well as being a
Rocking Horse Maker, he was also an Undertaker. Three insurance
policies have been found in relation to his property and are as follows;

23rd Dec 1824 John Allison   Policy 1023894

John Allison of W17 Chalcroft
Terrace Great Charlotte Street Blackfriars
Road, Undertaker & Rocking Horse
Manufacturer
On his household goods Wearing apparel
printed Books & plate in his now Dwel-
ling house only situate as aforesaid Brick
One hundred Pounds ------------------------   100
Stock & utensils Viz __ therein only One
hundred & fifty Pounds --------------------   150
& in Shed in Yard Brick & Timber Fifty   50
Pounds   £ 300

7th March 1826   John Allison   Policy 1043434

John Allison of W17 Chalcroft Terrace
Great Charlotte Street Blackfriars road Undertaker
Rocking Horse Maker
On his household goods wearing apparel printed
Books & plate in his now dwelling house only situate
as aforesaid Brick one hundred Pounds ------------------   100
Stock & utensils Viz __ therein only one hundred
& fifty Pounds --   150
In Shed in Yard behind Fifty pounds--------------------   50
Building of said Shed Brick & timber fifty pds   50
                                                            £ 350

30th Jan 1828 John Allison   Policy 1072306

John Allison of N19 Chalcroft Terrace
Great Charlotte Street Blackfriars Road Undertaker
& Rocking Horse Maker
On his household goods wearing apparel printed
books & plate in his now Dwelling house only situate
as aforesaid no work done therein / Brick one
hundred pounds--- 100
Stock & utensils viz : therein only two hundred pds   250
And in a Shed behind Brick & timber Fifty pds   50
Building of said Shed Fifty pounds----------------------   50
                                                    £ 450

Interestingly, in the last policy, 30th Jan 1828, it states that 'no work is done therein' which implies that he is to use that part of the premises purely as his domestic abode and not as a workshop. The 'Brick and Timber' shed in the Yard behind the property could well have been reserved for the rocking horse and undertaking business.

It should be noted that the 'bows' of a bow rocking horse are typically made from elm and elm was also commonly used in the construction of coffins. The wood was at one time available in wide width boards, a necessary requirement for both products.

Arnold, Joseph G.   - 1882 -

Address: 38, King William Street, London Bridge. E.C.

An excerpt from a Post office directory of 1882 states the following:

"Arnold Joseph G. archery, cricket, lawn tennis, nursery &
garden gymnasia & croquet warehouse & toy importer. rocking horse &
firework manufacturer(wholesale & shipping) 38 King William
street, London Bridge EC."

It would appear from this excerpt that Joseph Arnold was responsible
for a whole range of products, mainly imported, but also curiously a
manufacturer of **Rocking Horses** and fireworks, quite a combination.
With regard to his rocking horses, it is unknown what type that he
manufactured.

The swing stand rocking horse had been Patented in 1880 so he may
well have been manufacturing this or possibly the older type of 'English'
bow rocker.

As no other directory entries have been found for Joseph Arnold so one
would assume that his was a fairly short lived enterprise.

Aston (Worcester) Ltd., W. H. - 1914 -

Address: Reliance Works, James Street, Worcester.

W.H.Aston produced a variety of smaller wooden toys, which included
Beech Horses, Stool Horses, Hobby Horses and Horses and Carts.
An example of one of their beech horses can be seen in a 1914 advert
Fig.AN01

"RELIABLE BRITISH TOYS"

Beech Horses, Stool Horses, Hobby Horses, Horses
and Carts, Engines and Trucks, Barrows, Motors,
Push Chairs, Wood Hoops, Runabouts, The New Toy.

Tops and Skipping Ropes a Speciality.

W. H. ASTON, Ltd.,
RELIANCE WORKS, JAMES STREET,
— WORCESTER. —

From 1914 Trade advert

Fig.AN01

It is not known exactly when the company started or finished trading.
All adverts and trade editorial are dated 1914.
However, one point to note is that in the London Gazette of 1902
Fig.AN02 & 1903 *Fig.AN03* it was reported that a company 'W H Aston
(WORCESTER) Ltd. was advised and subsequently wound up. It is
unclear if this has any connection with the above toy making company.

In the Matter of the Companies Acts, 1862 to 1890, and
in the Matter of W. H. Aston, Worcester, Limited.
Extraordinary Resolution.
Passed 23rd July, 1902.
AT an Extraordinary General Meeting of W. H.
Aston, Worcester, Limited, duly convened, and
held at No. 9, Foregate-street, Worcester, on the 23rd
day of July, 1902, the subjoined Extraordinary
Resolution was duly passed:—
   That it has been proved to the satisfaction of this
Meeting that the Company cannot, by reason of its
liabilities, continue its business, and that it is advisable
to wind up the same, and accordingly that the Com-
pany be wound up voluntarily, and that Mr. G. W. Bull,
Accountant, Foregate-st set, Worcester, be and he is
hereby appointed Liquidator for the purposes of such
winding up.   H. A. OAINE, Chairman.

From 1902 London Gazette   Fig.AN02

W. H. ASTON (WORCESTER) Limited.
In Voluntary Liquidation.
NOTICE is hereby given, that in pursuance of section
142 of the Companies Act, 1862, a General Meeting
of the Members of the above named Company will be
held at No. 9, Foregate-street, in the city of Worcester,
on Wednesday, the 2nd day of December, 1903, at 4
o'clock in the afternoon, for the purpose of having an
account laid before them, showing the manner in which
the winding up has been conducted and the property
of the Company disposed of, and to hear any explanation
which may be given by the Liquidator; and also to pass
an Extraordinary Resolution, as to the disposal of the
books, accounts, and documents of the Company.—Dated
this 26th day of October, 1903.
·III   GEO. W. BULL, Liquidator.

From 1903 London Gazette   Fig.AN03

Ayres, F. H. 1810 - 1940

Address: 111, Aldersgate Street, London. EC
Seymour Road, Nuneaton, Warwickshire.

Incorporated: 29th Dec 1905 F H Ayres Ltd. Company No.87,040
See Also: Ayres Sports Goods Ltd.   William Sykes Ltd.

In 1810 Edward Ayres set up business as a cabinet maker in Great Bath Street, London and this was to become the beginnings of one of the most prestigious firms of rocking horse makers , F H Ayres. The initials F H stand for *Frederick Henry* and over the years there were four generations of 'F H' Ayres. The first F H Ayres, b. 1834, had eight children, not an uncommon size family at this time of high infant mortality. A wonderful letterhead of circa 1922 *Fig. AY00* confirms the early beginnings of the firm, 'Established in 1810'.

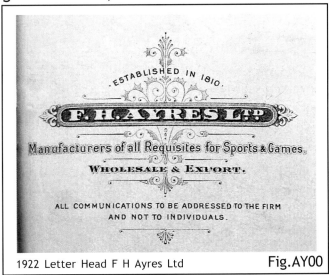

1922 Letter Head F H Ayres Ltd   Fig.AY00

In an 1841 trade directory, Thomas Ayres is also listed at 28 Great Bath Street London, as a Chess and Backgammon board maker. The Ayres name appears quite often over the years, and it is clear that it was very much a family run business. Different family members were listed under varying trades, including cabinet maker, ivory turner, lawn tennis, croquet, cricket, football, and every description of outdoor & indoor games and sports goods manufacture.

In 1864, F H Ayres registered his name as a trademark for balls and in 1885 registered his signature in full as a trademark for shuttlecocks, balls, rackets and a host of other items.

Up until the middle of the nineteenth century, Ayres had concentrated on mainly indoor goods, billiards, parlour games, toys etc. but with the advent of the popularity of outdoor games such as cricket, badminton, croquet and most importantly the game of tennis, as illustrated in their colourful adverts of the late 19c *Fig.AY02-AY04*, Ayres dramatically expanded their range. In 1875, F H Ayres moved to 111 Aldersgate Street and by 1881, 116-118 Aldersgate Street were also acquired, this expansion was greatly due to the new game of *Lawn Tennis* becoming *de rigueur* throughout the country. F H Ayres were quick to see the possibilities of producing quality items such as racquets but more importantly the introduction of the 'Championship' tennis ball. This was recognised as a market leader and gave the firm a world-wide reputation and cleared the way for a whole range of new products. These were not only for playing the game but also for the marking and setting out the court, even to the extent of 'boots' *Fig.AY01* for the horses, used in pulling rollers to level the courts. From 1880 for a further 22 years, F H Ayres supplied the All England Lawn Tennis and Croquet Club with tennis balls for the Wimbledon Championships. However, in

1902 a new Secretary was appointed to the club, and with his introduction it was decided that a new supplier should be sought and the up and coming firm of Slazenger were chosen to supply the balls from then on. Perhaps this was a pivotal moment for F H Ayres, seeing other 'younger' firms taking more and more of the market share.

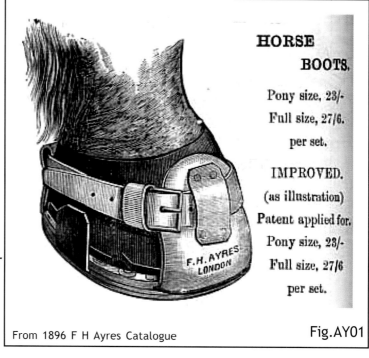

HORSE BOOTS.

Pony size, 23/-
Full size, 27/6.
per set.

IMPROVED.
(as illustration)
Patent applied for.
Pony size, 23/-
Full size, 27/6
per set.

From 1896 F H Ayres Catalogue

Fig.AY01

22

A selection of F H Ayres advertisements circa 1896 are shown below. The Croquet advert shows four people, possibly Queen Victoria and John Brown with Edward and Alexandria playing croquet at Osbourne.

1896 F H Ayres   Fig.AY02

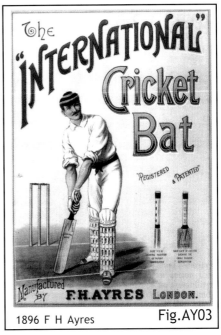

1896 F H Ayres   Fig.AY03

1896 F H Ayres   Fig.AY04

From an article in 1895 the Strand Magazine reported that

'In the vast establishment of F H Ayres, in Aldersgate St. one finds workshops covering three or four acres of priceless land, and a staff of nearly six hundred hands, who share between them in wages some £40,000 a year. The annual wood bill alone is more that £15,000.'

This gives us an insight into the scale of the firm at this time. The article goes on to mention various aspects of production of sporting goods, but no mention of rocking horses at all. This is a little curious as they were most definitely being produced at this time.

On the 29th December 1905, **F H Ayres Ltd.** (No. 87040) was formed with a nominal capital of £100,000 divided into 10,000 shares of £10 each and effectively took over the old firm which up until then had been known as F. H. & C. M. Ayres.
The shareholders at this time were;
Frederick Henry Ayres Snr., 111, Aldersgate Street. Manufacturer.
Frederick Henry Ayres Jnr., 4, Charterhouse Square. Manufacturer.
Sydney Frank Ayres, 4, Charterhouse Square. Manufacturer.
Rupert Stanley Ayres, 40, Elms Avenue. Billiard Table Manufacturer.
Clarence Montague Ayres, 4, Charterhouse Square. Manufacturer.
William Baxter Booker, 16, Godwin Road, Bromley. Commercial Clerk.
John Smith, 22, Park Avenue, Attleborough, Nuneaton. Sub Manager.

From around 1905, C.M. (Clarence Montague) Ayres lived in Nuneaton and ran the branch of the company known as C M Ayres & Co. (Late A W Philips & Co). They were listed as a 'Sports and Games Manufacturer' in various trade directories. The factory in Nuneaton was built in 1890 and situated at the end of Seymour Road,the building is still in commercial use today. A photograph *Fig.AY05* shows some of the Ayres staff preparing to take part in the 1931 carnival procession. They are gathered out side the Seymour road premises, and a more recent photograph *Fig.AY06* shows the same building, (photographed in April 2006). In the later picture, it is still possible to make out where the old Ayres sign was fixed to the front of the building.
One point of interest is that Nuneaton was regarded for its fine silk and many Ayres rocking horses have remnants of wonderful silk rosettes, perhaps these were supplied by a leading ribbon manufacturer such as Slingsby & Son.

Seymore Road premises 1931   Fig.AY05

Seymore Road premises 2006   Fig.AY06

By 1914 there were three directors of the company, Frederick (3rd), Rupert and Clarence, but around the end of 1915 Frederick had died leaving just two directors, Rupert who looked after the London part and Clarence who was in Nuneaton. In 1918, Lily Amelia, wife of Rupert became a director but was only recorded as such for 1 year up to 1919. In 1922 Frederick Henry (4th) and Stanley Stephen were listed as shareholders, but their professions were given as Farmers, they were probably the offspring of the late F H Ayres (3rd)(1915). F H Ayres(4th), farmer, was recorded as living in Kenya between 1923 and 1932 and then at an address in Somerset for a year, then to Oxford in 1933. In 1936 the business seemed to be struggling and a mortgage was taken out in early 1937 so as to inject some capital but this was to no avail. The bank obtained the appointment of a receiver, W H Cork & Co. on the 8th March 1938. In January 1940 the goodwill, trademarks and patents of F H Ayres Ltd were acquired by William Sykes Ltd, Sports and Games Manufacturers of Horbury Yorkshire. The acquired firm of F H Ayres Ltd was registered under the new title of **Ayres Sports Goods Ltd** on the 5th April 1940. The old F H Ayres Ltd. was finally wound up in 1948. Sykes were also manufactures of a wide range of sporting goods and had been established since 1866. Many of the Ayres work force stayed on and moved to Sykes' factories at Horbury, Ayres' factory having been a casualty of the blitz. However, in 1942 Slazenger acquired the share capital of the Sykes and Ayres firm to become the largest sports group in Europe with the result that the Ayres and Sykes brands were replaced by that of Slazenger. Rocking horses were still being offered in the 1949 Slazenger export list, albeit in only two versions, a painted and a skin covered option. How different things might have been if in 1902, the new club secretary of Wimbledon had not seen fit to change suppliers of the tennis balls from Ayres to Slazenger. After being in business in their own right for 130 years the name of F H Ayres will always be associated with first class quality goods, amongst which are some of the finest rocking horses ever produced.

A slogan *Fig.AY07* found on one of their products sums up the firm perfectly.

Fig AY07

   'The Best Is Good Enough'

It is unclear exactly when rocking horses were first manufactured by Ayres, certainly horses were made from circa 1880. There are hardly any directory references for Ayres producing rocking horses, which is most curious considering the range and volume of rocking horses that they had produced over the years. One small list of products *Fig.AY08* dated circa 1889 includes *'Hobby Horses, American Patent'* these being swing-stand horses and also *'Rocking Horses'* these being the older design of bow rocker. Also listed are *'Velocipede Horses'*, these are more commonly referred to as Tricycle horses. All three different types of horse were available in a variety of sizes as indicated by the price ranges on the list.

As with all of Ayres products, a large and varied range of rocking horses were available. Some of their products being well known and instantly recognisable, but many other more obscure and rarer items were also produced.

NEW PARLOUR GAMES, published by F. H. AYRES.

FANORONA.—A Game of Skill for two players, affording a great variety of combinations.— Price 1/-, 2/6.

LORIOTS, or, the DEVIL on TWO STICKS. An old Game, said to have come from China, but still fresh and amusing.— Price 2/6.

GOBANG.—A fashionable and highly interesting game of skill for two or more players.—Price 1/-, 2/6, 3/6, 4/6, 9/6, 12/6, &c.

RACE GAME.—One of the earliest of table games, but as great a favourite as ever.—Price from 6d. to 80/-.

ROULETTE GAME.—Any number of players can participate in the fun to be derived from a game that depends almost entirely on chance.—Price from 4/- to 50/-.

EXPERT ANGLER.—As the name implies, the player who is most skilful at hooking up the fish wins. A good round game.—Price 1/- to 8/6.

TABLE CROQUET.—The game of Croquet in miniature, and therefore capable of being played by any number on an ordinary dining table.—Price 1/- to 45/-.

HOBBY HORSES, American Patent.—These horses are constructed upon a novel principle, affording additional safety, security, and amusement.—Price 20/- to 85/-.

ROCKING HORSES.—Price from 16/6 to £6.

VELOCIPEDE HORSES.—Price from 36/- to 60/-.

JINRIKSHA, or JAPANESE CAR.—An elegant and serviceable little carriage for juveniles.—Price from 21/- to 30/-.

111, ALDERSGATE STREET, E.C.

F H Ayres Trade Advert c.1889   Fig.AY08

In 1897 F H Ayres' catalogue of 'Indoor and Outdoor Games & Sports' listed their entire range of horses. The **'Roadster, or Parlour Toboggan'** *Fig.AY09* was a novel idea, assuming the owner had sufficient space to operate such a device. From the catalogue description this was available in three different sizes and also intended as a form of exercise to *'promote muscular development and healthful training'*.

A photograph *Fig.AY10* taken in 1895 shows the interior of a dining room in a large country house where such a device, along with a host of other 'toys', including a large elephant, a bow rocking horse with end seats and a Punch and Judy type show tent, can all be seen.

THE ROADSTER, or PARLOUR TOBOGGAN.

PATENT.

The above consists of a Horse (constructed to seat a child) which runs upon a Track—as shown in the engraving. By the aid of a little mechanism it is made to run backwards and forwards by simply pulling the cords, enabling children or grown people to enjoy the ride. The exertion necessary to keep it in motion requires just sufficient exercise to promote muscular development and healthful training. Manufactured from the best materials, are exceedingly strong, and have been tested and proved equal to carrying a person weighing thirteen stone.

PRICES :—No. 1   31/6,   2   40/-,   3   50/-   each.

F H Ayres 1897 Catalogue   Fig.AY09

c.1895 Dining Room   Fig.AY10

The **'Alexandra Nursery Boat'** *Fig.AY11* was basically a swing stand with a double ended chair mounted on it, also listed was a version for three children, presumably the same but with a middle seat.

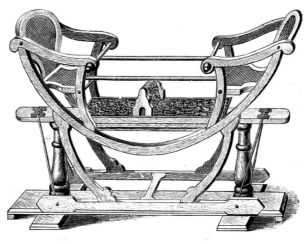

THE ALEXANDRA NURSERY BOAT.

For two children, 42/0.   For three children, 63/0.

F H Ayres 1897 Catalogue   Fig.AY11

The **'Nursery Yacht'** *Fig.AY12* was a similar device to the Alexandra Nursery Boat above, but built to be more along the lines of a bow rocker with its *free spirit* notion. The Nursery Yacht was available in various designs with the option of one or two carved horses. It is unsure how these were applied to the device.

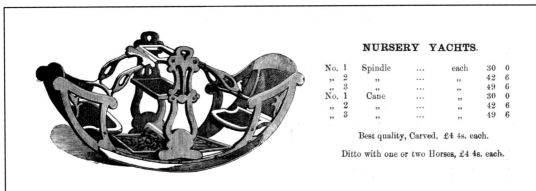

NURSERY YACHTS.

No. 1	Spindle	...	each	30	0
,, 2	,,	...	,,	42	6
,, 3	,,	...	,,	49	6
No. 1	Cane	...	,,	30	0
,, 2	,,	...	,,	42	6
,, 3	,,	...	,,	49	6

Best quality, Carved, £4 4s. each.

Ditto with one or two Horses, £4 4s. each.

F H Ayres 1897 Catalogue   Fig.AY12

The 'Merry-Go-Round' *Fig.AY13* was another variation of a theme, with a pair of carved horses instead of the usual seat arrangement. One assumes the centre post had to be buried deep in the ground so as to give the device a degree of stability.

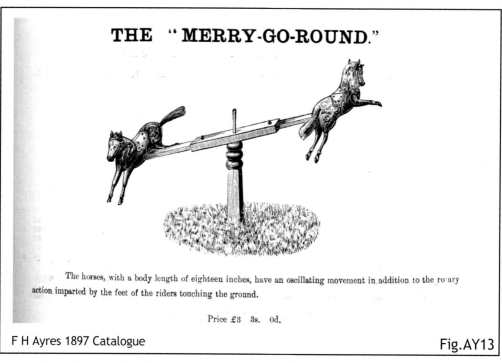

THE "MERRY-GO-ROUND."

The horses, with a body length of eighteen inches, have an oscillating movement in addition to the rotary action imparted by the feet of the riders touching the ground.

Price £3 3s. 0d.

F H Ayres 1897 Catalogue

Fig.AY13

Many smaller 'horse' related items were also produced by Ayres, such as **Painted Two-Horse Vans** in seven sizes, **White Wood Beech Horses & Carts** in nine sizes, **Cloth Donkeys on Wheels** in eight sizes, and **Hobby Horses** (stick) in seven sizes. **Beech Horses** with either pole or push handles, both in nine sizes, **Stool Horses on Castors** *Fig.AY14* in four sizes, and **Push Shaped Horses** with seat *Fig.AY15* in three sizes.

F H Ayres 1897 Catalogue   Fig.AY14

WITH SEAT.

F H Ayres 1897 Catalogue   Fig.AY15

Polished Pitch Pine Horses & Carts *Fig.AY16* in seven sizes. These were still being offered in Ayres' 1934 catalogue, although only in six sizes.

POLISHED PITCH PINE HORSES & CARTS.

F H Ayres 1897 Catalogue   Fig.AY16

Polished Birch Colonial Horses & Carts in six sizes.

Polished Pitch Pine Pair-Horse Van *Fig.AY17* in three sizes. These were still being offered in the 1934 catalogue, however, with a relative price increase from 31/6 in 1897 up to 70/- in 1934 for the largest size.

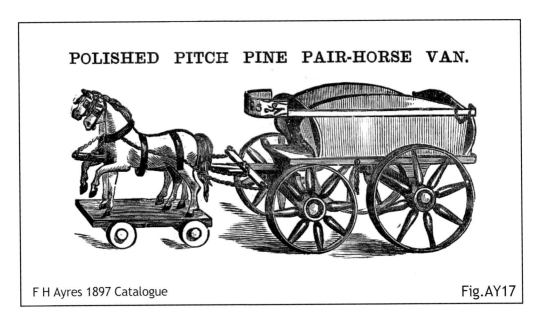

POLISHED PITCH PINE PAIR-HORSE VAN.

F H Ayres 1897 Catalogue   Fig.AY17

Painted Shaped Pole Horses with wooden wheels *Fig.AY18* available in six sizes and with bicycle-tyred wheels in three sizes. Another option

PAINTED SHAPED POLE HORSES.

F H Ayres 1897 Catalogue

Fig.AY18

for the Shaped Pole Horse was that of having it in up to 6 different sizes all 'with **Patent Movable Head**'. This was an invention that F H Ayres protected with a Patent in 1887 and he also applied this invention to his 'Velocipede' (Tricycle) Horses and the 'American Hobby or Rocking Horse'. 'Movable Head' horses will be described in full later on in the chapter.

Push Horses were also still being offered in the 1934 catalogue in various finishes (the 1939 catalogue no longer listed push horses). Three sizes were available in the more expensive 'Skin' covered option *Fig.AY19* and six sizes with painted bodies and wood wheels. A further choice of rubber-tyred wheels was available for the painted horses. Illustrated is a painted version *Fig.AY20* fitted with rubber-tyred wheels, circa 1920.

F H Ayres Ltd 1934 Catalogue   Fig.AY19

F H Ayres Ltd Push Horse circa 1920 Original Condition   Fig.AY20

In the 1934 F H Ayres Ltd catalogue, a **Combined Push & Rocking Horse** *Fig.AY21* was offered. It is not clear when these were introduced but they were not featured in 1939. The horse consisted of a stuffed body covered in an imitation skin. The horse was also available without the rocking base with or without push or pull handles, twenty options in all.

COMBINED PUSH AND ROCKING HORSES

These horses are strongly made, with well-shaped, stuffed bodies, covered with imitation skin. They are fitted with leather saddles, stirrup leathers, and irons. Each horse is mounted on a painted and varnished base, with varnished wooden wheels, bolts being provided to secure the board to the rocking base. Any of the sizes may be had without the rocking base if required. They will be found of very handsome appearance, and of excellent value.

Full height of Horse only.		Horse on stand with rocker. Each—s. d.	Horse on stand. s. d.
No. 1 (S)	15 inches	—	10 0
,, 2 (S)	19 ,,	19 6	15 0
,, 3 (S)	23 ,,	25 6	20 0
,, 4 (S)	28 ,,	35 0	27 6
,, 5 (S)	32 ,,	45 0	35 0

The above prices are for Horses without push handles, but push or pull handles can be fitted as follows:—
No. 1 .. **2s. 0d.**   No. 2 .. **2s. 6d.**   No. 3 .. **3s. 0d.**   No. 4 .. **3s. 6d.**   No. 5 .. **4s. 0d.** extra.

F H Ayres Ltd 1934 Catalogue   Fig.AY21

Another item offered in the 1934 & 1939 F H Ayres Ltd catalogues were the **Model Ponies** *Fig.AY22*. There were three sizes, all covered in real skin. The wheeled axles were fitted directly to the legs.

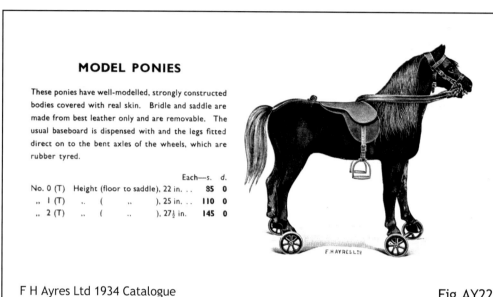

MODEL PONIES

These ponies have well-modelled, strongly constructed bodies covered with real skin. Bridle and saddle are made from best leather only and are removable. The usual baseboard is dispensed with and the legs fitted direct on to the bent axles of the wheels, which are rubber tyred.

			Each—s.	d.
No. 0 (T)	Height (floor to saddle), 22 in. ..		**85**	**0**
,, 1 (T)	,, (,,), 25 in. ..		**110**	**0**
,, 2 (T)	,, (,,), 27½ in.		**145**	**0**

F H Ayres Ltd 1934 Catalogue

Fig.AY22

Velocipede Horses *Fig.AY23* were offered in two different 'Qualities', an 'Ordinary Quality' in four sizes with wheel sizes from 12 inches up to 18 inches. Also in 'Best Quality' with 'Skeleton Wheels and India Rubber Tyres' in four sizes with wheel sizes of 14 inches up to 20 inches.
A polished metal Alarm Bell for the handle bar was also available at an extra 6d.

Very few Ayres velocipede horses are known to have survived as they were often left outside after play and did not last very long once they had got wet.

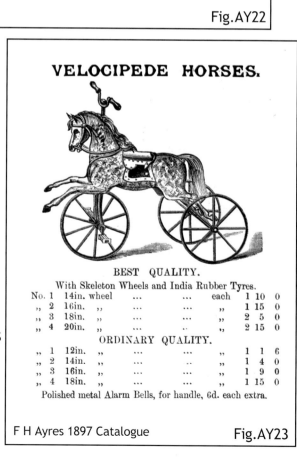

VELOCIPEDE HORSES.

BEST QUALITY.
With Skeleton Wheels and India Rubber Tyres.

No. 1	14in. wheel	...	...	each	1 10 0
,, 2	16in. ,,	...	...	,,	1 15 0
,, 3	18in. ,,	...	...	,,	2 5 0
,, 4	20in. ,,	...	..	,,	2 15 0

ORDINARY QUALITY.

,, 1	12in. ,,	...	...	,,	1 1 6
,, 2	14in. ,,	...	..	,,	1 4 0
,, 3	16in. ,,	...	...	,,	1 9 0
,, 4	18in. ,,	...	...	,,	1 15 0

Polished metal Alarm Bells, for handle, 6d. each extra.

F H Ayres 1897 Catalogue

Fig.AY23

Velocipede Horses with Patent Movable Head were available in four sizes with wheels from 14 inches to 20 inches. The colour illustration *Fig.AY24* is from a larger advert for Ayres horses and dates from around 1889. Although the picture is captioned 'Patent Movable Head', the horse does not show the leather 'flap' as it is described in the actual Patent 5395 text. An 1897 catalogue describes the movable head tricycle horse thus; *"By an ingenious pivot arrangement the horse's head is made to turn in whichever direction the rider desires to go -- another advance in the imitation of nature. They are manufactured of the best quality materials, and fitted with skeleton wheels and India rubber tyres, and in all respects a welcome present to a lad"*.

PATENT
MOVABLE HEAD

From F H Ayres Advert circa 1889   Fig.AY24

Shown below is the technical drawing for Ayres 'Patent Movable Head' *Fig.AY25* as applied to a Velocipede or Tricycle Horse. This model was

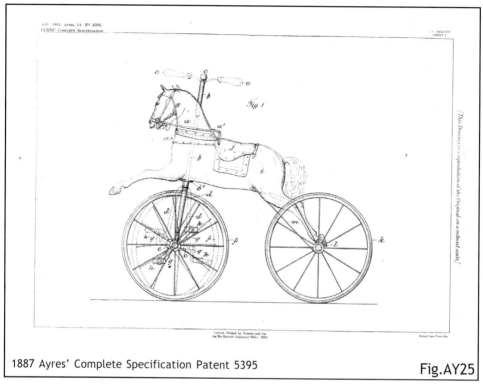

1887 Ayres' Complete Specification Patent 5395

Fig.AY25

only available in the 'best quality' as depicted in the illustration from the Ayres 1897 catalogue *Fig.AY26*.
It is unknown exactly when Ayres stopped producing the 'Movable Head' Velocipede horse but this was most likely to have been around 1900. This was generally in line with other products that had this option, as all examples of 'Movable Head' Hobby Horse date to around or before 1900. The ordinary tricycle horse was probably produced for some years after the cessation of the Movable head version. At the time of writing, no 'Movable head' velocipede horses are known to still exist.

VELOCIPEDE HORSES.

WITH PATENT MOVEABLE HEADS.

By an ingenious pivot arrangement the horse's head is made to turn in whichever direction the rider desires to go —another advance in the imitation of nature. They are manufactured of the best quality materials, and fitted with skeleton wheels and india rubber tyres, and are in all respects a welcome present to a lad.

No. 1	14in. wheel	...	...	each	1 12 6
,, 2	16in. ,,	...	...	,,	1 17 6
,, 3	18in. ,,	...	...	,,	2 8 0
,, 4	20in. ,,	...	...	,,	2 18 6

F H Ayres 1897 Catalogue

Fig.AY26

F H Ayres produced a variety of different 'models' of rocking horse and of course they were all supplied in a great choice of sizes. Some models were much more popular than others, some of them have only been seen in catalogue illustrations or advertisements. The beautifully illustrated colour advert *Fig.AY27* shows a small selection of the range of horse related items that were available at the time, circa 1889.

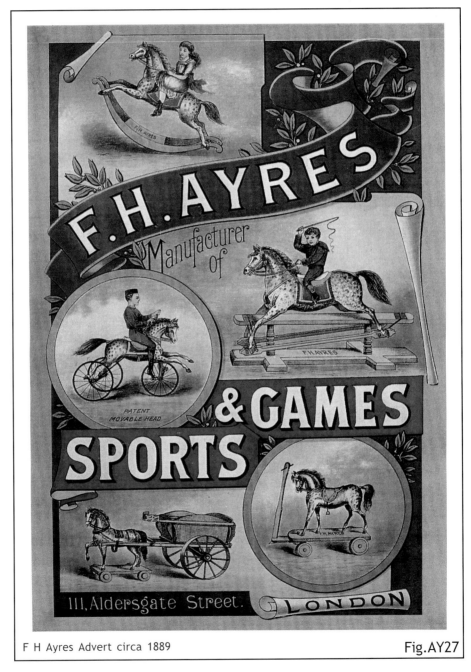

F H Ayres Advert circa 1889   Fig.AY27

The most popular of all the different types of rocking horse made by Ayres, and indeed probably of all rocking horse makers, was the design patented by the American, P Marqua, in January 1880, Patent No.395. This number is often found in the form of a stencilled label *Fig.AY28* on the base of the stand, and was thought to have been applied to some stands as late as the 1890's. Some early G&J Lines horses also have similar markings on some of their stands. This most important design is known by many different names, the swing-stand, the safety-stand, trestle rocker etc. but it was listed by F H Ayres in 1895 *Fig.AY29* as the **American Hobby** or **Rocking Horse.** America being the country where the design originated from. The 1895 listing describes the merits of this design over the old style bow rocker. The 'American Hobby' was originally offered in seven different sizes and illustrated as a dapple grey, but with no option for different qualities of finish. There were however two important extras available, firstly all sizes were available with the **Patent Movable Head,** and secondly **End Seats** could be fitted to the four largest sizes on offer. It is not clear if you could combine both of these extras, ie. a size No.7 with Movable Head and end seats. If this was the case, it would mean that from this page of the catalogue, some 22 different models of the American Hobby horse would be available. There is also a mention of 'Panniers with straps' but as there is no reference of the models they would fit, it could be assumed that they were suited to all the range. The illustration of the American Hobby horse *Fig.AY29* depicts what is now generally recognised as an 'extra carved' horse. A high quality rocking horse that at the time were fitted with pommels so that young 'ladies' could ride side saddle. The 'firmness' of the stand is referred to in the text and the illustration shows the heavy base construction, (a cross-halving type joint). These early models are rarely found. Over the years many different qualities and variations of the American Hobby were produced, but it is not known exactly when all these changes occurred. Changes were brought about by a variety of different factors such as a change of timber supplied, a new carver, a new set of more 'efficient' templates and updated manufacturing processes. Any one of these or other factors could have a profound effect on the 'look' of the end product.

1880 Patent 395 Stencil   Fig.AY28

AMERICAN HOBBY OR ROCKING HORSES.

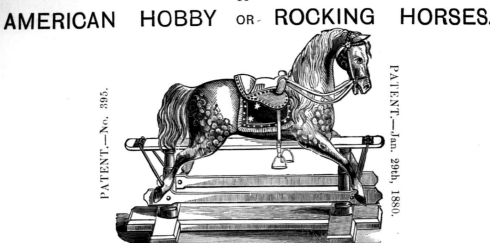

PATENT.—No. 395.

PATENT.—Jan. 29th, 1880.

These Horses are constructed upon a novel and unique principle, the chief objects attained being additional security, safety, and amusement to the rider, combined with freedom from danger to the feet of on-lookers. When in action the movement is at once graceful and natural, and its steadiness enables the rider to retain a firm seat. There is no possibility of the rider being thrown over its head or slipping off backwards. They are solidly constructed of well-selected wood and metal supports, suitably painted, and have substantial fittings. They are comparatively noiseless, the irregular thumping movement of the ordinary rocking horse, so frequently injurious to ceilings, being avoided by the firmness of the stands; whilst occupying much less space and being more portable, they will be found more suitable for the nursery.

| No. 2 | ... | 17 6 | each. | ,, 4 | ... | 24 0 | each. | No. 6 | ... | 44 0 | each. | ,, 8 | ... | 77 0 | ,, |
| ,, 3 | ... | 21 0 | ,, | ,, 5 | ... | 34 0 | ,, | ,, 7 | ... | 56 0 | ,, | | | | |

SKIN COVERED HOBBY HORSES.   No 4, 40/0 ;   5, 50/0 ;   6, 65/0 ;   7, 80/0 ;   8, 100/0

With **F. H. AYRES' PATENT MOVEABLE HEAD, 2/6** and **3/6** each extra.

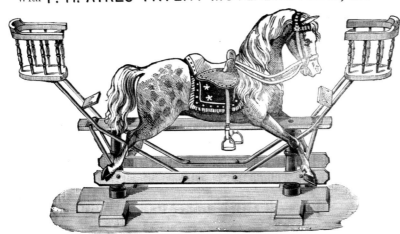

WITH SEATS AT EACH END.

No. 5	...	17/6
,, 6	...	19/6
,, 7	...	19/6
,, 8	...	22/6

extra.

Packing with Hay-bands for country transit—Nos. 3 and 4, 1/- ; 5 and 6, 2/- ; 7 and 8, 2/6, each, extra.

Panniers with straps, 9/0.

F H Ayres 1897 Catalogue

Fig.AY29

The hobby horse as illustrated in F H Ayres 1897 catalogue with the heavy base construction (a cross-halving type joint) was probably replaced very early on in production with the more conventional type of stand. This had the base bar resting on top of the cross pieces. The early heavy construction method would have been more time consuming to produce, required larger section timber and also to its detriment had a 'design fault'. If the base warped at all, the stand would not sit flat on the floor and the whole contraption could become unstable. This was obviously something that Ayres would have wanted to avoid, having praised the merits of the safety stand in the first place. However, a few examples of the heavy construction model have survived. A large restored 'hobby horse' *Fig.AY30* is shown below. It has had some replacement parts (the posts) fitted to the stand. The factory

F H Ayres Hobby Horse circa 1885   Fig.AY30

paint was covered over but this has now been revealed and retouched. The horse has also been reharnessed and fitted with new hair. While this horse is not in an original condition, it does give a good indication of what the early F H Ayres hobby horse would have looked like. As was typical of Ayres, the old catalogue illustration remained in place and was not updated for many years after the product had been modified.

An example of the the **Hobby Horse fitted with Seats at each end** is shown below *Fig.AY31*. This horse has its original heavy stand intact.

F H Ayres Hobby Horse with End Seats circa 1885   Fig.AY31

The only parts of this rocking horse that are not original are the actual wooden seats. The replacement seats are authentic copies of originals. As with many of the finely carved F H Ayres horses, the head *Fig.AY32* of this horse is turned to one side. Also note it has a high degree of extra carving including a carved tongue. Over the years it has lost its saddle cloth, but the outline can be traced by the brass nails that would have once held it in place.

Head Detail   Fig.AY32

Although the heavy design type stand appears to have been dropped after only a few years in the late 1890's, it was being used for a range of hobby horses referred to as **"D" Quality, Extra Best Make and Finish.** These were listed in the 1934 and 1938-39 F H Ayres Ltd catalogues. It is not known when the "D" quality horse was introduced. The "D" quality horse was listed with other rocking horses of different qualities and models, these being denoted by other letters "A", "B", "C" and "E". The 1934 and 1938-39 catalogues both had an illustration *Fig.AY33* of the "D" quality horse. The dimensions and prices were also listed *Fig.AY34*.

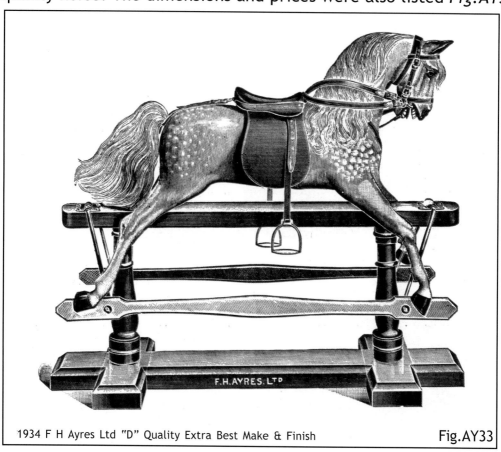

| 1934 F H Ayres Ltd "D" Quality Extra Best Make & Finish | Fig.AY33 |

" D " Quality, Extra Best Make and Finish (as illustrated).

Special workmanship and plated fittings throughout.   Each horse fitted with an exact reproduction in miniature of a full-size hunting saddle, both bridle and saddle being removable.

		Height from floor to saddle.	Length of body		Each.			Height from floor to saddle	Length of body		Each.
No. 5 (D)	..	35 in.	26 in.	..	**160 0**	No. 7 (D)	..	40½ in.	30 in.	..	**210 0**
„ 6 (D)	..	38 in.	28 in.	..	**189 0**	„ 8 (D)	..	44 in.	33 in.	..	**252 0**

1934 F H Ayres Ltd "D" Quality Extra Best Make & Finish Sizes & Prices   Fig.AY34

A number of examples of the "D" quality hobby horse have survived. A size 8 in original condition *Fig.AY35* stands 56" (142 cm) to the top of its head. Remarkably it still retains its original 'miniature' saddle, these are

F H Ayres Ltd Size 8 "D" Quality Extra Best Make & Finish circa 1934   Fig.AY35

often the first thing to be lost. As in the catalogue description, the metal work is chromium plated, this would also have included the bit, buckles and stirrup irons. When new this would have been very bright and given the rocking horse a very 'classy' and expensive look. This was not the ultimate, there was an option for a **Skin-Covered "E" Quality**. This was made to the same specification as the "D" but was advertised as *'covered with genuine calf skins. The greatest care and skill is used* *in covering, and the result gives an exceedingly life-like effect'*. The skin covered model "E" cost about 38% more than "D" model. Ultimately all qualities of hobby horse, were offered with the additional option of end seats, 'price on application'. This was still only part of Ayres' range, sixteen different versions of the best quality and only a year before the demise of the company, after which time its was reformed under W Sykes & Co Ltd. A size 7 example of the "D" model *Fig.AY36* clearly shows the high level of carving applied to these horses.

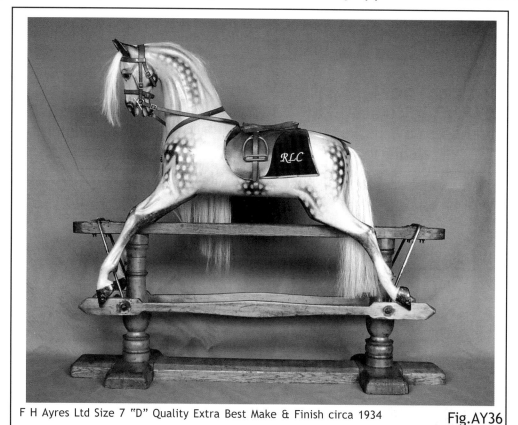

F H Ayres Ltd Size 7 "D" Quality Extra Best Make & Finish circa 1934   Fig.AY36

The horse has been restored, the smaller picture *Fig.AY37* shows its previous state, the original paint work was revealed and retouched and some new harness was fitted. The original saddle had just survived and was refurbished. These small saddles were built up around a wooden 'tree', a similar process to that of making a full size saddle.

Size 7 Before Restoration   Fig.AY37

A common feature of all Ayres top end or 'extra carved' hobby horses is that the runners (or rails) that the horse stands on are described as being 'thinned' or 'fluted' between the hooves. This would be a general guide to identify a better quality horse as opposed to a standard model with no thinning of the runners. However some variants have turned up, one such being that only the top of the runner is 'fluted' *Fig.AY38*. A few examples of this have been found, generally with the same body profile with the head in a lifted position. These and subsequent horses were now fitted to the lighter and more

F H Ayres Hobby Horse with Single Fluted Runners circa 1885   Fig.AY38

conventional stand. The horse shown below has been over painted and during restoration work the stencil '395 PATENTED JAN 29 1880' was uncovered on the base of the stand. This particular horse is not very detailed in its carving and unusually has no tongue.

Other similar examples have been more detailed and with a carved tongue suggesting that different qualities were now being offered. The date of manufacture would be circa 1885.

An good example of what might well be a natural design progression within F H Ayres' workshop is a horse *Fig.AY39* with its head up, on the lighter stand with 'double fluted' runners. The stand of the horse has the 395 patent stencil and is also marked with a '6' indicating its size.

F H Ayres Hobby Horse with Double Fluted Runners circa 1890   Fig.AY39

This horse has a tongue and is generally carved to a high standard. The paintwork of this horse is not original nor is the majority of the harness. Another general point about extra carved horses is that they run low on the stand, this is clear on the horse shown above. The later 'lighted carved' models all tended to run much higher on the stand. By altering the angle that the swinging irons hang affects the rocking motion of the horse as well as its stance. F H Ayres' extra carved horses generally have a good rocking motion but due to the closeness of the legs to the swinging irons, damage to the legs can occur if the bearing surfaces of the swinging components become worn.

A small F H Ayres horse *Fig.AY40*, probably a size 4, is extra carved but

F H Ayres Hobby Horse with Double Fluted Runners circa 1890   Fig.AY40

as can be seen in the detailed picture *Fig.AY41* it has no tongue. However, this was quite normal with the smaller sizes as it would be too fiddly and not cost effective to carve such fine detail. The horse is fitted to the lighter model of stand with the double fluted runners. This horse has been restored, the original paint work has been retouched and some of the harness replaced. The large fancy nail holding the rosette in place is original, these were fitted to all of Ayres' horses. The larger and better quality horses had more of them fitted to all areas of harness, the smaller horses had them fitted to the bridle and chest rosettes only.

Head Detail   Fig.AY41

Another slightly different version of an 'extra carved' horse *Fig.AY42* has 'F H AYRES' stencilled on its belly, this and other marks will be discussed later in the chapter. This horse is very similar to that shown in Fig.AY39 but it has far less detailed carving and no tongue.

F H Ayres Hobby Horse with Double Fluted Runners circa 1890   Fig.AY42

In the 1934 F H Ayres Ltd catalogue, three different qualities of painted hobby horses were available, "A", "B" & "D". the last we have already discussed. The model "A" was a cheaper option to the model "B" and while there is no accompanying illustration to the text *Fig.AY43*, the "B" was an in between model similar to the plainer 'extra carved' horses produced around the 1900's, such as that shown above *Fig.AY42*. It is unclear when the models "A", "B", "C" etc. were introduced as no catalogues between 1897 and 1934 have been discovered. The three different qualities of horse offered in 1934 would have required three different sets of templates but the "A" and "B" appear to share some dimensions. The "B" model was not listed in the 1939 catalogue, by omitting this model it would probably mean that all horses could be derived from one set of body sizes, reducing material and labour costs.

1934 F H Ayres Ltd "A" and "B" Quality Specification   Fig.AY43

An example of a "B" quality horse *Fig.AY44* in original condition has a '5' stencilled on the stand. The horse has some extra carving and pommel holes and has fluted runners on the stand. Compare this to an "A"

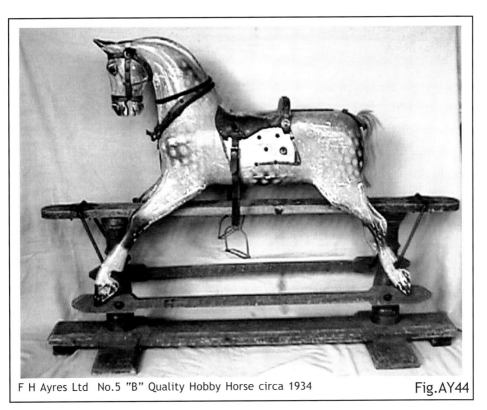

F H Ayres Ltd No.5 "B" Quality Hobby Horse circa 1934   Fig.AY44

quality horse *Fig.AY45* from around the same period. Notably the runners are not fluted at all. This is generally a good indication of a standard model without any extra carving. There are many other details

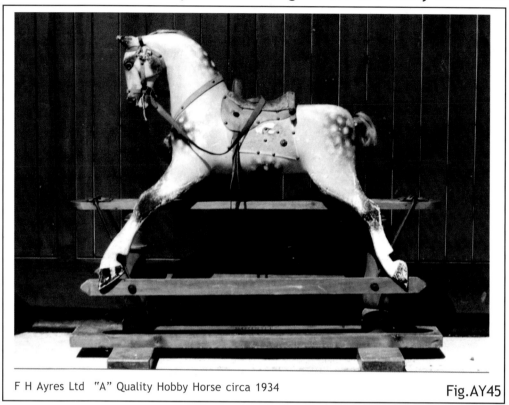

F H Ayres Ltd "A" Quality Hobby Horse circa 1934   Fig.AY45

that make up differences between the various qualities, for example the edges of the base were left square cut on the cheaper models, whereas the more expensive models had 'chamfered' edges *Fig.AY42*. Smaller horses also had some different components compared to the larger models, such as the turned posts of the stand. They were of a much simpler design as can be seen on a small horse *Fig.AY46* standing only 29" (74cm) to the top of its head. Another horse 34"(86 cm) tall *Fig.AY47* also has the simpler post. After the take-over by Sykes in 1940 all the horses were fitted with this simpler design of post. A standard or light carved horse dated to 1904 *Fig.AY48* certainly has a different look to the later models and is more like the earlier extra carved horses. It has plain runners and square edges to the base of the stand, typical features of a light carved model. The horse has no extra carving but does have a fine look all the same. This could be due to most horses of around 1900 being extra carved models and also by the 1930's, a new 'generation' of carvers were being employed.

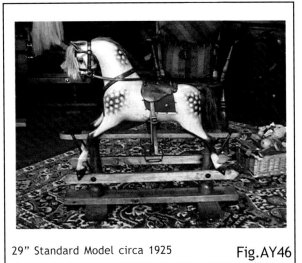

29" Standard Model circa 1925   Fig.AY46

34" Standard Model circa 1925   Fig.AY47

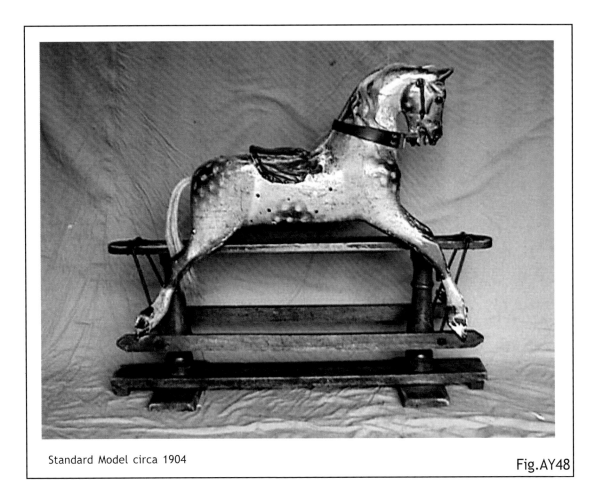

Standard Model circa 1904

Fig.AY48

Although the majority of F H Ayres' hobby horses fall into certain categories, over the years there have been many small production changes. This has given rise to a number of horses that seem to fall outside these categories, although they are certainly made by FH Ayres.

The first is a light carved horse *Fig.AY49* that has an unusually short body giving it a rather 'stumpy' look. Apart from this it is standard in all other aspects. It was mounted on a conventional swing stand. Manufactured circa 1920.

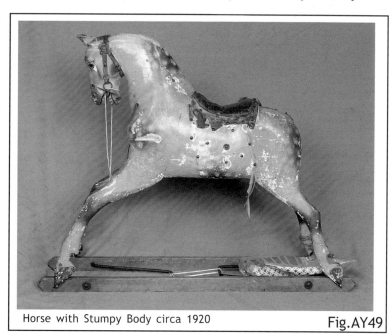

Horse with Stumpy Body circa 1920   Fig.AY49

The second is a horse that was made around 1900 *Fig.AY50* and is generally a 'fine' horse with a degree of extra carving but it does not have a carved tongue. It is fitted on a type of stand that would normally be associated with a light carved model. The runners are not fluted and the edges of the base and cross pieces have been left square cut. The horse also sits low on the stand as typical of the extra carved models of the time.

Extra Carved Horse fitted on Basic Stand circa 1900   Fig.AY50

The third slightly unusual horse *Fig.AY51* is basically a Quality "A" horse, size 4, manufactured circa 1930. It appears to be standard apart from the head. This head has what could be described as a 'hollow' throat. When the head was cut out, the area above the chin has been cut much deeper than usual.

The fourth example of an unusual horse *Fig.AY52* was made around 1900. It has no extra carving but it is fitted with a detachable saddle, normally associated with the "D" quality horses mentioned earlier in this chapter. The horse sits high up on the stand as a light carved model. The runners are not fluted but the base and cross pieces have chamfered edges as on extra carved models.

It is unclear why these four horses are not 'standard' and quite possibly there are many more that have yet to be discovered.

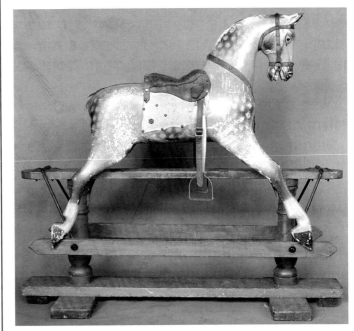

"A" quality horse with Hollow Throat circa 1930   Fig.AY51

Light Carved Horse Detachable Saddle
Part Extra Carved Type Stand circa 1900   Fig.AY52

The **American Hobby Horse with Patent Moveable Head** was produced from around 1887, some may well have been manufactured in 1886. The patent (1887 No.5395) was applied for in April 1887 and accepted in Jan 1888. A couple of examples have been found with a "PATENT APP FOR' stencil *Fig.AY53* applied to the body of the horse on both sides just above the back legs. This would imply these horses were made before the patent was accepted, maybe to indicate to possible competitors what F H Ayres intentions were regarding this invention and to put off others from copying it. The principle of the design was that the head of the horse was able to turn from side to side when the reins were pulled, on release of the reins, the head was returned to the forward position by means of a spring. This can be seen in the technical drawing *Fig.AY54* that went with the patent description. The idea, which was applied to other F H Ayres' horses, most likely derived from the tricycle horse.

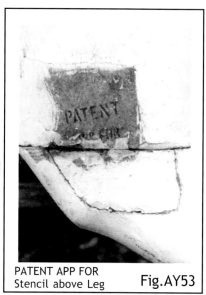

PATENT APP FOR
Stencil above Leg   Fig.AY53

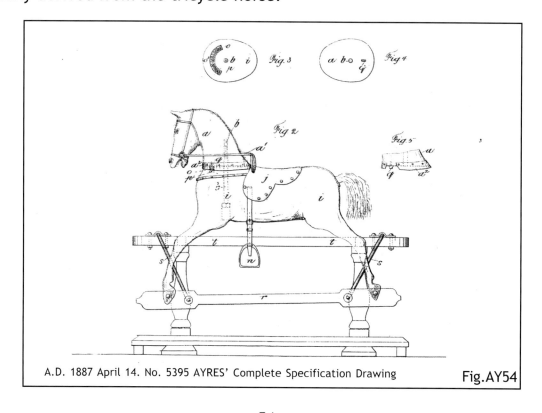

A.D. 1887 April 14. No. 5395 AYRES' Complete Specification Drawing   Fig.AY54

With the handle bars passing up through the head, it would not have been difficult to imagine the head of the horse turning as the tricycle horse was steered from side to side. A natural progression would then be to apply the idea, with a little modification, to a range of horses. Indeed, within the text of the specification, the 'moveable head' when applied to a hobby horse was described as a 'modification of the invention'. It would be worth noting that in the technical drawing, the stand is of the lighter design and all known examples of hobby horses with 'moveable heads' have been fitted to this lighter design of stand. This could well indicate that the early heavy stand was dropped by the end of 1886. There are however moveable head horses with different body profiles as with early standard hobby horses. The 'moveable head' was only an 'extra' after all and was not produced as a separate range in its own right.

The photograph *Fig.AY55* was taken some years after the horse's manufacture. This is evidenced by the later coat of paint that has been applied to the horse, tack and all.
The horse has its head up as that shown in Fig.AY39. The join where the 'moveable head' and neck meet is covered by a couple of pieces of leather, this is how they were originally finished. This was described as a 'curtain or flap' in the 1887 specification on the previous page and it is also illustrated in the 1887 drawing, labelled 'a²' on *Fig.2* & *Fig.5*.

F H Ayres Hobby Horse with
Patent Moveable Head circa 1887   Fig.AY55

A variety of hobby horses with 'moveable heads' are known to exist, one of which is pictured below *Fig.AY56*. This is a small horse that has a '3' stencilled on the stand, indicating its size. Also applied to the

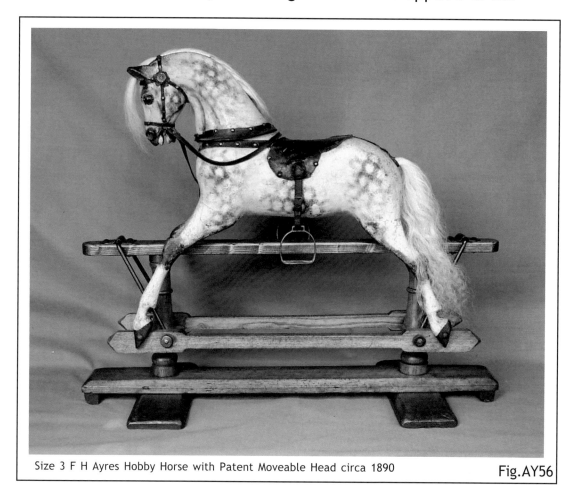

Size 3 F H Ayres Hobby Horse with Patent Moveable Head circa 1890   Fig.AY56

base of the stand is the '395 PATENTED 29TH JAN 1880' stencil. This has also been found on a number of the other 'moveable head' horses. It is not known if this was applied to all stands, as some examples of the 'moveable head' horses do not have all their original stand components. The size 3 horse has its original neck 'curtain' and saddle and a couple of decorative nails that hold the rosettes in place. Some other pieces of harness have been replaced. The paintwork is not original but has been retouched. The stirrup irons, mane and tail are also replacements but despite this the overall appearance is one of being an 'antique' horse.

A line up of three 'moveable head' horses *Fig.AY57* brought together again after about a hundred years since manufacture around 1887. They are all the same size horse, probably a size No.7, although only one of

Three F H Ayres Moveable Head Hobby Horses circa 1887   Fig.AY57

them is shown mounted on its stand. All three horses have various identity marks, the horse with on the left has an 'F H AYRES' stencil applied to its belly and a '2' stamped to its fore head. The horse in the centre has the F H Ayres belly stencil. The over painted white horse has the F H Ayres belly stencil, a '1' stamped to its fore-head and also the 'PATENT APP FOR' *Fig.AY53* stencilled above the rear legs. These markings will be discussed later in the chapter. None of the three horses pictured above is in an original condition. The two dappled horses have both had restoration work carried out, although the original paint work was preserved and retouched. The white horse was over painted some years ago but it does still have some original stand components, although they are not pictured here. All these horses are of the same profile with the head in a 'down' or low position. One possible reason for this change could be that by lowering the head it would save a small but not insignificant amount of timber during the manufacturing process. If it was only an inch per horse the saving after making hundreds, if not thousands of horses would be considerable. The majority of rocking horse makers produced horses with their heads in a relatively low position, perhaps for this very reason.

The horse shown pictured on the left in Fig.AY57 has subsequently had

F H Ayres Moveable Head Hobby Horse circa 1888

Fig.AY58

all traces of any later coats of paint removed to reveal the original factory paintwork *Fig.AY58*. This picture also shows some aspects of the extra carving and also note how low the horse sits on the stand. Some elements of the stand have been replaced, namely the base and cross pieces, the 'new' components have been made to the original specifications and 'aged' so as to blend in.

Some detailed views of a 'moveable head' horse show the body viewed from above with the head removed *Fig.AY59* The return spring can clearly be seen and the head *Fig.AY60* has a metal tab that locates in the spring. The hole in the centre of the head and body surface areas

Return Spring Mechanism   Fig.AY59

Underside of Head   Fig.AY60

is where the 'bolt' *Fig.AY61* passes through and acts as a pivot. On examination these 'bolts' have been found to have been fabricated, maybe not enough 'movable head' horses were made to warrant a

Moveable Head Fabricated Pivot Bolt   Fig.AY61

specific component to be made. The head of the bolt was rebated into the underside *Fig.AY62* of the horses body, and when the 'movable head' was fitted, the head of the bolt was covered over by a piece of timber. The horse was then gessoed and painted thus totally hiding all the workings.

Pivot Bolt Rebate Fig.AY62

Because of this, quite possibly some 'moveable head' horses would not have been recognised for what they were and may well have had their 'loose' heads repaired. The method of covering the head of the pivot bolt may have been well intentioned, but any subsequent repairs or servicing of the moving parts was made very difficult without possible damage to the horse. It is not certain when F H Ayres stopped producing horses with the 'moveable head' option, but due to the limited number that are known to exist, and subsequent examination of these, around 1900 is thought to be likely cessation date.

A colloquial term that is often used wrongly to describe F H Ayres 'moveable head' horses, is the term **'Swivel-Head'**. The term Swivel-Head was used originally by David & Noreen Kiss to describe their exacting replica of an original F H Ayres 'movable head' hobby horse. David and Noreen have produced their Swivel-Head horse *Fig.AY63* in limited numbers since 1990 after carrying out extensive research and subsequent restoration of a number of F H Ayres originals.

1990 Swivel-Head (F H Ayres Moveable Head Replica) by David & Noreen Kiss   Fig.AY63

F H Ayres were probably one of the most innovative of rocking horse makers, always looking for new ideas, some of which were not altogether very successful but one of their designs which was received quite well was the **International Patent Spring Rocking Horse** that was first catalogued in 1895 *Fig AY64*. As can be seen in the picture, the patent had been applied for (in 1895) and was accepted in September 1896. Patent No 20,747 *Fig.AY65*. The Spring Horse was described in the

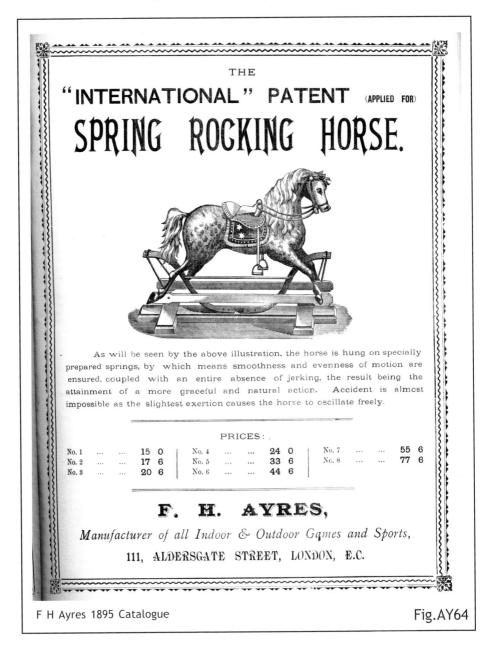

THE

"INTERNATIONAL" PATENT (APPLIED FOR)

SPRING ROCKING HORSE.

As will be seen by the above illustration, the horse is hung on specially prepared springs, by which means smoothness and evenness of motion are ensured, coupled with an entire absence of jerking, the result being the attainment of a more graceful and natural action. Accident is almost impossible as the slightest exertion causes the horse to oscillate freely.

PRICES:

No. 1	...	...	15 0	No. 4	...	...	24 0	No. 7	...	...	55 6
No. 2	...	...	17 6	No. 5	...	...	33 6	No. 8	...	...	77 6
No. 3	...	...	20 6	No. 6	...	...	44 6				

F. H. AYRES,

Manufacturer of all Indoor & Outdoor Games and Sports,

111, ALDERSGATE STREET, LONDON, E.C.

F H Ayres 1895 Catalogue   Fig.AY64

application thus; *This invention relates to improvements in hobby, or rocking horses, nursery yachts and the like toys, especially of the character known as "American Hobby Horses". In carrying out my invention I dispense with the rigid pedestals which ordinarily support the platform which carries the metal slings and sling bearings and in place thereof I mount the horse or body of the toy on the built up plate springs or equivalent forms of spring support adapted to give a swing motion thereto in a fore and aft direction but not in a direction from side to side, or these directions of play and rigidity may be transposed. By these means an action graceful and natural whilst free from unpleasant jerks can be imparted to the body, with a steady support. The apparatus will be enabled to work without noise or danger.*

The Spring Horse was first offered in their catalogue of 1895 in eight sizes but by the end of 1896 the smallest size was not listed any more, perhaps it was just too fiddly to produce. It is not known how long the Spring Horse was in production for, but it was still listed in the 'Bazaar' section of the 1907 Army and Navy catalogue and was thought to have been made up to World War One. The horse itself would have been made alongside their other 'hobby horses' and as such there were many slight variations from one model to another. The catalogue picture shows the construction of the timber base as by means of a 'cross-halving joint', this is the most elaborate and costly method of production, a few examples of this style have been found *Fig.AY66* but most known examples have the simpler and much more typical overlapped type of stand as in Fig.AY67.

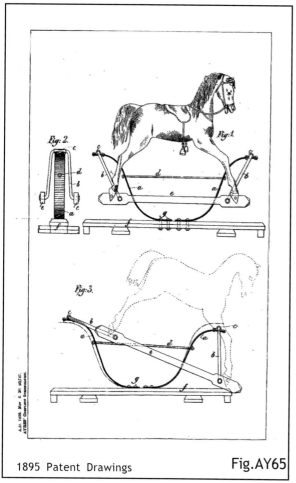

1895 Patent Drawings   Fig.AY65

Of the three Spring Horses pictured, the top *Fig.AY66* is the same as in the 1895 illustration with the cross-halving joint type stand and would date to around 1895. The horse has a tongue, is extra carved and stands on fluted runners.

The middle picture *Fig.AY67* is of a horse on the simpler type of stand, the horse is extra carved, has no tongue and stands on fluted runners.

The third picture shows another model of Spring Horse *Fig.AY68* that is from a different pattern than the previous two horses and is quite possibly the same pattern as the F H Ayres "D" quality hobby horse of the 1930's range. This would have originally had a detachable miniature of a full-size hunting saddle and also a detachable bridle. This Spring Horse also has the heavier 'cross-halved' type stand and it is interesting to note that all the known "D" model horses have this type of stand. They also have fluted runners but with the additional widening feature at the centre of the runner. The "D" model has not been known to have been fitted with pommels, unlike the earlier horses.

F H Ayres Spring Horse circa 1895   Fig.AY66

F H Ayres Spring Horse circa 1900   Fig.AY67

F H Ayres "D" Style Spring Horse   Fig.AY68

From this it may be reasonable to assume that the horse in Fig.AY68 was a revival of the earlier model of horse, and may have been produced as a top quality horse alongside the hobby horse "D" model of the 1930's.

As with all the range of F H Ayres' horses relevant sized fittings were used, such as 3 bolt swing iron brackets on the smaller size models. One such small Spring Horse Fig.AY69 had on the underside of the swing iron bracket 'No 2' marked in the casting Fig.AY70. It is not known if this referred to the model size of the horse or if it was a bracket size.

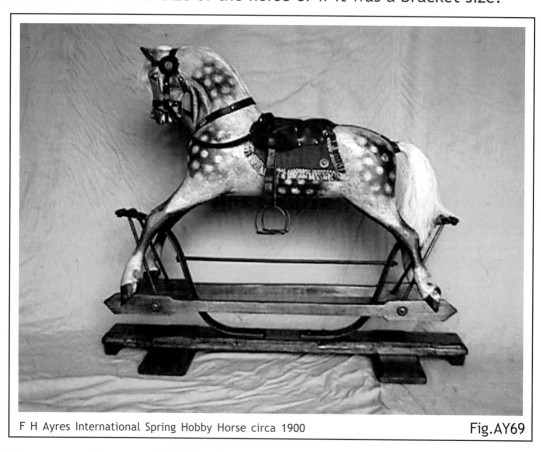

F H Ayres International Spring Hobby Horse circa 1900   Fig.AY69

F H Ayres catalogue of 1895 referred only to model numbers but did not list any corresponding sizes. This small horse is extra carved but has no tongue, in keeping with small horses. It is pictured in a restored condition, the original paint-work was covered by later coats of paint but the original has been revealed and retouched. All the harness and hair has been replaced. The horse did still retain a number of decorative nails that were refitted.

Another component that was marked on the small Spring Horse *Fig.AY69* was one of the 'springs' which had 'W O .. ROTHERHAM' stamped on the underside *Fig.AY71*. This stamping is not very clear but most certainly refers to the manufacturer of this particular component.

F H Ayres would have produced as many items as they could in their own workshops but sometimes specialist items would have to have been bought in. These 'springs' were most certainly one such item requiring skill and experience to produce a suitably reliable component.

(*A brief search was carried out for 'WO... Rotherham' but without result. There would have been many companies allied to the steel trade in that area as Rotherham is located by Sheffield, the 'steel' capital of Britain in the 1900's.*)

The 'springs' of these horses have been found with traces of maroon paint with applied yellow pin lining *Fig.AY72* which would have been very bright and eye catching when new.

Another marking found on some 'spring horses' is a stencil, **'International Spring Hobby Patent'** that is applied to the base of the stand.

Swing Iron Bracket Detail No2   Fig.AY70

Spring 'WO Rotherham' Detail   Fig.AY71

Spring Yellow Pin Line Detail   Fig.AY72

A rather nice photograph *Fig.AY73* of a couple of children sitting on a F H Ayres 'Spring Horse', probably taken around 1910.

F H Ayres International Spring Hobby Horse circa 1900   Fig.AY73

F H Ayres first mention of the **Skin Covered Hobby Horse** was in an 1897 catalogue and they appear to have been an available option throughout the company's existence. Even after F H Ayres Ltd was reformed as Ayres Sports Goods Ltd, a catalogue produced under the Slazenger title in 1949 offered a 'skin covered' horse, the last production year of any rocking horse linked to F H Ayres.

The 'skin covered' horses could be a version of any F H Ayres hobby horse, both ordinary and also extra carved models were used as a basis. In F H Ayres 1938 catalogue *Fig.AY74* the 'skin covered' horse was still

---

SKIN-COVERED HOBBY HORSES

The following ranges of Hobby Horses are covered with genuine calf skins.   The greatest care and skill is used in covering, and the result gives an exceedingly life-like effect.

" C " Quality, Ordinary.
Constructed of well-seasoned and selected wood, with best quality leather strappings, saddle and fittings.

	Height from floor to saddle.	Length of body	Each		Height from floor to saddle.	Length of body	Each
No. 2 (C) ..	23½ in.	16½ in.	.. 67 6	No. 6 (C) ..	38½ in.	28 in.	.. 150 0
„ 3 (C) ..	27 in.	19 in.	.. 77 6	„ 7 (C) ..	40½ in.	29 in.	.. 180 0
„ 4 (C) ..	30 in.	21½ in.	.. 100 0	„ 8 (C) ..	44½ in.	33 in.	.. 220 0
„ 5 (C) ..	34½ in.	25 in.	.. 126 0				

" E " Quality, Extra Best Make and Finish.
Special workmanship and plated fittings throughout. Each horse fitted with an exact reproduction in miniature of a full-size hunting saddle, both bridle and saddle being removable.

	Height from floor to saddle.	Length of body	Each		Height from floor to saddle.	Length of body	Each
No. 5 (E) ..	35 in.	26 in.	.. 210 0	No. 7 (E) ..	40½ in.	30 in.	.. 270 0
„ 6 (E) ..	38 in.	28 in.	.. 240 0	„ 8 (E) ..	44 in.	33 in.	.. 320 0

1938 F H Ayres Ltd "C" & "E" Quality Skin Covered Hobby Horses   Fig.AY74

---

being offered in two qualities. The "E" quality was top of the range, a 'skin covered' version of the the "D" extra best dapple grey. The other version available in the 1938 catalogue was the "C" quality, this was a 'skin covered' version of the "A" quality dapple grey, this was the most basic at this time. It is interesting to note that earlier in 1934 the "C" quality 'skin covered' horse was based on the "B" quality dapple grey, a middle quality dapple grey that was subsequently dropped some time after 1934 and before 1938.

The 'skin covered' horses were always a more expensive option than their counterpart dapple greys, the acquisition of suitable calf skins and the skilled labour required were both contributory factors. There is however a slightly ironic side to the 'skin covered' horse. With the production of normal dapple greys, during the blocking up stages, timber would have been used up as it arrived. This would have naturally led to some horses having 'knots' in areas of the horse's body that may well affect the subsequent gessoing and painting. Large knots in timber can lead to resin 'bleeding' from a knot and also possible weakness, cracking or splitting. To be able to use these 'questionable' bodies as a basis for a 'skin covered' horse was a perfect solution. The bodies of some 'skin covered' horses when they have had the skin removed at a later date have been found with unusually high degree of knots. An example of this is a horse that has a large knot *Figs.AY75 & AY76* just where the front leg is fitted, this is not an ideal candidate for painting.

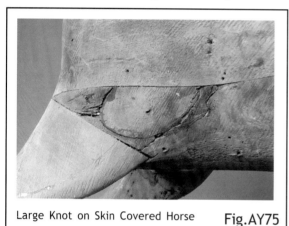

Large Knot on Skin Covered Horse   Fig.AY75

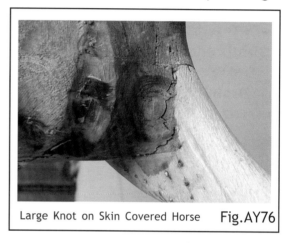

Large Knot on Skin Covered Horse   Fig.AY76

A number of 'skin covered' horses have survived but they are all generally in poor condition. A 'skin covered' horse *Fig.AY77* dating from

F H Ayres Skin Covered Hobby Horse circa 1900   Fig.AY77

1900 is in a shabby condition. It has also lost its lower jaw, possibly due to poor timber. The skins dry out and split, they can also wear leaving a bald effect, in general they do not age as well as a dapple grey might. Due to high refurbishing costs, most aged 'skin covered' horses end up being painted as dapple greys.

Occasionally an old and tired skin covered horse *Fig.AY78* gets a new lease of life and is recovered *Fig.AY79* with a new skin, giving an insight as to how smart a 'skin covered' horse would have looked when new. This example is probably a "C" quality horse made around 1930. The horse has a reasonable amount of extra carving, a detail that is often lost on a 'skin covered' horse. The stand has fluted runners and chamfered edges to the base and cross pieces. This appears to be generally in line with the specification on the "B" quality horse used as a basis for the "C" quality skin covered horse in the early 1930's.

F H Ayres "C" Quality Skin Covered Hobby Horse circa 1930   Fig.AY78

Refurbished "C" Quality Skin Covered Hobby Horse circa 1930   Fig.AY79

The small 'skin covered' horse *Fig.AY80* is a "C" quality horse dated to around 1938 and corresponds with the cheaper quality "A" model of painted horse. There is no evidence of extra carving and the stand has plain runners and square edges to the base and cross pieces.

F H Ayres "C" Quality Skin Covered Hobby Horse circa 1938   Fig.AY80

The **New Patent Swing Hobby Horse** *Fig.AY81* was a most curious foot operated hobby horse, another ingenious F H Ayres invention.

THE NEW PATENT SWING HOBBY HORSE.

Patent applied for.

Price, No.   5, 42/6 ;   6, 53/6.   7, 66/- ;   8,   87/-

1895 F H Ayres New Patent Swing Hobby Horse   Fig.AY81

It was certainly featured in F H Ayres' 1895-1897 catalogues, but it is not known if it survived after 1897. Although the illustration states 'Patent applied for', no record of this has been found. This would generally indicate that the patent was not granted or the application was withdrawn. As for the device itself it was offered in four sizes, these probably matched those of the conventional hobby horses of the day, and uniquely, it was controlled by means of a foot operated pedal. The detailed picture *Fig.AY82* shows there to be a series of pivoted rods connected to a 'shuttle' device on the top bar. The pedal and rod system is housed in a specially adapted post of the stand. The swinging irons are joined at their lower end to what appear to be metal brackets attached to the lower face of the runners. This arrangement created a much longer swinging iron than usual, and this would undoubtedly be a crucial element as to the overall performance of the device.

Pushing the foot pedal down would push the horse forwards, so by a continuous pushing of the pedal the horse would rock backwards and forwards. It does seem a highly elaborate way of achieving the horse to rock. A novelty certainly, but it may well have had a serious application with regards to a disabled child who could not operate a regular rocking horse. Unfortunately there is no descriptive text so it will remain a mystery for the time. Sadly, no examples of this curious device are known to exist at the time of writing.

Foot Pedal Detail
1895 F H Ayres New Patent Swing Hobby Horse   Fig.AY82

Another rocking horse invention *Fig.AY83* that was granted a patent in 1915 was compiled by F H Ayres and Thomas Freeman. Patent No.18,070 On the application Thomas Freeman is described as a draughtsman at the same address as F H Ayres, and most probably employed by Ayres. The basic design of the device consisted of a regular horse that was mounted on a stand that comprised of a series of metal bars and springs. It was described in the patent specification as being;

An extremely simple and cheap form of support for a rocking horse is in this manner provided.

Although the description states the device is simple, it does look to be made up from a considerable number of components. The horse also looks a little precarious mounted only by the tips of its hooves. There would undoubtedly be a large amount of strain on the leg joints of the horse.

It is not known whether the device ever went into production or not. For there are no known records of any models in existence. The design may well have been 'shelved' with the advent of the First World War.

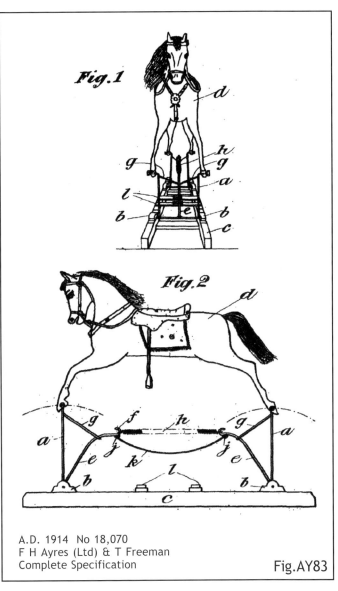

A.D. 1914 No 18,070
F H Ayres (Ltd) & T Freeman
Complete Specification

Fig.AY83

The old style bow rocking horse *Fig.AY84* was referred to in the F H Ayres catalogue of 1895 simply as a **Rocking Horse**, this being the forerunner of all the different subsequent rocking horse designs.

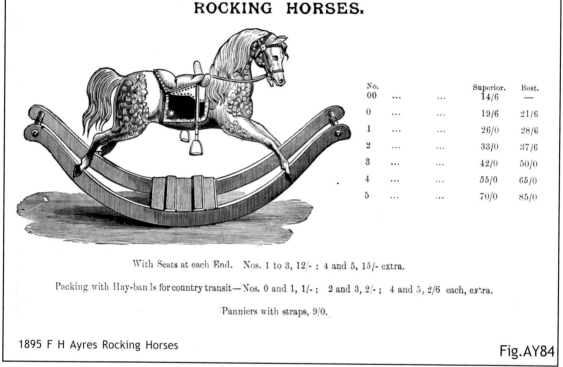

ROCKING HORSES.

No.			Superior.	Best.
00	...	...	14/6	—
0	...	...	19/6	21/6
1	...	...	26/0	28/6
2	...	...	33/0	37/6
3	...	...	42/0	50/0
4	...	...	55/0	65/0
5	...	...	70/0	85/0

With Seats at each End. Nos. 1 to 3, 12/- ; 4 and 5, 15/- extra.

Packing with Hay-ban ls for country transit—Nos. 0 and 1, 1/- ; 2 and 3, 2/- ; 4 and 5, 2/6 each, extra.

Panniers with straps, 9/0.

1895 F H Ayres Rocking Horses

Fig.AY84

The 'rocking horses' were available in seven sizes and of two different qualities. The 'superior' was the cheaper option and the 'best' was the top range. The smallest size '00' was not available in the 'best' finish. There is no text explaining the differences of quality but most likely the best was 'extra carved' and with possibly different detailing about the bow rocker. The 'rocking horse' was also offered with the option of having 'Seats at each End', these could be fitted to the five larger models. 'Panniers with strap' was another available option.

The 'rocking horse' was still available in 1938 as shown in F H Ayres Ltd catalogue *Fig.AY85* although now in only six sizes and in one quality. At this time it was identified by the letter "M" within the catalogue. Note that the same drawing from 1895 has been used in 1938 to depict the 'rocking horse'. There are some differences of saddle heights if the 1938 list is compared with an earlier 1934 list. This seems to tie in with a general streamlining of the complete rocking horse range within F H Ayres Ltd around 1934. This was a difficult time for the company.

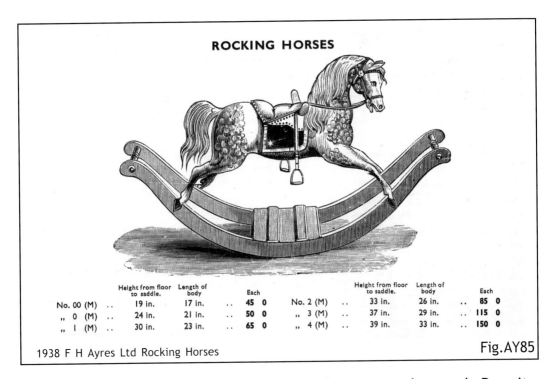

ROCKING HORSES

	Height from floor to saddle.	Length of body		Each			Height from floor to saddle.	Length of body		Each	
No. 00 (M) ..	19 in.	17 in.	..	**45**	**0**	No. 2 (M) ..	33 in.	26 in.	..	**85**	**0**
,, 0 (M) ..	24 in.	21 in.	..	**50**	**0**	,, 3 (M) ..	37 in.	29 in.	..	**115**	**0**
,, 1 (M) ..	30 in.	23 in.	..	**65**	**0**	,, 4 (M) ..	39 in.	33 in.	..	**150**	**0**

1938 F H Ayres Ltd Rocking Horses   Fig.AY85

It is not clear when the option of two qualities was dropped. Despite the fact that 'rocking horses' were produced in reasonable quantities, there are not a large number of survivors. 'Rocking horses' are not as strong as the swing stand rocking horse. Repairs to 'rocking horses' are not straight forward, many repairs consisting of unsightly metal straps or odd support posts. The bow rockers were most commonly made from elm, a timber favoured by woodworm. All of these elements conspired to destroy a large number of 'rocking horses' over the years. An example of a 'rocking horse' with a 'flattened' bow *Fig.AY86* and the

Size No4 F H Ayres Rocking Horse circa 1910   Fig.AY86

75

rear legs pulled out of their sockets is quite typical. This is a large lightly carved horse, probably a size 4 and made around 1910. It has not only broken but also suffered the effects of being damp. This has caused the gesso to start crumbling and also the glass eyes to come out. It would now require a great deal of work to either preserve or restore before it completely disintegrates.

A 'rocking horse' that has fared a little better Fig.AY87 has had its original paint work retouched. It still has some vestiges of the factory saddle and martingale. The horse has no extra carving so would likely be

Superior Quality (Cheaper) F H Ayres Rocking Horse circa 1900   Fig.AY87

a 'superior' model, the cheaper option. The bow has been painted at some time, usually they are varnished from the factory. Where the stretcher fits at the end of the bow, a decorative wooden rosette Fig.AY88 is applied to the outside of the bow to hide the large construction nails that hold the stretcher in place. This also give the appearance of being the end of the stretcher as well. These rosettes have been

Rosette Detail.   Fig.AY88

found on a number of 'rocking horses' but appear to be fitted to earlier models. A head-on-view of the 'rocking horse' with the 'flattened bow' shows the stretcher in place and also the one remaining rosette *Fig.AY89* to the right.

The 'rocking horse' *Fig.AY90* pictured below has been extensively restored and had a replacement bow rocker made. The horse is extra carved and would have been classed as a 'best' model when sold. It has been repainted and fitted with new harness, mane and tail.

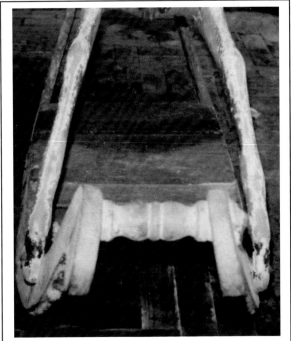

Stretcher & Rosette Detail   Fig.AY89

Restored F H Ayres size 2 Best Quality Rocking Horse circa 1900   Fig.AY90

F H Ayres produced not only rocking horses but a huge variety of sporting goods and games and were always keen to promote the name of the firm. Most sporting goods were marked with the company name, 'F H Ayres' was registered as a trade mark itself, and the name was always associated with quality products. Unfortunately many of their rocking horses are not marked, and marks are not always obvious on some that are. It would seem that initially the great majority were marked, but for some reason for many years they were not marked at all. However, towards the end of the company's existence there was a revival in marking them. All the known marks *Fig.AY91* are shown below.

F H Ayres Identification Marks

Fig.AY91

The two brass plaques '1' & '2', which are subtly different, were both found on early hobby horses. They were pinned to the base in the middle of the stands. Both of these hobby horses were made circa 1895 and also had the 395 patent stencil on the stand. These brass plaques are a little vulnerable and could easily 'catch' on something. A number of horses have been found with evidence of them being previously fitted by evidence of two small pin holes left in the base. The plaques are about two and a half inches across and were fitted with small brass escutcheon pins (brass nails). Occasionally just the pins survive.

The 'F H AYRES' stencil, '3' was applied to the belly of horses and is probably the most common of the markings. This was applied to a variety of early horses and is thought to have been in use up to around 1900, or just a little later. It can be over looked due to its position and it is also often covered over by later coats of paint. Restoration work has uncovered a number of these stencilled markings. In December 1905 F H Ayres became a limited company and after this date they marked their sports products appropriately with 'F H Ayres Ltd'. However, this practice was not applied to any of their rocking horses and they remained unmarked for many years. The only marks found between the approximate dates of 1906 and 1940 are either the hobby horse size number stencilled to the stand, ie.1,2,3,4, etc. and /or a retailers name such as Harrods *Fig.AY92*.

| Harrod's Knightsbridge and size 5 Stencil circa 1930 | Fig.AY92 |

A number of hobby horses have been found with a plastic label '4' fitted to the front of the top bar of the stand. These have all had the letters 'F H' and 'Ltd' cut away. They were fitted to horses that were produced at the time of W Sykes Ltd take-over of F H Ayres Ltd in 1940. Sykes acquired the trade marks of F H Ayres Ltd but could not use the 'Ltd' in conjunction with the Ayres name, this was an official matter.

The horses with the cutaway label were the last to be produced in London. World War Two effectively stopped production and F H Ayres' premises were destroyed in the blitz. After the war, F H Ayres was now under control of W Sykes Ltd and a limited rocking horse production was carried out at Horbury, Yorkshire. The firm had been reformed as 'Ayres Sports Goods Ltd' and rocking horses were marked with the old 'F H Ayres' signature trade mark, one of many trade marks acquired by Sykes. The signature *F H Ayres* label was an applied transfer '5', this was fitted to the top bar of the stand. This ceased with the end of rocking horse production at around 1950.

Another set of curious markings that has been found is a 'number' stamped on the horses forehead *Fig.AY93*. The 'numbers' have ranged

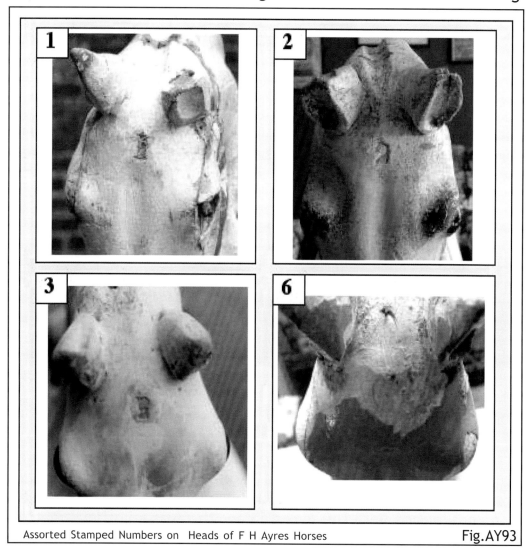

Assorted Stamped Numbers on Heads of F H Ayres Horses   Fig.AY93

from 1 to 6 and have been applied to horses made up to around 1900. These 'numbers' are generally not apparently visible as they are initially obscured with gesso, and then with the leather brow band of the bridle. This would imply they had a significance during production. Not all horses made before 1900 are marked. The 'number' does not relate to the size of the horse, those illustrated with the 'numbers' '1' and '2' are the same size horse and worth noting are both 'moveable head' horses. The horse with the 'number' '3' was a very large extra carved hobby horse. The horse with the 'number' '6' was also a large horse. One possible explanation is that the 'numbers' were to do with productivity. Many of the staff at F H Ayres would have worked piece rate, getting paid for what they produced and its thought likely this would have especially applied to the 'carvers'. A 'number' for each carver, as there would have been many, would stop any confusion as to who had carved what. This is very important when your weekly wage depended on it.

A component that can help with the identity of an F H Ayres hobby horse is the swinging iron bracket. There were two basic styles of bracket, one had four bolts to fix it down, the other had three bolts. A number of slight variations of both types of bracket *Fig.AY94* have been discovered. A good quality bracket is a vital part of a rocking horse, and F H Ayres made these to a very good standard. The early four bolt brackets were 'cast' as in examples *1,2&3*. Usually they were made in steel, but one example has been found that was cast from brass. The four bolt brackets were fitted to the larger hobby horses. At some time around 1905 the brackets were changed to pressed steel. A quicker and cheaper method, and most probably carried out within Ayres own workshops. The cast items would most likely have been bought in. The pressed brackets were used right up to the end of the companies existence, note that some of the very last used were quite roughly cut out. After World War Two the brackets were painted silver, before the war they had been black. The only exception to this were brackets fitted to the top range "D" quality horses, these were described as being 'chromium plated'. The larger horses horses also had an additional square metal 'plate' fitted under the bracket, which acted as a much wider bearing surface than the standard 'staple' bearings. The smaller horses were fitted with a three bolt bracket, examples *8 &9*. One is cast, the other pressed. The cast example *Fig.AY70* had 'No.2' marked on the underside, the only known marked example of an Ayres bracket.

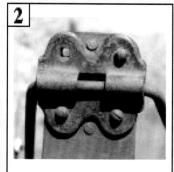

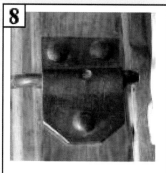

1. Cast Steel 4 Bolt + Steel Bearing Plate   Extra Carved Hobby   c.1890
2. Cast Steel 4 Bolt   Spring Stand Hobby   c.1895
3. Cast Brass 4 Bolt   Extra Carved Hobby   c.1900
4. Pressed Steel 4 Bolt   Light Carved Hobby   c.1920
5. Pressed Steel Chrome Plated 4 Bolt +BP   "D" Quality Hobby   c.1930
6. Pressed Steel Silver Painted 4 Bolt   Light Carved Hobby   c.1945
7. Pressed Steel Silver Painted (Roughly Cut Out) Light Carved Hobby   c.1948
8. Pressed Steel 3 Bolt   Small Moveable Head Hobby   c.1890
9. Cast Steel 3 Bolt   Small Spring Stand Hobby   c.1900

Variations of Swing Iron Brackets Fitted to F H Ayres Hobby Horses   Fig.AY94

The turned posts of F H Ayres hobby horses were made to one of three basic designs *Fig.AY95*. The post '*1*' was the simplest and was fitted to

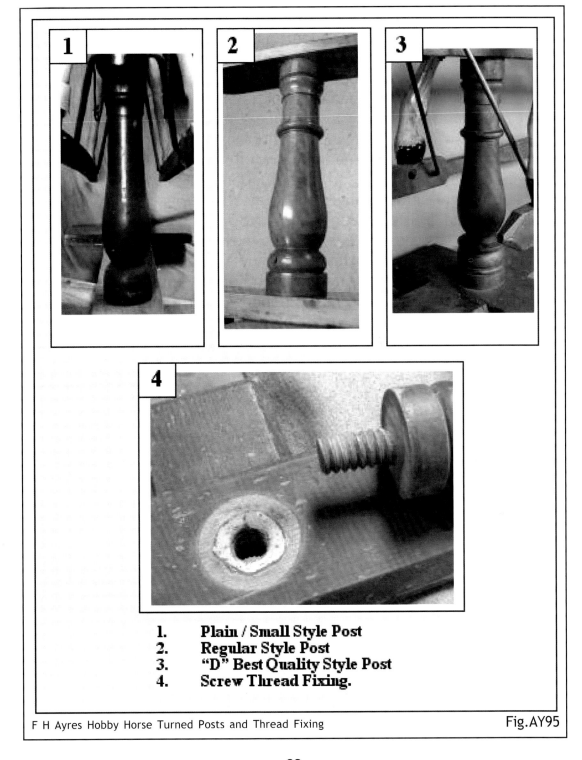

1. Plain / Small Style Post
2. Regular Style Post
3. "D" Best Quality Style Post
4. Screw Thread Fixing.

F H Ayres Hobby Horse Turned Posts and Thread Fixing   Fig.AY95

small horses of all qualities. After 1940 this simple pattern was used for all hobby horses. The 'regular' '2' post was used for the great majority of hobby horses from when they were first produced up to 1940. The only hobby horses they were not fitted to were the small horses and also the "D" quality horses. The best quality "D" horses had the most elaborate post '3'. This had additional turning near the base. There are however always exceptions, a "D" quality horse has been found with the 'regular' posts. It is not clear if this was intentional or a mistake. With the volume of hobby horses F H Ayes produced, it would be expected to have a few oddities. Both the 'regular' and the 'best' quality posts had 'threaded' spigots '4' on the lower fitting and these were screwed into the base of the stand. The top spigot was slotted and held in the top bar by a 'wedge'. In all this was the most secure method of stand construction.

Most manufacturers used 'fancy' nails as a final decoration to the harness and F H Ayres were no exception. A number of different styles of 'fancy' nail have been used over the years but the pattern most often found is shown below *Fig.AY96*. Different sizes of the popular

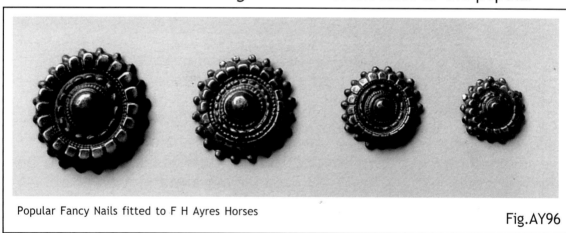

Popular Fancy Nails fitted to F H Ayres Horses

Fig.AY96

style were used on various areas of the harness. Larger ones for ribbon rosette centres, smaller ones around the bridle. However these same style 'fancy' nails were also used by other manufactures so identification on this one item alone should not be considered. The fancy nails would have been produced by an independent firm who would have been at liberty to sell them to any purchaser.

Ayres Sports Goods Ltd.   1940 - 1986

Address: 1, Old Street, London. E.C.1

Incorporated: 5th April 1940   Company No. 360,359

See also: F H Ayres.   W. Sykes Ltd.

Ayres Sports Goods Ltd was formed by William Sykes Ltd on the 5th April 1940 from the acquisition of the estate rights and interest, the goodwill, trademarks and patents of F H Ayres Ltd. Sykes had bought the troubled firm of Ayres mainly for their sporting goods which were of world-wide renown. Fig.AG01 is of a 1940 letterhead from the new company.

AYRGAMES
THE SIGN OF QUALITY

AYRES SPORTS GOODS LIMITED

Telephones: Clerkenwell 4644 & 4645
Telegraphic Address:
"Progress, Barb, London."

I OLD STREET
LONDON, E.C.I

Cables: "Progress, London."
Codes: Marconi, and A B C (5th and 6th Editions).

OUTDOOR SPORTS AND GAMES

Terms: { Approved Accounts 3½%
7 Days

CONFIDENTIAL TO THE TRADE
Accounts under 20/- strictly nett

2½% 30 days from invoice date

Circa 1940 Letterhead   Fig.AG01

Before 1940 the production of rocking horses from Ayres was quite busy with a range of rocking horses still available. However, the company faced difficult times. With the advent of the take over and WWII production would have ceased, not only for Ayres but other rocking horse makers.

 A number of horses have been found with an applied label made from a type of plastic *Fig.AG02* which are inscribed *Manufactured by...Ayres...London*, but notably all these labels have had sections cut out, this being the 'FH' and 'Ltd', so it would be a safe assumption that these horses were made when F H Ayres Ltd were trading, but sold after the take over by William Sykes, obviously the Ayres name was still of great importance and prestige.

After the war, horses were produced again at Sykes' factory in Horbury but in much smaller numbers as 'tin horses' were now taking a much greater share of the market. The fact that Sykes still had 'wood working' departments for their range of sports goods, was probably the only reason rocking horses were still manufactured. Rocking horses that were produced after the war had a transfer 'FH Ayres' *Fig.AG03*

Label C.1940   Fig.AG02

Label 1940 - 1950   Fig.AG03

applied to the same position as the cut out label, to the front of the top bar of the stand. In 1942 Slazengers and their subsidiary Gradidge, acquired the share capital of Sykes and Ayres and all products came under the control of Slazenger, however, rocking horses as well as other sports goods were still sold under the 'Ayres' brand. A 1949 Slazenger export list had as subheadings the names of Sykes, Ayres and Gradidge, these four firms were an amalgamation of the leading sports goods makers of their day and this became the largest sports manufacturing group in Europe. The 1949 Slazenger list is also the last known reference to the supply of rocking horses *FigAG04* and it is very interesting to note that only two horses were available, both the same size, but one was a skin covered horse at an extra 40% in cost. The rocking horse of 1949 was certainly a far cry from its predecessor of the 1880's.

ROCKING HORSES

29003 Beautifully finished hand carved models mounted on firm wooden stands and suitable for children between the ages of 5 and 12. Approximate sizes : Floor to saddle, 30 in. ; Length of body excluding head, 21½ in.

PAINTED WOODEN   ..   ..   .. **130/-** ea.

29014 SKIN COVERED   ..   ..   .. **180/-** ea.

From 1949 trade export Catalogue   Fig.AG04

These post war horses were probably made initially in three sizes, small, medium and large but reduced to just one size, medium by 1949. Fig.AG04 is picture of a painted horse as described in the 1949 list and would date to around 1948. These horses were much simpler than the

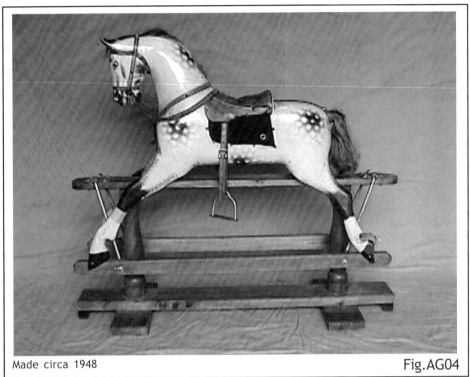

Made circa 1948   Fig.AG04

earlier models with basic light carving, but they still had carved teeth and generally balanced proportions apart from the eyes which were particularly small *Fig.AG05*.The horses were still had real leather tack with adjustable stirrup leathers. Saddle blankets were of a red wool based material and tended to wear quite quickly. The stands, although basic, were still of good construction, turned posts with spigots were used so as to give long life. The swinging irons and top plates of these horses were painted silver, a change from black of the prewar horses and top plates were a lighter pressing of the classic Ayres four bolt pattern.

The production of 'Ayres' rocking horses, now owned by the Slazenger group, ceased in 1950 but Ayres Sports Goods Ltd. traded up to 1983.

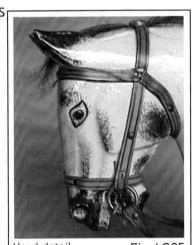

Head detail   Fig.AG05

Baby Carriages Ltd.   1906 - 1963

Address: 165-167, Duke Street, Liverpool.

Incorporated: 1906 Baby Carriages Ltd. Company No. 88,015

Trade name: 'Rambler'

See also: Hill & Harrison   1884 - 1906

In 1906, Baby Carriages Ltd. was incorporated, this new name was given
to the old firm of **Hill & Harrison** and as such continued producing as
before. As the company name suggests, their main business was the
manufacture of perambulators and other allied wheeled items, but they
offered a variety of other goods which included foot cycles, coasters,
snow sleighs, express wagons, tricycles and a range of carved horses,
including **Swing Horses**, **Pole Horses**, **Stool Horses** and **Tricycle Horses**.
The firm was also known for supplying riding schools with larger horses,
special animal chairs for hairdressers and also undertook coach painting
work. In 1916 six sizes of both pole horses and swing stand rocking
horses were offered. An advert from 1916 *Fig.BY01* lists some of their
products that were available at the time and also it also shows a
somewhat strange view of their workshops. It's not clear what buildings

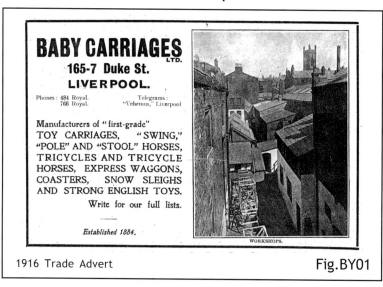

1916 Trade Advert   Fig.BY01

were used, but views of the inside of various departments show us that many small 'workshops' were occupied. Conditions seem far from ideal, all rather cramped and somewhat gloomy. The Horse Shop *Fig.BY02* is

Horse Shop Circa 1916   Fig.BY02

an interesting view, with various leg templates hanging from the ceiling, a stack of components on the bench, behind which are two very large horse heads and also horses being worked on by the three workmen. The joiners shop *Fig.BY03* and the blacksmiths shop *Fig.BY04* are also equally as busy, with materials and components everywhere.

Joiners Shop Circa 1916   Fig.BY03

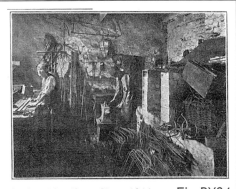

Blacksmiths Shop Circa 1916   Fig.BY04

With the company being based in Liverpool, it is not surprising that one of their markets was to supply horses for ships nurseries to some of the many shipping lines based in Liverpool. The P&O line was certainly one customer. Fig.BY05 is of a BCL horse in the tourist nursery aboard the 'Maloia', this ship was in use between 1923-1954. Another was aboard the P & O ship the 'Strathnaver', in use between 1931-1962. The horse

Tourist Nursery P & O Maloia Circa 1923   Fig.BY05

pictured aboard the Maloia looks quite standard apart from thicker swing irons and heavier top plates than those fitted to a regular horse, probably to take account of the impending intensive use and combined ships movement. Its interesting to note that the horse is not fixed down at all, perhaps it was safer this way. The horse also has pommels, and used as a pair gave very small children an 'added sense of security' as they were more or less balanced on top of what to them would be a huge rocking horse. Young 'ladies' would not have ridden astride but used the pommel as in conventional side saddle riding.

Throughout Baby Carriages' existence, they regularly placed small advertisements in trade publications, these typically were accompanied with a small illustration, but because of the firms main business, these were often of perambulators or carriages. Occasionally an illustration of a small combination rocking horse was used *Fig.BY06*. Apart from this

BABY CARRIAGES LTD.
167, Duke St.
LIVERPOOL.
—:—
Send for our lists of
Shaped Wood Horses,
Foot Cycles,
Carriages,
and
Strong Toys.

1915 Trade Advert   Fig.BY06

illustration and the somewhat unclear images of horses in the 'Horse Shop' picture *Fig.BY02* no further authentic pictures of BCL horses have been found. Fortunately the company did mark some of their top plates *Fig.BY07*. The top plate shown is of a design specific to BCL, but not all of these were marked, the reason for this is unclear. By using these identified examples it is possible to recognise others that were not marked. Later BCL horses were sold under the '*Rambler*' trademark and a small transfer *Fig.BY08* was applied to the base of the stand.

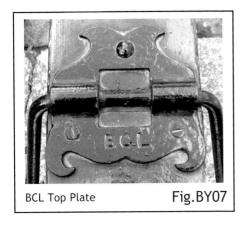

BCL Top Plate   Fig.BY07

Rambler BCL Trademark   Fig.BY08

Around the time the firm was incorporated, 1906, the shape of the horses was changed and they were then produced with their heads tucked back. Fig.BY09 is of a smaller BCL swing horse that measured

Small BCL Swing Stand Horse Circa 1910   Fig.BY09

34 inches tall and has its head back. As was often the case with smaller horses, the eyes were metal studs *Fig.BY10* but with very delicate painting around them. The stand has chamfered edges to the base and cross pieces and also fairly ornate turned posts, *Fig.BY11* one of at least three different patterns that were used until the advent of square posts, this is thought to be towards the end of the 1920's.

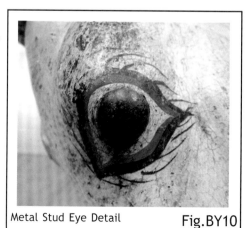

Metal Stud Eye Detail   Fig.BY10

Post
Detail   Fig.BY11

A large 52 inch tall BCL horse *Fig.BY12* also has its head tucked back

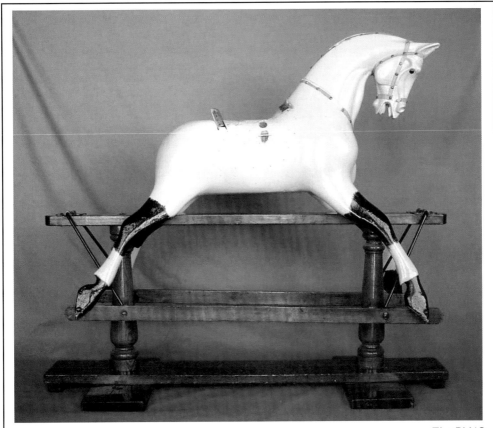

Large BCL Swing Stand Horse Circa 1910

Fig.BY12

the same as the smaller 34 inch horse. The posts are the most ornate style used, *Fig.BY13* the same as on earlier Hill & Harrison horses. This horse was fitted with the BCL top plates in Fig.BY07. One curious point about the stand is that the base and cross pieces are square edged which is not in keeping with the fact that many other aspects of this horse are much more elaborate, the horse also having a degree of extra carving to the head and neck. Ayres style decorative nails were used to cover the nails fixing the posts to the top bar. The horse was originally a typical dapple grey but has been over painted at a later date. This horse also has holes drilled just above the stirrup staples, to fit pommels.

Fig.BY13

A 42 inch tall BCL swing stand horse *Fig.BY14* with its head tucked back

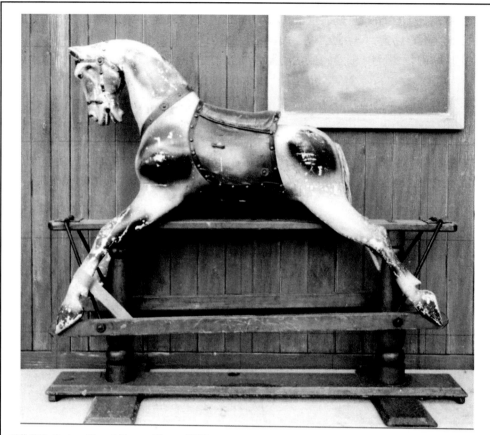

42" BCL Swing Stand Horse Circa 1910

Fig.BY14

differs slightly to the previous horse, the posts are of a much simpler design *Fig.BY15* but have been found on other BCL horses. The top plates are of the unique style as in Fig.BY07 but do not have any markings. The base and cross pieces are chamfered, odd as the horse is not extra carved and has the simpler posts. Again, Ayres style decorative nails were used to cover the nails fixing the posts to the top bar. The horse would have originally been a dapple grey but has been over painted at some time. It is not clear as to why these differences were made. Looking back to the old workshop pictures does not conjure up a vision of great organisation, perhaps items were changed as a new 'batch' was made or possibly different workmen employed.

Fig.BY15

Around the end of the 1920's, square posts became the norm on the entire range of swing stand horses, still thought to have been available in six sizes. Various examples survive, a very large 54+ inch model *Fig.BY16* is a very powerful looking horse. Unfortunately it is not in its original condition, but would have been a dapple grey fitted on a plain

54+" BCL Swing Stand Horse Circa 1930   Fig.BY16

varnished stand when new. Another change was that the design of the top plate. This reverted to a more standard style *Fig.BY17* although as can be seen in the picture, the Ayres type fancy nails were still used to cover construction nails and were also used on the horses as well. The larger horses still had pommel holes as the horse in Fig.BY05 in the nursery of the Maloia. Typically after years of production, not only of BCL but generally all manufacturers, production methods were streamlined and products become standardised, usually accompanied with a reduction in sizes and options available. This course of events happened within BCL and ultimately, sold under the trade name of 'Rambler',

Top Plate Detail

Fig.BY17

only a few sizes of horse were available, but in several different finishes. The standard dapple grey Rambler *Fig.BY18* was probably the most popular at 41 inches tall. As can be seen, the design has been

41" BCL Rambler Swing Stand Horse Circa 1937   Fig.BY18

slightly changed and the head is not tucked back as much as that of its predecessors. The construction of the horses was one of the most basic employed within the trade, the legs were only glued and nailed into notches cut in the body of the horse, all BCL and Hill & Harrison horses were made in this way. However, this was never apparent to the buyer, only the top finish was seen and BCL paid attention to their detail of finish. The glass eyes used were very good quality, the colour actually 'fired' to the glass so as to avoid 'silvering' which was a problem with eyes that had painted backs. The painting around the eye was still very similar to the early horses as in Fig.BY10, compare this to the Rambler eye painting, Fig.BY19. This picture also shows that the heads were well carved and also applied with two of three different types of decorative nails used on the Rambler horse *Fig.BY20.* The harness was a mixture of leather, used on the strap work, leather cloth for saddle blanket and flaps and type of plush velvet was used to cover the saddle *Figs.21&22.* The horse shown has a blue saddle and cloth, red was also an option.

Rambler dapple grey, circa 1937, fitted with blue cloth and saddle.

Head & Eye Detail   Fig.BY19

Decorative
Nails   Fig.BY20

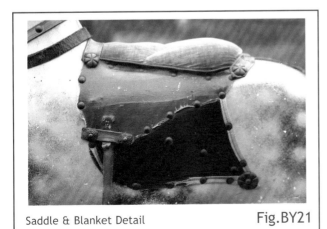

Saddle & Blanket Detail   Fig.BY21

Saddle Top Detail   Fig.BY22

Other options available for the Rambler were a 'Chestnut' painted horse, this had white 'socks' and a white flash on its head and was tacked up as a standard Rambler. The most dramatic option was the spotted polychrome horse *Fig.BY23*. This was not the first BCL model

BCL Spotted Polychrome Rambler Circa 1937   Fig.BY23

to be painted in this style, as an earlier dated horse, circa 1925 is shown in Fig.BY24. This is a larger horse than the Rambler and had pommel holes, a feature that was dropped before the production of the Rambler range. The horse shown has been restored but the colours and placement of spots are true to the original layout. It also has new harness that differs from the factory original.

BCL Spotted Polychrome Circa 1925 Fig.BY24

A number of examples of the Rambler Spotted Polychrome horse are known to exist. All of these are painted in the same format, with the same colour spots in the same places Note the hooves are painted green. One unusual example was found, a horse with no stand, but with marks and screw holes in its belly, implying that it was at one time fitted up for another purpose other than a rocking horse. BCL were not alone in producing these spotted horses and at least two other manufacturers produced similar styled horses. The inspiration for this is not known, but perhaps some social event was the catalyst.

It is unclear when the last rocking horses were made. They were probably produced after WWII for a number of years, but with changing trends and expanding production costs the rocking horse was now not as popular with either producers or the buying public. Fig.BY25 is thought to be an example of the last in the line of BCL horses, the only real discernible difference from earlier Rambler horses is the lack of decorative nails. This is possibly compensated by many more ordinary upholstery studs being applied. In common with all Rambler horses and those just predating them, wooden 'diamonds' were fitted to the top of the stands *Fig.BY26* to hide the construction nails. The earlier horses used the Ayres style decorative nail for this purpose.

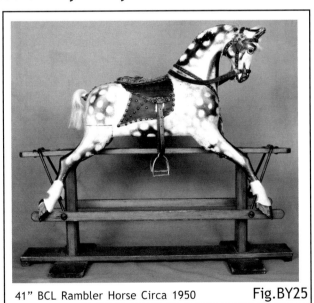

41" BCL Rambler Horse Circa 1950   Fig.BY25

Diamond Detail   Fig.BY26

Baby Carriages Ltd went into voluntary liquidation in 1963 after trading initially as Hill & Harrison, for all but 80 years, a great achievement.

Baker, W.H.

Baker, W.H.   1859 - 1938

Address: 168 & 170, Bethnal Green Road, London. E.

                  98, Gossett Street, Bethnal Green, London. E.

Various trade directories from the 1880's onwards list William Harding Baker as a toy maker and wholesaler, and also mentioned is that he established his business in 1859. **Shaped Horses and Carts** are first mentioned in a trade directory in 1910, but these may well have been made earlier. Trade directories usually only list a persons profession, listed items were the result of paying for 'additional' listing.

In a list of exhibitors at the 1916 British Industries Fair, Baker is described as a well-known toy manufacturer, and amongst his many lines, '**Wooden Horses**' are mentioned. Other items listed are, military and toy drums, battledores, toy rackets, tennis rackets, skipping ropes and a variety of similar items.

It is unknown what form the 'wooden horses' referred to above actually are. It is quite possible that they would be smaller models, as are most of his other items. Mr Baker exhibited regularly at the British Industries Fair up until around 1938, this was an event that many of the country's leading manufacturers used as a major sales platform. These Fairs would have been attended by many of the countries retail 'buyers' and it would have been possible to take enough orders for the whole season.

Barker. Wm. Late Norton & Barker   1932 - 1935

Barker, W. & Sons Ltd.   1935 - 1972

Address: Victory Works. 157, Irving Street, Birmingham.

Incorporated: 1935 W. Barker & Sons Ltd. Company No. 311,044

See Also: Norton and Barker.

The firm of W Barker carried on trading from the now defunct firm of 'Norton & Barker' at around the end of 1931. It is not known what happened to the 'Norton' part of the old firm.
The first recorded advert is from 1932 *Fig.BW01* and this mentions that the firm is *Late Norton & Barker*. The advert also states the firm is the best known maker of toy horses in Britain and goes on to list some of its products. **Rocking Horses, Pole Horses, Push Horses, Stool Horses, Hobby Horses** and **Combination Rocker and Pull Horses.**

In 1935 the firm was incorporated and then referred to as W Barker & Sons Ltd. Early in the firm's career, production was confined to the previously mentioned horses and other strong wooden toys but in 1944 they were also listed as wood turners and wood workers as well. 1947 was the last mention of rocking horses in a trade directory and in 1948 they were listed as packing case manufacturers, joiners and woodworkers. From 1956 up to

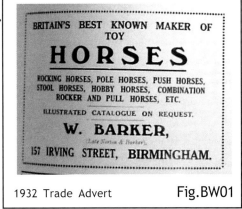

1932 Trade Advert   Fig.BW01

1970 they were listed as furniture makers and in 1965 they had moved to Camden Drive, Birmingham. In November of 1970, the London Gazette recorded that the company had ceased trading and that Mr F R Barker was Chairman at the time. One assumes that he was one of the 'sons' of the original firm. The company was finally dissolved in 1972.

Some of W. Barker's products have been found with the company's trade label, this was a thin transfer applied to the stand in the case of rocking horses. Despite these being rather fragile, a number of horses have survived with the transfer intact *Fig.BW02*. The label consists of the makers initials W B and an illustration of a British bull dog, the Union Flag and captioned 'British Made'. This would certainly date the item to between around 1932 to 1935. It not clear if this same label was used after the firm became incorporated in 1935. With this piece of evidence, it is possible to identify a range of swing stand horses that were made by the company as they shared some very distinctive features. These were common through the range of horses and its thought that at least five or more sizes were offered.

W Barker Makers Label Circa 1935   Fig.BW02

Fig.BW03 is of a small W Barker horse that has the WB transfer, as shown above, applied to the centre of the base. As can be seen, the horse is very upright, as if on tip-toes, and quite simply carved. The smaller horses had no teeth, but with the increase in size, so more detail was carved. The larger horses had teeth and a very large example even had a tongue. Despite the simple look they were quite well made, with mortise and tenon leg joints and all fitted with glass eyes.

Small W Barker Swing Stand Horse Circa 1935   Fig.BW03

Two further examples of small Barker horses *Figs.BW04 & BW05*. The black horse is not original, but was over painted some years ago.

Small Barker Swing Stand Horse   Fig.BW04

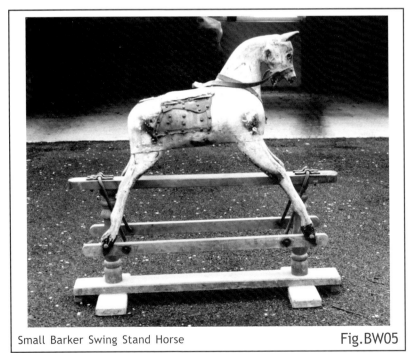

Small Barker Swing Stand Horse   Fig.BW05

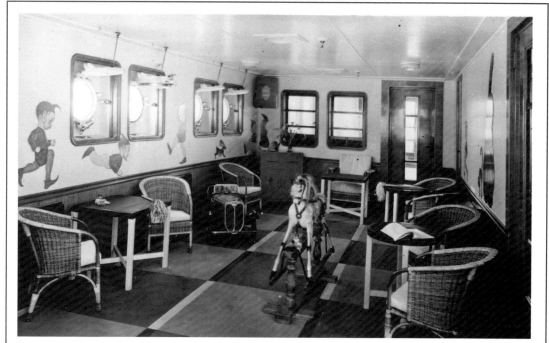

First Class Nursery P&O Ship Canton   Fig.BW06

As with some other manufacturers, mainly based in Liverpool, it would appear that W. Barker also supplied shipping lines with rocking horses. A view *Fig.BW06* of the first class nursery aboard the P&O ship Canton. More effort seems to have been made towards looking after adults than the children, with only two playthings. The picture was probably taken around 1938 when the ship was first commissioned as everything looks new. Certainly the horse in the detailed picture *Fig.BW07* is new. This would correspond to the time when Barker was a limited company. Note that the horse is not fixed down at all, this may have been safer.

Detail Nursery Horse   Fig.BW07

Another small swing stand horse *Fig.BW08* is in original condition. All of the illustrated small horses differ slightly in a number of areas.

Small Barker Swing Stand Horse   Fig.BW08

Three different styles of top plates have been found on Barker rocking horses *Fig.BW09*. The simplest form is two strips of steel bent as hump back bridges, the second is regular one bolt and two screw cast type bracket. A couple of horses have had a 'squared' version of the cast bracket. This squared version has been found on other makes of horse.

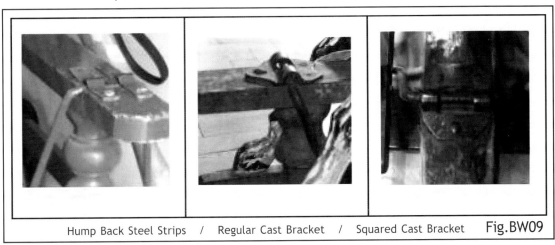

Hump Back Steel Strips   /   Regular Cast Bracket   /   Squared Cast Bracket   Fig.BW09

The posts of Barker horses varied from a fairly plain pattern *Fig.BW10* to a much more elaborate style *Fig.BW11*. There were other variations in between, but they all looked as if an 'extra' and slightly incongruous piece was added to the top, this gives them their distinctive look.

Plain Post Style   Fig.BW10

Elaborate Post Style   Fig.BW11

As previously mentioned, the legs were tenoned, with most horses having both front and back legs fitted square to the body but some horses have been found with the front legs fitted to the body at an angle, this generally being the most popular method employed within the trade. It is not clear if this angled leg model was earlier or later as exact dates for any Barker horse are a little illusive.

A very nice period photograph *Fig.BW12* captioned on the back *'The rocking horse workshop of W Barker & Sons Ltd.'* would date it to after 1935 when Barker was incorporated. Interestingly the horses in the picture are with their legs fitted square into the body.

The workshop scene of W Barker & Sons Ltd. where it is quite possible

Workshop of W Barker & Sons Ltd.   Fig.BW12

that it is actually William Barker and his sons pictured, surrounded by a great number of horses. Most of the horses are various sizes of the swing stand type, but to the left are a number of stool horses. It all seems a little cramped and rather precariously balanced. In the centre of the picture is a partly made horse, the head is fully carved and the legs are shaped, this work being done before assembly. This was usual practice within the trade, being generally the most efficient production method.

Fig.BW13 is the saddle detail of a larger horse, note that it does not have a saddle block. Most Barker horses are in this style but a few have been found with a block fitted.

Saddle Detail   Fig.BW13

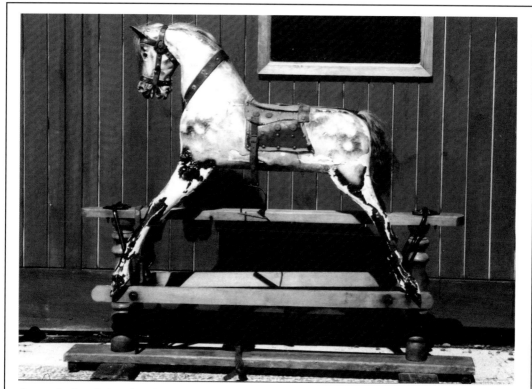

Large Barker Swing Stand Horse
Fig.BW14

The large decorative nails used on the saddle are quite common to Barker horses. Fig.BW14 is a side-on view of the larger horse that is about 48 inches tall. This has the same general 'look' as the smaller horses, with straight legs and looking as if up on tip toes. Fig.BW15 is a detailed view of the head, note the use of the same style of decorative nail as on the saddle. It has carved teeth and the ears and nose are scooped out. This was quite usual on the larger model horses, but these details were left plain on the smaller models.

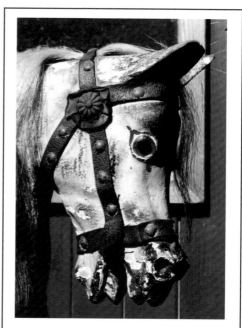

Head Detail
Fig.BW15

Bashall, Betty.

(Thames Vale Industries)

1933 - 1940

Address: 8, Queen's Drive, Thames Ditton, Surrey.

Agents: J K Farnell & Co. 1, New Union Street, London. E.C.2

In 1933, Betty Bashall, wife of a retired naval Officer and keen woodworker, bought a fret saw, cut out a small wooden horse and painted it, at once it became her children's favourite toy. She thought that there may be a demand for her toys and commenced production in her garage. Soon she had to take on workers and move to more suitable premises. Her husband joined her in the business and also her uncle, Mr Roberts, who was sales manager. All the new prototype toys that were made were given to her children to see what sort of response they received, if it were unfavourable, the toy in question did not go into production. One of the first and most popular toys produced was the **Spring horse,** this was available in a variety of sizes and models *Fig.BB01* all being brightly painted for use in the nursery.

Betty Bashall 1935 Trade advert   Fig.BB01

Soon after Betty Bashall had started her business, she found that as she had no showroom or stockroom. A travelling van *Fig.BB02* was the answer to this problem, and it was advertised that upon sending a postcard, a buyer would be visited and the whole range of toys could be viewed. Before the travelling van was acquired, the story goes that a converted Bentley was used for moving and delivering stock.

After only a relatively short time in business, the range of toys also included the **Self-propelling Go-along Horse,** as well as **Spring** and **Rocker Horses.** In a view of the workshop *Fig.BB03* amongst the numerous items being produced, many **Toddler's Horses** can be seen. A pair of Spring horses *Fig.BB04* that are being test ridden by her children.

Betty Bashall 1934 Trade advert

Fig.BB02

Because of the general increase of her business, it was decided in January 1938, that Messrs. J. K. Farnell & Co. Ltd were to be the sole selling agents for her range of wooden toys and nursery furniture.

With the onset of WWII, as with all toy manufacturers, a change of direction was required and the firm produced parts for the Mosquito aircraft. At the end of hostilities, Betty Bashall sold the factory, designed and built a boat, called Mellona and sailed through the French waterways to the Mediterranean and onto Majorca where she retired.

It was known that amongst her many skills Betty Bashall was a keen photographer and undoubtedly she took many pictures including the two shots below.

Workshop circa 1937

Fig.BB03

Betty's children 'test' riding, circa 1935

Fig.BB04

Two Spring horses *Fig.BB05* were originally bought as a pair in 1935 and have remained together their entire existence up to the present day. Some early examples of Betty's toys were signed by her. Both of these Spring horses bear her signature *Fig.BB06*.

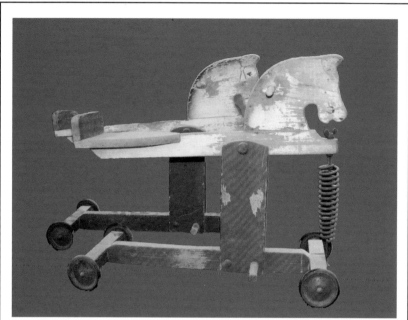

Spring Horses made 1935   Fig.BB05

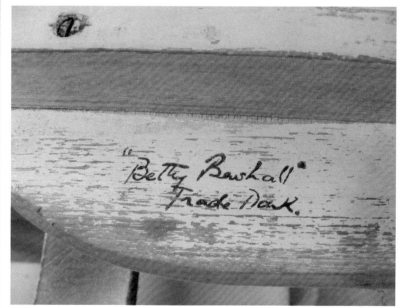

"Betty Bashall" Trade Mark Signature 1935   Fig.BB06

Berwick & Co.   - 1934 -

Address: South Hunter Street, Liverpool.

An advert from 1934 *Fig.BE01* tells us that Berwick & Co. produced a range of goods and toys, amongst which were simple **Swing Horses** and also **Stool Horses** on wheels. The advert was aimed at potential buyers attending their stand at the forthcoming British Industries Fair of 1934.

Berwick & Co.1934 Trade advert   Fig.BE01

The products illustrated do not look to be of very good quality and it is not known if the Fair was a success for these or any of their other products. No further reference to the firm has been found.

Berwick & Co.   - 1934 -

Address: South Hunter Street, Liverpool.

An advert from 1934 *Fig.BE01* tells us that Berwick & Co. produced a range of goods and toys, amongst which were simple **Swing Horses** and also **Stool Horses** on wheels. The advert was aimed at potential buyers attending their stand at the forthcoming British Industries Fair of 1934.

Berwick & Co.1934 Trade advert   Fig.BE01

The products illustrated do not look to be of very good quality and it is not known if the Fair was a success for these or any of their other products. No further reference to the firm has been found.

Bonner, George & Co.   - 1882 - 1899

Address: 106, Albert Street, Regents Park, London. N.W.

See also: Pegram, H.   Abbott, Bonner & Co.(late H Pegram)

Between approximatly 1880 and1900 George Bonner and Henry Pegram seem to have had some sort of business ties. Various directory entries list them as individuals and also listed together, both names are associated with **Rocking Horse Making**, perambulators and also **Life Size Horses** and **Roundabouts**

In 1882, George Bonner is listed as a rocking horse maker and also as *'Pegram, Bonner & Co. 187 Gt Portland St, life size model horses roundabouts'*.
In 1884, he is listed as 'Bonner George & Co.' both as a rocking horse maker and also as a perambulator maker.
The last entry found, in 1899, is *'Abbott, Bonner & Co.(late H. Pegram) established 50 years. 320 Euston Rd. NW; life size model horses'*

It is not clear who was established for 50 years, whether it was George Bonner or Henry Pegram or both.

No known products have been attributed to this maker, despite obviously being productive for eight years, and quite possibly a great deal longer.

Bosworthick, James.　　　　　1940 - 1986

Address:　　　　Kersey, Suffolk, East Anglia.

To supplement his half-crown weekly wage as an apprentice at the Medway dockyards of Kent, James Bosworthick made a small range of toys. These included **Rocking Horses**, model Spitfires, aerodromes and forts. All of which were made in his tiny workshop and sold to a local corner shop. The pattern he used for the rocking horses was acquired from an AFS man he met at the outbreak of war, who was unfortunately killed during the blitz.

James Bosworthick later moved to Wiltshire and then emigrated to Kenya where he was called up into the prison service and subsequently taught the convicts how to carve rocking horses. Then on returning to England some years later, he set up his workshop in Kersey, East Anglia.

The method of construction is that the horses were blocked up by first notching a thick base board and fixing the legs by screws, the rest of the body was built up and the head and neck glued last. Fig.BK01 shows this construction. One of the main timbers used on the bodies was lime, a timber that was renowned as a good carvers wood, beech or ash was used for the legs. The stands for the horses were made from a variety of timbers, depending on availability. Three sizes of swing stands were made and also a bow rocker type, was also available *Fig,BK02*.

James Bosworthick carving.　　　　Fig.BK01

It would be worth noting that James Bosworthwick was an uncle of the 'Stevenson Brothers' and that Tony Stevenson served a short apprenticeship with his uncle. As a result of this very early Stevenson Brothers horses were made in the same fashion and with a similar look.

James Bosworthick Bow rocker

Fig.BK02

Fig.BW03 is a detail picture of the head of the bow rocking horse *Fig.BK02*. Note the slightly unusual style of head carving that was employed by James Bosworthick which will help to identify the make.

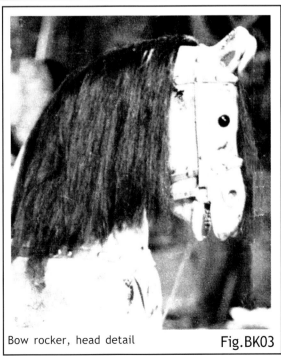

Bow rocker, head detail

Fig.BK03

Brassington & Cooke.　　　1875 - 1937

Address:　1877　　135, Oldham Street, & 27/29 Henry Street.
　　　　　　1879　　135, Oldham Street, & 8 Loom Street, Ancoats.
　　　　　　1886　　Cable Street Mills, Cable Street, Ancoats.

Incorporated:　March 30th 1920.　　Registered No.165,720

The earliest listing for Brassington & Cooke is under the heading of perambulator manufacturer, one of eighteen such manufactures in Manchester alone. Despite the competition, the firm expanded along with their range of products and by 1915 they proudly announced that they were manufacturers of over 100 different toys, as shown in their advert *Fig.BC01*. Some of their products are shown around the border

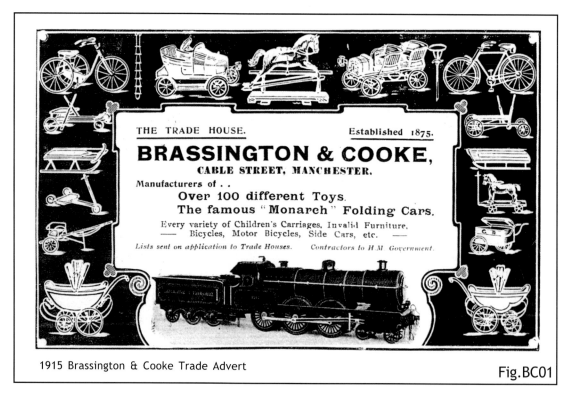

1915 Brassington & Cooke Trade Advert

Fig.BC01

of the advert, including a **Swing Stand Rocking Horse** and also a **Pull-along**. The firm became incorporated in 1920 and was then known as

Brassington & Cooke Ltd. They only dealt with the Trade on a wholesale basis and were regular attenders of trade fairs such as the British Industries Fair of May 1915. A picture of their 'shared' stand *Fig.BC02* shows a range of toys, including a **Rocking horse,** a **Horse & Gig** and some other smaller horses. From the picture, we can make out the distinctive style of the rocking horse and identify the maker.

1915 British Industries Fair Shared Trade Stand   Fig.BC02

A trade supplement of 1921 listed a variety of the company's products. Amongst these were some horse related items and they included, **Swing Rocking Horses, Tricycle Head Horses, Pole Horses, Push Horses Stool Horses, Hand Propelled Trotting Gig & Horse** *Fig.BC03* and a **Horse and Gig** *Fig.BC04*. The hand propelled trotting gig was no doubt

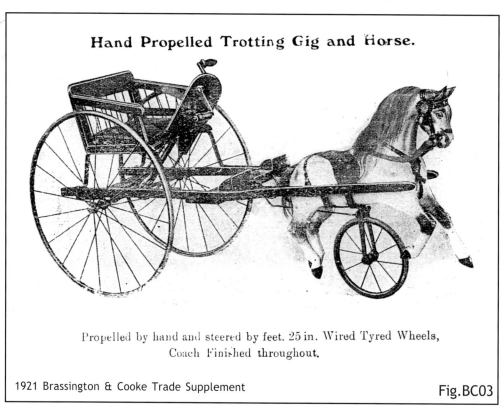

Hand Propelled Trotting Gig and Horse.

Propelled by hand and steered by feet. 25 in. Wired Tyred Wheels, Coach Finished throughout.

1921 Brassington & Cooke Trade Supplement

Fig.BC03

HORSE & GIG

Highly finished in Polished Wood, nicely fine lined, Hand Carved Horse with leather Harness, Strong Levers and Handle. Comfortable Chair with Loose Cushions.

1921 Brassington & Cooke Trade Supplement

Fig.BC04

a result of the company's interest in the manufacture of bicycles and the like, this being a natural hybrid and looking for a niche in the market. Their rocking horses were stocked by various large stores and amongst them was 'Barr's' of Deansgate, Manchester. Examples have been found with this supplier's name stencilled on the base *Fig.BC05* and also some with the store's applied metal label *Fig.BC06*. The metal label also referred to a 'Children's Paradise'. This was widely used in descriptions of the Manchester store which was reputed to be the country's largest toy store at the time.

Barr's Applied Stencil   Fig.BC05

Barr's Applied Metal label   Fig.BC06

Swing stand horses were made in a range of sizes and various examples are known to exist. A lovely photograph taken in 1915 *Fig.BC07* is of a smaller horse with a group of children in attendance. A close up view of

Brassington & Cooke Horse 1915   Fig.BC07

the front of the horse *Fig.BC08* shows a number of identifiable features. The head is raised up and is of good proportion, wide by the ears and tapering to the mouth, carved to a good quality and fitted with glass eyes *Fig.BC09*. The front legs widen just after the join with the body before narrowing to the knee. This feature is constant with all sizes of Brassington & Cooke horses, as is the way that the horses are dappled. The dappling is applied all over the body and neck but is generally very light.The back-ground colour is cream as opposed to the grey used by most other makers.

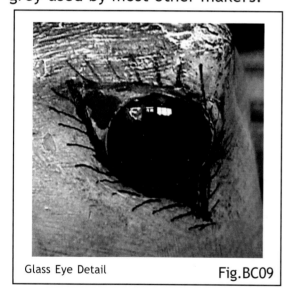

| Glass Eye Detail | Fig.BC09 |

Head and Leg Detail Fig.BC08

A general side view *Fig.BC10* of a basically original but lightly restored horse shows what it would have been like when first purchased. One feature that is very noticeable is the saddle blanket that runs down to a long thin point, finished with a decorative nail. The harness is all leather with the exception of the saddle top and blanket. One point is that the horses were not fitted with a separate bit. The reins were attached by means of rings that were in turn fitted to small threaded

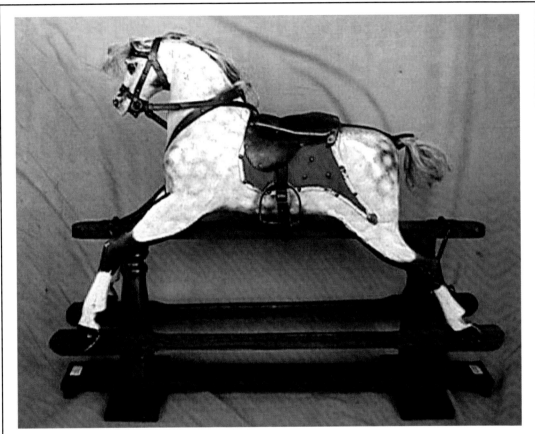

No.2 Brassington & Cooke Swing Stand Circa 1915   Fig.BC10

posts and screwed into the head just above the mouth *Fig.BC11*. The leather strap that ran down the head, passed through the mouth and back up the other side of the head. As was usual at this time, pommels were certainly fitted to the larger horses. Fig.BC12 shows an original pommel in place, note how it is covered in both red and cream so as to match the saddle and cloth. When the pommel was not in place, a small leather flap covered the hole. The pommel hole was drilled through into the hollow center of the horse and was a magnet for children to easily 'post' small items into the belly of the horse, but almost impossible to retrieve. Often during restoration work, typically when a horse is turned upside down, some items make a reappearance. Also during restoration work of B & C horses, some have been found with the bodies made from different types of timber, not good practice and this has resulted in delamination, often a problem found with this maker.

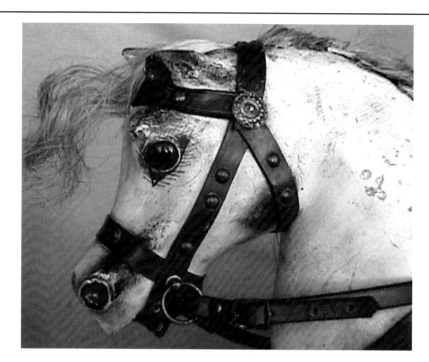

Rein Fixing Detail Brassington & Cooke Horse
Fig.BC11

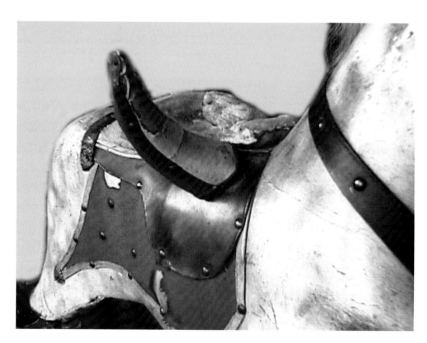

Pommel Detail Brassington & Cooke Horse
Fig.BC12

The stands of most B&C horses have been found to be made out of pitch pine. This is a hard and heavy timber that finishes really well but is a little prone to splitting. The top plates consisted of no more than

No 2 & Top Plate Detail   Fig.BC13

Post Detail   Fig.BC14

a strip of steel, bent as a hump back bridge *Fig.BC13*. Two of these were fitted at each end of the stand. Also in the same picture can be seen the lack of hoof notches and the large '2' stencilled to the end of the stand. presumably with reference to its size. All known Brassington & Cooke horses have had turned posts of the same or very similar style as in Fig.BC14. It would be worth noting that some other makers produced posts of a very similar pattern. In all, their rocking horses would have been very impressive looking when new.

Brierly & Co.

- 1924 -

Address: 12, Theobalds Road, London. W.C.1.

From a trade advert of 1924, Brierly & Co would appeared to have been in business for a while, describing in their advert that they had recently moved to a more centralised position at Theobolds Road.

They made quite a range of smaller mechanical toys, dolls, soft toys and novelties.

The item pictured in the advert *Fig.BY01* would best be described as a novelty, the **Rodeo Broncho,** was a horse's head with a flexible neck that allowed the 'jockey' to turn the head in any direction. The device was held in place by straps, the child, with a little imagination, becoming both the horse and rider.

No further information has been found about Brierly & Co and it is not known how long they continued trading.

BRIERLY & CO.

beg to notify the trade that their Office and Showrooms have been removed to more centrally situated premises at . . . .

12, Theobalds Rd., W.C.1

where an extensive range of Toy Samples can be seen. Deliveries from stock or forward as desired

卐

We hold stocks of MECHANICAL TOYS, HESSMOBILES, MECHANICAL BOATS, DOLLS, SOFT TOYS and NOVELTIES

Apply for Terms which are the most generous in London

卐

RODEO   BRONCHO

Flexible Neck, allowing the head to be turned in any direction.
Sample on request, post free, 1/6.

1924 Trade advert   Fig.BY01

Burlington & Co.   - 1917 -

Address: Unknown

A small entry in a 1917 trade journal reporting on Toy Horses exhibited at a trade fair reads

*"Amongst the sound made-to -last wooden toys manufactured by Messrs. Burlington and Co. **Beech Horses** were prominent"*

No subsequent mention of this firm has been found.

Burrows, G.

Address: 110, Great Saffron Hill, Hatton Garden, London. E.C.

See also: Burrows, W.

From an undated trade card for G Burrows *Fig BG01* it would be reasonable to suggest that there was a family connection to W Burrows, it is not proof positive, but likely that G Burrows preceded W Burrows from the known sequence of address' for both G & W Burrows.

Undated Price List   Fig BG01

G. BURROWS,
Riding Car, Rocking & Toy Horse
MANUFACTURER,
110, GREAT SAFFRON HILL,
HATTON GARDEN. EC.
Old Rocking Horses repaired & repainted,
Country Orders promptly attended to.

		£	s	d
No 0 Rocking Horse, Common		0	6	6
" 1 do		0	12	4
" 2 do		0	18	0
" 3 do		1	4	0
" 4 do		1	14	0
No 0 Rocking Horse, Best Make		0	12	0
" 1 do		0	17	0
" 2 do		1	5	0
" 3 do		1	15	0
" 4 do		2	10	0
No 1 Pole Horses		0	2	?
" 2 do		0	3	3
" 3 do		0	4	6
" 4 do		0	5	6
" 5 do		0	7	0
" 6 do		0	11	0

The card states that G Burrows is a manufacturer of the following: 'Riding Car, **Rocking and Toy Horses'**.
It goes on to list five sizes of 'Common' rocking horse, five sizes of 'Best Make' rocking horse and finally six sizes of **'Pole Horse'**.

The 'Riding Car', as also mentioned in the 1855 advert of W Burrows, is open to speculation, as there is no illustration of the device.

Rocking horses 'Common' and 'Best Make' would have been of the bow rocking type and it is interesting to note the price mark between the two different qualities, this varies from approximatly 60%-75%.

'Pole horses' most likely refers to stick horses with carved heads, and quite a comprehensive range of sizes as well. Obviously to cater for all ages of children. Apparently no 'one size' fits all in those days.

'Old' rocking horses were also advertised as being able to be
'repaired and painted'.

Burrows, W.   1843 - 1855-

Address: 1852-   4, Peter Street. Great Saffron Hill, London.

             1855-   21, Charles Street, Hatton Garden, London.

See also: Burrows G.

The first found mention for W Burrows, is from a trade directory of 1852 in which he is listed as a **Rocking Horse Maker**, but it is known that he started in business around 1843 as an advert of 1855 *Fig.BR01* states his

---

W. BURROWS,
21, CHARLES STREET, HATTON GARDEN, LONDON,
ROCKING HORSE AND TOY MANUFACTURER,
WHOLESALE, RETAIL, AND FOR EXPORTATION;
SOLE MANUFACTURER OF THE IMPROVED AND COMBINED ROCKING HORSE AND RIDING CAR,
FOR THE AMUSEMENT OF ONE, TWO OR THREE CHILDREN, WITHOUT ATTENDANCE,
FROM ONE GUINEA AND A HALF; MADE TO ORDER, TWO GUINEAS UPWARDS.
Small-shaped Horses, Pole Horses, &c. Country Orders promptly Executed.
Old Rocking Horses Repaired.
MERCHANTS & SHIPPING AGENTS LIBERALLY TREATED WITH.

W. B. offers his sincere thanks for the patronage conferred upon him during twelve years past, and embraces this opportunity respectfully to solicit an extension of favours from the Nobility and Gentry, the Trade, and Public in general, hoping to deserve a continuance of their kind support.

W Burrows 1855 Trade Advert   Fig BR01

---

gratitude for *'patronage conferred upon him during twelve years past'.* It is also thought that he followed on from Burrows G in the same business, as there seems to be a very close continuity of products and address'.

Within the advert there is much more information regarding W Burrows business. He supplied wholesale, retail and trade orders and was the sole manufacturer of **"The Improved and Combined Rocking Horse and Riding Car"**. This appears to have been able to be played with up to three children, ..unsupervised.   What this device was is open to speculation, as no illustration of it was provided. It is worth noting on a trade card of a *'Burrows G.'* there is also mention of a *'riding car'.*

Prices started from 'one guinea and a half' and made to order started at 'two guineas'.

Other goods supplied included **'Small Shaped Horses, Pole Horses**, etc. and a repair service for 'Old rocking horses' was also offered.

Quite a thought that in 1855 'Old' horses were being repaired.

No further information regarding W Burrows has been found.

The two streets as mentioned in the different address' for W Burrows are geographically very close to each other.

Cadby, T & Sons (1921) Ltd. 1921 - 1923

Address: 389-397, Farm Street, Birmingham.

This little known firm seemed to have manufactured a great variety of tricycles and scooters, but also as described in a 1922 advert *Fig.CY01* **'A Chain Drive Horse Tricycle'** was also offered.

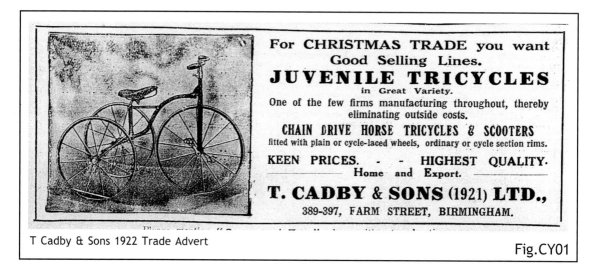

T Cadby & Sons 1922 Trade Advert

Fig.CY01

The firm advertised the fact that they 'manufactured throughout', but this was obviously to no avail, because by February of 1923 it was reported in the London Gazette that the firm had been voluntarily wound up, and because of its liabilities could not continue in business.

Calton, Robert.   - 1845 -

Address: 14, Low. Kennington Green, London.

See also: Leach P.

A Post Office directory entry for Robert Calton in 1854 lists him as a
Rocking Horse Maker, unfortunately this is the only known reference.

However, in 1854 Paul Leach (Rocking Horse Maker) also has a listing at
14 Low. Kennington Green. The significance of this is unclear, although
we do know that earlier in 1826 Paul Leach did serve an apprenticeship
to learn about rocking horse making, perhaps he later took over or
bought out Robert Calton.

Carlton, Richard. 1838

Address: 6 Webber Street, New Cut, London.

Recorded as a producer of **Rocking Horses**. No further information.

Cartwright, F.A. & Co.   1896 - 1956

Address: Justice Works, 178, Charles Henry Street, Birmingham.

Export Agents: T.J.Walsh & Son. 18, Cullum St. Fenchurch St. London.

Primarily, from their Birmingham factory *Fig.CT01* F A Cartwright were manufacturers of bicycles and tricycles, but their production also included juvenile toy motor cars and **Tricycle Horses**. The majority of items produced are done wholly on site, apart from the production of the rubber tyres which are bought in.

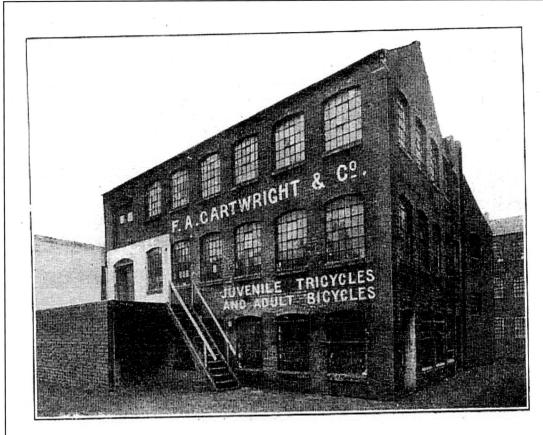

F. A . Cartwright Factory circa 1912   Fig.CT01

The tricycle horse was shown as Model No.53 *Fig.CT02* in their list and was described thus;
The bodies are made of best pine, while the legs are of birch and glass eyes. The saddles are padded, and enamelled in black (or art colours). It can be had with either cemented or wired on rubber tyres.

F. A. CARTWRIGHT & Cº

JUSTICE WORKS,
CHARLES HENRY STREET, BIRMINGHAM.

All kinds of Toy Motors, Horses,

etc., made in all sizes.

Our
Model No. 53.

From 1915 Trade advert

Fig.CT02

It is unknown if the tricycle horse was available in different sizes, or if the choice was purely that of tyre type. Fig.CT03 shows one of the firm's juvenile toy motor cars.

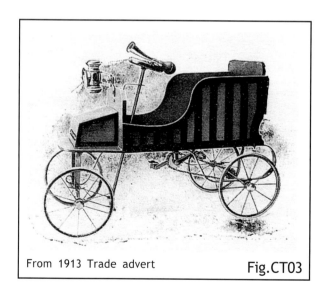

From 1913 Trade advert   Fig.CT03

Cartwright & Watkins.

- 1914 -

Address: 10, Bissell Street, Birmingham.

Export agent: G Heiser & Co., 27, Barbican, London. E.C.

The firm of Cartwright and Watkins manufactured juvenile tricycles, cycles, frames, and **Tricycle Horses** *Fig.CW01* around 1914 when this illustration was published. It is not known when the firm started or finished. A trade report of the time reported *'that the lines are turned out extremely well, particular care being given to the finish. The workmanship is excellent, while the value is apparent'*.

Cartwright & Watkins Illustration circa 1914   Fig.CW01

Cheshire, John.

Address: 11, Jackson's Row, Manchester.

John Cheshire is listed in an 1863 Slater's Directory of Manchester and Salford as a **'Rocking Horse Maker'**. No other listings or information have been found

Chinn & McMillen   - 1920 -

Address: 23, St James Road, Kingston-on Thames, London.

Trade name: "Chimac"

Just one small trade advert dated January 1920 is all the information
that is known about Chinn & McMillen. From the advert it would be fair
to assume that the firm had just started as they were looking for
representatives for various parts of the country.
The 'Chimac' **Rocking Horse** *Fig.CM01* is of a basic design and would
have been aimed at the lower end of the market. The firm also
produced other items including the "Chimac" Propellor Car and Rolls
Royce Scooter. It is not known how long the firm stayed in business as
no further information has been found.

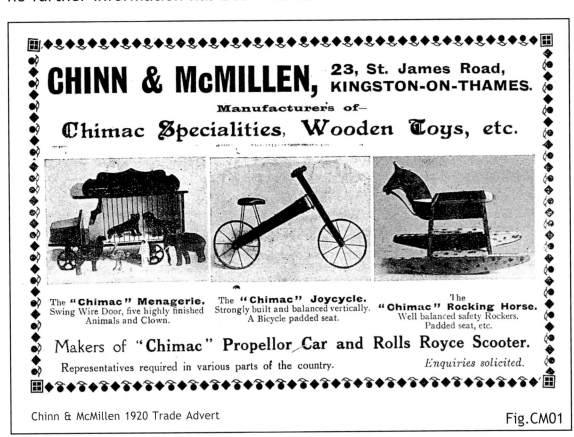

Chinn & McMillen 1920 Trade Advert

Fig.CM01

Churchward, John George.   - 1891 -

Address: 280, Cambridge Road, London. E.

John George Churchward is listed in an 1891 London Post Office directory under the heading of **'Rocking Horse Makers'**. No other listings or information has been found.

Collinson, J. & Sons.   1836 - 1994

Address: 1853   56, London Road, Liverpool.
                  1920   Richmond Terrace, Liverpool.
                  1935   Great Georges Road, Liverpool.
                  1965   465, Smithdown Road, Liverpool.

The firm of Collinson was one of the longest established **Rocking Horse** makers in the UK. Reputedly set up around 1836 by William Collinson who was a cabinet maker by trade, his father was also thought to have been in the trade as well. Very little factual information is known about the early years, stories are told and handed down, but can be muddled. It is thought that William decided to make toys as this was possibly more lucrative than cabinet making and having recently married, aged 21, money was an issue. Small items such as **Horse and Carts** were thought be have been produced at first. An interesting anecdote from this time was told thus.

*One day, a certain Mr William Gladstone, of Rodney Street, Liverpool, visited Mr Collinson to order a horse on a stick. "What do you call them" Mr Gladstone asked the proprietor. "Nothing in particular, I just make them as a hobby", was the reply. "Then we must call them **Hobby Horses**" said the man who was to become one of England's most famous Prime Ministers.*

Another popular story is that to honour a visit by Queen Victoria to Liverpool in 1851, rocking horses made by Collinson's were from then on to be painted as dapple greys, the colour of the horses pulling Queen Victoria's coach. Up to this time they were apparently all painted black.

One of the first known directory entries is from 1853 and lists William Collinson as a **Toy Manufacturer** at 56 London Road, Liverpool.

From the outset, the firm was very much a family business, William's wife joined him and also their children. The family name 'Jervis' gave rise to the 'J' in J Collinson & Sons, the firm having gone on for five generations, all the time employing family members, wives, brothers, sisters, and occasionally at busier times taking on a few out-workers. One such worker was reputed to be a young Tommy Handley who went on to become one of Britain top entertainers of stage and radio. Whatever the stories, Collinsons supplied a sizable proportion of the British and overseas market for a longer period than any other maker. All the rocking horses produced by Collinson's up to 1880 would have been the old style bow rocker, but no information regarding these has been found. Very little if any information about any of their products appears to have been catalogued making identification of early models difficult.

A small amount of documentation from the 1950's onwards gives us a little more insight as to the latter years. It was reported in 1959 the firm was producing up to 700 horses a year. As a small family run firm that had not really changed much since 1900 one can assume that production over the years would have been reasonably constant, even if the 1959 production figure was high, an average of at least a couple of hundred horses a year would be plausible. By this reckoning there should be a considerable number of similar looking horses awaiting identification. This appears not to be the case. From the 1950's demand would have appeared to be quite steady, with multiple orders from many department stores up and down the country. Other special orders were also takensuch as Collinsons supplying some of the Liverpool based shipping lines with rocking horses. One such order in 1959 was for the 'Windsor Castle' Liner, launched by the Queen Mother from Cammell Laird's shipyard at Birkenhead. Occasionally these 'ocean going' horses were painted in bright polychome colours, though it was not reported what colour or model of horse was supplied to the 'Windsor Castle'.

From around 1970 many of the 'family' department stores closed down with a change in retailing as supermarkets came to the fore. With these closures so Collinson's orders began to slowly diminish and ultimately the firm announced its closure in 1994. This news had two effects, firstly the old firm was 'bought' by a local businessman and secondly it inspired a musical to written. The musical was written by John Robinson who had fond memories of his 'school' rocking horse that was allowed to be ridden as a reward for good behaviour. The musical was called 'Shipperbottom's' and was based on the ups and downs of Collinsons. A fitting tribute to the longest serving British rocking horse maker. While Collinsons were at the Great Georges Road workshops, three generations of Collinsons were working together.

The most senior family member was Jervis(I) *Fig.CN01.* He was generally reported as being William's son, but this must be an error. William, going by dates thought to be accurate, would have been born at the latest in 1820, this would make him 60+ at the time of Jervis(I) birth! Perhaps a generation has been skipped. Jervis(I) worked almost up to the time of his death, his later years spent carving the horses heads. His son Jervis(II) was also involved with the carving and is seen 'roughing out' *Fig.CN02* the bodies of the horses. Note that they have been put together with almost all of the components carved. This was a method of production favoured by many rocking horse manufacturers. The horse's legs

Jervis (I) Collinson
1881 - 1965   Fig.CN01

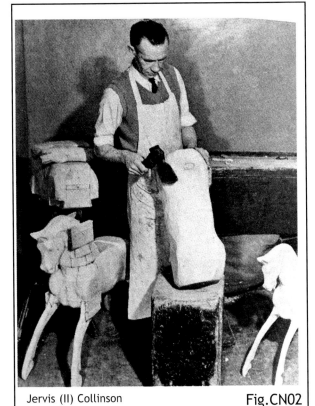

Jervis (II) Collinson   Fig.CN02

were assembled using a method that used nails to fix the legs. The horse body by Jervis'(II) elbow has been 'notched'. The legs would have been glued and nailed into place. This was a much quicker and therefore cheaper option than the more sophisticated mortise and tenon leg joint. It is not known what method of construction was used on their early bow rocking horses, certainly anything other than a mortise and tenon joint would be very short lived. Although the family members did all have some 'specific' jobs within the firm, they were all able to carry out many of the different tasks that would have been required. Jervis (III) is busy painting horses *Fig.CN03* with what is likely to be gesso. This is the base coat, consisting of a calcium carbonate powder (whiting) and an animal glue, that was applied to most rocking horses as primer and substrate coat before the colour coats were applied. Jane (wife of Jervis II) is occupied with the finishing of the horses *Fig.CN04*. Although the picture is a little posed, she was responsible, amongst other things, for the making up of the saddles and harnessing the horses and also the fitting of the manes and tails.

Jervis (III) Collinson

Fig.CN03

Mrs Jane Collinson

Fig.CN04

Swing stand horses have been made in twelve different sizes over the years, but some of the smaller and larger sizes have been 'specials' and made in very limited numbers. The 'sizes' of the horses were defined by the length of the horses body (measured in inches) and would have been referred to as such during manufacture. The sizes made were as follows: **12", 15", 17", 19", 21", 23", 25", 27", 30", 33", 36", 39'**. The smallest 12" horse was produced briefly in the mid 1980's and only about a dozen were made. Only a couple of the largest 39" horse were thought to have been made, one of these may well have been 'Blackie'. Blackie was housed in the children's clothing department of Blacklers department store in Liverpool and stood over 5' tall. During Collinsons busiest period of production, thought to be around the 1950's, up to nine of the sizes would have been produced on a regular basis. After this the choice was lessened to around three by the 1980's. The horses made after the Second World War were quite discernible but before this is not as clear. A 19" swing stand horse *Fig.CN05* made around 1920 or perhaps earlier can be recognised by the characteristic profile of a 'Collinsons' horse. The paint work and glass eyes are not original and should be discounted for identification purposes. All the basic timber

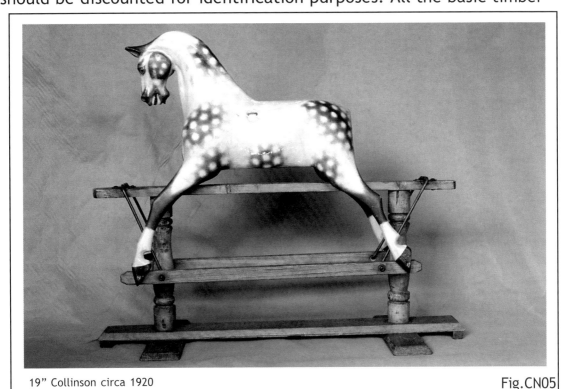

19" Collinson circa 1920   Fig.CN05

elements of both the horse and the stand are original. The posts *Fig.CN06* are turned, this may well have been a standard format in the early 20th century, but almost all other known Collinson horses have square cut posts *Fig.CN07*.

An interesting feature about the stand with the turned posts is that the base and cross pieces have chamfered edges. Again this may well have been a regular feature of the earlier stand.

Round Post Detail — Fig.CN06

Square Post Detail — Fig.CN07

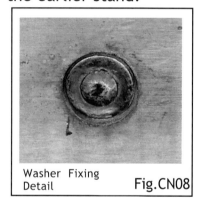

Washer Fixing Detail — Fig.CN08

On the early stand, the swinging irons were held in place in the runners with a washer fitted over the end of the iron *Fig.CN08* and then the end of the iron has been 'peened' over to stop the washer from coming off. This method of fixing was used by Collinson up to around the mid 1950's. After this a 'starlock' fitting was used *Fig.CN09*. This is a 'one fix' toothed push fitting designed to fit onto a round bar. The picture shows the outside and inside faces of a typical starlock. The original swing iron brackets were missing from the early horse *Fig.CN05* so it is not clear what design they were, possibly not of good quality, hence their demise.

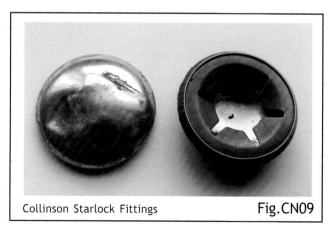

Collinson Starlock Fittings — Fig.CN09

A photograph taken around 1915 *Fig.CN10* shows a horse on a swing stand, the horse is in a worn condition indicating it was made some years earlier, circa 1905. The stand of this horse is almost identical to that in Fig.CN05. From this it would be reasonable to assume they are

Attributed to Collinson circa 1905   Fig.CN10

from the same firm. However, the horse in the picture above is of a slightly different profile to the other horse. This may well be due to a general change of 'patterns' within the workshops, this is known to have occurred within other companies. Later Collinsons horses do have a characteristic 'arched' neck, this style is even evident in the smaller push and pole horses they produced. The quality of Collinsons horses, as with other makes, slowly dropped over the years but they were still easily recognisable.

Pictured below is a large 30" horse that was made around 1950 and has

30" Collinson Swing Stand Rocking Horse circa 1950   Fig.CN11

survived quite well in its original condition *Fig.CN11*. The horses were reasonably well carved at this time, and the larger models were still fitted with pommels *Fig.CN12*, unfortunately the family dog had chewed at these. Glass eyes were no longer fitted but now had 'wooden' eyes that were set into the head to give a realistic look *Fig.CN13*.

The wooden eyes, which must have been an awkward and time consuming task, were replaced in the mid 1950's with various types of upholstery nails, depending upon the size of the horse.

Pommel Detail   Fig.CN12

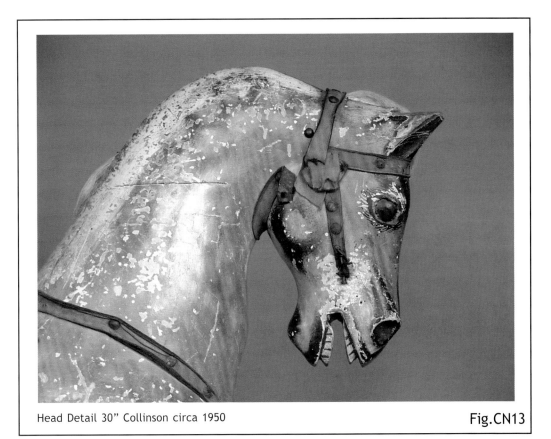

Head Detail 30" Collinson circa 1950   Fig.CN13

The saddle was made up with a velvet material top, also used to cover the pommels, and had leather cloth flaps. The saddle blanket was also made from leather cloth with a frilled edging, *Fig.CN14*. Note also the small leather flap that is above the pommel hole. This was designed to cover the hole when the pommel was not in use. Very often small items were 'posted' through the pommel holes ending up inside the body of the horse. Once inside they were almost impossible to retrieve, only being rediscovered during restoration work.

Saddle Detail 30" Collinson circa 1950   Fig.CN14

A selection of Collinsons horses in different body sizes, all in worn but original condition.

15" body *Fig.CN15*.

15" Collinson Swing Stand Rocking Horse circa 1954   Fig.CN15

17" body *Fig.CN16*.

17" Collinson Swing Stand Rocking Horse circa 1954   Fig.CN16

A selection of Collinsons horses in different body sizes, all in worn but original condition.

19" body *Fig.CN17.*

19" Collinson Swing Stand Rocking Horse circa 1960   Fig.CN17

21" body *Fig.CN18.*

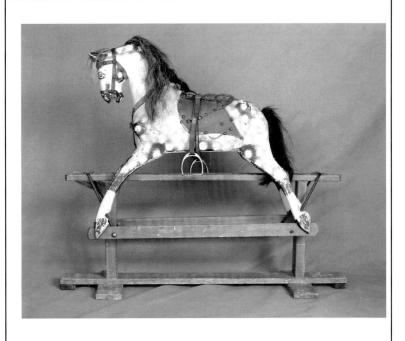

21" Collinson Swing Stand Rocking Horse circa 1960   Fig.CN18

A selection of
Collinsons horses
in different body
sizes, all in worn
but original
condition.

23" body *Fig.CN19*.

23" Collinson Swing Stand Rocking Horse circa 1965   Fig.CN19

25" body *Fig.CN20*.

25" Collinson Swing Stand Rocking Horse circa 1955   Fig.CN20

A selection of Collinsons horses in different body sizes, all in worn but original condition.

27" body *Fig.CN21*.

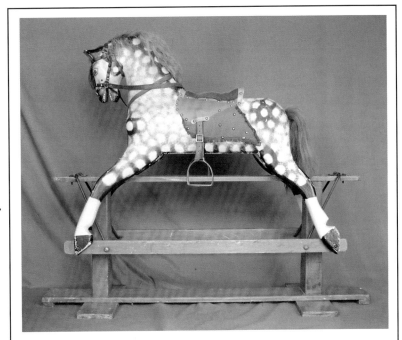

27" Collinson Swing Stand Rocking Horse circa 1965   Fig.CN21

30" body *Fig.CN22*.

30" Collinson Swing Stand Rocking Horse circa 1965   Fig.CN22

The top horse is the third largest produced with the 33" body, standing at almost five foot tall. This example has had some restoration work.

33" body *Fig.CN23*.

33" Collinson Swing Stand Rocking Horse circa 1952   Fig.CN23

All the previous horses have been of a similar style of dappling, however in the late 1970's Collinsons changed their style of painting to that of the 27" example shown here.

27" body *Fig.CN24*.

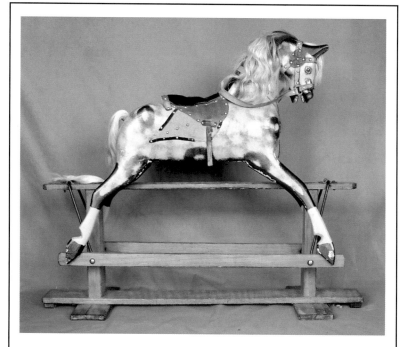

27" Collinson Swing Stand Rocking Horse circa 1978   Fig.CN24

Spotted Polychrome Horses *Fig.CN25* were reported as being supplied to shipping lines. These were basic horses that had just been painted in a different style than normal. A couple of other manufacturers also produced similar painted horses. Other slight changes such as stronger swing iron brackets were often used as well, to cope with additional strain. Collinsons also produced a number of **Fabric Covered Horses** *Fig.CN26* around the 1970's This was a basic standard horse that had a brown 'plush' material applied directly over the wooden body. It seems an odd thing to do, as normally a plush horse is seen as a cheaper option to a painted horse and at the time a number of British firms specifically produced cheap plush horses.

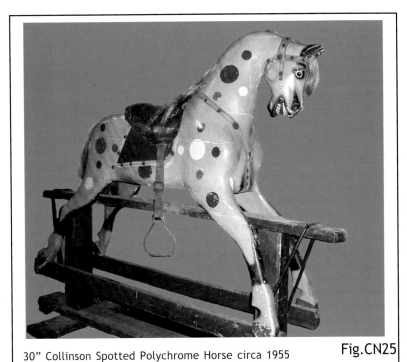

30" Collinson Spotted Polychrome Horse circa 1955   Fig.CN25

25" Collinson Fur Fabric Covered Horse 1970   Fig.CN26

Although Collinsons 'carved' rocking horses were generally placed at the cheaper end of the market in comparison to other makers of the day, they themselves offered cheaper options within their own range.

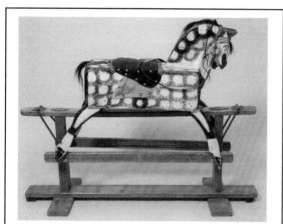

Simple Square Box
Collinson circa 1965

Fig.CN27

Simple Streamlined Box
Collinson circa 1955

Fig.CN28

At least two different **Box Type** models were made, both quite small. They used a regular stand from a 17" body size horse. One version *Fig.CN27* has an almost square body, this was made from boards simply nailed together with the edges rounded off. There was no board fitted to the underside face of the body, this was left open. The head was cut out from two inch thick timber, roughly shaped and nailed to the body. The legs were cut from thin board, edges rounded and nailed to the body. Another version was more streamlined *Fig.CN28*, made in the same way as the other horse but with much shallower sides. The sides had the lower edge cut so as to suggest the horse had a belly. The simple box horses were painted in a similar way to their carved counterparts. They were also harnessed and fitted with real hair manes and tails. Cows tails were used for the manes and tails, not only on the simple box horses but on all of their shaped horses. Cow hair is discernible from horse hair in that it is generally quite curly. However, the mane is usually the first thing to disappear from an old horse, as it is 'loved' away by the constant attention of the young rider.

The eyes of the box horses were painted on the head and had an upholstery nail in the centre representing a pupil. This was the same method of creating an eye as that used on the carved horses, only the very early horses appear to have had glass eyes.

156

The painting of the eyelid and lashes changed over the years from one family member took over from another. A selection *Fig.CN29* of painted eyes show some of the variations, from really delicate to very crude.

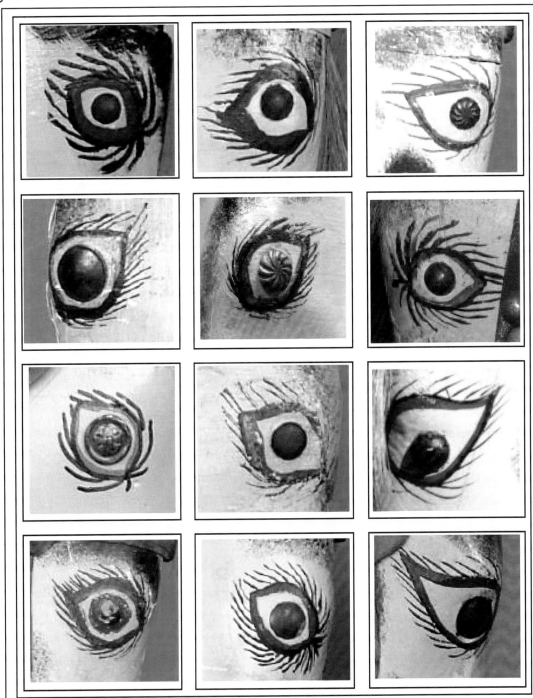

Selection of Collinson Eye Painting

Fig.CN29

The stands of Collinson's horses have several points of recognition, possibly the best known is the 'diamond' shaped piece of plywood or hardboard that is fitted to the top bar of the stand directly above the posts. This is to cover the large nails used to hold the stands together. Another point is that the swinging irons were painted red on horses made from the mid 1950's. There were also various types swing iron brackets *Fig.CN30* used over the years. Older horses have been found with composite brackets, these were made up of four pieces, two flat strips holding down two 'humped' shaped pieces. Small 15" horses have

Composite 'Humped' Bracket

Small Double 'Humped' Bracket

Chrome Double 'Humped' Bracket

Small Cast Bracket

Large Cast Bracket

Large Cast Bracket Markings 'J & GL'

Selection of Collinson Swing Iron Brackets

Fig.CN30

had painted 'humped' brackets fitted. Many horses were fitted with the chrome 'humped' brackets but these were really not up to the task and were often replaced at a later date. Cast brackets were also used and generally fared much better. They are found in two sizes, both of which are copies of brackets made originally by G&J Lines as can be seen on the underside of the large bracket illustrated.

As with all makers a few oddities turn up, one such is a standard 23" body horse mounted on a conventional stand *Fig.CN31*. Peculiarly the swinging irons had no fixings on the end where they fitted the runner. The irons were bent as usual but the ends were cut short so as not to protrude through the runner. The outside was covered by a 'diamond' as used on the top bar. The 'diamonds' were found with writing on the reverse, some old workshop information perhaps.

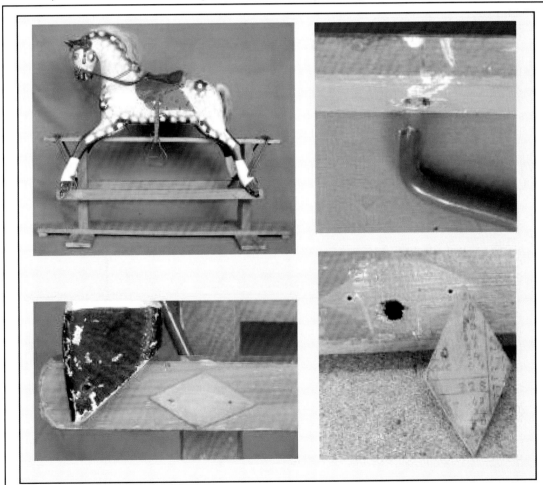

23" Body Collinson Horse with Diamond Covers on Runners

Fig.CN31

Collinsons also produced a variety of smaller wooden horses, one of which was the **Pull Along** *Fig.CN32*. The horse shown has the distinctive arched neck associated with the make along with a 'notched' body to accept the nailed-on legs, it has a body length of 17". They were obviously made from some rocking horse components wherever possible, certainly utilising the same 'bodies' of the smaller horses. The horse is original although somewhat worn but the wheels may well be later replacements.

17" Collinson Pull Along circa 1950

Fig.CN32

Another small horse variation was the **Pole Horse** *Fig.CN33*. This is a 17" body model, has a pivoting front axle and is fitted with cast iron wheels. (The handle is lost) It is in original condition with delicately painted eyes *Fig.CN34* and has its factory saddle *Fig.CN35*. The red top is a type of leather cloth and is fitted with real leather flaps.

17" Collinson Pole Horse circa 1938   Fig.CN33

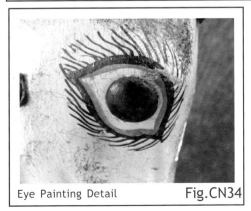

Eye Painting Detail   Fig.CN34

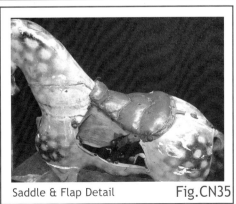

Saddle & Flap Detail   Fig.CN35

Push horses were also a popular version of the small horse. The model

15" Collinson Push Horse circa 1955   Fig.CN36

shown *Fig.CN36* has lost its push handle, which would have consisted of two metal rods fixed to the base, running up to the horses back leg and above then joined by a wooden stretcher. It is possible to see the metal brackets on the rear leg. This horse also had a paper label stuck to the underside of the platform *Fig.CN37*, handwritten with Harrod's address.

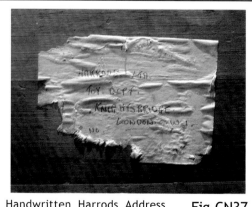

Handwritten Harrods Address   Fig.CN37

Cox, Henry.   -1870-1881-

Address: 53, Bedford Street, Belgrave Gate, Leicester.

Various Leicestershire directory entries have been found for Henry Cox at 53 Bedford Street listing him as a **Rocking Horse Maker** and wood carver and are as follows;

1870	Rocking Horse Manufacturer
1875	Rocking Horse Maker
1875	Wood carver, and Rocking Horse Maker.
1876	Rocking Horse Maker
1878	Wood carver and Rocking Horse Maker
1880	Wood carver and Rocking Horse Maker
1881	Rocking Horse Maker

No other records or information about Henry Cox have been found, but listed as a rocking horse maker for eleven years, he must have produced a reasonable number of rocking horses.

A recent visit to the area, discovered that a relatively modern industrial building had been erected at No.53 Bedford Street and no trace of the old was left.

Crossley Brothers.   -1914 - 1979

Address: Station Works, Blackpool, Lancashire.

Crossley Brothers originally started their business in Yorkshire, but after the Great War they moved to Blackpool and over the years built up one of the largest mills in the north employing at one time up to 600 workers. The firm described itself as Woodware manufacturers, with the mainstay of the business supplying gas producing companies with timber purifying grids for the production of coal gas, this was more or less an ongoing theme as the grids needed regular replacement. Crossley's premises were adjacent to the railway which was an advantage when receiving the huge quantities of timber involved in their work. Fig.CY01 is from the cover of their 1935 brochure and shows a wonderful panorama of the works beside the railway. The main building was by all accounts very impressive, with its entrance to the offices reminding the visitor perhaps of the foyer of a high class cinema, with the firms initials **'CB'** proudly set into the timber floor.

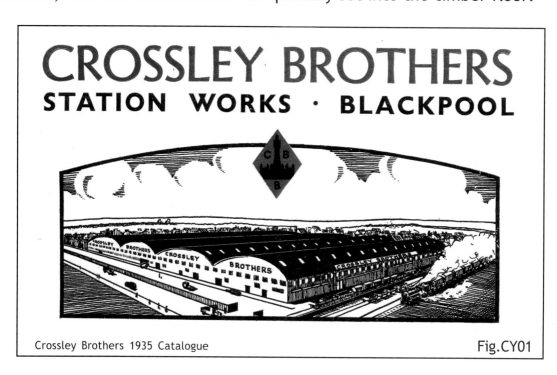

Crossley Brothers 1935 Catalogue   Fig.CY01

Around the beginning of the 1930's it was decided that a range of toys were to be made and to promote this new venture for the firm a stand was taken at a 1933 British Industries Fair in London. Fig.CY02 is a picture of the stand which was used in a trade advert, this has a **Rocking Horse** on display which was admired by her Majesty the Queen (Mary) during her visit to the fair.

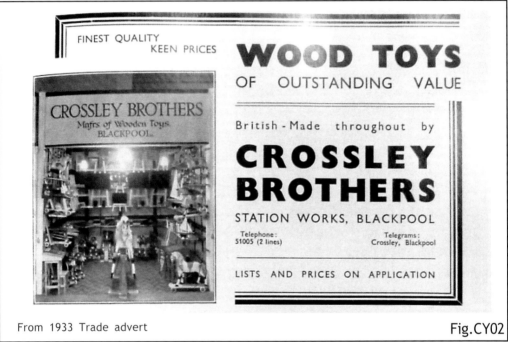

From 1933 Trade advert   Fig.CY02

The production of toys was carried on up to the outbreak of the second world war, and as with other toy manufacturers this was then stopped, but Crossley's were kept busy throughout the war with essential supplies such as tent poles, duck boards and sheds. After hostilities ceased they did not resume toy making, but stuck with the production of domestic woodware along side the timber yard and manufacture of gas purification grids. However, during the 1930's Crossley Brothers range of toys was quickly built up to a creditable range of well made items that were popular with the trade, their range included engines, wheelbarrows, sandcarts, child's desks, boards and easels, scooters and a large range of model yachts.

The author has had the opportunity to discuss the company with former employees and accounts are given of how some of the men worked during the evenings painting the toys. Harry Aspin, (foreman painter) and John Preston being just two of the hundreds of staff at the works.

A very touching first-hand account, recorded in 2008, by Gladys Narcott described a little of her time at Crossley Brothers between the years 1934 and 1946.

"*I worked there from 1934 to 1946, so I am knocking-on a bit. I remember the rocking horses we use to make. There was just one man Tommy Turtum that worked on the heads, shaping the nose ears mouth, he made a beautiful job. We had the job of painting them white & dappling them, also painting the nostrils & eyes. We worked on household goods such as steps, ironing boards, card tables, rubbing boards, knife boxes & sea grass stools & chairs. They came up from the machine shop already shaped & the girls use to nail them together. I am or use to be a dab hand with a hammer & nails & a screwdriver. When it got to September we went on making toys. Wheelbarrows, engines, little trucks & little horses on wheel. We use to start work at eight in the morning until half past five with one hour for lunch which we ate at our benches. I use to catch the half past seven train in the morning. It came from Fleetwood. I got on it at Burn Naze. The driver use to give us a whistle when he came round the bend, that was to tell us to start running if we were not already on the platform. We could get a rail contract for two shillings and sixpence that lasted us a month & you could travel as many times as you liked all the way to Blackpool if you wished. We use to get off at Bispham where Crossleys bridge is. My wage when I started was seven and sixpence a week. We worked overtime near Christmas and I got nine shillings and eleven pence. Our wages went up one shilling a year until we got to twenty-one and that was our wages. During the war we went on war work, tent poles, duck boards and sheds. I met my husband at Crossleys. He was fourteen and I was fifteen and we have been married sixty two years in January. Ron use to leave Crossleys during the summer to work on deck chairs and come back in the winter. From the train you could see all the timber stacked up all being seasoned.*"

Ron Narcott also gave account of working alongside Tommy Turtum, who was a man very much to himself, occasionally putting his hand out to be passed some tool or other, or perhaps the glue pot whilst assembling the horses. Ron also recorded that the horses were given several coats of whiting and were fitted with cows tails for the hair and that the horses were wrapped in brown paper and protected by simple wooden frames for delivery in Crossley's own vans or lorries.

A range of horse based items were manufactured and included twelve different variations of **Push and Stool Horses.** Fig.CY03 is from their 1935 catalogue and lists the range. These were aimed at the cheaper end of the market and interestingly there was an option mentioned on the price list to have a hair mane fitted at 1d. on No.1 horses, 1½d. on No.2 horses and 2d. on No.3 horses.

CROSSLEY BROTHERS - BLACKPOOL

STOOL PUSH HORSES.

Turned hardwood wheels in two colours, dappled grey Finished in leather-cloth, well upholstered, shaped head and legs, varnished.

No. 0.	Height to top of handle	19 in.
No. 1.	Do. (as illustrated)	20¼ in.
No. 2.	Do.	22¼ in.
No. 3.	Do.	23¼ in.

Super No. 4. Chamfered legs, solid platform, superior finish, stained and varnished, height to top of handle 24 in.

No. 20. ROCKER. A No. 1 Push Horse, as above, but with wide axles and rockers in place of handle and platform.

No. 21. COMBINATION. Exactly as No. 1 Push Horse, but with detachable rockers.

SAFETY SWING STOOL HORSE. A safe Swing Horse, built on a substantial stand, with mane and steel swing fittings. Height to head 26 in., length of stand 36 in., height of stand 14 in.

STOOL HORSES.

Cast wheels, flat seat, dappled grey, leather-cloth finish, shaped head.

No. 01.	Height to top of head	10 in.
No. 02.	Do.	12 in.
No. 03.	Do.	14 in.

SHEET No. T.2

Crossley Brothers 1935 Catalogue

Fig.CY03

167

In the middle of the range were the **Semi Shaped Horses**, these were available as **Push Horses** *Fig.CY04* and as **Combination Push & Rocking Horse** *Fig,CY05* . The combination horse was basically a push horse that was fitted to a simple bow, being easily removable to be used on its own as a push horse.

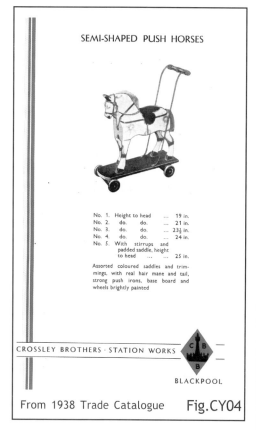

SEMI-SHAPED PUSH HORSES

No. 1. Height to head   ...   19 in.
No. 2.   do.   do.   ...   21 in.
No. 3.   do.   do.   ...   23½ in.
No. 4.   do.   do.   ...   24 in.
No. 5. With stirrups and
        padded saddle, height
        to head   ...   ...   25 in.

Assorted coloured saddles and trimmings, with real hair mane and tail,
strong push irons, base board and
wheels brightly painted

CROSSLEY BROTHERS · STATION WORKS

BLACKPOOL

From 1938 Trade Catalogue   Fig.CY04

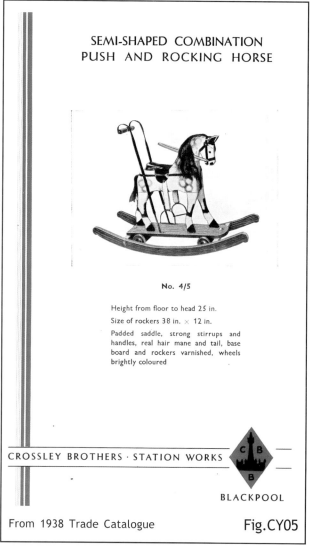

SEMI-SHAPED COMBINATION
PUSH AND ROCKING HORSE

No. 4/5

Height from floor to head 25 in.

Size of rockers 38 in. × 12 in.

Padded saddle, strong stirrups and
handles, real hair mane and tail, base
board and rockers varnished, wheels
brightly coloured

CROSSLEY BROTHERS · STATION WORKS

BLACKPOOL

From 1938 Trade Catalogue   Fig.CY05

The largest in the **Semi Shaped** range were the **Swing Horses** *Fig.CY06* and these were available in three sizes.

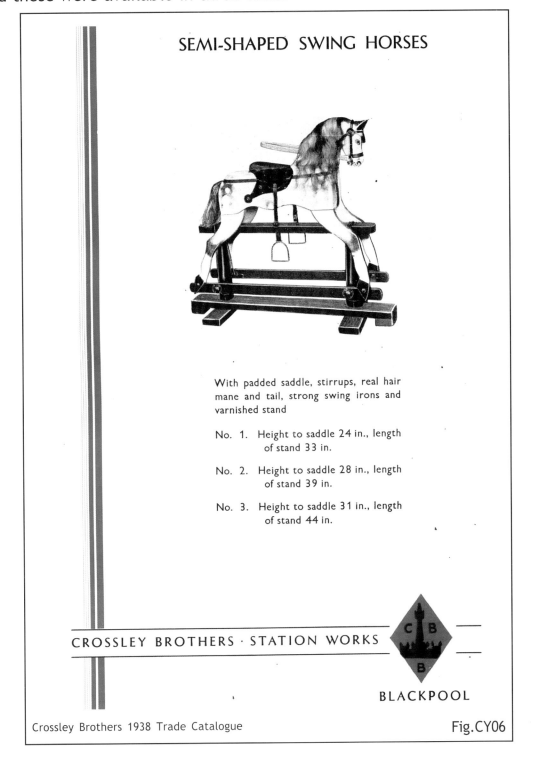

SEMI-SHAPED SWING HORSES

With padded saddle, stirrups, real hair mane and tail, strong swing irons and varnished stand

No. 1. Height to saddle 24 in., length of stand 33 in.

No. 2. Height to saddle 28 in., length of stand 39 in.

No. 3. Height to saddle 31 in., length of stand 44 in.

CROSSLEY BROTHERS · STATION WORKS

BLACKPOOL

Crossley Brothers 1938 Trade Catalogue

Fig.CY06

The **Semi Shaped Horse** was a simple box type construction made from thin boards and fitted with a carved head and mounted on a regular swing stand *Fig.CY07*. This is a No.3 model comparisoned to the 1938 trade catalogue. They were a cheaper option compared to the shaped horse but did share many stand components. The carved heads were

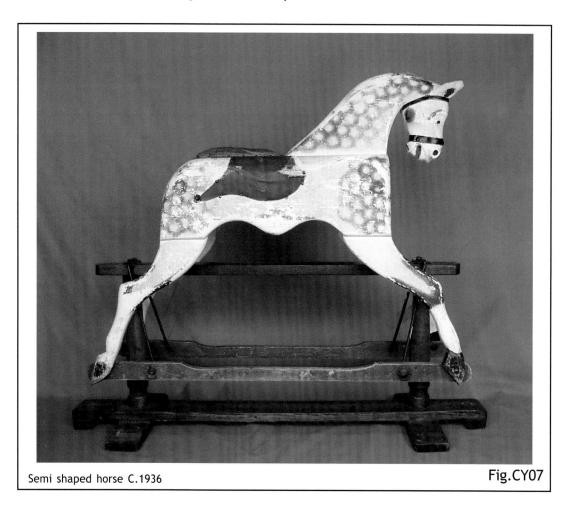

Semi shaped horse C.1936

Fig.CY07

not fitted with glass eyes, but used a nail instead *Fig.CY08* as was the practice with the shaped push horse. The horse *Fig.CY07* above has been over painted. Also note the saddle blanket is of the same material (there were remnants of red edging *Fig.CY10* under the saddle top) as the shaped horse in Fig.CY21. Despite being a cheaper option, turned posts were fitted *Fig.CY11* and these appear to be just a plainer version as those fitted to the shaped horse. The ends of the swinging irons are also protected with bowler hats.

Semi shaped horse, C 1936.

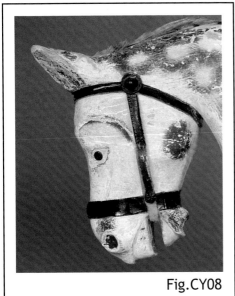

Fig.CY08

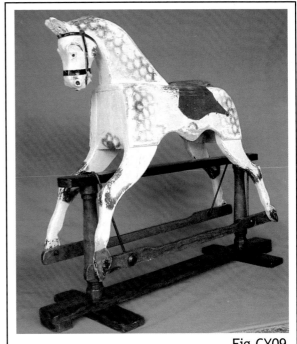

Fig.CY09

Fig.CY10

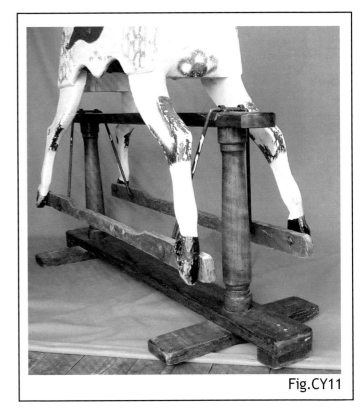

Fig.CY11

The semi-shaped swing horse was sold through many outlets, one of them being the famous Gamages store in London. The horse was illustrated in their 1936 Christmas advert *Fig.CY12* and sold for 39/6. This would have been a popular choice with parents as a fully shaped horse of the same size would have cost over £5, two and a half times more expensive.

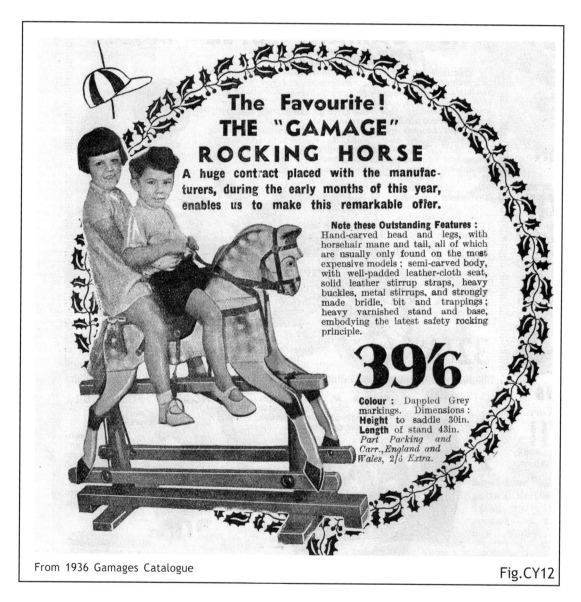

The Favourite!
THE "GAMAGE"
ROCKING HORSE

A huge contract placed with the manufacturers, during the early months of this year, enables us to make this remarkable offer.

Note these Outstanding Features : Hand-carved head and legs, with horsehair mane and tail, all of which are usually only found on the most expensive models : semi-carved body, with well-padded leather-cloth seat, solid leather stirrup straps, heavy buckles, metal stirrups, and strongly made bridle, bit and trappings ; heavy varnished stand and base, embodying the latest safety rocking principle.

39/6

Colour : Dappled Grey markings. Dimensions : Height to saddle 30in. Length of stand 43in. *Part Packing and Carr.,England and Wales, 2/6 Extra.*

From 1936 Gamages Catalogue

Fig.CY12

A range of **Shaped horses** were also manufactured in three different styles, the **Shaped Push horse** in the 1935 catalogue *Fig.CY13* was offered in five different sizes with largest being a **Combination Rocker** which was 30 inches tall. Described as being 'correctly modelled' it was

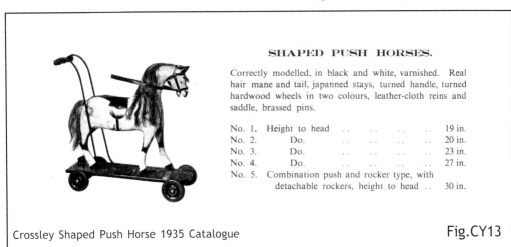

SHAPED PUSH HORSES.

Correctly modelled, in black and white, varnished. Real hair mane and tail, japanned stays, turned handle, turned hardwood wheels in two colours, leather-cloth reins and saddle, brassed pins.

No. 1.	Height to head	..	..	..	..	19 in.
No. 2.	Do.	..	..	..	..	20 in.
No. 3.	Do.	..	..	..	..	23 in.
No. 4.	Do.	..	..	..	..	27 in.
No. 5.	Combination push and rocker type, with detachable rockers, height to head				..	30 in.

Crossley Shaped Push Horse 1935 Catalogue   Fig.CY13

certainly as good as anything else on the market. These push horses were described as being black and white, but from the catalogue picture its clear this is dappled paint work as can be seen on the Crossley Shaped Push Horse *Fig.CY14*, the underside of the base confirming it to be a size 4 *Fig.CY15*. One notable feature about the construction of these horses is that the top face of the rear legs are cut to an angle where fitted to the body, this is common to front leg fittings but unusual on the rear. This method of leg fixing was also

Size 4 Shaped Push Horse   Fig.CY15

Crossley Shaped Push Horse   Fig.CY14

applied to the **Shaped Swing Horse** , this construction can be clearly seen on an extremely dilapidated size No.3 horse *Fig.CY16*. The swing

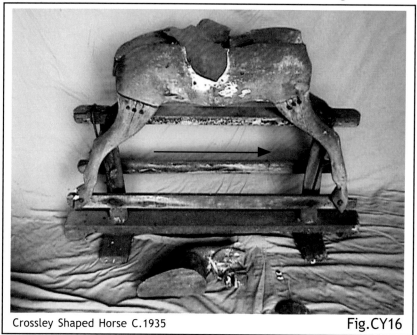

Crossley Shaped Horse C.1935   Fig.CY16

horse was advertised in the 1935 brochure *Fig.CY17* as being made in five sizes, the largest being a good size at 40 inches to the saddle. Crossley horses have many discernible features. A very interesting point is that all the shaped horses were carved by the same workman, Tommy Turtum, this would presumably give them all a common characteristic.

SHAPED SWING HORSES.

Correctly modelled, dappled grey, varnished. Real hair mane and tail, japanned swing irons, leather-cloth trimmings, padded saddle, shaped stirrups, turned platform columns.

No. 1.	Height to saddle				24 in.
No. 2.	Do.				28 in.
No. 3.	Do.				31 in.
No. 4.	Do.				35 in.
No. 5.	Do.				40 in.

Crossley Brothers 1935 Catalogue

Fig.CY17

174

A more detailed view of the shaped swing horse from Crossleys 1935 catalogue *Fig.CY18.*

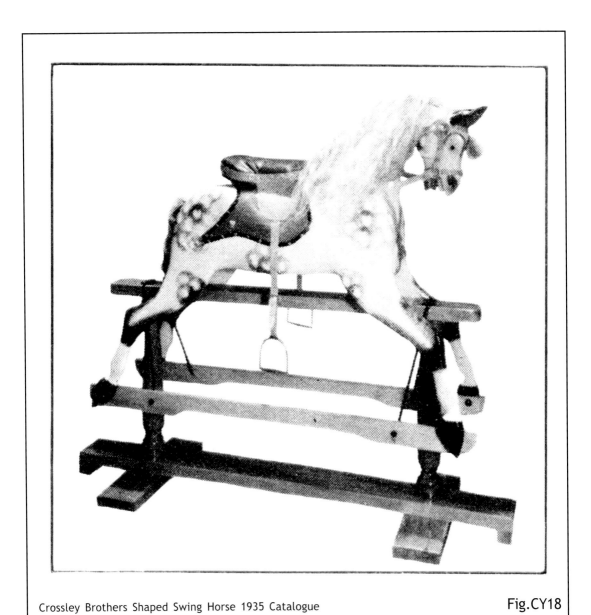

Crossley Brothers Shaped Swing Horse 1935 Catalogue   Fig.CY18

The heads were carved to a distinctive style, with 'ridged eyebrows' *Fig.CY19* while the rest of the body and legs were generally quite plain.

A general view *Fig.CY20* of a No.4 horse that shows the upright stance of this model. The hooves are notched, so as to stand on the runner and are held in place with coach bolts. Glass eyes were also certainly fitted to the larger sizes, but not on the shaped push horses. Harness, as mentioned in the 1935 details was made from leather cloth.

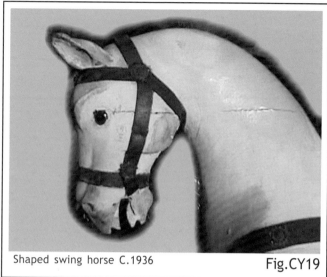

Shaped swing horse C.1936

Fig.CY19

Shaped swing horse C.1936

Fig.CY20

The saddle was of an unusual arrangement *Fig.CY21 in* that it looked very much like a detachable saddle but was in fact nailed to the body of the horse . Also note the elongated saddle blanket. The horse would have originally been fitted with metal stirrup irons on leather straps. The stands of the shaped horses were conventional, with tall thin turned posts *Fig.CY22* although there were slight variations depending on the model size of the horse. The base and cross pieces were plain square cut timber, the top bar had rounded ends.

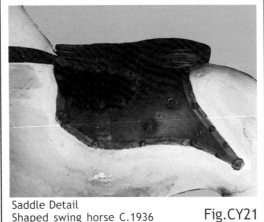

Saddle Detail
Shaped swing horse C.1936   Fig.CY21

The runners were of different designs, again depending on model size. The horse in the 1935 catalogue illustration *Fig,CY17* has shaped runners indicating a large size horse while the smaller sizes were plain with round ends, The swinging iron brackets were plain humped strips of steel, two per end. The swinging irons had a long drop and also tended to be on the narrow side . Fig.CY23 is a general head view of the horse as seen in Fig.CY20.

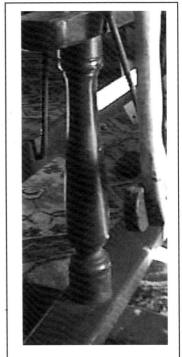

Post Detail   Fig.CY22

Shaped swing horse C.1936 Fig.CY23

Dalston Baby Carriage Company Ltd.
1910 - 1934

Address: 544, Kingsland Road, London. E.8.

Incorporated: 1910   Company No. 117,542.

The principle area of manufacture of this company, as the name implies,
is that of Baby Carriages, but they also manufactured a range of other
products, including, bath chairs, engines, barrows and **Beech Horses.**
A picture from a 1919 advert *Fig.DN01* is of one of their Beech Horses.
In 1934, the company was struck off the Companies Register.

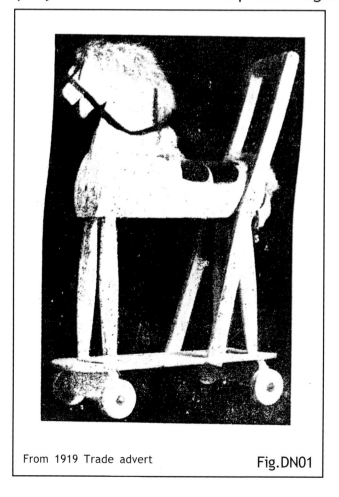

From 1919 Trade advert   Fig.DN01

Davies. Alfred, & Co.   1895 - 1927

Address: Penn Rd Works, 5-9 Penn Rd Mews, Caledonian Rd. London.

This London based firm was established in 1895 and produced a variety of wooden toys, which included wheel barrows, pole waggons, motor cars (in many styles and finishes), motor 'buses, dolls' houses, wood engines, **Push Horses**, **Horses & Carts**, **Hobby Horses**, **Tricycle Horses** and **Rocking Horses**. Two adverts from 1915 *Figs.AD01 & AD02* list some of these products.

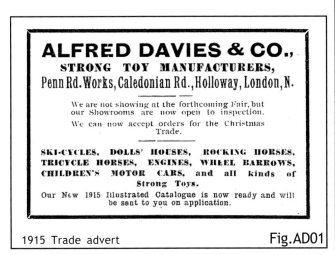

1915 Trade advert   Fig.AD01

1915 Trade advert   Fig.AD02

The firm seemed to be aware of changing trends and produced items such as a model of a street ice cream barrow, brewers drays, model taxicabs and the 'Skacycle', which was very popular at this time.

In August 1923, a new company was formed under the name of The "New" Alfred Davies Toy Co., Ltd, Company No.192,147. The new company appears to have taken over the old firm and produced an even larger variety of wooden toys. At this time, the leading line for the company was the **'Safety Rocking Horse'** *Fig.AD03* which was described as beautifully carved and finished with the best leather reins saddle, etc., and wicker panniers or seats for rocking could be supplied if required. The Safety Rocking Horse was made in a number of sizes to suit all classes of buyers. The illustration *Fig.AD03* has 'A.D.& C.' on

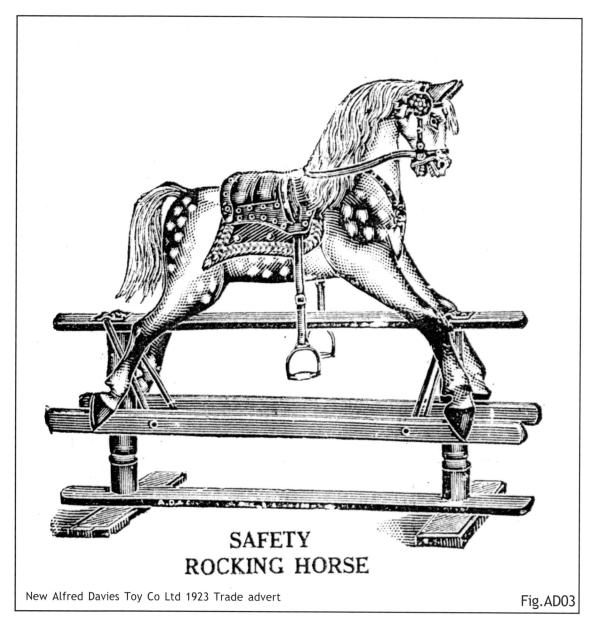

SAFETY
ROCKING HORSE

New Alfred Davies Toy Co Ltd 1923 Trade advert

Fig.AD03

the side of the based bar, indicating that this was one of the firms own drawings and likely to be quite accurate. Other favourites were still being produced, items such as the **Push and Pole Horses** *Fig.AD04* and the Tricycle horse. The company also manufactured some other horse related items, such as the **Gig Horse** which was supplied in three sizes, all with rubber tyred wheels. A **Galloping Gig** was also available as well as a **Combination Rocking Horse,** the latter also being available in three sizes and easily adapted to either use. **Stool Horses** and **Beech Horses**

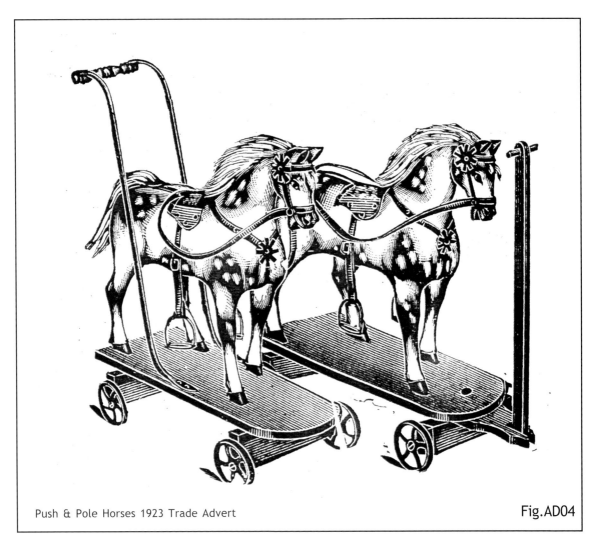

Push & Pole Horses 1923 Trade Advert   Fig.AD04

were also available in a variety of sizes.
Despite this wide and varied range of products, or perhaps because of it the company had problems. It was announced in the London Gazette in November 1926 that the company would be removed from the register. This became the case in February the following year, 1927. This action was usually the result of the failure to provide up to date 'books' due to financial problems.

Davies, George.   - 1882 - 1884 -

Address: 109, Kingsland Road, London. E.

There have been two entries found for George Davies listed under the heading of **'Rocking Horse Makers'** and one as a 'Perambulator' maker.

1882   Davies George   109, Kingsland Rd. E.   Rocking horse maker.

1884   Davies George   109, Kingsland Rd. E.   Rocking horse maker.

1884   Davies George   109, Kingsland Rd. E.   Perambulator maker.

George Davies was like many other tradesmen mentioned in this book, in that he was involved with both rocking horses and perambulators.

No further information has been found.

Davison & Hilditch.   - 1854 -

Address: 21, North Street, Pentonville, London.

Only one entry has been found in a Post Office directory of 1854 for Davison & Hilditch as a **Rocking Horse Makers.**

Unusually there are two other separate listings under the surname of 'Davison' also as 'rocking horse makers' around 1852 -1854. It is not known if there is any connection between them at all or if it is just pure coincidence

Davison, George & Walter. - 1854 -

Address: 2, Cannon Street Road, London.

Only one entry has been found in a Post Office directory of 1854 for George and Walter Davison as a **Rocking Horse Makers.**

Unusually there are two other separate listings under the surname of 'Davison' also as 'rocking horse makers' around 1852 -1854. It is not known if there is any connection between them at all or if it is just pure coincidence

Davison, Joseph.   - 1852 -

Address: 2, Back Hill, Hatton Garden, London.

Only one entry in a commercial directory of 1852 for Joseph Davison as a **Rocking Horse Maker** is known of,

1852 Davison Joseph, rocking horse ma. 2 Back hill, Hatton grdn.

Unusually there are two other separate listings under the surname of 'Davison' also as 'rocking horse makers' just a couple of years later in 1854. It is not known if there is any connection between them at all or if it is just pure coincidence

De La Rue, Evelyn.   1813-1906-Present

Address: 110, Bunhill Row, City, London.

Patent: No.7379   Accepted, May 1906.

See also: Gamage, A.W.

The long running firm of De La Rue were mainly noted for printing social stationary, stamps and playing cards, however Evelyn De La Rue applied for, and was subsequently granted a patent in 1906 for

'Improvements in Rocking Horses and Like Toys.'

This was an adaption for making a rocking horse move forwards while rocking. A drawing from the Patent is shown below *Fig.DL01*.

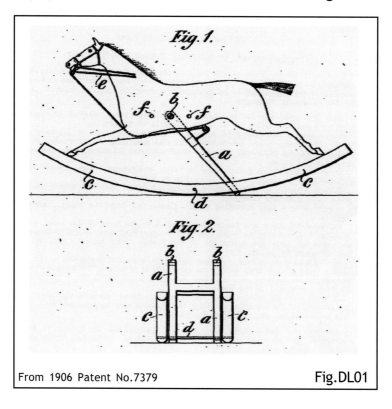

From 1906 Patent No.7379   Fig.DL01

This patent design was put into production by way of the 'Galapa' and sold through the retail outlet A W Gamage who advertised it as the 'Gamages patent Galapa Horse' and was illustrated *Fig.DL02* in their 1906 catalogue along with size details Fig.DL03. It was claimed it could canter, gallop and answer to the reins, but it was not relisted in any

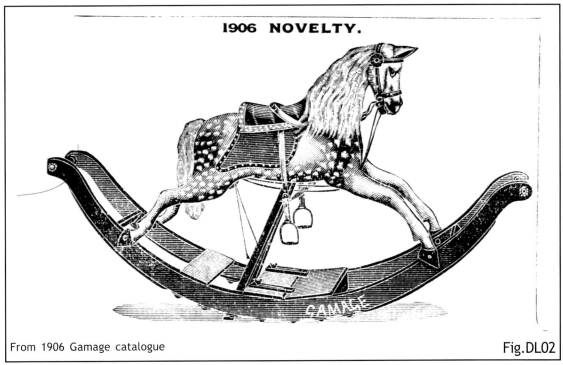

1906 NOVELTY.

From 1906 Gamage catalogue

Fig.DL02

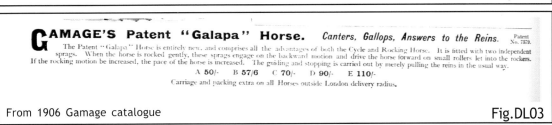

GAMAGE'S Patent "Galapa" Horse. *Canters, Gallops, Answers to the Reins.* Patent No. 7379.

The Patent "Galapa" Horse is entirely new, and comprises all the advantages of both the Cycle and Rocking Horse. It is fitted with two independent sprags. When the horse is rocked gently, these sprags engage on the backward motion and drive the horse forward on small rollers let into the rockers. If the rocking motion be increased, the pace of the horse is increased. The guiding and stopping is carried out by merely pulling the reins in the usual way.

A 50/-   B 57/6   C 70/-   D 90/-   E 110/-

Carriage and packing extra on all Horses outside London delivery radius.

From 1906 Gamage catalogue

Fig.DL03

other following lists. It may be concluded that it was not a particular success. This may well have been due to its ability to move around, possibly causing untold damage. The Galapa would have been made by a supplier to Gamages, as neither they or De La Rue were actual manufacturers. However, there is a strong possibility that the Galapa was produced by the same firm that supplied the 'Bronko' rocking horse, who were the 'Swan' brand manufacturers, an alliance between the Star Manufacturing Co. and Simpson, Fawcett & Co. The Galapa was offered in five different sizes, but its not known if any examples of any of these still exist.

Dear, J. C.

- 1851 - 1852

Address: 191, Bishopsgate Without, London.

J C Dear was listed as an exhibitor in a catalogue for the 1851 Great Exhibition under the heading ' Miscellaneous Manufacturers and Small Wares'. North Transcept Gallery, as a manufacturer of **Rocking Horses**.

The actual listing is shown *Fig.DR01* below.

From 1851 Great Exhibition catalogue   Fig.DR01

> 128   Dear, J. C.   191   Bishopsgate Without,   Manu.–
> Rocking-horse: and walking-sticks carved.

A couple of Post Office directory listings have been found and are as follows;

   1852 Dear & Warrener, toy importers, 191 Bishopsgate without.

   1852 Warrener James, importer of toys, see Dear & Warrener.

Both of these confirm that J C Dear was involved not only with rocking horses but also seem to have other toy business ties with a James Warrener as well.

Two earlier Post Office listings of 1841 that may or may not have any relevance with J C Dear.

   1841 Dear John Cox, ironmonger, reflector & lamp maker, also stove maker & smith, 102 High street Marylebone.

   1841 Walton H. M. 191 Bishopsgate without, Imp. of toys, &c

Derby Patent Hobby Horse Co. Ltd.

1885 - 1894

Address: 9, Hammerton Street, Burnley, Lancaster.

Incorporated: 26th March 1885 Company No.20,954

Although not a rocking horse maker, but with such a curious and closely allied name, *'The Derby Patent Hobby Horse Company Limited'* just had to be included herein.

The company was initially set up in March 1885 by a group of eight shareholders all of whom were living in and around Burnley, the group included two husband and wife partners. The main shareholder was a John Mosedale, described as a Foundry engineer, the other share holders were quite a mix, a painter, farmer, and Innkeeper. The nominal capital was £1,980 divided into thirty three £30 shares. An excerpt from the company memorandum of association is as follow;

'The objects for which the Company is established are:-

The acquisition of a Patent recently obtained or for which a Provisional Protection has been secured for certain improvements in **"an improved toy apparatus for imitating horse racing"** of which John Mosedale of Burnley in the County of Lancaster is the Patentee and the manufacturing, making, buying etc.....'

Later, in June 1885 there were a few changes amongst the share holders, but it would seem the company was not successful as in 1891. the official registrar wrote to the company asking for returns for 1886-1890. In 1894 the London Gazette reported that the company would be struck off the register

It is not really clear what the 'apparatus' referred to above was, or if it was ever produced at all, it certainly must have seemed like a good idea at the time for the partnership to form and money put into the venture.

Dobby Horse Exploitation Syndicate

- 1922 -

Address: 38, Parliament Street, Whitehall, London. S.W1.

Trade name: 'Dobby Horse'

Quite possibly the most bizarrely named firm in the world of toy horses. The Dobby Horse Exploitation Syndicate appeared to have only one product, which was a horse's head with a flexible neck. This could be purchased either as a complete toy, or as a head on reins to attach to the waist, or supplied for fitting to an existing item.

Their advert of 1922 *Fig.DS01* claimed that it would be the "one and only" toy to have for Christmas and described the item as,

The "Dobby" has a flexible neck which gives it a realistic appearance that no other toy horse possesses,

but despite these bold statements, the firm appears to have lasted only a year or so and no further reference to them has been found.

Also, no trace of the supposed 'universal protection' has been located despite a thorough search through the Patent records.

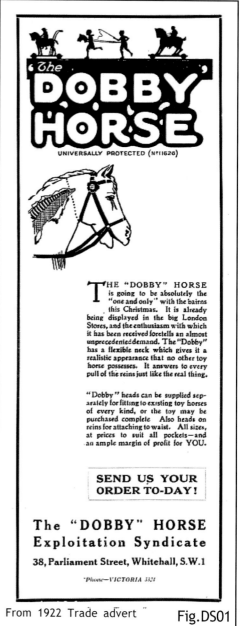

THE "DOBBY" HORSE is going to be absolutely the "one and only" with the bairns this Christmas. It is already being displayed in the big London Stores, and the enthusiasm with which it has been received foretells an almost unprecedented demand. The "Dobby" has a flexible neck which gives it a realistic appearance that no other toy horse possesses. It answers to every pull of the reins just like the real thing.

"Dobby" heads can be supplied separately for fitting to existing toy horses of every kind, or the toy may be purchased complete. Also heads on reins for attaching to waist. All sizes, at prices to suit all pockets—and an ample margin of profit for YOU.

SEND US YOUR ORDER TO-DAY!

The "DOBBY" HORSE Exploitation Syndicate

38, Parliament Street, Whitehall, S.W.1

'Phone—VICTORIA 3321

From 1922 Trade advert   Fig.DS01

Dunkley, W. H.   1874 - 1964

Address: Jamaica Row. Birmingham.

                76 Houndsditch. London. E.C.

The name, William Henry Dunkley will always be synonymous with the manufacture of prams, the first reference to his name being in Birmingham in 1874. Over the years W H Dunkley's firm expanded into the manufacture of powered vehicles, some being truly bizarre, such as the 'Moke' of 1896 *Fig.DY01* which was powered by compressed coal gas and the 'Pramotor' *Fig.DY02* which was basically a pram driven by an engine. Unsurprisingly, neither of these were produced for very long.

Dunkley's Moke   Fig.DY01

Dunkley's Pramotor   Fig.DY02

Dunkley's created many subsidiary companies, such as Dunkleys (Sales) and Dunkleys (Manufacturing) etc., but during the 1930's these went into liquidation. After this the firm also ventured into the more conventional motor cycle manufacture, but this also failed and the final reference to pram manufacture was in 1964, which was the winding up of W.H.Dunkley of Eltham Ltd (Pram Manufactures).

However, in earlier times Dunkley's also produced a range of horse based items including **Swing Stand Rocking Horses, Tricycle Horses, Bow Rocking Horses,** and **Steam Circuses & Roundabouts with Organ Complete** which were illustrated in the 1890's advertisement *Fig DY03*.

DUNKLEY'S

Steam Circuses & Roundabouts, with Organ
COMPLETE.
DUNKLEY'S MAIL CARTS, 14/6.

21/.

WINTER BASSINETTE, 45/.

30/.

From 21/

15/6.

DUNKLEYS NEW SAFETY

30/.

21/.

76 Houndsditch, LONDON, E.C.   Jamaica Row, BIRMINGHAM.

Dunkleys advert circa 1890

Fig.DY03

In 1885, Dunkleys had a splendid store in Birmingham *Fig.DY04* in which

DUNKLEY'S EXPORT PERAMBULATOR AND ROCKING HORSE MANUFACTORY, BIRMINGHAM.

Dunkleys Store 1885

Fig.DY04

some of their products can be seen on display, bow rocking horses are in the two-left hand ground floor windows.

From the information available, its thought that rocking horses and the like were only produced for a limited period of time, approximately 1880 to around 1915. Certainly Dunkley's are listed in an 1882 directory, specifically as rocking horse makers. Despite the potentially large scale production the firm was capable of, none of Dunkley's horses have been identified. It is also not known if the images on Fig.DY02 were accurate representations of their products, so identification from these would be unadvisable without further information.

Edinburgh Toy Factory Ltd. -1916 -1923

Address: 121-123, Fountainbridge Road, Edinburgh, Scotland.

Incorporated: 1917. Company No.SC9599

Very little is known about the Edinburgh Toy Factory with the exception that around 1916 they produced **Stool Horses** on wheels and also **Double Rocking Horses**.

In December 1923, it was reported in the Edinburgh Gazette that the firm had been struck off the companies register.

Elderkin, T.   - 1883 - 1911 -

Address: 371, Oxford Street, Manchester. (Works)
                         192, London Road, Liverpool.

Incorporated: 1898 Elderkins Ltd.   Company No.57,30763

Thomas Elderkin started trading around 1880 and was initially a Bassinette and Perambulator maker. Trade directories from this time also tell us that he was involved with the manufacture of Bicycles, Iron and Brass Bedsteads, and Washing, Wringing and Mangling Machines. Elderkin's advert of 1885 below *Fig.EN01* also lists him as a maker of **Rocking and Velocipede Horses.** This is the only reference to rocking horses that has been found.

From 1885 Trade advert   Fig.EN01

It would appear that Elderkin Ltd was formed around 1900 and that the manufacture of Washing, Wringing and Mangling Machines became the mainstay of the company, but it was reported in the London Gazette that the company had filed for bankruptcy in 1905. An application to have debts discharged in 1908 was rejected by the court on the grounds that Thomas Elderkin tried to defraud his creditors. 'Elderkin & Co' appear to have been trading (washing machines etc.) in 1911.

Elite Toy Manufacturing Co.   - 1916 -

Address: Salt Street, Manningham, Bradford, Yorkshire.

As reported in the 1916 British Toymaker, The Elite Toy Manufacturing Company, under the management of Mr Harry Holdsworth, was a recently formed business set up to take advantage of the lack of imported German toys, due to the War. Two posed photographs show the same **Rocking Horse** but there is no further evidence in the workshop picture *Fig.EE01* to suggest their manufacturer or is there any mention of their production within the article.

From 1916 Trade Journal   Fig.EE01

The picture of finished toys *Fig.EE02* shows the same rocking horse but it is difficult to make out clearly. Fig.EE03 is an enlarged view which shows the horse to be of conventional swing stand design, with turned posts in a very similar style to that of G&J Lines. Indeed, the overall appearance is reminiscent of an early G &J Lines rocking horse.

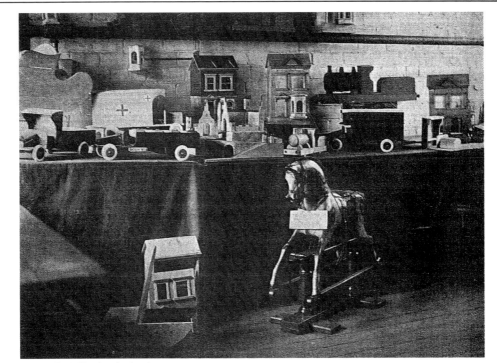

From 1916 Trade Journal   Fig.EE02

One area for identification is that the horse has no block at the rear of the saddle.

However, from the evidence that is supplied in the article, it cannot be assumed that this firm were actually in the process of manufacturing their own rocking horses, but may well have 'borrowed' one for the purpose of suggesting what they may make in the future. No further information has been found for the Elite Toy Manufacturing Company.

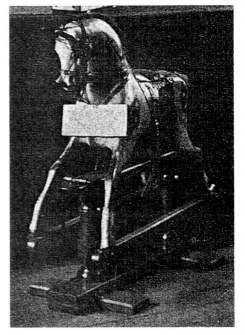

Detail of Rocking horse   Fig.EE03

Evans, Joseph & Son.   - 1841 - 1884 -

Address: 1841 -   114, Newgate Street, London.

                                101, Temple Street, Bristol.

            -1881   31 & 33, Old Street, London. E.C.

The earliest known record for Joseph Evans was in 1841 and gave the firm two addresses, one in London and one in Bristol, the entry read:

Evans Joseph & Son, importers of foreign, manufacturers of English toys, and fancy articles. 114 Newgate St. & 102 Temple St. Bristol.

This would imply that the firm was of a size and that it was probably formed some years previous. In 1844, Evans & Son were listed as 'Toy Manufacturers' at 101, Temple Street. Curiously another company under the heading of 'Toy Manufacturers' was next door at 102, Temple Street. No further listings for the firm of Evans in Bristol after 1844 have been found. They quite probably carried on all their business in London from then on.

It was reported in the London Gazette that a partnership between Joseph Evans, John Huntley, Arthur Foy and William Todd trading as 'Joseph Evans and Sons' was dissolved on the first of January 1881 and that the firm would be carried on by Joseph Evans under the old name. Note that previous to 1881 it was 'Son', after 1881 it was 'Sons'. It is not clear if this is a print error or an additional son joined the firm.

The 1882 London Post office directory also lists the firm as tooth, nail, hair, cloth & fancy brush manufacturers, and that the firm was 'late of Newgate Street'. Also in 1882, Joseph Evans and Sons, 31 & 33, Old Street were listed as **Rocking Horse Makers.**
1884 is the last known record for the firm with a small listing under the heading of Toy Makers and Wholesale Dealers.

Farmer, Lane & Co.   - 1888 - 1901

Address: 77 & 79, New Oxford Street, London. W.C.

     Works;   Carrier Street, Bucknall Street, London. W.C.

During the fairly short duration of the firm 'Farmer, Lane & Co.' there had been no less than four partnership changes, as recorded by the London Gazette. In December 1888, the partnership between George Farmer, Arthur Lane and William Trigg was dissolved. Its not clear when this partnership was first formed, but it was noted as being a *'Children's Carriage and Chair and Invalids Furniture Manufacturer'*. George Farmer continued and went into partnership with Thomas Drever and William Milburn, this partnership lasted until 1892 when William Milburn left and a new firm was formed by Farmer, Drever and new partner Albert Hobbs. In 1893 Thomas Drever left leaving Farmer and Hobbs who continued until 1900. When Hobbs left another new partner Walter Gardiner joined forces with Farmer. This only lasted a year and in 1901 solicitors for Gardiner had the firm dissolved. It is unclear what happened to George Farmer who was the mainstay of the firm throughout its existence.

The first directory entry for Farmer, Lane & Co. was in 1891 and the firm was listed under two headings, these were 'Perambulator makers' and **'Rocking Horse Makers'**. Subsequent directory listings from 1895 and 1899 also have them listed under the heading of Rocking Horse Makers. Nothing is known of their products or of the firm generally, other than the varied partners. However, that they must of been a reasonably sized firm with office and probably showroom space in New Oxford Street, whilst their works were literally just round the corner off Bucknall Street.

Francke, B. & Co.

1912 - 1933

Address: 1912 London Works, Villa Street, Hockley, Birmingham.

            1914   London Works, Wellesley Street, Hockley, Birmingham.

1915: **The Frankby Manufacturing Co**. Wellesley Street, Hockley.

            1924 London Works, Tyburn Road, Erdington, Birmingham.

A 1913 advertisement Fig.FE01 for B. Francke & Co. states that it is

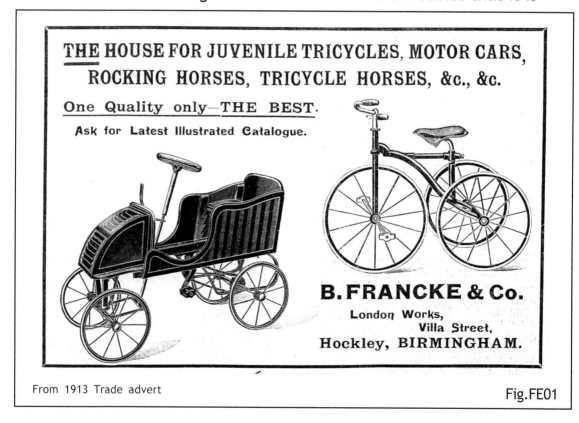

THE HOUSE FOR JUVENILE TRICYCLES, MOTOR CARS, ROCKING HORSES, TRICYCLE HORSES, &c., &c.

One Quality only—THE BEST.

Ask for Latest Illustrated Catalogue.

B. FRANCKE & Co.
London Works,
Villa Street,
Hockley, BIRMINGHAM.

From 1913 Trade advert

Fig.FE01

The house for various items, including juvenile tricycles, motor cars, **Rocking Horses, Tricycle Horses** etc. This recently formed firm were very positive in the advertising of the high quality of their products.

Although the 1913 advert does not mention that the firm are manufacturers, this is confirmed in an advert of 1914 *Fig.FE02* and also in a brief entry in a 1914 trade journal which states, *Messrs. B Francke & Co. can offer our readers some splendid values in juvenile bicycles, motor cars, rocking horses, tricycles, cycle horses, road skimmers etc. That are actual manufacturers of these goods.*

1914 is the last known mention of rocking horses, but the firm did continue in business and at this time, a Mr Bertram E Jones was the proprietor.

Around 1915 the firm changed its name to 'The Frankby Manufacturing Company'. It is not known exactly why the name was changed, but during the time of the Great War the public may have been sensitive to German sounding names. The name Francke may well have deterred potential purchasers.

In 1924 the firm moved to Erdington, a north suburb of Birmingham and were at this time described as a 'Wheel, Toy and Steel-Folder Manufacturer'. 1933 saw a Mr Francis Jones start Bankruptcy proceedings and the firm closed down.

As to the rocking horses and other similar products, no further information has been found and identification is not possible at this time.

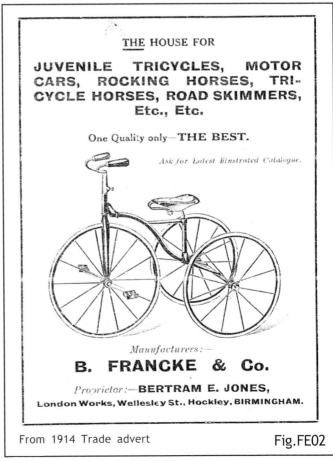

THE HOUSE FOR

JUVENILE TRICYCLES, MOTOR CARS, ROCKING HORSES, TRI- CYCLE HORSES, ROAD SKIMMERS, Etc., Etc.

One Quality only—THE BEST.

Ask for Latest Illustrated Catalogue.

Manufacturers:—

B. FRANCKE & Co.

*Proprietor:—*BERTRAM E. JONES, London Works, Wellesley St., Hockley, BIRMINGHAM.

From 1914 Trade advert   Fig.FE02

Gabriel, William.   - 1784 -

Address;   9, Wards Court, 43, Goswell Street Rd, Islington. London

A trade card of circa 1784 names William Gabriel as a **Rocking Horse Maker** and seller and also that he offers '*Signs and Horfes on wheels*'

An entry in Wrightsons Triennial Directory of Birmingham of 1818 lists William Gabriel as shown in the excerpt below *Fig.GL01*. Other items that he produced are 'Bath chairs for invalids' and also 'children's carriages'. However, it is not clear if this is the same person. There is

Gabriel William, manufactory for Bath chairs for invalids, rocking horses, children's carriages, &c. Islington

1818 Birmingham Directory   Fig.GL01

an Islington in the Birmingham area and it would be very unlikely to be listed in area unless you were resident.

Other Birmingham directory entries have been found for the surname of Gabriel and may or may not be relevant.

1808 - 1815 Gabriel, William. Broker and Cabinet Maker. Snow Hill.

1821   Gabriel, Thomas. **Rocking horse, &c. maker**, Moland Street.

1835 - 1839 Gabriel, William. Mangle and Bath chair manufacturer.
                               99, Coleshill Street & 11, Caroline Street

1843 - 1847 Gabriel, Thomas. Mangle maker, 21 ct. Coleshill Street.

Galway Toy Industry.   1919 - 1927 -

Address: Galway, Ireland.

See also: Shillelagh Wood Industry

Not a British firm, but it is important to record the Galway Toy Industry as it exhibited and sold many of its products in the UK and as such deserve to be mentioned.
Recently resigned from the Shillelagh Wood Industry Mr R Hunter was employed to take over the management for the Congested District Board of Ireland, of the newly formed Galway Toy Industry. This was set up to employ the discharged soldiers and workers of the Great War. The old National Shell Factory in Galway, covering some 18,000 sq ft, was used for the purpose and Mr Hunter quickly organised the workers into producing large quantities of strong toys that were ready for the British Industries Fair in early 1920. It was reported that up to a 1000 shaped horses were being produced a week. Amongst the items produced were

Pole Horses,
Push Horses,
Stool Horses,
Horses & Carts,
Safety Swing Rockers,
Ordinary Rockers,
Combination Rocking
Rockaways and
Combination Rockers.
A picture shows *Fig.GY01*
a safety swing rocker
from a 1920 advert for the
firm. It should be noted
that the horse illustrated
is similar in appearance to
a G&J Lines horse of
around 1900. However,
this same horse is also

From 1920 Trade advert   Fig.GY01

pictured in another totally separate publication, indicating that it is a genuine portrayal of their product. As the Galway firm shared the same tutor as the Shillelagh firm, it would be very likely that there would be similarities between the products of the two firms.

In 1923 the Galway Toy Industry exhibited at the British Industries Fair and put on a great show of horses *Fig.GY02* but sadly the picture is

Exhibit at 1923 British Industries Fair   Fig.GY02

just not quite clear enough to make out any discernible points for identification. Also in 1923 it was reported that a UK distribution centre was being considered so as to speed up delivery times but it is unclear if this came to fruition. In 1924 the factory temporarily closed due to the "varnish question", import duty being the issue. This was later refuted and a statement was made saying the temporary closure was for stock taking and to the contrary they were opening a new department for toy and model cars. The last known report about the firm was in 1927 when a further extension to the factory's scope was announced in that it would also produce furniture and other goods.

Gamage, A.W.   1878 - 1972

Address: 116 - 128, Holburn, London. E.C.

See Also: Simpson, Fawcett & Co.   ('Swan' Toys)
                    Star Manufacturing Co.   ('Swan' Toys)
                    De La Rue Patent No.7379 re Gamage 'Galapa'.

Registered Design: No. 467,670 ("Bronko") 23rd October 1905

Although Arthur Walter Gamage was not an actual manufacturer, it is important to list the name of the Firm here as they sold amongst their wide range of toy horses, this 'unique' rocking horse.

The **"Bronko" Safety Hobby Horse, (Regd. No 467,670)** was first announced in Gamage's 1906 Catalogue *Fig.GE01* and it was offered in four different sizes specially constructed to Gamage's own design with cowboy saddle and stirrups. The design was registered in October 1905,

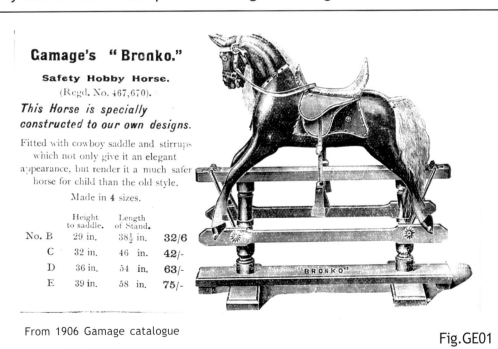

Gamage's " Bronko."

Safety Hobby Horse.
(Regd. No. 467,670).

This Horse is specially constructed to our own designs.

Fitted with cowboy saddle and stirrups which not only give it an elegant appearance, but render it a much safer horse for child than the old style.

Made in 4 sizes.

	Height to saddle.	Length of Stand.	
No. B	29 in.	38½ in.	32/6
C	32 in.	46 in.	42/-
D	36 in.	54 in.	63/-
E	39 in.	58 in.	75/-

From 1906 Gamage catalogue

Fig.GE01

so by the time it appeared in the store, none of their competitors could produce a 'like' item without infringing upon their registered design. The copyright was extended in October 1910, presumably for another five years. The copyright was certainly still in force in 1914 as an illustration *Fig.GE02* from their catalogue of that year still shows the registered number.

However, by 1924 the copyright seems to have expired as it is only referred to by its name, 'Gamage's Celebrated Bronko Hobby Horse' with no mention of the registered number Fig.GE03.

Also, it was now being offered in only two sizes as opposed to the original four in 1906.

Examples of 'Bronko' horses have been found with the registration number 467,670 printed onto the saddle flaps *Fig.GE04* and all Bronko horses have a small metal

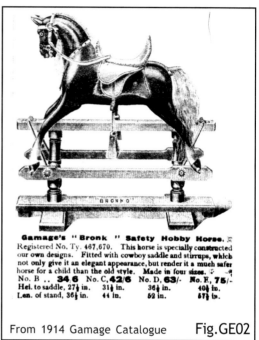

Gamage's " Bronk " Safety Hobby Horse.
Registered No. Ty. 467,670. This horse is specially constructed our own designs. Fitted with cowboy saddle and stirrups, which not only give it an elegant appearance, but render it a much safer horse for a child than the old style. Made in four sizes.
No. B .. **34/6** No. C, **42/6** No. D, **63/-** No. E, **75/-**
Hei. to saddle, 27½ in. 31½ in. 36½ in. 40½ in.
Len. of stand, 36½ in. 44 in. 52 in. 57½ in.

From 1914 Gamage Catalogue Fig.GE02

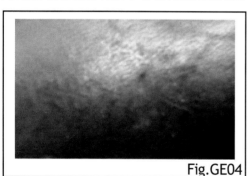

Fig.GE04

label with an individual serial number pined to the horse, this is usually found under the leather saddle covering *Fig.GE05*.

Fig.GE05

" Gamage's" Celebrated Bronko Hobby Horse

Very strong, made and finished in best style. Quite safe and practically unbreakable.

No.	Price	Length of Stand.	Height to saddle.
1	63/9	41 ins.	31½ ins.
2	90/-	52 „	37 „

From 1924 Gamage Catalogue Fig.GE03

The 'Bronko' was manufactured alongside **'Swan'** Toys which was the joint trading name used by 'The Star Manufacturing Company' and also 'Simpson. Fawcett and Co. Ltd'. A catalogue of The Star Manufacturing Co. stated that

" By mutual agreement, the designs shown in this catalogue are also manufactured in Leeds by Messrs Simpson Fawcett & Co. Ltd." .

By this mutual agreement, it would be possible to maximise production and sales, and it is thought most likely that the horses would have been produced at the works of The Star Manufacturing Co, in London and that Simpson, Fawcett were more likely producing items such as prams etc. in Leeds.

In a 1912 'Swan' toys catalogue *Fig.GE06* is an illustration of their regular swing-stand rocking horse which has many identical features to the 'Bronko'. The most obvious being the posts and runners of the stand but also its general style and appearance.

From 1912 'SWAN' Catalogue   Fig.GE06

One important point that is not apparent from these pictures is that all 'Swan' horses have the same type of metal label, with a serial number, attached to the horse, although sometimes fitted in a different position. This is the only manufacturer of the day that is known to have fitted serial numbers to its products. Fig.GE07 shows the timber construction of the saddle, exposed during the restoration of a 'Bronko' *Fig.GE08*. The serial number plate can be seen between the front and rear raised sections of the saddle.

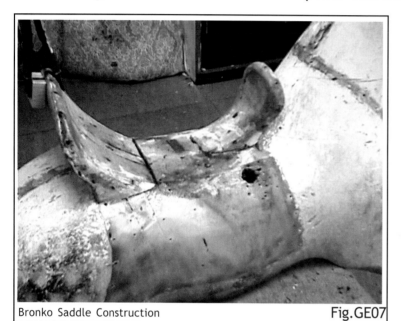

Bronko Saddle Construction   Fig.GE07

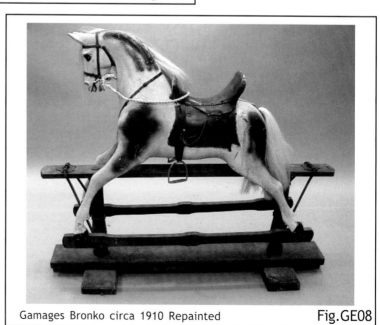

Gamages Bronko circa 1910 Repainted   Fig.GE08

Gamages Bronko circa 1910 Restored   Fig.GE09

The restored 'Bronko' *Fig.GE09* retained its original A W Gamage
brass label and some of the fine decorative nails Fig.GE10.
The leather stirrups are authentic replicas.

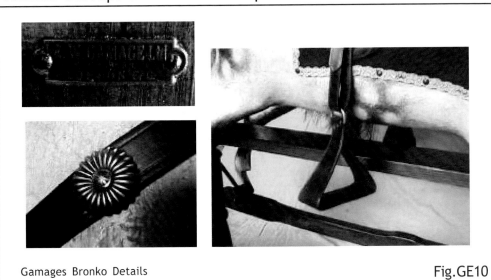

Gamages Bronko Details   Fig.GE10

Another unique rocking horse that Gamages sold was the 'Gamages patent Galapa Horse' which was claimed could canter, gallop and answer to the reins and was illustrated in Gamages 1906 catalogue *Fig.GE11* and was offered in five different sizes *Fig.GE12*. This horse

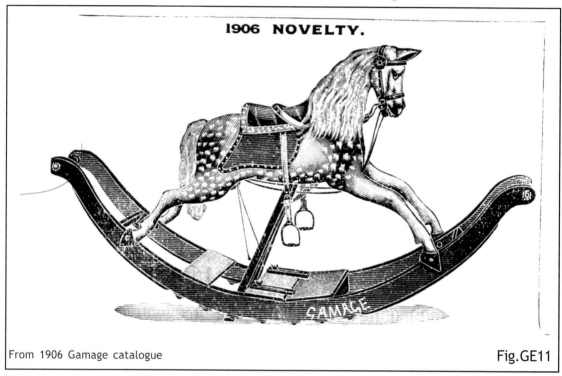

1906 NOVELTY.

From 1906 Gamage catalogue

Fig.GE11

GAMAGE'S Patent "Galapa" Horse. *Canters, Gallops, Answers to the Reins.* Patent No. 7379.

The Patent "Galapa" Horse is entirely new, and comprises all the advantages of both the Cycle and Rocking Horse. It is fitted with two independent sprags. When the horse is rocked gently, these sprags engage on the backward motion and drive the horse forward on small rollers let into the rockers. If the rocking motion be increased, the pace of the horse is increased. The guiding and stopping is carried out by merely pulling the reins in the usual way.

A 50/-   B 57/6   C 70/-   D 90/-   E 110/-

Carriage and packing extra on all Horses outside London delivery radius.

Galapa Description and Sizes

Fig.GE12

was made to Patent No.7397 which had been granted to the firm De La Rue. The 'Galapa' would have been made by a supplier to Gamages, as neither they nor De La Rue were actual manufacturers. However, there is a strong possibility that the 'Galapa' was produced by the same firm that supplied the 'Bronko' rocking horse who were the 'Swan' brand manufacturers, the alliance between the Star Manufacturing Co. and Simpson, Fawcett & Co. It is not known if any examples of the 'Galapa' are still in existence or how many were ever sold. The 'Galapa' was probably its own worst enemy, having the ability to move around and to wreak havoc as it went,... a child' dream, ...a parents nightmare.

Goblin Toy Co. Ltd.   1914 - 1922

Address: Unknown.

Incorporated: 1914   Company No.137,962

The Goblin Toy Company was reported to have exhibited a line of **Horses on Wheels** at a 1917 Trade show, unfortunately no illustration accompanied the report.

In June of 1922 the London Gazette reported that the company had been struck off the register.

Greenwood, Charles & Co. -1833 - 1882-

Address: 14 & 15, Great Street, Thomas Apostle, London. E.C.

In a relatively short space of time, quite a few partnership changes were made in connection with Mr Charles Greenwood.

In 1833, two partnerships were dissolved and from this a new firm under the title of *Lea, Greenwood and Lindop* was formed. This would mean that the former partners, particularly Charles Greenwood, were in business some time before 1833, the firm was described at the time as a 'Toy-Merchants'.

In 1839 the partnership of *Greenwood and Lindop* was dissolved, the absence of Mr Lea from this would imply that he had left some time previously.

In 1841 the firm *Greenwood, Ebbs & Co.* was listed and from 1852 onwards the firm was listed as *Charles Greenwood and Co.*

A catalogue form circa 1875 describes the firm *Fig.GD01* as Wholesalers and exporters, manufacturers of English and importers of foreign Toys and fancy goods. Within the catalogue is listed a wide range of items *Fig.GD02* including, **Rocking horses, Skin Covered Horses, Spring horses, Velocipede Horses, Carriage Horses with pole, Shaped horses,** and many other horse related items. Its not clear if these were some of the items actually manufactured by the firm, as mentioned on the front of the catalogue, or if they were another manufacturers products, and that Greenwood was an agent.

The firm was listed up until 1882, after which no further information has been found, suggesting that it had ceased trading soon after that date.

Circa 1875 Catalogue   Fig.GD01

Charles Greenwood & Co. catalogue from circa 1875

SUNDRY TOYS.

Rocking Horses for Boy or Girl
   No. 1, 2, 3, 4,
Ditto   ditto   with seats at
   end of Rocker
Skin covered Rocking Horses
Spring Horses
Mechanical or Velocipede Horses
Perambulators, single & double
   in great variety
Nursery Yachts
Carriage Horses with pole, best
Ditto   ditto   common
Wood Horses, plain and painted
   in various sizes
Shaped Horses
Ditto   Rocking
Ditto   Trotting
Hobby Horses in all sizes
Large Donkeys
Registered Cloth Donkeys in
   all sizes
Dressed Figures on Donkeys
Punch on Donkey
Stables with 2, 4, 6, and
   8 horses
Cow Stalls with 2, 4, and
   6 Cows
Baby Houses, all sizes
Furnished Dressers
Furnished Kitchens
Ditto   ditto   tin
Tin Bath Rooms, with pump
Mahogany Chests of Drawers
Ditto Bookcases
Butchers Shops
Basket, Grocer, Confectioner,
   Berlin Wool & Milliner do.
Tin Gigs and Carriages, in va-
   riety
Ditto with moving-leg Horses
Pumps
Dolls Baths
Dolls in Bath, with dresses, &c.

Toy Perambulators, wicker and
   wood
Oak Money-boxes, single and
   double
Ditto gilt mounted
Ditto steel ditto
Magic Lanterns 3/0 2/0 0 1
   2 to 8
English ditto, best quality
Slides for ditto—Astronomy,
   Natural History, Chroma-
   trope, &c.
Magic Ships and Boats
   ,,   Steamers
   ,,   Fish, 1, 2, 3, and 4
   ,,   Ditto large
   ,,   Swans and Ducks
Drums, all sizes
Ditto in nests for exportation
French Drums
Ditto Mechanical or Tattoo
Tambourines
French ditto
Guns and Pistols
Self loading ditto
Swords in variety
Whips in variety
Riding ditto
Boys Reins
Kit Fiddles and Bows
Kaleidoscopes
Globes, various sizes
Magic Warblers
Bubble Blowers
Fine painted Carts with shaped
   Horses
Waggons and Chaises
Hay Carts
Dust ditto
Errand ditto
Loaded ditto
Pickford's ditto, with 3 Horses
Drays with 1 and 2 Horses

Circa 1875 Catalogue   Fig.GD02

Hammond Manufacturing Co., Ltd.
1915 - 1919

Address: Mosley Street, Burton-upon-Trent, Staffordshire.

Incorporated: 1914.   Company No.137,963

The Hammond Manufacturing Company was set up in 1915 and from the outset was designed to be a large concern. The premises *Fig.HM01* were situated at Mosley Street, Burton-upon-Trent and covered an area of two acres and was capable of housing 1,500 work people. In hindsight, this was not the best time to be setting up a new business, with shortages of raw materials and of labour. However, after a few months

Hammond Factory circa 1915   Fig.HM01

of contractors getting the premises ready, work began on toy production. Because of the war, the factory was mainly staffed by women and the first items to be produced were along the lines of soft toys such as rags dolls, teddy bears and other animals. Once the woodworking plant had been installed, wooden painted and varnished toys were produced. As can be seen **Rocking Horses** *Fig.HM02* were also being produced. In the foreground of the picture there are two

Hammond horses 1916

Fig.HM02

distinctive shaped horses, one with its head down and the other with its head up, this typically representing both swing stand and bow rocking types of horse. By 1917 it was reported that the company's trade exhibit comprised of an extensive range of horses, **Beech Horses (Push or Pole), Shaped Horses, Safety Rocking Horses** of improved pattern, **Rocking Horses** of ordinary type, **Pair-Horse Carts** and **Stool Horses**. Also a new item that is as clever as it is original, the **"Live" Horse**. This was in the form of a horse on wheels and there is movement of the head every time the horse is pulled along. This was but a small selection from the company and it seemed that the original goal of the company had been realised. However, by April of 1919 a general meeting was held and it was agreed to reconstruct the company so as to avoid liquidation, but in September 1919, it was reported in the London Gazette that the company, because of its liabilities, had been voluntarily wound up.

Curiously, it was reported that the Hammond Manufacturing Co. was showing a range of strong wood toys at the White City Fair of 1921.

Hart & Ventura Co. (Ltd). - 1914 - 1923

Address: 31 & 32, Beech Street, Barbican, London. E.C.

Incorporated: 1919   Company No.15,787

1914 is the first known report of the firm Hart & Ventura Co. which was made up of the partnership between Joseph Ventura and John Hart.

In 1917 a trade journal reported the following;

    'Horses were included in the wooden combined push, pull or rock "carved" toys displayed by Messrs. Hart and Ventura. Foot-cycles--- horses on the lines of skicycle---were also unique and clever in design.

It is not clear if the company actually produced these items or were just manufacturers agents.

The firm was incorporated in 1919 but ran into financial difficulties in 1922 and was eventually dissolved in 1923.

Hearson, Charles & George. -1822-1824

Address: High Street, Barnstaple.

An archived document of 2nd January 1821 records that a John Harvey Greenwood, aged 15, was apprenticed to George Hearson, cabinet and chair maker, Barnstaple.

An 1822-3 trade directory lists both Charles Hearson and George Hearson of Barnstaple as;

'**Rocking Horse** & Fancy Chair Manufacturers' High Street.

It would appear that the two (brothers?) were indeed partners as in February 1824 The London Gazette reported that;

'the partnership which lately subsisted between George Hearson and Charles Hearson, of Barnstaple, in the county of Devon, Cabinet-makers, Turners, and Fancy Chair-Manufacturers, is dissolved by mutual consent.'

Other trade directory listings found are in 1844 for a George Hearson of Litchdon Street, Barnstaple, under the heading of 'Cabinet Makers' and also under 'Auctioneers'

Between 1843 and 1856 the London Gazette mentions a George Hearson, Auctioneer, Litchdon Street, Barnstaple. It is not known if this is the same George Hearson of the 1822, but 'Hearson' is a relatively uncommon name.

Hill & Harrison.   1884 - 1906

Address: 1884   167, Duke Street, Liverpool.

                    1900   165 & 167, Duke Street, Liverpool.

See Also: Baby Carriages Ltd. 1906 - 1963

Harold Cheetham Hill and William Harrison traded together from around 1884 as 'Hill & Harrison' and were principally perambulator makers. A number of Liverpool trade directories confirm this. In 1900 they are also listed as bath chair manufacturers, hand cart builders and makers of hospital ambulance appliances and invalid furniture makers. A point to note is that in 1900 another firm, Hitchings Ltd was also listed under the same trades at the same address,165 &167 Duke Street as well as 74 Bold Street, only a short distance away from Duke Street. This was obviously some sort of collaboration but details of this are not known. In 1906 the firm was incorporated under the new name of **Baby Carriages Ltd**. and continued trading up to around 1963. In 1922 a Patent was applied for by Baby Carriages Ltd, and in the document, Harold Cheetham Hill is noted as a director of BCL, confirming the company to be one and the same. **Rocking Horses** were produced at the time the firm was known as Hill and Harrison, and a few examples have turned up. These have had some sort of makers identification, usually on the top plates, two examples are *'H&H LP'* marked on the top *Fig.HH01*. The other is *'HL' Fig.HH02* marked on the underside.

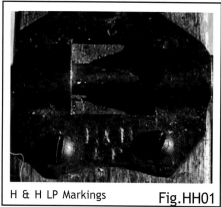

H & H LP Markings   Fig.HH01

H L Markings   Fig.HH02

Changes were common, especially as a new firm would be 'fine tuning' their products. Items such as top plates would have been bought out, the suppliers of which may well have been changed, thus supplying a slightly different product. Even some years after the firm became Baby Carriages Ltd., some significant changes were made to the style of the horses and the stands as well. The horse shown *Fig.HH03* has the top plates marked '*H&H LP*' and is in original condition. The horse is well carved but the construction is secondary, with the legs only being

Hill & Harrison Swing Stand Rocking Horse   Fig.HH03

nailed to the body. This method of construction was quicker and therefore cheaper to produce but not as long lasting as a mortise and tenon type leg joint. Good quality glass eyes, black pupils surrounded with dark brown, were certainly fitted to the larger models, Fig.HH04 shows this detail. Leather harness was used and also large decorative nails were applied to the saddle, martingale and bridle. These nails are the same type that are also found on F H Ayres horses of the same period and can be seen in Fig.HH06. Also in this picture of the saddle there is provision for a pommel and just below is the staple for the stirrup leather.

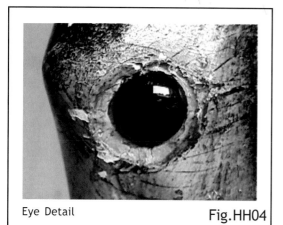

Eye Detail
Fig.HH04

Post Detail
Fig.HH05

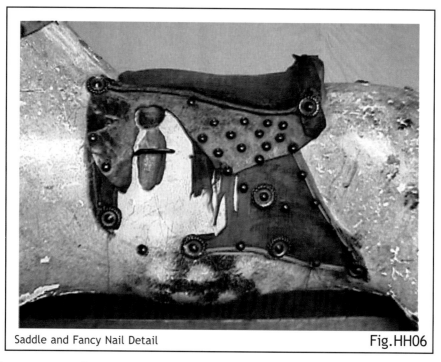

Saddle and Fancy Nail Detail
Fig.HH06

The stands appeared to be reasonably well made with fancy turned posts *Fig.HH05*. However, nails were also used to hold the posts in place, another cheaper alternative to the superior spigot type fixing.

These horses had long swinging irons, this would give a good rock. The horses hooves were notched to fit on the runners, the best method. Another Hill & Harrison horse *Fig.HH07* has 'HL' on the top plates. This horse is smaller than the one previously illustrated but does share many details, although there are some differences. Legs are nailed, as

Hill & Harrison Swing Stand Rocking   Fig.HH07

are the posts of the stand. The post nails are disguised by fitting a couple of fancy nails over them, the same type as used on the horse, Fig.HH08. The posts are all but the same pattern *Fig.HH09* as the larger horse. One notable difference is that this smaller horse is not fitted with glass eyes, as can be seen in the detail picture of the head *Fig.HH10* but it is fitted with the fancy nails as before.

Curiously the saddle *Fig.HH11* is fitted with a different style of fancy nail to the head, both are thought to be original.

Stand Fancy Nail Detail   Fig.HH08

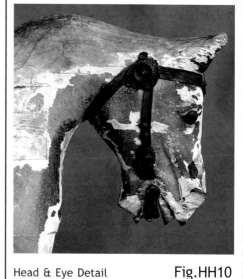

Head & Eye Detail   Fig.HH10

Post Detail   Fig.HH09

Saddle & Fancy Nail Detail   Fig.HH11

Other Hill and Harrison horses have been found, and these all have slight changes, but the overall shape remained constant. It did however change after the firm incorporated as Baby Carriages Ltd. These horses and other products are described in the relevant Baby Carriages Ltd. chapter.

Hitching T. H Brooke.   - 1884 - 1891

Address: 19, 21, 23, Ludgate Hill, Ludgate Sq. & Holyday La. E.C.

Brooke Hitching & Co. Ltd. 1885   Company No.21,765

Hitching & Wynn.   1891 - 1899

Address: 19, 21, 23, Ludgate Hill, E.C. 3 & 9, Ludgate Square E.C.
                  73, Berners Street, W.   116, Oxford Street. W.

Hitchings Ltd.   c.1899 - 1936?

Address: 29, Ludgate Hill. E.C.   198, Oxford Street. W.
                  28, St. George's Place S.W.
     1910--   56 New Bond St. 329, 331 Oxford St. 45, Knightsbridge.

Affiliated: *1896?   Company No:*52718?

As can be seen from the above, the firm is thought to have been set up by a T.H. Brooke-Hitching and has gone through many changes.

The firm is primarily listed in trade directories as a manufacturer of perambulators, but in 1891 as Hitching & Wynn, they are listed as **Rocking Horse Makers**. No further reference to rocking horses has been found in any of the subsequent listings, and it appears that the company concentrated on the manufacture of perambulators.

In 1936, The London Gazette reported on a meeting of shareholders of Hitchings Ltd but it is not known what the result of this was or how long the company continued trading.

Honey, James & Co.   - 1914 - 1919

Address: 1914   73, Sydenham Road, London. S.E.
             1917   61, Sydenham Road, London. S.E.

Affiliation: See Honey, R.E & E.T.

It was reported that in 1914 James Honey & Co. were manufacturers of **Wooden Horses and Carts**, bicycles and prams. Various trade directory listings have put the firm under the heading of Fancy repository and also cycle makers.

In April 1919 The London Gazette reported that,

'The Partnership subsisting between James Honey, Robert Ernest Honey and Edward Thomas Honey, carrying on the business as Cycle Makers and Repairers and Fancy Goods and Toy Dealers under the style or firm of JAMES HONEY & CO. has been dissolved by mutual consent as and from the 19th day of March, 1919'.

In 1922, two of the previous partners, Edward and Robert Honey took out a Patent relating to **Rocking Horses**. See Honey, R.E. & E.T.

Honey, R.E. & E.T.   1922

Address: Robert;   11, Tredown Road, Sydenham, London. S.E.

                  Edward;   49, Girton Road, Sydenham, London. S.E.

Affiliation: Honey, James & Co.

Patent: No. 196,434. Granted, 26th. April 1923.

In February 1922, after the break up of the partnership of 'James Honey & Co.', Robert and Edward Honey, who were both 26 and thought to be brothers, applied for a Patent described as,

*'Improvements in or relating to **Rocking Horses** and the like Devices'*.

The invention relates to an improved construction of rocking horse or other animal toy, and has for its object to provide a rocking horse, which will be caused to travel along the ground with a galloping motion if the rider sways alternately backward and forward in the saddle. See Fig.HY01 which shows the arrangement of the device.

The Patent was granted on the 26th April 1926, but it is not known if this device was put into production and if so, whether there are any surviving examples.

Drawing of Patent No.196,434.

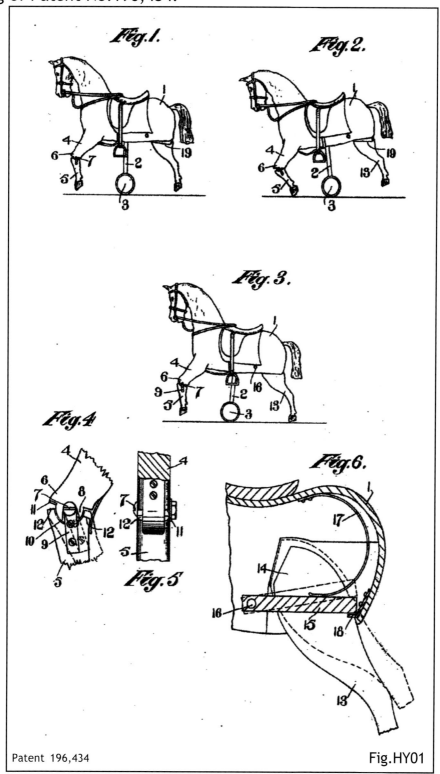

Patent 196,434

Fig.HY01

Hooper. H. S. Ltd. 1916 - 1924

Address: 54, Great Eastern Street, London. E.C.2.

Incorporated: 1917 Company No.147,448

H.S.Hooper (London) Ltd. 31st January 1920. Company No.163,544

H. S. Hooper Ltd. was run by Herbert Studdy Hooper and Edgar Jay and was a subsidiary of a larger company, John Warrilow Ltd. of Birmingham. In 1917, H. S. Hooper Ltd. took over the games manufacturing branch of the company J Frenkel & Co. Ltd., this along with a large output of games and toys from Warrilows, the new company of H S Hooper Ltd. very quickly became a major toy producer.

Initially the items produced were the smaller games and toy books, but in a trade fair review of March 1921, it was reported that the company had inaugurated a new department for the manufacture of wood toys and many of these were on show. Particular attention was drawn to a series of **Rocking Horses** and one special number was made on a new principal *Fig.HR01*. This was described;

    'Instead of the ordinary swing-stand, the horse was mounted on strong springs and wires, so that a child on one of these horses would go through the same action as riding a live horse. This has a great value,and has an advantage over the ordinary rocking horse,inasmuch as a child is easily able to learn to ride a real horse with one of these models.'

It would be worth noting that 'The "Invicta" Toy and Doll Works Ltd. (previously Kent Toy Works) displayed a very similar product some months earlier in February 1920. It is not clear which of the two companies, if indeed either, had come up with the design, however, Invicta had described their product as a 'Specially Mounted Rocking Horse, Patent Pending'. Unfortunately, no patent relating to this design has been found.

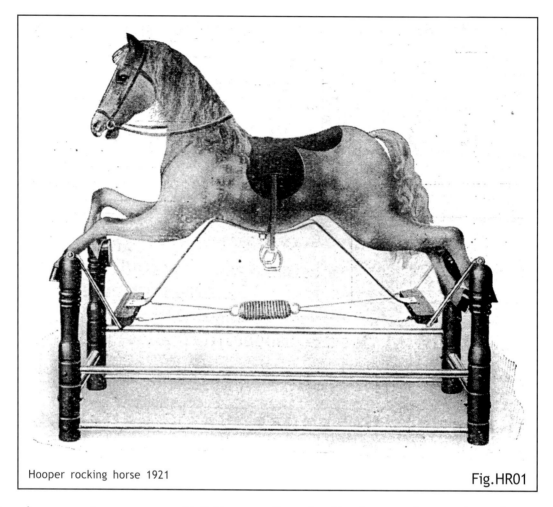

Hooper rocking horse 1921   Fig.HR01

A subsequent company, H S Hooper(London)Ltd. was formed at the beginning of 1920, and acted as a selling agent for the products of the previous firm H S Hooper Ltd. In March 1924, H S Hooper(London)Ltd. were compulsory wound up with many creditors. The Official Receiver criticised some of the business practises of the company.

Two years on in 1926, Edgar Jay and Herbert Studdy Hooper appeared at the Old Bailey on charges of fraud, Jay was further charged with falsifying stock sheets and destroying documents with intent to defraud. Jay pleaded guilty and was sentenced to six months' imprisonment. The prosecution offered no further evidence against Hooper and he was found not guilty and was discharged.

No subsequent information about Herbert Studdy Hooper has been found.

Howard, G.
(Late Howard E.)

1870 - 1920

Address: 46a, London Road, Downs Road, Lower Clapton. E.5.

An advert *Fig.HD01* from a 1920 trade journal lists some of the products made by George Howard and also tells us that the he has carried on business from E. Howard who may well have been his father.
Among the items listed are **Hobby Horses,** and while this was used as a description for a rocking horse, it is more likely that in this context it refers to a stick horse but this is speculation. No other reference to either E. Howard or George Howard has been found.

From 1920 Trade Advert   Fig.HD01

Hughes, G.H.   - 1882 - 1897 -

Address: St. Stephen Street Works, Birmingham.

From the directory entries and the advert of 1882 *Fig.HS01* it can ascertained that the main area of production of George H Hughes was that of a wheel and bicycle maker. However, in 1896/7 he was listed under the heading of 'Toys and Games' and as a tricycle maker.

In the advert of 1882 a **Tricycle Horse** is pictured, but it is unclear if the whole item was produced or if this as just one of the many items that his wheels were supplied for.

The last known directory entry for George H Hughes was in 1897 and he was listed under the headings, 'Toys & Games' and also 'Perambulator Fittings(Wheels)'

From 1882 Trade advert

Fig.HS01

Hurst, T.   - 1903 - 1911 -

Address: 133, Bolton Road, Clifton, Manchester.

Thomas Hurst was listed in various trade directories with the job description **Hobby Horse Maker.** This is the only known reference found of a 'Hobby Horse Maker' in a trade directory.

A hobby horse can refer to a variety of different items, including a 'stick horse' and also a 'swing-stand' rocking horse, but it is not clear as to what was being referred to in this case.

No further information about Thomas Hurst has been found.

Industria Ltd.

- 1920 - 1923

Address: Bank Chambers, 97, Old Street, London. E.C.1.

It is thought that Industria Ltd started trading around 1920 with a variety of products that were made in their Hounslow and Hackney factories. Amongst the items they produced were **Composition Horses** which were described as 'The Best in the World' and their advert, *Fig.IA01* also advised against buying German 'rubbish' in this line. This was a fairly common type of statement of the time due to recent hostilities with Germany.

Also advertised were the 'very best' **Rocking Horses**, but it is not known in what form these took.

The company was fairly short lived and in November 1923 The London Gazette reported that a meeting of creditors was to take place as required by the liquidator.

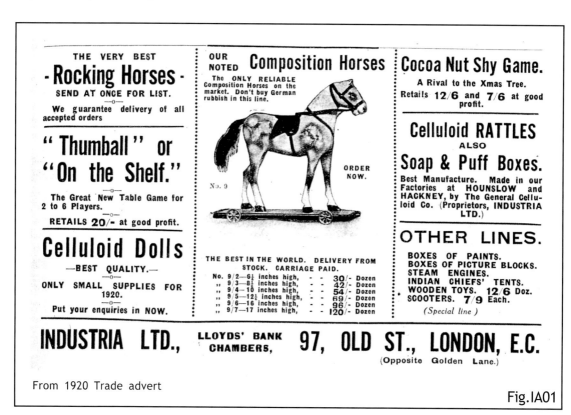

From 1920 Trade advert

Fig.IA01

Invicta Toy & Doll Works Ltd.

Late; Kent Toy Works.   1919 - 1925

Address: Eridge Road, Tunbridge Wells, Kent.

Incorporated: 1920   Company No.169,661

The Invicta Toy and Doll Works Ltd., which originally traded under the name of the Kent Toy Works was set up by an ex army officer, Mr A S Williams. While still in the Army, he mentioned to some fellow officers of his desire to start a business manufacturing toys after being demobilised, and this is exactly what happened. One of his new partners already had some experience of the toy trade and the new firm started in July of 1919 by producing simple items such as black boards and counting frames. It was decided that the firm should exhibit their products at the 1920 British Industries Fair as this was popular within the toy trade. The firm increased their range of products and made a handsome display at the fair, as can be seen in the illustration in their advert *Fig.KW01*. Amongst the new items produced were a range of **Shaped Horses** *Fig.KW02* these were available in four qualities, **Stool Horses** and **Rocking Horses with Special Mounting** *Fig.KW03*.

'Phone : 1089 Tunbridge Wells.

KENT TOY WORKS
ERIDGE ROAD, TUNBRIDGE WELLS, KENT.
LONDON SHOWROOMS :
5, SOUTHWARK STREET, LONDON BRIDGE, S.E.I.
MANUFACTURERS OF

THE 'CANNON' DOLLS.

Don't Fail to See This Line.

Exceedingly well made and perfectly finished.

Specially Mounted
ROCKING HORSES
(Patent pending)

A call at our London Showrooms will be worth your while.

An Illustration of our Stand at the British Industries Fair.

OTHER LINES.
Railway Engines, Scooters, Wooden Spades, Cricket Bats & Stumps, Beech Horses, Rolling Stock, Dolls' Furniture, "Cannon" Mechanical Coaster.
ALSO
CHILDREN'S ROCKER.
PLACE ORDERS EARLY.

From 1920 Trade advert   Fig.KW01

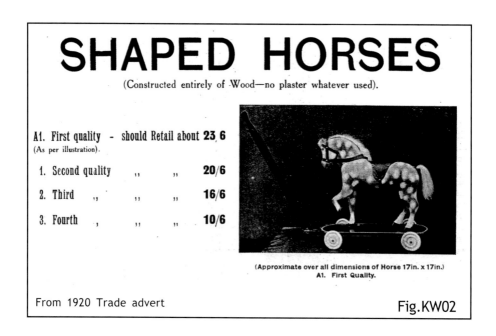

SHAPED HORSES

(Constructed entirely of Wood—no plaster whatever used).

A1. First quality - should Retail about **23 6**
(As per illustration).

   1. Second quality   ,,   ,,   **20/6**

   2. Third   ,,   ,,   ,,   **16/6**

   3. Fourth   ,   ,,   ,,   **10/6**

(Approximate over all dimensions of Horse 17in. x 17in.)
A1. First Quality.

From 1920 Trade advert

Fig.KW02

The Fair was a great success, so much so that the newly formed company had to build a new factory which was carried out by Mr Williams and his own staff, which took only six weeks to complete. Additional lines were added to their range, including Railway Engines, Cricket Bats and Stumps, and also a range of composition Dolls. It would appear that this initial burst of sales was only relatively short lived, for it was reported in the London Gazette that the company had been struck off the Companies register in February 1925.

The 'Shaped Horses' were offered in four different qualities, the illustration above is of the 'First' quality and it is described as being made entirely of wood and no plaster whatever. It certainly appears to be a well finished item with harness and possibly a horse hair tail. The fourth quality horse was less than half the price of the First, so it must have been of a very basic finish indeed.

It would be worth noting that the rocking horses made by the company H S Hooper Ltd. were of a very similar design as those of Invicta, but were marketed about a year later. It is not clear who had originally come up with this new type of mounting for a rocking horse, or if it was just a known modification of an existing item. The basic principle of the Invicta and Hooper rocking horse is the same as that popularly known as the 'Jubilee Rocker' which was patented by G&J Lines in 1887, (Patent No. 2938), some thirty three years earlier.

The rocking horses although being carved, were quite plain in their finish, for example the mouth was formed simply by means of sawing, no further carving with regard to teeth was carried out, also they were finished with 'painted' eyes, as opposed to the more elaborate horses with glass eyes. They are painted as dapple greys and finished with what looks like a plain leather saddle. The bridle looks like some type of

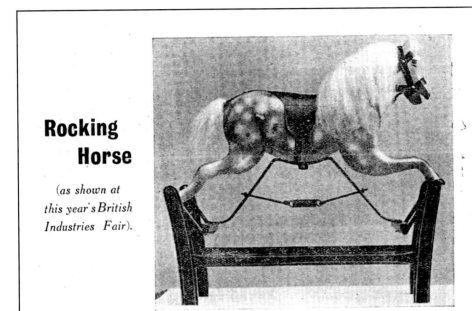

Rocking Horse

(as shown at this year's British Industries Fair).

NOTE Special Mounting which, in addition to ordinary movement, gives up-and-down motion

From 1920 Trade advert

Fig.KW03

'oilcloth' or other manmade material The mane and tail look to be of horse hair.

It is not known how many were produced, but it is unlikely to be a great number due to the short time the company traded for, and is also unknown if any examples still survive.

Kain (Late Jones)   - 1808 -

Address: 25, Ludgate Street, London.

From a small undated trade card trade *Fig.KN01* **Rocking Horses** with improved Manes and Tails were being offered. There were also various other items on offer from the Toy and Tunbridge Warehouse at Ludgate Street and these were Dolls of every description and a great variety of Work Boxes, the latter most likely being Tunbridgeware boxes which were very popular at this time.

Trade card circa 1808   Fig.KN01

The card also refers to Kain, 'Late Jones', a trade directory listing from 1808 has been found and reads,
                 'Jones Richard, Toyman, 25 Ludgate-ftreet'.
This is obviously the Jones referred to in the trade card but it is not known if the Rocking Horses were produced by either of Kain or Jones, quite possibly they were agents for another manufacturer.

Kaye Toy Co.   - 1917 -

Address: Lockner Road, Kingsland Road, London. N.E.

The only known information about the Kaye Toy Company is from a advert of 1917 *Fig.KE01* which lists a whole variety of items that the firm made.

Amongst these are **Beech Horses** and also the advert has a picture of two **Pull and Push Horses**. There is however, no reference to these pull and push horses within the advert text. Quite often a publisher would use a 'typical' illustration to give an 'idea' of what a firm produced, this said, this picture is not known to have been used elsewhere so it could well represent the actual products of this firm.

It would be reasonable to assume that this firm did trade for a number of years either side of 1917 as it describes itself as the *Premier Wood Toy House*. This sort of claim would generally take a few years to acquire.

From 1917 Trade advert   Fig.KE01

Kendrick, R. & F.W.   - 1920 -

Address: Bedford Street, Loughborough, Leicestershire.

Patent: No.142,279   Accepted: 6th May 1920

Agent, North: C.P.Marrison. Orchard Chambers, Church St. Sheffield.

Agent, South: S.C.Smith. Quorn, Nr. Loughborough, Leicestershire.

In 1919, Robert Kendrick applied for a Patent for a 'New' type of
Rocking Horse that was advertised as the 'New Riding Horse', this was
to mark a 'new era' in nursery toys, the Patent was granted in 1920.

This new item was exhibited at the 1920 British Industries Fair and it
was reported in the trade that,

*The new invention of Messrs.Kendrick, which they call the
"Perfect" riding horse, threatens the popularity of the rocking horse,
and this exhibit was the centre of interest during the whole period of
the Fair. It is a toy horse with a see-saw motion, although it is not
necessary for the child's feet to touch the ground, and besides
affording the greatest amount of pleasure it teaches a child to ride,
and it is recommended by the medical profession as an aid to physical
development. All the models are mounted on wheels, and a pole is
attached to two types so that they may be drawn along while the child
is riding, and the third model is propelled by the natural action of
bumping the saddle. The "Perfect" riding horses will appeal to
children of all ages.*

In their advert of May 1920 *Fig.KK01* two models were being advertised,
quite possibly it was decided to reduce the number of different
models, three had been on display at the recent Fair, so as to keep
costs down.

Despite have a good review at the Fair nothing further is known of the firm or how many of the much acclaimed 'New' Riding Horses were actually produced.

The Arrival of the 'NEW' RIDING HORSE has marked a new era in nursery toys. Recommended by the Medical Profession, the 'New' Riding Horse provides a permanent source of healthy, muscle-making, nerve-building, *instructive* enjoyment.

The finest toy ever invented for a child, it is strongly made in two models, as illustrated, for nursery use. Certain of the appreciation of the youngsters and the approval of their parents, it is a line certain of big sales. Send for illustrated catalogue.

Manufactured by R. & F. W. KENDRICK, Bedford St., Loughborough.

C. P. MARRISON, Orchard Chambers, Church Street, **SHEFFIELD,**

Agent for Yorkshire, Derbyshire, the North, and Ireland.

S. C. SMITH, Quorn near **LOUGHBOROUGH,**

Agent for Midlands and South of England.

From 1920 Trade advert   Fig.KK01

Fig.KK02 is part of the Kendrick's original Patent 142,279 drawing.

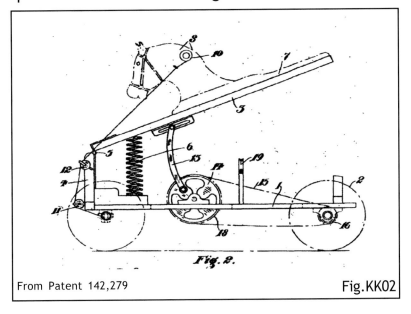

From Patent 142,279   Fig.KK02

Kennedy, W. S.

Address: 16, Talbot Terrace, Westbourne Park, Bayswater, London.

Patent No. 578.   Applied for;   7th March 1861.
                         Sealed;   30th August 1861

William Saddler Kennedy was by all accounts an entrepreneur, although not very successful it seems. His professions around 1857 were described as Licensed Victualler, Family Hotel keeper and dealer in Enamel Colours for Glass and Porcelain but in 1858 it was reported that he was in a debtors prison owing money to a Wine Merchant and a Meat Purveyor amongst others. It appears that he sorted his affairs in 1860 and in March of 1861, William Kennedy applied for a Patent for his invention described in the following manner;

*"An Improved Method of an Apparatus for Imparting the Motion of Riding to **Wooden or Metal Horses**, Part of which is applicable to Cradles and other similar Appliances".*

His invention was quite a simple affair in that it was no more than a horse, or other item, mounted on springs. His drawings, Fig.KY01, showed a variety of modifications of his idea which was also applicable in part to a baby's cradle. If a horse were to be mounted in this way the ride would be a little awkward, probably resulting in no more than a mild bouncing sensation. However, despite his inventions possible shortcomings, the Patent was 'Sealed' in August 1861 and therefore protected from any rivals. However, in March 1864 he failed to pay the additional Stamp Duty of £50 before the expiration of the third year anniversary of being granted the Patent and it therefore became void.

As a note, in the meantime in April 1863 he had also applied for another Patent for the invention of " *an improved method of, and apparatus for, applying fomentations and other external remedies to the throat".*
If nothing else, William Kennedy certainly had a curiously varied life.

Different drawings *Fig.KY01 - Fig.KY04* that accompanied William Kennedy's Patent 538 of 1861.

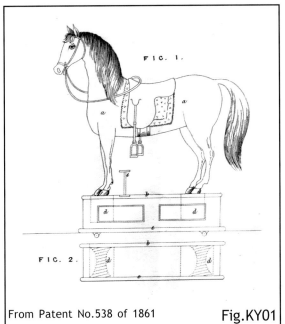

Fig.KY01

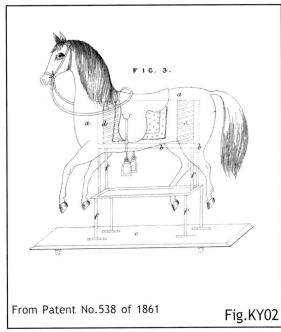

Fig.KY02

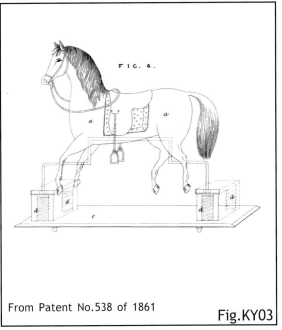

Fig.KY03

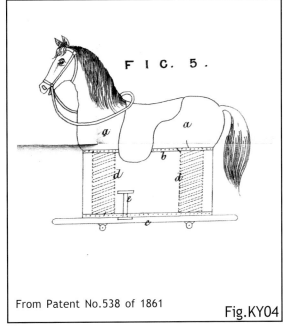

Fig.KY04

Leach, George.   -1900 - 1904-

Address: 47½, Bishop Street, Birmingham.

Leach, Walter Edward.   1906 - 1915

Address: 47½, Bishop Street, Birmingham.

        1912   49, Bishop Street, Birmingham.

The first known mention for George Leach is from 1900 when he is listed as a **Rocking Horse Maker** in a Birmingham directory. He is also listed under the heading of toy manufacturer. The last reference to George Leach that has been found is from 1904 and throughout this time has had the unusual street number of 47½, Bishop Street. In a 1903 directory another tradesman, James Davis, ferrule maker, is also listed at this same address. This may imply that this was a shared workshop of some kind.

In 1906, directory listings refer to a Walter Edward Leach, again at 47½, Bishop Street. One may assume that this is most probably a relative, a brother or son perhaps. Walter is listed at this address, both as a **Rocking Horse Maker** and also a toy manufacturer up to 1912. After 1912 Walter's address changes to 49, Bishop Street. This is continued up to 1915. After this date no further reference has been found for Walter Leach. Neither has any information regarding the products that were made by either George or Walter Leach.

Leach, Paul.   -1826 - 1891

Address: 1826 (Apprentice) 18, London Terrace, Hackney Rd.
              1852   14, Low. Kennington Green, London.
              1882   305, Euston Road, London. N.W.
              1886   305, Euston Road, London. N.W.
              1886   69, Warren Street, Tottenham Court Rd.

Leach, Paul & Co.   1891 - 1899
              1891   11, Ecclestone Street, London. S.W.
              1895   12, Hindon Street, London. S.W.

Leach, Mrs Paul.   1899 -
              1899   214, Vauxhall Bridge Road, London. S.W.

See Also: Palmer, S.   Calton, Rt.

The first known record of Paul Leach was in 1826 when he was called as a witness to the Old Bailey. The case surrounded the theft of a truck from a Stephen Palmer, who was a rocking horse maker. In Paul Leach's evidence, he stated that he was an *'Apprentice to Mr. Palmer'* who had been in the trade a number of years previously. It was quite typical to learn a trade by way of an apprenticeship, and it is wonderful to have clear documented evidence of such an event.

The next listing for Paul Leach was as a **Rocking Horse Maker** in 1852 and up to 1886 in his own right, after which the firm is referred to as Paul Leach & Co. It is interesting to note that in 1845 Robert Calton, who was listed as a rocking horse maker, also had the same address at 14 Low, Kennington Green seven years before Robert Leach. Perhaps Leach took over from Calton after his apprenticeship with Stephen Palmer. From 1886 up to 1891, it would appear that his main business address was at 305 Euston Road.

An example of a very fine large bow rocking horse has a brass plaque fitted to the front of the platform. This plaque is stamped 'P LEACH Manufacturer 305 Euston Road LONDON' *Fig.LH01.*

From 1891 onwards the firm is referred to as P Leach & Co. and also has a new address, If Paul Leach was still alive at this time, he would be about 79 years old, assuming he was 14 or so when he served his apprenticeship. Perhaps the change of name marked his death

P. Leach applied label   Fig.LH01

He was certainly alive in 1886 because he signed *Fig.LH02* an Indenture with a Charles Hayward. This is a revealing document in that it states Paul Leach is a '**Rocking Horse, Perambulator and Toy Manufacturer**'

Paul Leach

Paul Leach signature 1886   Fig.LH02

and that he is of 305 Euston Road and also 69 Warren Street. The indenture was basically that Paul Leach was to repay monies owed to Charles Hayward or his firm Gedge & Co. (A brief search, 1884, came up with Gedge & Co. Varnish/Lacquer Makers. 90, St Johns St.) The loan was secured against various chattels, at Euston Road. '*Seven work benches, Five vices, Six Gas brackets and all other trade fixtures and fittings*' and at 69 Warren Street, '*Four tables, One chest of drawers, Two bedsteads and bedding, One washstand, two armchairs, Eight pictures, Two clocks, Three Vices, Three benches - One lathe and all other trade fixtures and fittings.*

From this inventory it would appear that Paul Leach was probably employing a handful of men between the two addresses so as to occupy all these workbenches etc.

While referred to as P. Leach & Co there were two moves, approximately four years at each address and then the last known reference is in 1899 to a Mrs Paul Leach of 214, Vauxhall Bridge Road.

With regard to the actual items produced by Paul Leach, the large bow rocking horse that was previously mentioned is the only known example that exists with the makers label and there is nothing to suggest that this is anything but a true example of Leach's work and as such, other identification from this would be justified. Fig.LH03 shows a general view of the bow rocking horse, which from its brass identification plaque would date its manufacture between 1852 and 1891. The horse has been over painted at some time and has now lost its original tack.

P. Leach bow rocker circa 1880

Fig.LH03

It is well carved, the head *Fig.LH04* which is turned to the right, has teeth and a tongue, long elegant ears and glass eyes. The body of the horse is of a typical box type with pommel holes and has mortise and tenon leg joins. The legs are of particular note in that they have very unusual accentuated fetlocks, and the rear legs also have carved

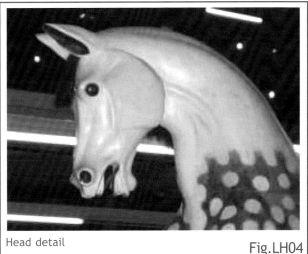

Head detail

Fig.LH04

hocks and also prominent stifles.

All of these points would be consistent across the range of similar quality horses, whether it is a bow rocker or the later safety stand. The rocker itself is typical of a Victorian item, with elm sides and a pine platform, which in this case has four top boards and three cover strips and on its own would be difficult to discern from many other makers, the only element that might be specific to Leach is the style of stretcher *Fig.LH05* although other makers may well have produced a very similar turned pattern.

Bow 'Stretcher' detail

Fig. LH05

A few examples of safety stand horses that have striking similarities to the bow horse have turned up and have been attributed to Paul Leach. One point about the safety stand horses is that while the horse is of first class manufacture, the stands always seem to be lacking in one way or another.

Two swing stand horses attributed to Leach *Figs.LH06 and LH07* are of very similar size horses with all the same characteristics as the previously mentioned bow horse. Fig.LH08 shows the unusual accentuated fetlock of the horse in Fig.LH07 and also shows two other special points regarding the swing stand horses. The very individual shape of runners which have pointed ends and are relieved between the hooves with a long wavy finish to the top and bottom of the bar. (Some smaller examples have only one wavy side to the runner.) The other individual item is the way in which the runners are held on the swinging irons by means of nuts, in turn locked with a cotter pin. See Fig.LH09 for a dismantled view of the components. The small hole in the thread is to take the cotter pin, sometimes this is not obvious as a broken pin and paint can obscure this feature. Almost every swing stand is different, although they all share the features mentioned above. The horse in Fig.LH07 was originally purchased in 1889, this is evidenced by a 'note' placed under the saddle by its then owner in 1959 who at the time 'restored' it. At that time, most of the stand was

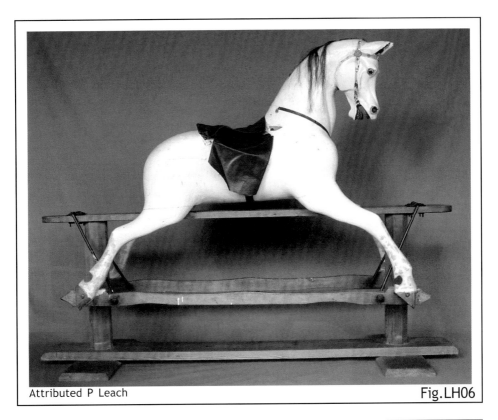

Attributed P Leach   Fig.LH06

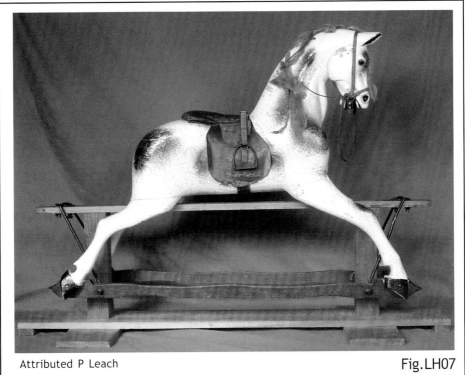

Attributed P Leach   Fig.LH07

247

Fetlock detail   Fig.LH08

Swinging iron nut detail   Fig.LH09

replaced but was apparently based on the original. A subsequent restoration *Fig.LH10* has revealed traces of Leach's fine dappling on the neck.

Fig.LH11 is of the horse 'restored' and is now finished to represent how it would most likely have looked when first made.

Revealed original paint dappling   Fig.LH10

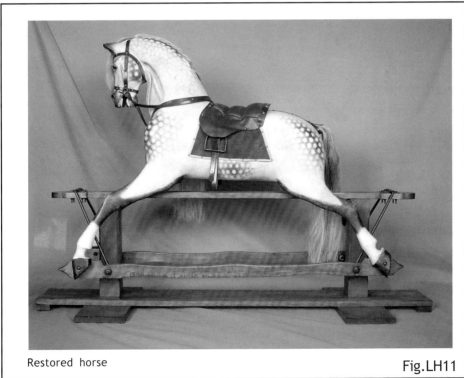
Restored horse   Fig.LH11

Another swing stand horse that is attributed to P Leach *Fig.LH12* is smaller and lighter than the two previously mentioned, has the same accentuated fetlocks and also the wavy runners and 'nut' fittings to the swinging irons. The stand is all original and has turned posts and is

Attributed P Leach   Fig.LH12

generally of much better finish than other stands, but the 'top plates' are still of poor quality. Other examples of this model horse are known of and also a smaller version as well.

An example of a smaller version *Fig.LH13* is generally simpler in its carving and more in the style of the horse in Fig.LH12 and still has the accentuated fetlocks, nut fixing to the swinging irons and also has turned posts and poor quality top plates. See Fig.LH14 for detail. Its thought that the last two horses mentioned were made later, probably dating from the very end of the 19th century. Because of the constant changing throughout their production, it is difficult to identify P Leach horses as it appears that almost everyone is an 'individual'.

Attributed P Leach   Fig.LH13

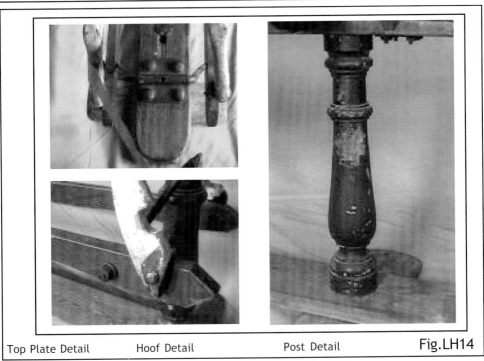

Top Plate Detail   Hoof Detail   Post Detail   Fig.LH14

251

Lines, G & J.

c.1860 - 1931

Address: 1860   Bagnigge Wells, Kings Cross, London.
           1876   'Steam Works' 457, Caledonian Road, London. N.
           1886   27, Hackney Road, London. (Allen's)
           1895   North Road & Roman Road, London.
           1914   'Thistle Works', Down Lane, Tottenham, London.

Patent: 1887   No.2938   'Jubilee Rocker'

Incorporated: 1907   G & J Lines Ltd.   Company No. 97,581

Trade Name: 'Thistle Brand'.

See Also: Allen C & J.   Hughes G H.   Lines Bros.Ltd.   Woodrow G.

One of the best known names in the British toy trade is that of 'Lines' and around 1860 George Lines set himself up in business. George had premises at Bagnigge Wells, a Spa in north London, and from the outset he produced strong toys and baby carriages. In 1876 his younger brother

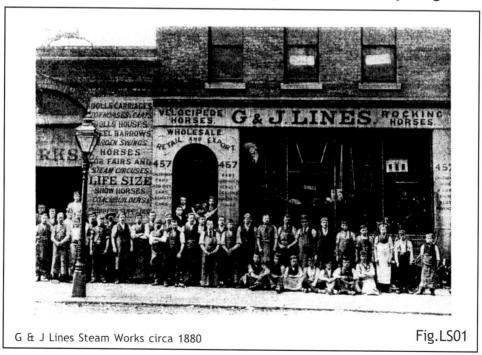

G & J Lines Steam Works circa 1880   Fig.LS01

Joseph joined him at the newly acquired 'Steam Works' factory in the Caledonian road, by which time over one hundred and fifty men were employed by the now named 'G&J Lines'. Fig.LS01 shows some 44 members of the staff posing outside the 'Steam Works', Caledonian Road. This is a most informative picture which shows us the showroom frontage of the 25,000 sq.ft. factory with a sign written inventory. Among the staff who are posing for the picture are Joseph Lines in the bowler hat stood in the doorway. Jack the Sawyer in the ten gallon hat, Hacko, Charlie Mackenzie, Pat Murphy, Alsop, Hacko, Chillman, Peacock, etc. As can be seen on the outside of the building a great number of their services and products were advertised, this was a common practice in those days. Listed are dolls carriages, **Toy Horses & Carts**, dolls houses, wheel barrows, garden swings, **Horses for Fairs and Steam Circuses, Life Size Show Horses, Velocipede Horses** and **Rocking Horses**. They also undertook coach building and were happy to deal with wholesale orders to the trade, export and retail sales. At this time G&J Lines were the largest toy factory in Great Britain, and still growing. Subsequently further premises were acquired in North Road, Penn Road, St Georges Road and Roman Road. Around 1886 the old established firm of 'Allen & Co.' was also acquired. Allen's was founded in 1817 by John Allen and among the products they made were rocking horses and child carriages. Walter Lines, son of Joseph and one of four brothers, started at his father's factory only a couple of days after leaving school in 1896 aged 14. For a while he went to Allen & Co.'s in Hackney Road to learn how to make prams. Walter and his brothers also attended a local college learning about building, carpentry and cabinet making. This was to later have a big influence on both the firms of G&J Lines and the yet to be formed 'Lines Brothers'.

On the 31st December 1903 George Lines officially retired from the business and left Joseph to continue running things as before. This was to become a bone of contention with his young and ambitious sons. Joseph was all for keeping the *Status Quo*, producing the same old models in what had now grown to seven factories spread over the north of London. However, in 1913 after much persuading the brothers succeeded in getting Joseph to purchase four and a half acres of land beside the railway at Tottenham. The new factory was roughly based on a wooden model that Walter had made earlier but an architect was also employed in order that the new buildings could be planed so as to meet all the special requirements of the business. The new factory was divided by a wide private road with manufacturing departments on one

G&J Lines Ltd Thistle Works Tottenham Circa 1914   Fig.LS02

side and the offices warehouses and showrooms on the other. Fig.LS02 is a view of the rear of the buildings with the loading platform on the far right. Fig.LS03 is an artist's aerial drawing showing the whole of the site. This new site was to become popularly known as the 'Thistle Works'. the 'Thistle' brand having been established some years previously. The new factory was a model of its time having a north

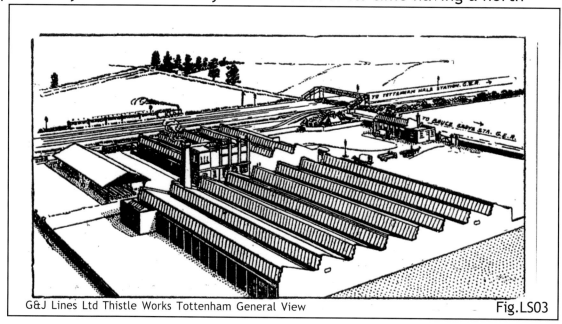

G&J Lines Ltd Thistle Works Tottenham General View   Fig.LS03

facing skylight in every department, a far cry from the dark and gloomy workshops of the past. The adjacent railway siding was of great foresight. This allowed large quantities of raw materials, such as timber to be delivered from all over the UK right to their doorstep. Before, the packers had to load up ten or a dozen times a day on horse vans to take goods to the station. Now with a platform long enough to accommodate half a dozen trucks at a time, the company could load up directly and the trucks were removed once a day. Fig.LS04 shows the private siding just off the main rail line. Inside the factory the various workshops were positioned so as to run smoothly, allowing raw materials to be

G&J Lines Ltd Private Siding Tottenham circa 1914   Fig.LS04

transformed through the various production stages, turned into goods, and eventually packed and dispatched via the railway. Local goods, within 50 miles of the factory, were sent out using either the company's own horses and vans or their motor lorries, these can be seen parked up in the previous Fig.LS02. By this time the company employed around 300 staff and within the main manufacturing departments, each man would have his own station. Fig.LS05 is a photograph taken inside one of the toy fitting departments with the men at their 'stations'. They would have been supplied, by a team of young lads, with basic components and also be overseen by a shop foreman. One such employee can also be seen in Fig.LS05, second person back on the left holding his clip board. Fig.LS06 is a view of a woodworking department, probably taken during an official break-time such as lunch. On the right, shelves can be seen stacked with a great array of raw materials awaiting assembly.

Toy Fitting Department circa 1914

Fig.LS05

Wood-Working Department circa 1914

Fig.LS06

The manufacture of any product is nothing without their display and subsequent sale. G&J Lines had always accounted for both of these and for a while still continued to run their Caledonian Road showroom after setting up at Tottenham. However after a while this was closed and goods could be viewed at the new works at Tottenham. Fig.LS07 is a view inside the well-lit and well-stocked showroom. Various types of

G&J Lines Ltd Showroom Tottenham circa 1914   Fig.LS07

horses can be seen including **Tricycle Horses**, **Push Horses**, **Rocking Horses**, **Pole Horses** and a small mountain of **Horse and Carts** piled up on the table. Besides these are other items, engines, wagons, carts, prams and a good range of toy motor cars, the toy car being the most recent 'must have' for Christmas. Since about 1912, sales of toy motor cars had become one of the firms principle specialities, with no less than seventy different types on offer. These ranged from 15s up to £19 for the latest up to date electric powered model with pneumatic tyres, electric lights and horn. The toy horse was now slowly but surely being replaced as the nursery favourite by the 'car' in its many guises.

The firm was incorporated in 1907, after George Snr. had retired, and subsequently called 'G&J Lines Ltd'. Joseph was chairman and the joint managers were William and Walter, Joseph's two eldest sons.

By 1914 production was now well underway at the new Tottenham factory, only to be interrupted by the start of the World War One. This was a drain on their staff, many of the younger men being called up or enlisting. This even extended to the management, with Walter along with his brothers George and Arthur joining the cause, leaving their eldest brother William, who was over age, to help their father keep things running throughout the War. Despite the hostilities toy manufacturing continued, even taking advantage of the situation in some cases as there were no direct German imports. This did not affect the Lines company as much, Britain always had the upper hand in producing strong toys such as rocking horses. Fig.LS08 is a photograph of their stand at a 1915 British Toy Fair with Mr Joseph Lines in

G & J Lines Ltd Exhibit 1915   Fig.LS08

attendance, (second from right). It is not known who the other members of staff were. However a fantastic display of their products is on show, rocking horses of all sizes including a very large horse fitted with end chairs, (below the 'L' in Ltd of their stand name board). As the War progressed it became more difficult to get adequate supplies of some materials and orders were only accepted on the condition that that there was no guaranteed delivery. At the end of the War the brothers returned but the old issues came up. With no agreement possible with their father, the three brothers, William, Walter and Arthur decided to take a chance and go their own way. They immediately set up their own firm **'Lines Brothers'** which eventually went on to surpass their forebears and became the largest toy manufacturer in the world. The fourth brother, George, took up farming on his return from the War but after some years returned to help his father at Tottenham, around 1924. G&J Lines Ltd continued to develop their products to keep up with new trends, only being briefly distracted from this by events such as a fire that broke out in April of 1923. Luckily, this was confined to a relatively small part of the premises and the damage was repaired in only a short time. On the 31st of December 1931 Joseph Lines *Fig.LS09* died aged 83. He had been working at the Tottenham factory up to within a few days of his death, no doubt just 'sorting out' after the Christmas period. This effectively ended the company 'G&J Lines Ltd', and this was officially wound up in early 1932. At the time of Joseph's death, a Mr George Woodrow was an acting director and secretary to the firm. On the cessation of G&J Lines Ltd, he set up his own company, G Woodrow & Co.Ltd, also in Tottenham. The majority of staff joined him, this probably being their best offer of continued employment. At this time Mr George Lines (junior) joined his brothers at Lines Bros Ltd. who had subsequently acquired the trademarks and goodwill of their father's company. Lines Bros Ltd. also made it known in the trade press that Woodrow's had not taken over the old G&J Lines Ltd company.

Joseph Lines 1848-1931   Fig.LS09

The range of items produced by George Lines started with **Push Horses, Pole Horses, Rocking Horses** and the like but by the time G&J Lines was formed the range had become very extensive. Fig.LS11 is a list of **Old Style Rocking Horses** from 1895, these were the bow rocker type as shown in the illustration *Fig.LS10*. This style would have been produced from the beginning of the firms existence but it is not known if they

G & J Lines Old Style Rocking Horse   Fig.LS10

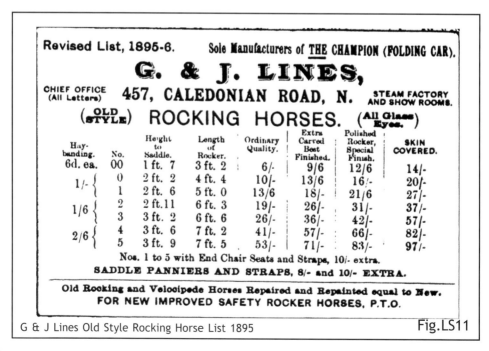

G & J Lines Old Style Rocking Horse List 1895   Fig.LS11

looked the same and were from the same templates as in the drawing. The illustrated horse was produced up to around the time of the firm's incorporation in 1907 after which a new set of templates were introduced and continued to be marketed as the ever popular 'Thistle' brand. Both bow rocking horses and swing stand horses were updated at this time with an 'improved' design. However, some of the old illustrations continued to be used, showing an impression rather than the exact look. An advert from 1931 uses an illustration first seen in the early 1890's. Fig.LS12 is an 'extra carved' 'old style' rocking horse that

G & J Lines Extra Carved Old Style Rocking Horse   Fig.LS12

was made around 1900. The picture above is of the horse in a restored condition, the old paintwork having been revealed from later coats of paint, then repaired and retouched. The harness and hair are also new, the original having succumbed long ago. The bow rocker had also been painted over but has now been returned to its former polished state. It now looks more or less as it would when first purchased. This particular horse was supplied by Hamley's, London and has the suppliers applied label *Fig.LS13* fitted to the centre of the platform. Walter Lines recalled that the 'dappling' of the horses was to resemble those that were portrayed in Rosa Bonheur's "Horse Fair". The detailed picture *Fig.LS14* of the head taken before restoration shows the 'extra' carving and also the type of fancy nails *Fig.LS15* that were used. The fancy nails were

Hamley's Applied Label   Fig.LS13

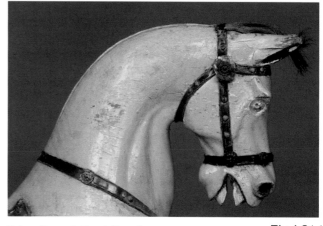

Extra Carved Head Detail   Fig.LS14

used as decoration all around the horse, on the martingale, crupper, bridle, saddle and blanket. They were also used to hold the ribbon rosettes in place. The rosettes were hand sewn and some used old trade cards as a backing. Fig.LS16 shows the remains of cards that were discovered during restoration. It is just possible to make out where the one on the top left would have been cut out from an old card such as that in Fig.LS11.

Fancy Nail   Fig.LS15

Rosette Backing Card   Fig.LS16

The earlier style of horse, both swing stand and bow, produced by G&J Lines had many distinguishing features. The heads with their dished faces, flared nostrils and long elegant ears. Bodies that were of quite a square nature and the legs had distinctive fetlocks, hooves that were generally notched all help to identify the brand. This early style of horse is often referred to as a 'J&G' type, some swing stand model having JG initials stamped into their top brackets in this order. Another example of the earlier style is a size 4 extra carved horse, Fig.LS17. This horse

G & J Lines Size 4 Extra Carved Old Style Rocking Horse   Fig.LS17

has been well used and also been over-painted at some time, but this does not hide the powerful look of the horse. The fetlocks of this horse are not cut as seen on the previous horse, this could well indicate a change within the workshop as this less accentuated fetlock is so much easier to cut out than the earlier example. It is worth noticing that there are two stretchers *Fig.LS18* at each end of the bow. This was the norm on the larger of the horses, smaller horses had only one stretcher per end and on the smallest size 'OO' these were often left plain *Fig.LS19* without any turned pattern at all. Fig.LS20 is another example of the double stretcher and Fig.LS21 shows a single stretcher that was fitted to the bow of a smaller size 2 horse.

The stretchers were generally all turned to the same principle design.

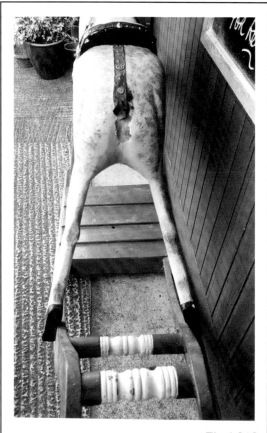

Double Stretcher Size 4   Fig.LS18

Single Stretcher Size OO   Fig.LS19

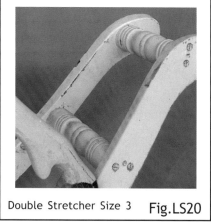

Double Stretcher Size 3   Fig.LS20

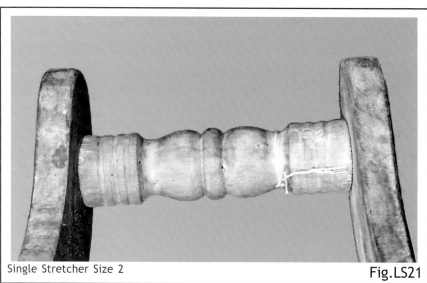

Single Stretcher Size 2   Fig.LS21

The old style rocking horses were not only available in seven sizes and four different finishes but could also be fitted with *'End Chairs and Straps'*. This allowed the horse to be used as a see-saw, usually under the supervision of a nanny. The horse illustrated *Fig.LS22* is fitted

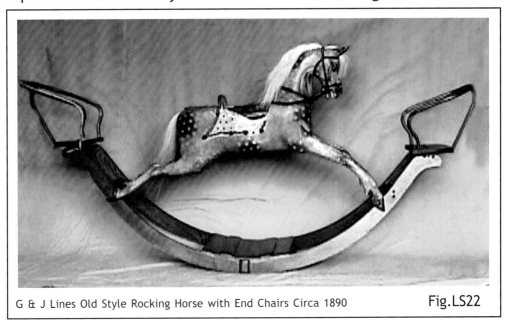

G & J Lines Old Style Rocking Horse with End Chairs Circa 1890   Fig.LS22

with bamboo type end chairs, although some of this is now missing. Many items made by G&J Lines incorporated the use of bamboo, a material that was well suited to carriages and the like. Another material used for end chairs was wicker, as shown in the illustration *Fig.LS23.* and this horse also has a Pannier *Fig.LS24* fitted. Panniers were extras that could be supplied in a variety of sizes and styles.

At the very top end of the range was the **Scots' Greys Cavalry Old Style Rocking Horse.** These were available in five sizes and fitted with
>Real detachable Cavalry harness, with Shoe Cases, Valise,
>Holsters. Martingale, Saddle cloth, Military Bridle, etc.

This type of horse was listed in G&J Lines Ltd 1914 catalogue and was obviously aimed at the children of those involved with the armed forces, the war giving impetus for many military based products. The high specification military option was also available on a range of swing stand horses and also the pole horse and push horse.

Old Style Rocking Horses with End Chair Seats.

Size.	Ordinary Finish.	Best Finish. Brown Harness.	Polished Rocker. Spcl. Finish.	Real Skin Covered to order only.
1	50/6	58/-	65/-	81/-
2	62/-	75/-	85/-	104/-
3	77/-	96/-	108/-	—
4	99/-	120/-	146/-	—
5	112/-	145/-	164/-	—
6	137/-	174/-	200/-	—

Well packed for Country at no extra charge.

Saddle Panniers   as illustrated, small, for Nos. 1 and 2,   Price **17/-** extra.
see page 6   ,,   larger, ,,   ,, 3 and 4,   ,, **21/-** ,,
,, extra large, ,,   ,, 5 and 6,   ,, **27/-** ,,

Old Style Rocking Horse with End Chairs 1914 G & J Lines Ltd Catalogue   Fig.LS23

Panniers.   No. 515.

These can be supplied from stock in various sizes (see below). They are constructed of strong Buff Wicker, and have three Straps.

No. 1 suitable for Nos. 1, 2
and 3 Horses   Price **17/-**

,, 2 suitable for Nos. 3, 4
and 5 Horses   ,, **21/-**

,, 3 (to order only) for Nos. 5,
6 and 7 Horses   ,, **27/-**

Or for Child to *face forward*, cross saddle, same prices. To order only (three days).

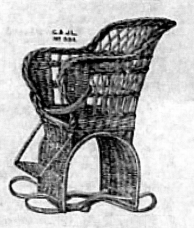

Panniers from 1914 G & J Lines Ltd Catalogue   Fig.LS24

Although illustrations in their catalogues remained unchanged in respect of the old style rocking horse, there was a change made to the product around the early 1900's. This seems to roughly correspond with the introduction of the trade name of 'Thistle'. There are however some of the earlier models with the applied Thistle label. Before the introduction of the swing stand horse in 1880, all their rocking horses were the bow rocker (old style) type with their typically outstretched legs. This arrangement was not suited to the 'new' swing stand model, so these were made with a much more upright leg arrangement. This situation of producing two different models was obviously reviewed and a new design was brought out. A horse with it legs arranged so that it would fit the new swing stand and also accommodate the old style bow rocker, thus roughly halving the number of different basic horses that needed to be produced. These new models were then referred to in their catalogues as the **Improved Old Style Rocking Horse, No.41a** and the **Improved Safety Rocking Horse, No.21.** Fig.LS25 is a picture of a latter 'improved' model bow rocker, this was originally fitted with end end chairs. The flat board instead of a stretcher at the end of the bow denoting where the chair was fitted. Another item that was revised around this time was the platform of the bow with plywood now replacing the earlier timber boards, a quicker and cheaper option.

G & J Lines Ltd 'Improved' Old Style Rocking Horse circa 1915   Fig.LS25

From their 1914 catalogue *Fig.LS26* is the 'Improved' Old Style rocking horse, still with the old illustration. The range has been increased to

Improved Old Style Rocking Horses. No. 41a.

These Rocking Horses are an improved type of the original Horse. They are well known for their high finish, strength and low cost.

Size.	About height to Saddle.	Length of Rocker.	Ordinary Quality.	Extra Carved Best Finish, Brown Harness.	Polished Rocker, Special Finish.	Real Skin Covered to order only.
oo	1ft. 7in.	3ft. 2in.	13/6	20/-	26/-	31/6
o	2ft. 1¼in.	4ft. 4in.	22/-	28/6	33/6	47/-
1	2ft. 6in.	5ft.	30/6	38/-	45/-	61/-
2	2ft. 11in.	6ft. 3in.	42/-	55/-	65/-	84/-
3	3ft. 3in.	6ft. 6in.	57/-	76/-	88/-	—
4	3ft. 5in.	6ft. 10in.	74/-	95/-	121/-	—
5	3ft. 8in.	7ft. 2in.	87/-	120/-	139/-	—
6	3ft. 11in.	7ft. 5in.	112/-	149/-	175/-	—

1914 List of Improved Old Style Rocking Horses No.41a   Fig.LS26

eight sizes, one more than on the 1895 list. Fig.LS27 is of a size 'OO' Improved Old Style Rocking Horse in exceptional original condition.

G & J Lines Ltd 'Improved' Old Style Rocking Horse size OO circa 1920   Fig.LS27

The '00' was the smallest size available but despite this was still well carved. Fig.LS28 is a detailed view of the head, note the absence of a bit, the reins being simply nailed to the head. The size of the horse is clearly marked on the underside of the platform *Fig.LS29*. Also marked on this horse were both stirrup irons, stamped *G & J L Ltd* along the side of the foot plate *Fig.LS30*.

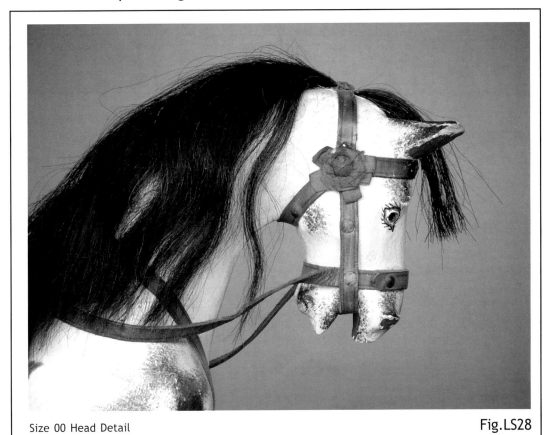

Size 00 Head Detail   Fig.LS28

Size 00 Stencil Detail   Fig.LS29

G & J L Ltd Stirrup Detail   Fig.LS30

It is uncertain when G&J Lines first started to make swing stand rocking horses. Originally referred to as **Hobby Horses** or **Safety Rockers**, the earliest references are from around 1890 although this new invention was introduced into the UK in 1880. Fig.LS31 is from a 1902 A W Gamage catalogue, but the 'G & L L' illustration, as it is marked on the drawing, is known to have been used from at least 1896. It has also been used over the years by other rocking horse manufacturers and G&J Lines Ltd used it in 1931, their last year of advertising.

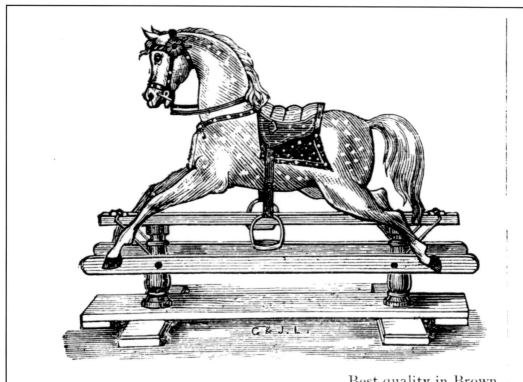

No.	About Height to Saddle.	Length of Stand.	Price.	Best quality in Brown or Cream beautifully finished.
1A	2ft. 2in.	2ft. 8½in.	19/6	25/9
2B	2ft. 7in.	3ft. 1½in.	26/6	34/6
3C	2ft. 11in.	4ft. 0in.	38/6	47/6
4D	3ft. 4in.	4ft. 7½in.	46/-	63/-

English-made Real Skin-covered Hobby Horses.
Sizes as above.

No. 1 AS, **33/6**   No. 2 BS **42/-**   No. 3 CA **63/-**

From 1902 Gamage's Catalogue   Fig.LS31

While not a true representation, the drawing was obviously based on a G&J Lines horse. The posts of the stand are more or less correct and although the horse is not entirely accurate, it does impart the look of an actual G&J Lines horse. These early horses were based on designs carried over from the earlier bow rocking horses, such as those shown in Figs.LS10 & LS12. An example of a small dapple grey 'hobby horse' *Fig.LS32* of this earlier style has an unusual feature in that the ends of

Early type G&J Lines 'Hobby Horse'   Fig.LS32

the runners are painted black where the hooves rest. This horse had no maker's label, the only mark being a 'Patented Jan 29 1880' stencil applied to the base. The saddle blankets of the earlier horses, both swing stand and bow rocker types, were very pointed as shown in Figs.LS10 & LS31. Some early swing stand horses have been found with small brass chest plaques, decorated with a thistle, a rose and the word 'Caledonian'. This probably refers to the factory that was in the Caledonian Road and is most likely to be to the forerunner of the 'Thistle' brand.

Another type of chest plaque that has been found on the earlier type of swing stand has a thistle in the centre and circled by a buckled strap *Fig.LS33*. Later versions had '*G.&J. L. Ltd LONDON*' inscribed around the strap *Fig.LS34*. This was obviously after the firm was incorporated in 1907, but horses made after this time have been found with the plain plaque. Another version is that fitted to the 'Scots Grey' *Fig.LS35*, these are nickel plated to match the other nickel fittings of the horse and the one illustrated is of the plain design. The brass plaques were not always fitted to the horse as many have been found applied to the stands, generally fitted over the tops of the turned posts. The 'Thistle' brand incorporated all the products made by G&J Lines Ltd but it would have been far to extravagant and also impractical to apply brass plaques to all items. Colourful paper labels *Fig.LS36* were applied to many products, the one illustrated being on a Tip Cart. The company also used the 'Thistle' image *Fig.LS37* at every opportunity in their ongoing advertising campaign.

Plain Brass Thistle   Fig.LS33

G & J L Ltd Thistle   Fig.LS34

Plain Nickel Thistle   Fig.LS35

REGISTERED TRADE MARK.

THE SIGN OF QUALITY.

THE SIGN OF QUALITY.

THE THISTLE BRAND TOYS.

Advertising Thistle   1926   Fig.LS37

Paper Thistle   Fig.LS36

A unusual type of brass plaque to have been used on early swing stand horses had a Lion and Unicorn either side of a Royal crest *Fig.LS38*. These were pinned to the stands over the tops of the posts. The stand this was applied to also had the 'Patented' stencil to the base and

Lion & Unicorn Brass Plaque   Fig.LS38

Horse with Lion & Unicorn Brass Plaque   Fig.LS39

was fitted with bowler hats *Fig.LS39*. The horse is extra carved with the original paint work intact. Note the outline of the pointed saddle cloth, shown up by the remaining decorative nails.

At the top end of the range was the **'Real Skin Covered'** version, Fig.LS40 is an example of one in original condition. This horse has both

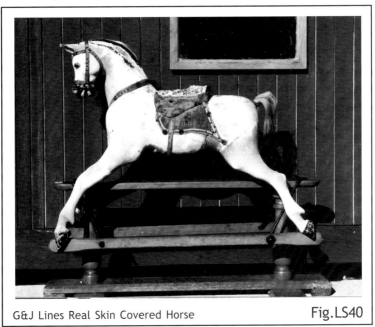

G&J Lines Real Skin Covered Horse   Fig.LS40

an applied retailers label, Hamleys, and also a plain Thistle plaque, both attached to the stand *Fig.LS41*. The harness was used to cover joins of the hide and this is shown well in the detailed picture *Fig.LS42* of the head. The bridle strap covers the joins allowing different colour pieces of hide to be used to great effect. The harness was also decorated with fancy nailing but surprisingly the saddle top was only made from a type of 'leather cloth' *Fig.LS43* as opposed to actual leather.

Hamleys & Thistle detail Fig.LS41

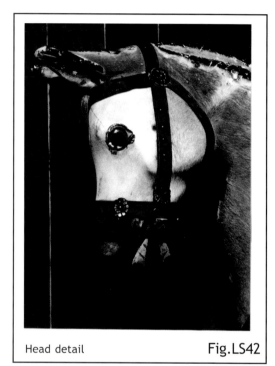

Head detail Fig.LS42

Saddle & Fancy Nailing detail Fig.LS43

Other examples of the earlier style of G&J Lines hobby horse are as in Fig.LS44 which is only 34 inches to the top of its head. This little horse has been over painted at some time and is probably an 'ordinary' finish horse. Fig.LS45 is a 52 inch tall horse in its original condition, this is extra carved and has the 'Patented' stencil on the base. Despite the huge difference in size, both horses share a very similar profile as do the rest of the range of early shaped 'hobby horses'.

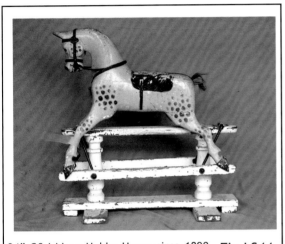

34" G&J Lines Hobby Horse circa 1890   Fig.LS44

52" G&J Lines Hobby Horse circa 1890   Fig.LS45

The patent stencil *Fig.LS46* appears on many G&J Lines horses, some of these were made well after the actual patent No.395 had expired. The reason for this is unclear, maybe it was to deter other makers from producing this type of rocking horse. The only other known maker to have applied a similar mark was the firm 'F H Ayres' of London.

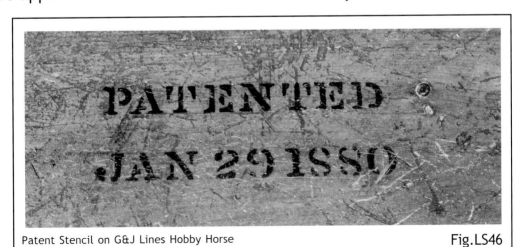

Patent Stencil on G&J Lines Hobby Horse   Fig.LS46

275

Not all rocking horses were painted dapple grey, another option was a 'chestnut' *Fig.LS47* coloured horse. This horse is mainly painted in chestnut but has a small amount of dapple on its cheeks. The hooves,

G&J Lines Chestnut Hobby Horse circa 1900   Fig.LS47

knees and parts around the head are shaded black with red detail to the nostrils and ears. There is a white flash on the face and it also has white socks. The harness is all leather except for the saddle top, this is a type of 'leather cloth' as on the 'skin' covered horse. The saddle blanket is a patterned material *Fig.LS48* and is very pointed in shape as were those of other G & J Lines horses at the time.
One unusual feature of this horse is that the swing irons are almost in the vertical position, making it quite a difficult rock for the rider.

Saddle & Blanket Detail   Fig.LS48

The **No.21 Improved Safety Rocking Horse** was introduced in the early 1900's and as illustrated below *Fig.LS49* was available in eight sizes with

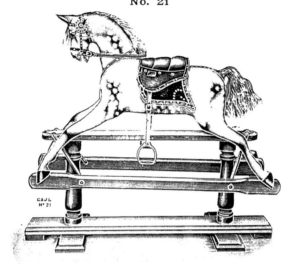

ROCKING HORSES.

Improved Safety Rocking Horses.
No. 21

Our Horses are world renowned. Every point has been studied which can possibly improve their Lasting qualities ; long Stands for safety ; bone dry Timber ; non-poisonous paint ; high-class Harness ; all go to make an unequalled Horse.

Nicely finished Cap is now fitted over end of hanger iron.

Packing.	No.	About Height to Saddle.	Length of Stand.	Ordinary Finish.	Best Finish.	Spcl. Best Finish.	Real Skin Covered. To order only.
1/- each ...	0	1 ft. 11 in.	2 ft. 6½ in.	24/-	28/-	33/-	38/-
	1	2 ft. 3½ in.	3 ft. 0½ in.	28/-	35/-	43/-	52/-
2/- each ...	2	2 ft. 7½ in.	3 ft. 8 in.	39/-	48/-	54/-	68/-
	3	3 ft. 0½ in.	4 ft. 4 in.	57/-	66/-	76/-	106/-
3 - each ...	4	3 ft. 4½ in.	4 ft. 9½ in.	73/-	86/-	96 -	...
	5	3 ft. 6½ in	5 ft. 3½ in.	110/-	136/-	144/-	...
5/- each ...	6	3 ft. 10 in.	5 ft. 10½ in.	144/-	160/-	172/-	...
7/6 each ...	7	4 ft. 0 in.	6 ft. 2 in.	188/-	208/-	248/-	..

NOTE INCREASED SIZES AND REDUCED PRICES.

Old Rocking Horses of every description can be repaired, and made like new. Estimates Given.

1909 G&J Lines Ltd No21 Improved Safety Rocking Horse List

Fig.LS49

up to four different finishes, depending upon the size. This illustration is from a 1909 G&J Lines Ltd. catalogue and the horse is an accurate likeness of the middle of the range best finish. Smaller horses tended to be not as detailed, no teeth, simpler stands etc. Fig.LS50 is of a size 1 restored example. The paintwork is original but it has been fitted with new harness and hair. Mention is made of a 'Nicely-finished Cap' fitted over the end of the swinging iron. This is colloquially referred to as a 'bowler hat' and can be seen on the size 1 horse below. The new model was constructed in the same way as before, with the advantage of being able to fit either a bow or swing stand. Changes were made to the legs, the angle they were fitted into the horse and the actual leg shape. This was made less acute, certainly around the fetlocks. The head and neck were also modified through the range, all the new 'Improved' horses had the same general profile, in the way of the earlier model.

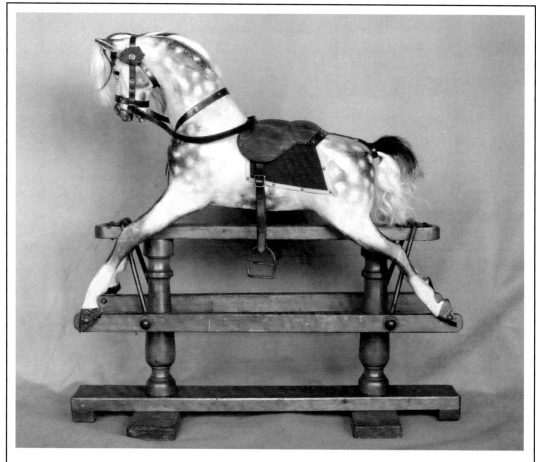

Size 1 G&J Lines Ltd Improved Safety Rocking Horse No.21 circa 1910   Fig.LS50

Fig.LS51 is of a size 6 'special best' finish horse in original condition. Note the extra carving and decorated harness, both being signs that

Size 6 G&J Lines Ltd Improved Safety Rocking Horse No.21 circa 1910　　　Fig.LS51

it is a 'top of the range model'. The varnish is quite dark on this horse, possibly due to the fact that the special best had more coats of varnish than the lesser models. This stand of this horse was fitted with a plain Thistle plaque. Because of the size of the stand, the swinging iron brackets were of a larger size than usual, see top right picture, Fig.LS53 As one of the most prodigious makers, the quantity of components produced would have been in their thousands and items such as swinging iron brackets would have been changed and modified over the years. The following are different examples that have been found. Some of these were also used and or copied by other makers, the **bold** text adjacent to the picture is that of the text that is in the casting.

1H
J&G L
L

Fitted to small
'improved' type

J&GL
L
3

Fitted to 'early'
type, also had
1887 Jubilee
plaque on horse

1
J&GL
L

Fitted to small
'early' type

3
J&GL
L

Fitted to 'early'
type

2
J&GL
L

Fitted to small
'early' type
Chestnut
Thistle model,
Fig.LS47

J&GL
L

Fitted to size 6
'early' type

2?
J&G
L

Fitted to small
'early' type

2H
G& JL LD
L

Fitted to small
'improved' type

3
J&GL
L

Fitted to 'early'
nursery swing
stand type,
Patent on stand.

4
G& JL LD
L

Fitted to (2?)
medium size
'improved' type

Selection of Swing Iron Brackets off 'Lines' Horses   Fig.LS52

280

??

Fitted to large
'Scots Grey'
Nickel plated

??

Fitted to size 6
'improved' type
as in Fig.LS52

W F
2 3/4

Fitted to small
'improved' type
with plain
Thistle plaque

2
G& JL LD
L

Fitted to early
'Lines Bros SP2'

W 3 F
3

Fitted to
'Lines Bros SP3'

2
G& JL LD
L

Fitted to
'Swallow' by
G Woodrow & Co.
as in Fig.WR08

W No 4 F
53/4 31/4

Fitted to
'Lines Bros SP5'.

LB LTD SP2

Fitted to a
'Lines Bros SP2'

W F   **2**

These two brackets are marked
differently and were fitted to an 'Ajoy'
rocking horse as seen in Fig AJ04

Selection of Swing Iron Brackets off 'Lines' and other Related Horses   Fig.LS53

Several examples of the 'Improved' Safety Rocker have been found with part detachable tack. The horse shown below *Fig.LS54* has a detachable saddle, not unlike that used on 'Lines Bros Sportiboy' horses.

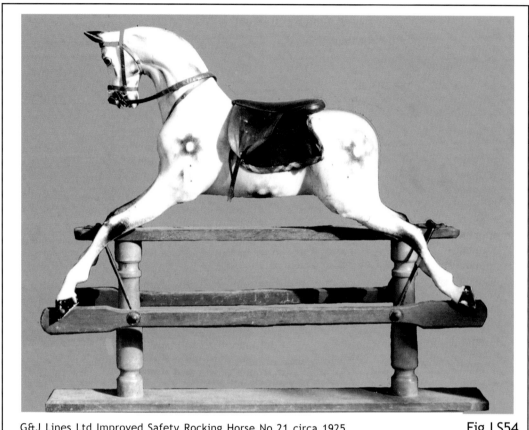

G&J Lines Ltd Improved Safety Rocking Horse No.21 circa 1925   Fig.LS54

The saddle cloth and colourful edging are the same type that fitted to the size OO bow rocking horse in Fig.LS27. The bridle and martingale are nailed on in the conventional way. The horse is partly 'extra carved', though not as much as some older models. The paintwork is in original condition and has been only lightly dappled, the stand is also in its original condition. The horse was supplied by the famous London toy store Hamley's as can be seen by the retailer's applied label *Fig.LS55*. The label is made from an early type of plastic as opposed to brass that would have been used for older labels.

Hamleys Applied Label   Fig.LS55

As with the old style rocking horse, there was a **Scots' Greys** version *Fig.LS54* of the safety stand rocking horse. The main differences

THE SCOTS' GREYS ROCKING HORSE.

Real Detachable Cavalry Harness, with Shoe Cases, Valise, Holsters, Martingale, Saddle Cloth, Military Bridle, etc.

Plated Metal-work on Stand.

Special Finish Horse and Stand. Harness as above.

No.	Height to Saddle.			Length to Stand			Price.
2 ..	.. 2 ft. 7½ in.	..	..	.. 3 ft. 8 in.	..	..	.. **55/-**
3 ..	.. 3 ft. 0½ in.	..	..	.. 4 ft. 4 in.	..	..	.. **75/-**
4 ..	.. 3 ft. 4½ in.	..	..	.. 4 ft. 9½ in.	..	..	.. **95/-**

Special Clothing **for these Horses in Royal Blue and Red with Braided edges, etc.**

No. 2, 3/6 each ; No. 3, 4/6 each ; No. 4, 5/6 each,

G&J Lines Ltd Scots Greys List from 1914 Catalogue   Fig.LS54

between this and the 'improved' horse was that the Scots Greys had more authentic military harness and that the stand was fitted with nickel plated metal work. Very few examples of the Scots Greys are known to have survived, as the detachable harness became easily lost leaving only the stand's nickel fittings to indicate the model.

End seats had been an option on the safety rocker since it was first produced and was illustrated in G&J Lines Ltd 1914 catalogue *Fig.LS57* and was titled the **Improved Safety Rocker with End Seats No.39**. The earlier model would have been referred to as a Hobby Horse with end seats. The illustration below is of the earlier style horse and it is fitted

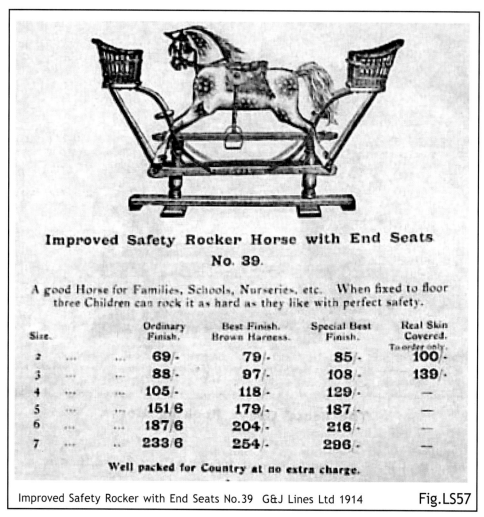

Improved Safety Rocker Horse with End Seats No. 39.

A good Horse for Families, Schools, Nurseries, etc. When fixed to floor three Children can rock it as hard as they like with perfect safety.

Size.			Ordinary Finish.	Best Finish. Brown Harness.	Special Best Finish.	Real Skin Covered. To order only.
2	...	...	69/-	79/-	85/-	100/-
3	...	..	88/-	97/-	108/-	139/-
4	...	...	105/-	118/-	129/-	—
5	...	...	151/6	179/-	187/-	—
6	...	...	187/6	204/-	216/-	—
7	...	..	233/6	254/-	296/-	—

Well packed for Country at no extra charge.

Improved Safety Rocker with End Seats No.39 G&J Lines Ltd 1914   Fig.LS57

with cane seats. The first models would have been fitted with bamboo seats and the later with wicker. An early type Hobby horse with end seats *Fig.LS58* that is in a dilapidated state has lost its original bamboo end seats. Compare this to the later 'Improved' model *Fig.LS59* that is in an original condition with its wicker seats still intact. The latter has a plain Thistle plaque on its chest and is only lightly carved, so would probably have been sold as an 'ordinary finish' model.

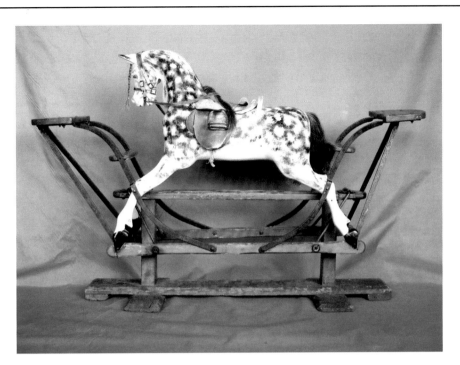
G&J Lines Hobby Horse with End Seats circa 1895   Fig.LS58

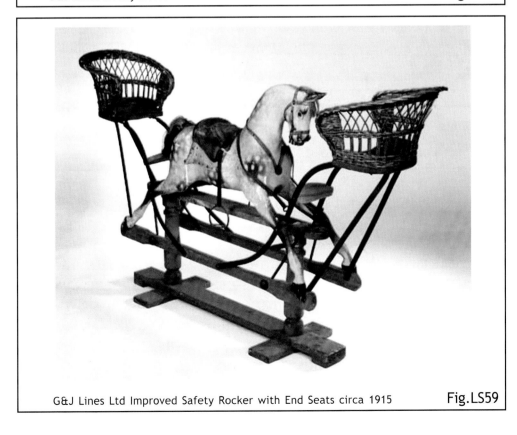
G&J Lines Ltd Improved Safety Rocker with End Seats circa 1915   Fig.LS59

In 1887 G&J Lines applied for and were subsequently granted a Patent for 'Improvements Connected with Rocking Horses, Rocking Chairs and such like Manufactures'. This invention was popularly referred to as the **Jubilee Safety Rocking Horse**, 1887 being the year of Queen Victoria's golden jubilee. This new device differed from other rocking horses in that the horse was not mounted at its feet but on its body. Curved pieces of wood are attached to the body and these are in turn attached to a fixed frame by means of swinging irons. The illustration *Fig.LS60* shows how the new invention was organised. It was however

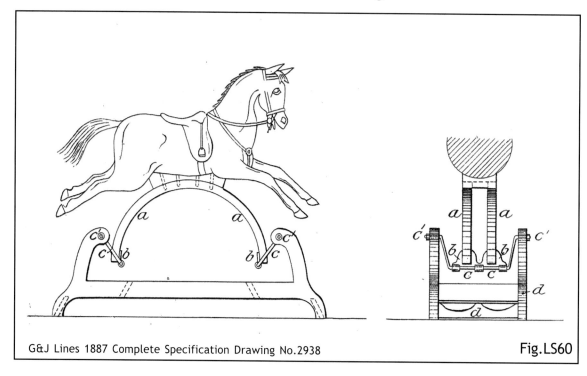

G&J Lines 1887 Complete Specification Drawing No.2938   Fig.LS60

not particularly successful in the UK although it was marketed up until at least 1915, as can be seen from a G&J Lines Ltd catalogue *Fig.LS61* of that date. At that time the Jubilee was offered in two finishes and in five different sizes. Its model was a No.42 within the G&J Lines range. This 'Jubilee' design was however very successful in the US where its production far exceeded that of Marqua's US 1878 Safety Swing Stand design, this ironically being far more popular in the UK.
The type of horse used on the Jubilee range was the same as G&J Lines' early hobby horse and bow rocker, with the exception of the legs. These appeared to be even more out stretched, in a 'flying' position, than those of the bow rocker.

A number of examples have survived and these were found to have

Jubilee Safety Rocking Horse. No. 42.

Size.	About Height to Saddle.	Length of Stand.			Best Finish. Brown Harness.	Special Best Finish.
1	2ft. 2in.	2ft. 11in.	...	...	49/-	57/-
2	2ft. 5in.	3ft. 6in.	...	...	72/-	78/-
3	2ft. 10in.	3ft. 11in.	...	...	95/-	103/-
4	3ft. 2in.	4ft. 6in.	...	...	126/-	134/-
5	3ft. 6in.	5ft. 7in.	...	...	168/-	183/-

Well packed for Country at no extra charge.

Jubilee Safety Rocking Horse G&J Lines Ltd 1914   Fig.LS61

been fitted with a brass plaque denoting the Royal Letters Patent No. 2938 *Fig.LS62*. One such horse that has recently been restored *Fig.LS63*. This is a size 4 horse and because of the amount of extra carving, is most likely to be a 'Special Best Finish' model. The horse has retouched paintwork and also been fitted with replacement harness and a new horse hair mane and tail.

Patent 2938 Brass Plaque   Fig.LS62

This horse also has another brass plaque fitted to its chest *Fig.LS64.*

G&J Lines Size 4 Jubilee Safety Rocking Horse circa 1887   Fig.LS63

This has a picture of Victoria encircled with the words '*Empress of India, Queen of Great Britain and Ireland. Jubilee 1887*'. Its not known if the 'Jubilee' plaque was fitted only during 1887 or if it was used throughout the entire production run. This plaque has been found fitted to a G&J Lines hobby horse which may well imply that it was fitted to a variety of products for the jubilee year only. If this is the case, it would mean that an exact date of manufacture can be established.

Detail of Jubilee Plaque   Fig.LS64

Of all the manufacturers of rocking horses, G&J Lines were one of the best at labelling their products. Aside of all the standard marks and plaques previously mentioned, a couple of more rather obscure marks have also been discovered during restoration work. Two examples of a letter "G" have been found. One of these was on an old style bow rocker *Fig.LS65* and the other on an early swing stand horse *Fig.LS66*. These were both written by the same hand in the wet gesso under where the saddle was later fitted, and therefore not apparent when

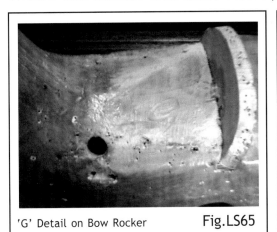

'G' Detail on Bow Rocker   Fig.LS65

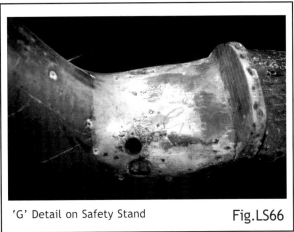

'G' Detail on Safety Stand   Fig.LS66

the horse was sold. A young George Lines, Joseph's third son, may well have been responsible as both of these horses date to the early 1900s. George was born in 1888 and like his brothers would have spent time on the shop floor the learning the 'trade'. The other obscure marking found are the initials 'JG' stamped on the back *Fig.LS67* of an early swing stand horse. The detailed picture *Fig.LS68* shows that the initials were stamped three times. They were obviously not designed to be seen and would have originally been filled with gesso, the purpose is unclear.

'JG' Markings on back of Horse   Fig.LS67

'JG' Detail   Fig.LS68

Besides rocking horses G&J Lines made a huge variety of other strong wooden toys, a great number of these being horse related.

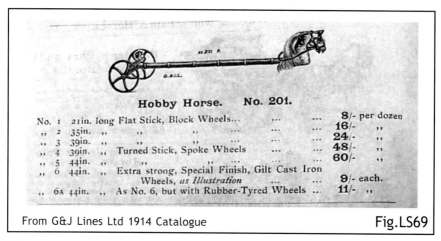

Hobby Horse.   No. 201.

No. 1	21in. long Flat Stick, Block Wheels...	...	...	8/-	per dozen
„ 2	35in. „ „ „ ...	...	...	16/-	„
„ 3	39in. „ „ „ ...	...	...	24/-	„
„ 4	39in. „ Turned Stick, Spoke Wheels	...	...	48/-	„
„ 5	44in. „ „ „ ...	...	...	60/-	„
„ 6	44in. „ Extra strong, Special Finish, Gilt Cast Iron				
	Wheels, as Illustration	...	...	9/-	each.
„ 6A	44in. „ As No. 6, but with Rubber-Tyred Wheels ..		...	11/-	„

From G&J Lines Ltd 1914 Catalogue   Fig.LS69

The **Hobby Horse No.201** *Fig.LS69* may well be a confusing title without the illustration. Earlier swing stand horses were also called hobby horses, perhaps 'stick horse' would have been a better title. They were seven different options for the Hobby (stick) Horse.

The **Wobbling Goblin** *Fig.LS70* was a sprung loaded seat that could be made to imitate a trotting motion. Sold as a novelty and could be used as a practical joke, a heavier person would think that the stool had given way under their weight.

Stool Horses on Runners *Fig.LS70* were offered in two qualities of finish and in three different sizes. They appear to be quite fragile and as such very few are likely to have survived the rigours of boisterous children. The great majority of the smaller horse related items failed to survive.

The **'Old Time' Hobby Horse** *Fig.LS70* was probably one of the first of these smaller items to have succumbed to an early demise.

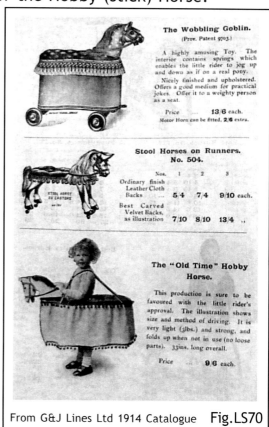

The Wobbling Goblin.
(Prov. Patent 9703.)

A highly amusing Toy. The interior contains springs which enables the little rider to jog up and down as if on a real pony.
Nicely finished and upholstered. Offers a good medium for practical jokes. Offer it to a weighty person as a seat.

Price   ...   13/6 each.
Motor Horn can be fitted, 2/6 extra.

Stool Horses on Runners.
No. 504.

	Nos.	1	2	3
Ordinary finish Leather Cloth Backs	...	5/4	7/4	9/10 each.
Best Carved Velvet Backs, as illustration		7/10	8/10	13/4 „

The "Old Time" Hobby Horse.

This production is sure to be favoured with the little rider's approval. The illustration shows size and method of driving. It is very light (3lbs.) and strong, and folds up when not in use (no loose parts). 33ins. long overall.

Price   ...   9/6 each.

From G&J Lines Ltd 1914 Catalogue   Fig.LS70

The **Head and Chair Rocking Horse No.135** *Fig.LS71* was available in two different sizes. curiously with not much difference between them.

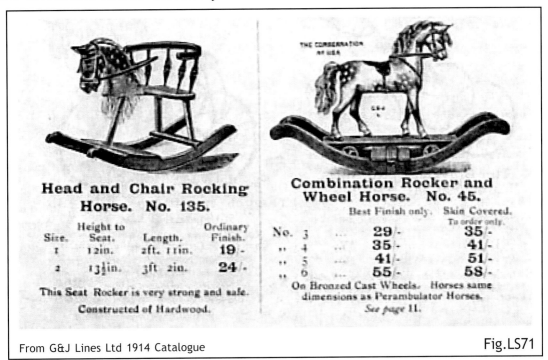

Head and Chair Rocking Horse. No. 135.

Size.	Height to Seat.	Length.	Ordinary Finish.
1	12in.	2ft. 11in.	19/-
2	13½in.	3ft 2in.	24/-

This Seat Rocker is very strong and safe.

Constructed of Hardwood.

Combination Rocker and Wheel Horse. No. 45.

Best Finish only.   Skin Covered.
To order only.

No.		Ordinary	Skin Covered
,,	3	29/-	35/-
,,	4	35/-	41/-
,,	5	41/-	51/-
,,	6	55/-	58/-

On Bronzed Cast Wheels. Horses same dimensions as Perambulator Horses.
See page 11.

From G&J Lines Ltd 1914 Catalogue   Fig.LS71

The **Combination Rocker and Wheel Horse No.45** *Fig.LS71* was produced as a dapple grey and also in a 'Skin covered' version. Both of these could be had in four different sizes. The basic horses were used in a number of applications so as to keep the number of different models to a minimum. The **Pole Horses No.138** and **Push Horses No.133** would have been an example of this, they in turn were made in upto eight sizes with a choice of three different wheel styles *Fig.LS72*.

Pole Horses, No. 138.

Good Shape.   Ordinary Quality.

No.	Height to Saddle About.	Wood Wheels.	Milo Wheels.	Cast Iron Wheels.
00	8½in.	3/4	—	—
0	11½in.	4/10	5/4	6/-
1	13½in.	5/10	6/4	7/-
2	16in.	8/-	9/-	10/-
3	18in.	10/6	11/6	12/-
4	20in.	13/6	14/6	16/-
5	22½in.	16/6	17/6	19/-
6	25½in.	25/-	27/-	28/-

No. 6 has a Padded Saddle.

Push Horses, No. 133.

Same Measurements as Pole Horses.

Ordinary Finish.

No.	Wood Wheels.	Cast Iron Wheels.	Milo Wheels.	Spider Rub. Wheels.
0	6/-	7/6	6/6	—
1	7/-	8/6	7/6	—
2	9/6	11/6	10/6	16/6
3	12/6	14/6	13/6	19/6
4	15/6	18/-	16/6	23/-
5	18/6	21/6	19/6	27/-
6	27/-	30/-	29/-	39/-

No. 6.—Very Large with Padded Saddle.

From G&J Lines Ltd 1914 Catalogue   Fig.LS72

The smallest pole horse was tiny at only 8 1/2 inches to the saddle. Fixed to the end of a pole must have made it extremely vulnerable. At the other end of the scale was a horse that was over two feet to the saddle and quite capable of carrying a small child. Middle of the range horses *Fig.LS73* were the most popular.For the discerning customer, the **British Cavalry Horse** *Fig.LS74* would have been the ultimate, an equal of the Scots Greys rocking horse. The British Cavalry horse was carved to a very high standard and then fitted with the very best quality harness.

Pole Horse.   **Push Horse.**

G.&J.L.

From G&J Lines Ltd 1914 Catalogue   Fig.LS73

British Cavalry Horses.

(Large.)

These Horses are far superior to the usual carved Horse. The proportions are exceptionally good.

The Harness is magnificently made of splendid material, it is all detachable and is made on the Cavalry Model, with all fittings as shown. Sandow Wheels and Handles are fitted. Will be the pride of any boy or girl lucky enough to receive one.

No.	Height to top of Head.	As Illustrated.	With Push Handles.
1B	19in.	21/- each.	23/- each.
2B	22½in.	27/- ,,	29/- ,,
3B	24 in.	33/- ,,	35/- ,,
4B	25½in.	39/- ,,	41/- ,,
5B	27½in.	45/- ,,	47/- ,,

From G&J Lines Ltd 1914 Catalogue   Fig.LS74

Royal Gig Horses No. 22 like all of G&J Lines products were available in many options *Fig.LS75*. Two basic styles of finish, each in four sizes and then with the choice of different wheels. The 'ordinary' finish horse was fitted with a hard wood seat, whereas the 'best' finish was fitted with a strong buff wicker seat. This resulted in twenty two variations available for the Royal Gig alone.

The new **Galloping Horses No. 138a** *Fig.LS76* was a tandem version of the **Pair Horse Galloping Gig** *Fig.LS78*. Obviously designed with twins in mind. As the gig was pushed along, the pair of horses moved in a 'galloping' motion. There was no choice with this item, just an option of having a brass jointed hood, upholstered if so required.

The **Velo-Trailer Gig No. 134** *Fig.LS77* was much more of a toy than the other gigs. Being designed so that two children could play with it, the other gigs were really to be operated by an adult. A well made and relatively costly item compared to the other gigs.

Royal Gig Horses. No. 22.

	Ordinary Finish.	Hardwood Seats.		Best Finish, as *illustration.* Strong Buff Wicker Seats.		
No.	Cast Wheels.	Iron Spider Wheels.	Rubber Wheels.	Iron Spider Wheels.	Rub.	Rub. Wheels. Skin Covered. *To order only.*
1	19/-	23/-	25/-	26/-	28/-	35/-
2	22/-	25/-	28/-	30/-	32/-	40/-
3	—	29/-	32/-	37/-	40/-	47/-
4 large seat	36/-	40/-		44/-	—	—

No. 4. Best Finish, with large Perambulator Handle, also Foot Rest, on 10in. ½in. Rubber Wheels and strong Steel Axles 52/- 62/-

From G&J Lines Ltd 1914 Catalogue Fig.LS75

THE TANDEM Nº 138

The New Galloping Horses. No. 138a.

With Two Seats—Tandem.

Best finish only, with Reed Seats, Cushions and Straps, fitted Wired-on Rubber-tyred Wheels.

As Illustrated 88/-

Brass-jointed Hoods, 16/- each.

If Upholstered, 13/- extra.

From G&J Lines Ltd 1914 Catalogue Fig.LS76

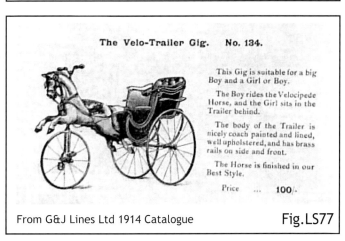

The Velo-Trailer Gig. No. 134.

This Gig is suitable for a big Boy and a Girl or Boy.

The Boy rides the Velocipede Horse, and the Girl sits in the Trailer behind.

The body of the Trailer is nicely coach painted and lined, well upholstered, and has brass rails on side and front.

The Horse is finished in our Best Style.

Price ... 100/-

From G&J Lines Ltd 1914 Catalogue Fig.LS77

The **Galloping Scooter** *Fig.LS78* was also designed to be used solely by a child although there was an option for push handles. The **New Pair-Horse Galloping Gig No.121** and the **No.127** *Fig.LS78* are basically the same item, the former just being a larger and more elaborate version. A charming picture *Fig.LS79* taken in 1930 is of the smaller size pair horse galloping gig. This was a 'best' finish with cream painted horses and a cane seat. In 2004 this actual galloping gig was sympathetically restored *Fig.LS80* retaining the great majority of its original factory finish. It had been purchased from Hamleys toy store in London.

The Galloping Scooter.

Prov. Patent
No. 23415.

A Great Novelty.

The Rider propels the toy by means of pedals and chain and the horses gallop as the toy moves along. Lamp and Horn provided. Suitable for Children 6 to 10 years.

No. 23415 ... **75/-**

Push handles fitted behind when required, extra **5/-**

New Pair-Horse Galloping Gig.

Handle about 3ft. high.

No. 121 (Full Size).

With Wicker Seat and Cushion, as illustration with Grey Horses, suitable for perambulator... ... ... **147/-**

Best Finish, with pretty White Reed Seat and Side Wings, upholstered in Crockett's Leather Cloth, fitted with Strap Cee Springs, Horses extra Carved, and either Grey, Brown or Cream colour... **157/-**

Hood, **20/-**; Apron, **7/-** extra.

No. 137 (Small Size).

Height of Handle about 3ft.

Ordinary Finish, Wicker Seat, two Horses painted Grey only **56/-**

Best Finish, Cane Seat, Two Horses painted Grey, Brown or Cream, with Brass Rail, Cushion Foot Mat, etc., as illustration... ... **67/-**

Hood, **16/-**; Apron, **6/-** extra.

No. 137a.

As small size, but with one (only larger) Horse Ordinary Finish **70/-**

Ditto, in Best Finish **80/-**

Handsome Brass Handle bars to any of the above, **6/-** extra.

From G&J Lines Ltd 1914 Catalogue

Fig.LS78

Galloping Gig 1930

Fig.LS79

Galloping Gig Restored 2004

Fig.LS80

Horses and Carts were available in great profusion *Fig.LS81 - Fig.LS84*

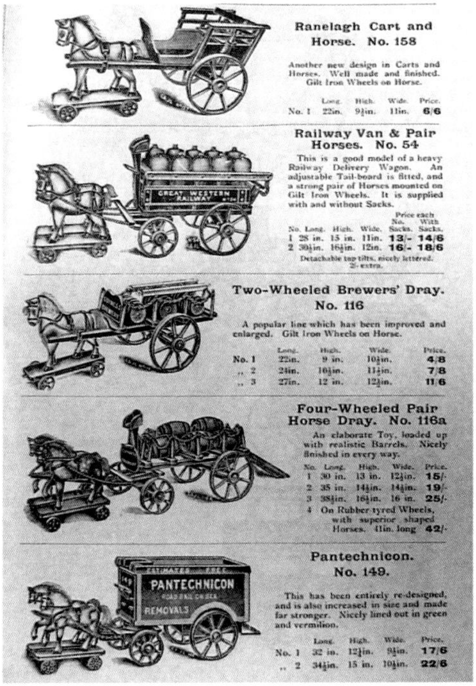

Ranelagh Cart and Horse. No. 158

Another new design in Carts and Horses. Well made and finished. Gilt Iron Wheels on Horse.

	Long.	High.	Wide.	Price.
No. 1	22in.	9¾in.	11in.	6/6

Railway Van & Pair Horses. No. 54

This is a good model of a heavy Railway Delivery Wagon. An adjustable Tail-board is fitted, and a strong pair of Horses mounted on Gilt Iron Wheels. It is supplied with and without Sacks.

No.	Long.	High.	Wide.	Price each No Sacks.	Price each With Sacks.
1	28 in.	15 in.	11in.	13/-	14/6
2	30½in.	16½in.	12in.	16/-	18/6

Detachable top tilts, nicely lettered. 2/- extra.

Two-Wheeled Brewers' Dray. No. 116

A popular line which has been improved and enlarged. Gilt Iron Wheels on Horse.

	Long.	High.	Wide.	Price.
No. 1	22in.	9 in.	10½in.	4/8
,, 2	24in.	10½in.	11½in.	7/8
,, 3	27in.	12 in.	12½in.	11/6

Four-Wheeled Pair Horse Dray. No. 116a

An elaborate Toy, loaded up with realistic Barrels. Nicely finished in every way.

No.	Long.	High.	Wide.	Price.
1	30 in.	13 in.	12½in.	15/-
2	35 in.	14½in.	14½in.	19/-
3	38½in.	16½in.	16 in.	25/-

4 On Rubber tyred Wheels, with superior shaped Horses. 41in. long 42/-

Pantechnicon. No. 149.

This has been entirely re-designed, and is also increased in size and made far stronger. Nicely lined out in green and vermilion.

	Long.	High.	Wide.	Price.
No. 1	32 in.	12½in.	9½in.	17/6
,, 2	34½in.	15 in.	10½in.	22/6

G&J Lines Ltd 1914 Catalogue Fig.LS81

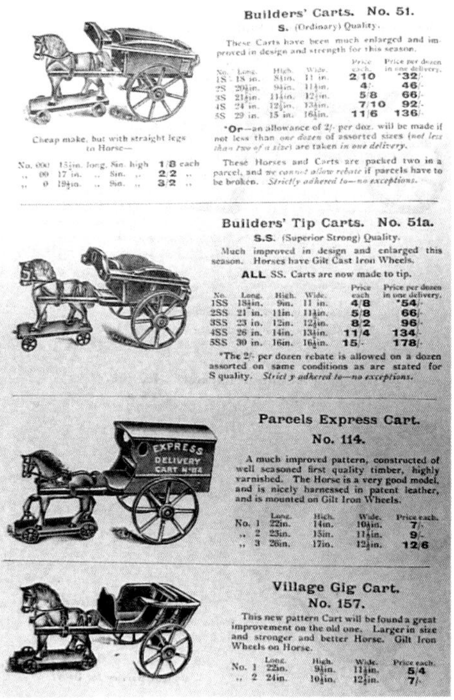

Builders' Carts. No. 51.

S. (Ordinary) Quality.

These Carts have been much enlarged and improved in design and strength for this season.

No.	Long.	High.	Wide.	Price each.	Price per dozen in one delivery.
1S	18 in.	8½in.	11 in.	2/10	*32/-
2S	20½in.	9½in.	11½in.	4/-	46/-
3S	21½in.	11½in.	12½in.	5/8	66/-
4S	24 in.	12¾in.	13½in.	7/10	92/-
5S	29 in.	15 in.	16½in.	11/6	136/-

*Or—an allowance of 2/- per doz. will be made if not less than *one dozen* of assorted sizes (*not less than two of a size*) are taken *in one delivery.*

Cheap make, but with straight legs to Horse—

No. 000	15½in. long, 8in. high	1/8	each
,, 00	17 in. ,, 8in. ,,	2/2	,,
,, 0	19½in. ,, 9in. ,,	3/2	,,

These Horses and Carts are packed two in a parcel, and *we cannot allow rebate* if parcels have to be broken. *Strictly adhered to—no exceptions.*

Builders' Tip Carts. No. 51a.

S.S. (Superior Strong) Quality.

Much improved in design and enlarged this season. Horses have Gilt Cast Iron Wheels.

ALL SS. Carts are now made to tip.

No.	Long.	High.	Wide.	Price each	Price per dozen in one delivery.
1SS	18½in.	9in.	11 in.	4/8	*54/-
2SS	21 in.	11in.	11½in.	5/8	66/-
3SS	23 in.	12in.	12½in.	8/2	96/-
4SS	26 in.	14in.	13½in.	11/4	134/-
5SS	30 in.	16in.	16½in.	15/-	178/-

*The 2/- per dozen rebate is allowed on a dozen assorted on same conditions as are stated for S quality. *Strict y adhered to—no exceptions.*

Parcels Express Cart. No. 114.

A much improved pattern, constructed of well seasoned first quality timber, highly varnished. The Horse is a very good model, and is nicely harnessed in patent leather, and is mounted on Gilt Iron Wheels.

	Long.	High.	Wide.	Price each.
No. 1	22in.	14in.	10½in.	7/-
,, 2	23in.	15in.	11½in.	9/-
,, 3	26in.	17in.	12½in.	12/6

Village Gig Cart. No. 157.

This new pattern Cart will be found a great improvement on the old one. Larger in size and stronger and better Horse. Gilt Iron Wheels on Horse.

	Long.	High.	Wide.	Price each.
No. 1	22in.	9½in.	11½in.	5/4
,, 2	24in.	10½in.	12½in.	7/-

G&J Lines Ltd 1914 Catalogue Fig.LS82

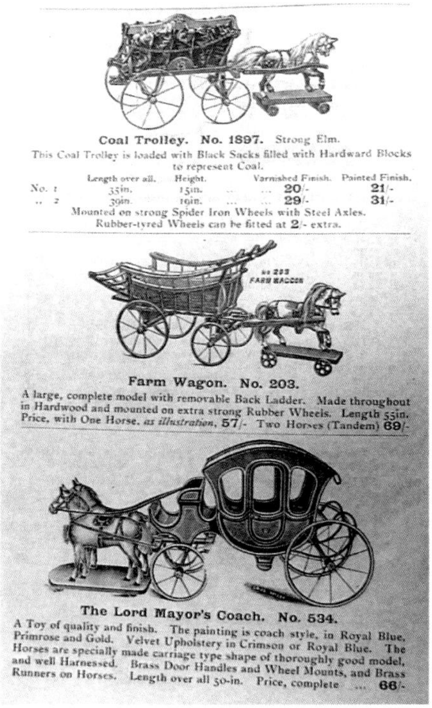

Coal Trolley. No. 1897. Strong Elm.

This Coal Trolley is loaded with Black Sacks filled with Hardward Blocks to represent Coal.

	Length over all.	Height.	Varnished Finish.	Painted Finish.
No. 1	35in.	15in.	20/-	21/-
,, 2	39in.	19in.	29/-	31/-

Mounted on strong Spider Iron Wheels with Steel Axles. Rubber-tyred Wheels can be fitted at 2/- extra.

Farm Wagon. No. 203.

A large, complete model with removable Back Ladder. Made throughout in Hardwood and mounted on extra strong Rubber Wheels. Length 55in. Price, with One Horse, *as illustration*, 57/- Two Horses (Tandem) 69/-

The Lord Mayor's Coach. No. 534.

A Toy of quality and finish. The painting is coach style, in Royal Blue, Primrose and Gold. Velvet Upholstery in Crimson or Royal Blue. The Horses are specially made carriage type shape of thoroughly good model, and well Harnessed. Brass Door Handles and Wheel Mounts, and Brass Runners on Horses. Length over all 50-in. Price, complete ... 66/-

G&J Lines Ltd 1914 Catalogue Fig.LS83

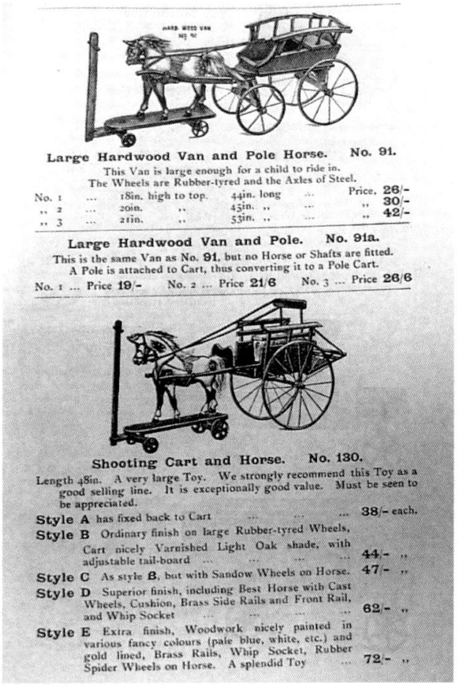

Large Hardwood Van and Pole Horse. No. 91.

This Van is large enough for a child to ride in. The Wheels are Rubber-tyred and the Axles of Steel.

No. 1 ...	18in. high to top.	44in. long ...	Price. 26/-
,, 2 ...	20in. ,,	45in. ,, ...	,, 30/-
,, 3 ...	21in. ,,	53in. ,, ...	,, 42/-

Large Hardwood Van and Pole. No. 91a.

This is the same Van as No. 91, but no Horse or Shafts are fitted. A Pole is attached to Cart, thus converting it to a Pole Cart.

No. 1 ... Price 19/- No. 2 ... Price 21/6 No. 3 ... Price 26/6

Shooting Cart and Horse. No. 130.

Length 48in. A very large Toy. We strongly recommend this Toy as a good selling line. It is exceptionally good value. Must be seen to be appreciated.

Style A has fixed back to Cart ... ... 38/- each.

Style B Ordinary finish on large Rubber-tyred Wheels, Cart nicely Varnished Light Oak shade, with adjustable tail-board ... ... 44/- ,,

Style C As style **B**, but with Sandow Wheels on Horse. 47/- ,,

Style D Superior finish, including Best Horse with Cast Wheels, Cushion, Brass Side Rails and Front Rail, and Whip Socket ... ... 62/- ,,

Style E Extra finish, Woodwork nicely painted in various fancy colours (pale blue, white, etc.) and gold lined, Brass Rails, Whip Socket, Rubber Spider Wheels on Horse. A splendid Toy ... 72/- ,,

G&J Lines Ltd 1914 Catalogue Fig.LS84

Horses and Carts *Fig.LS85 - Fig.LS90*

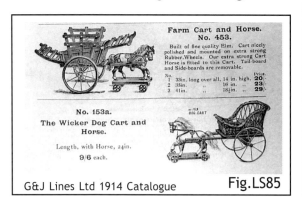

Farm Cart and Horse. No. 453.

Built of fine quality Elm. Cart nicely polished and mounted on extra strong Rubber Wheels. Our extra strong Cart Horse is fitted to this Cart. Tail-board and Side-boards are removable.

No.					Price.
1	33in. long over all, 14 in. high.				20/-
2	35in.	,,	16 in.	,,	23/-
3	41in.	,,	18½in.	,,	29/-

No. 153a.
The Wicker Dog Cart and Horse.

Length, with Horse, 24in.

9/6 each.

G&J Lines Ltd 1914 Catalogue **Fig.LS85**

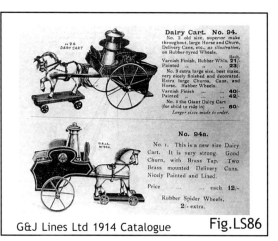

Dairy Cart. No. 94.

No. 2 old size, superior make throughout, large Horse and Churn, Delivery Cans, etc., *as illustration,* on Rubber-tyred Wheels.

	Each.
Varnish Finish, Rubber Whls.	21/-
Painted	,,	23/-

No. 3 extra large size, best make, very nicely finished and decorated. Extra large Churns, Cans, and Horse. Rubber Wheels.

Varnish Finish	each	40/-
Painted	,,	42/-

No. 4 the Giant Dairy Cart (for child to ride in) ... 80/-

Larger sizes made to order.

No. 94a.

No. 1. This is a new size Dairy Cart. It is very strong. Good Churn, with Brass Tap. Two Brass mounted Delivery Cans. Nicely Painted and Lined.

Price ... ... each 12/-

Rubber Spider Wheels, 2/- extra.

G&J Lines Ltd 1914 Catalogue **Fig.LS86**

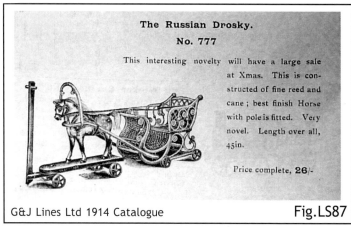

The Russian Drosky.
No. 777

This interesting novelty will have a large sale at Xmas. This is constructed of fine reed and cane ; best finish Horse with pole is fitted. Very novel. Length over all, 45in.

Price complete, 26/-

G&J Lines Ltd 1914 Catalogue **Fig.LS87**

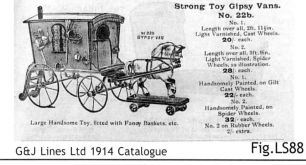

Strong Toy Gipsy Vans. No. 22b.

No. 1.
Length over all, 2ft. 11½in. Light Varnished, Cast Wheels.
20/- each.

No. 2.
Length over all, 3ft. 9in. Light Varnished, Spider Wheels, as illustration.
28/- each.

No. 1.
Handsomely Painted, on Gilt Cast Wheels.
22/- each.

No. 2.
Handsomely Painted, on Spider Wheels.
32/- each.
No. 2 on Rubber Wheels, 2/- extra.

Large Handsome Toy, fitted with Fancy Baskets, etc.

G&J Lines Ltd 1914 Catalogue **Fig.LS88**

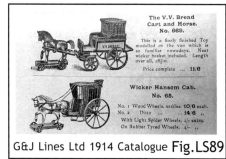

The V.V. Bread Cart and Horse. No. 669.

This is a finely finished Toy modelled on the van which is so familiar nowadays. Neat wicker basket included. Length over all, 28½in.

Price complete ... 11/6

Wicker Hansom Cab. No. 65.

No. 1 Wood Wheels, *as illus.*	10/6 each.
No. 2 Ditto	,,	14/6 ,,
With Light Spider Wheels, 2/- extra.	
On Rubber Tyred Wheels, 4/- ,,	

G&J Lines Ltd 1914 Catalogue **Fig.LS89**

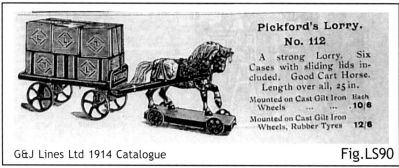

Pickford's Lorry.
No. 112

A strong Lorry. Six Cases with sliding lids included. Good Cart Horse. Length over all, 25 in.

	Each
Mounted on Cast Gilt Iron Wheels	...	10/6
Mounted on Cast Gilt Iron Wheels, Rubber Tyres	12/6

G&J Lines Ltd 1914 Catalogue **Fig.LS90**

Horses and Carts.
Fig.LS91 - Fig.LS95

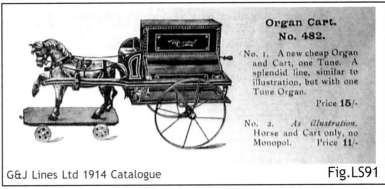

Organ Cart.
No. 482.

No. 1. A new cheap Organ and Cart, one Tune. A splendid line, similar to illustration, but with one Tune Organ.

Price 15/-

No. 2. As *illustration*, Horse and Cart only, no Monopol. Price 11/-

G&J Lines Ltd 1914 Catalogue — Fig.LS91

Timber Van
(Loaded).
No. 530.

A well-made article, fitted with strong Cart Horse and loaded with cut timber.

Price :
32in. long over all ... 16/-

G&J Lines Ltd 1914 Catalogue — Fig.LS92

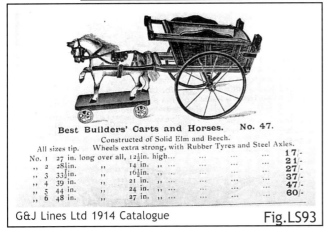

Best Builders' Carts and Horses. No. 47.
Constructed of Solid Elm and Beech.
All sizes tip. Wheels extra strong, with Rubber Tyres and Steel Axles.

No. 1	27 in. long over all, 12½in. high...	...	...	...	17/-
,, 2	28½in. ,,	14 in. ,, ...	...	...	21/-
,, 3	33½in. ,,	16½in. ,, ...	...	...	27/-
,, 4	39 in. ,,	21 in. ,, ...	...	...	37/-
,, 5	44 in. ,,	24 in. ,, ...	...	...	47/-
,, 6	48 in. ,,	27 in. ,, ...	...	...	60/-

G&J Lines Ltd 1914 Catalogue — Fig.LS93

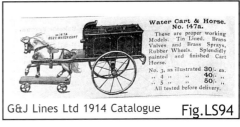

Water Cart & Horse.
No. 147a.

These are proper working Models. Tin Lined. Brass Valves and Brass Sprays, Rubber Wheels. Splendidly painted and finished Cart Horse.

No. 3, as illustrated 30/- en.
,, 4 ,, ,, 40/- ,,
,, 5 ,, ,, 50/- ,,
All tested before delivery.

G&J Lines Ltd 1914 Catalogue — Fig.LS94

The **Best Builder's Cart & Horse** *Fig.LS95* is a size No.2 and has a paper Thistle label *Fig.LS36* attached to the front of the cart.

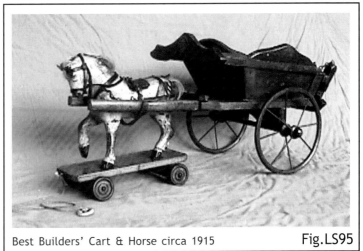

Best Builders' Cart & Horse circa 1915 — Fig.LS95

G&J Lines Ltd also produced a wide range of ordinary and superior finish **Velocipede Horses** *Fig.LS96* and at the cheaper end of the market was **The Startler** and the **Tricycle Head Horse** .

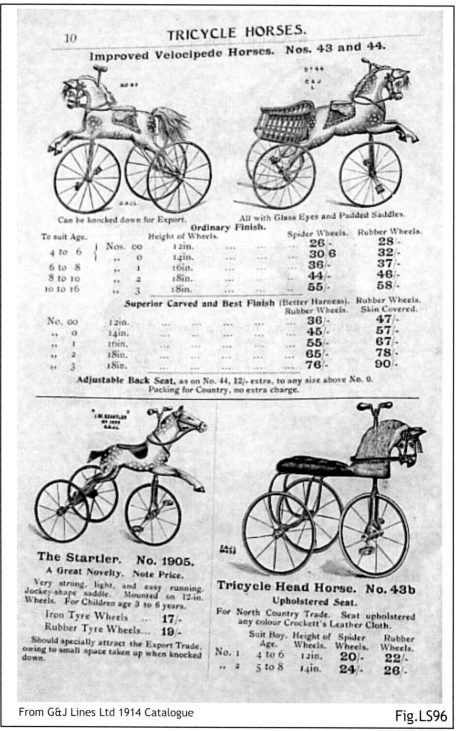

TRICYCLE HORSES.

10

Improved Velocipede Horses. Nos. 43 and 44.

Can be knocked down for Export.

All with Glass Eyes and Padded Saddles.

Ordinary Finish.

To suit Age.		Height of Wheels.				Spider Wheels.	Rubber Wheels.
4 to 6	Nos. oo	12in.	...	...	...	26/-	28/-
,, o	14in.	...	...	...	30 6	32/-
6 to 8	,, 1	16in.	...	...	...	36/-	37/-
8 to 10	,, 2	18in.	...	...	...	44/-	46/-
10 to 16	,, 3	18in.	...	...	...	55/-	58/-

Superior Carved and Best Finish (Better Harness). Rubber Wheels. Skin Covered.

						Rubber Wheels.	
No. oo	12in.	...	...	...	...	36/-	47/-
,, o	14in.	...	...	...	...	45/-	57/-
,, 1	16in.	...	...	...	...	55/-	67/-
,, 2	18in.	...	...	...	...	65/-	78/-
,, 3	18in.	...	...	...	...	76/-	90/-

Adjustable Back Seat, as on No. 44, 12/- extra, to any size above No. 0.
Packing for Country, no extra charge.

The Startler. No. 1905.
A Great Novelty. Note Price.
Very strong, light, and easy running.
Jockey-shape saddle. Mounted on 12-in.
Wheels. For Children age 3 to 6 years.

| Iron Tyre Wheels | ... | 17/- |
| Rubber Tyre Wheels | ... | 19/- |

Should specially attract the Export Trade, owing to small space taken up when knocked down.

Tricycle Head Horse. No. 43b.
Upholstered Seat.
For North Country Trade. Seat upholstered any colour Crockett's Leather Cloth.

	Suit Boy. Age.	Height of Wheels.	Spider Wheels.	Rubber Wheels.
No. 1	4 to 6	12in.	20/-	22/-
,, 2	5 to 8	14in.	24/-	26/-

From G&J Lines Ltd 1914 Catalogue

Fig.LS96

A proud lad poses next to his velocipede horse *Fig.LS97*. Note the 'Thistle' plaque fitted to the horses chest.

G&J Lines Ltd Velocipede Horse circa 1915

Fig.LS96

Lines Bros Ltd.   1919 - 1978

Address: 1919-25   Hatcham Works, Ormside St. Old Kent Rd. London.
                1921-35   9, Fore Street, London. E.C. (Showrooms)
                1922-25   761, Old Kent Road, London. S.E. (Factory)
                1925   Morden Road, Merton, London. S.W.19. (Factory)
                1927   Oldham, Lancashire. (Depot)
                1935   18, New Union Street, London. EC2 (Showrooms)
                1945   Merthyr Tydfil, Wales. (Factory)
                1946   Belfast, Northern Ireland. (Factory)

Incorporated: 1st May 1919 Lines Bros.Ltd.   Company No.154,775

Trade Names: 'Triangtois', 'Sportiboy', 'Tri-ang', 'Pedigree'.

See Also: Allen, C&G.   Lines, G&J.   Simpson Fawcett & Co.

Created out of frustration, three brothers, William, Walter and Arthur Lines decided to go their own way, set up for themselves, and in early 1919 they formed Lines Bros Ltd. Even in their wildest dreams they could not have envisaged what this company would go on to become. We have to go back some years to understand why they decided to set up for themselves. The brothers were three of four children of Joseph Lines, Joseph ran G&J Lines, probably the most experienced toy manufacturer in the UK, having been established around 1860. This is where the brothers learned their trade. Having all started on the shop floor, they progressed to areas of management but were constantly thwarted by their father's old ways and reluctance to move on. In 1914 on the outbreak of War, Walter, George and Arthur joined up, William was too old to enlist so he stayed on and helped his father run things. After the war it was immediately apparent that the situation had not changed so this is when the three brothers decided on their move. George went his own way and took up farming. It is important to note that Lines Bros Ltd and G&J Lines Ltd were separate companies and in direct competition with each other. It was a long time before the family rift was made good, in fact only a few years before Joseph's death and the subsequent closure of G&J Lines Ltd in 1931.

After the war property was scarce but the brothers eventually came across an old wood working factory in Ormside Street. The owners were retiring and agreed to a price of £28,000 for the freehold. This was agreed on the spot, the finances to be sorted out later. Work started on the reorganisation the following day, June 16th. This was all very unconventional, especially as the brothers did not have any funds at the time. However an appointment at Lloyds Bank to meet with Mr Risk, the Overdraft Manager, was arranged. After some time he agreed to their request and loaned the brothers the full amount. The excess plant, vans and horses were sold off and this gave the brothers enough money to start them on their way. The first toys were designed by Walter Lines and prototypes were made up in only a few days. Their first order was for export to an old South Africa acquaintance and this was followed by an order from Harrods and from then on orders flooded in. Many of these were from customers of G&J Lines who the brothers had met while working for their father. The Hatcham Works *Fig.LB01* was very soon at full swing and by October 1920 toys were sold under the 'Triangtois' trade name and applied with the Lines Bros Ltd triangle trademark.

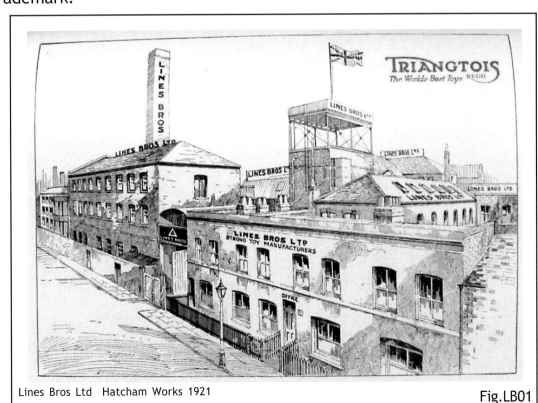

Lines Bros Ltd Hatcham Works 1921

Fig.LB01

The Lines Bros red triangle logo *Fig.LB02* was registered, No.391,682 in 1919. The first of many logos and trade names that would follow.

When the Hatcham works were acquired, they were fitted with kilns for drying the timber, usually the timber would have to be stored for a couple of years to 'dry' before being used. The kilns would achieve the same result in only a couple of weeks. This was another reason for Lines Bros ability to produce toys almost immediately on starting up in business. Most of the staff had been in the Army, and as such were reliable and well suited to the

Lines Bros Ltd
Regd. Trade Mark 1919   Fig.LB02

discipline of working as a team. By December 1919, only six months from starting up, nearly 200 staff were being employed, a work force that would continue to grow. From early on special machines, many of them automatic, were used to minimise labour while enabling large quantities of goods to be produced. They were installed in many of the different departments throughout the factory, from the mill where the basic machining of timber was carried out, through the engineering shops, fitting shops, painting shops, upholstery shops and many more right up to the dispatch department. One such machine was a huge double ended sandpapering machine which was 48 inches in diameter, the largest in the country. Copying lathes were used for 'roughing out' the bodies of the smaller shaped horses although the larger models were all done by hand. This work was carried out by a number of highly skilled workmen. The first operation carried out by means of a 'chopper' to rough carve the body of the horse, the head and other detailed areas were done by chisel and gouge. No machine being able to do this work. A view of the Horse Making shop *Fig.LB03* gives an indication of the volume of horses being dealt with at any given time. Most of these appear to be either **Pole or Push Horses**, some attached to platforms and others clearly showing the fixing dowel in the bottom of their hooves. The horse painting shop *Fig.LB04* is equally busy, a large **Rocking Horse** on the right is being dappled while all around horses of all sizes are waiting to be painted or are drying off. A young lad (centre) appears to be attending to portioning out the paint or gesso into more manageable sized buckets.

Lines Bros Ltd Horse Making Shop 1920   Fig.LB03

Lines Bros Ltd Horse Painting Shop 1920   Fig.LB04

Walter Lines described the Hatcham works as *'an archaic building and as inconvenient as you like'*. Despite this they soon had achieved maximum capacity, partly by knocking holes in walls and ceilings, and making chutes and hoists from floor to floor. In 1921 showroom premises were acquired at No.9 Fore Street *Fig.LB05*, an area associated with the toy retail trade. A Mr K J Turner and three assistants looked after sales, the brothers generally staying at the works to supervise production.

Lines Bros Ltd Showrooms 9 Fore St. London 1921   Fig.LB05

Despite the small appearance of the exterior, the Fore Street premises were spread over a number of floors giving adequate space to display their products. The property was well lit and no artificial light was normally required. However, if necessary it had been provided for with the most up-to-date metallic filament lamps. Electricity was still in its infancy. The showroom *Fig.LB06* is certainly well lit and a good range of **Rocking Horses**, **Horses & Carts**, engines and the like can be seen.

Lines Bros Ltd Showroom 9 Fore St London 1921   Fig.LB06

Although moving the showrooms from the Hatcham Works freed up some floor space, this was quickly used up so further workshop space was sought. In late 1921 further premises were acquired nearby at 761 Old Kent Road. This was operational by July 1922, running alongside the Hatcham Works. The new site was around 60,000 sq,ft. and a great deal of this area was taken up with metal presswork, stove enamelling and electroplating processes. Very soon this additional floor space at the Old Kent Road was also running at full capacity. The Hatcham Works were reorganised, this allowed for an extended wood working department, part of this was taken up with a horse making shop *Fig.LB07*.

Horse Making Department 1922   Fig.LB07

While the subject of this publication is rocking horses, Lines Bros Ltd were producing a huge range of other toys. The following illustrations give us an insight as to the extent of this company in only its third year of production. Over the following years this became ever more so, with metal toys becoming more popular, we will return to the subject in hand in further pages of this chapter.

Many women were employed and typically worked in areas such as the Upholstery *Fig.LB08* and Hood Making *Fig.LB09* departments.

Upholstery Department 1922   Fig.LB08

Hood Making Department 1922   Fig.LB09

Men in the Lining Out department *Fig.LB10* are fitting the interior trim to motor car and pram bodies after which they are assembled in the Pram Fitting department *Fig.LB11*. The Wood Toy Fitting department *Fig.LB12* was the final shop before the finished toys were sent on to

Lining Out Department 1922   Fig.LB10

Toy Pram Fitting Department 1922   Fig.LB11

Wood Toy Fitting Department 1922   Fig.LB12

the Packing Department *Fig.LB13*.
Of course none of these 'departments' would be viable without the appropriate administration controlled from the General Offices *Fig.LB14*.

Packing Department 1922

Fig.LB13

General Offices Old Kent Road 1922

Fig.LB14

Distribution was handled by Lines Bros Ltd fleet of vans and these were loaded from a newly constructed wharf *Fig.LS15* at the Old Kent Road site. Up to forty vans could be loaded from this new facility in an eight hour day. Fig.LB16 is a drawing of the Old Kent Road site and the

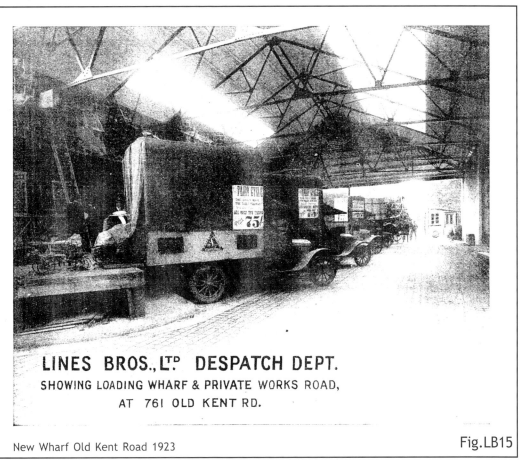

LINES BROS., LTᴰ DESPATCH DEPT.
SHOWING LOADING WHARF & PRIVATE WORKS ROAD,
AT 761 OLD KENT RD.

New Wharf Old Kent Road 1923   Fig.LB15

position of the new wharf is clearly visible. Not wanting to miss an opportunity, the vans were also used for advertising. The van in the centre has an advert for the new 75/- 'Fairycycle'. This was basically a bike with small wheels and it became very popular and much in demand by children of all ages. The advert also refers to the huge advertising campaign that was to be launched in the Daily Mail and Daily Express newspapers.

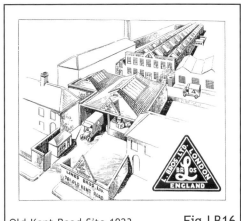

Old Kent Road Site 1923   Fig.LB16

The success and expansion of Lines Bros Ltd was quite unprecedented and by the end of 1923 the search was on for new premises. Looking for a suitable building was not an option. A new factory would have to be purpose built so an area of land was sought, preferably with access to the railway. After nearly a year a 47 acre site was found at Merton, south west of London. An initial 20 acres was purchased with a one year option on the remainder, fortuitously this was later acquired.

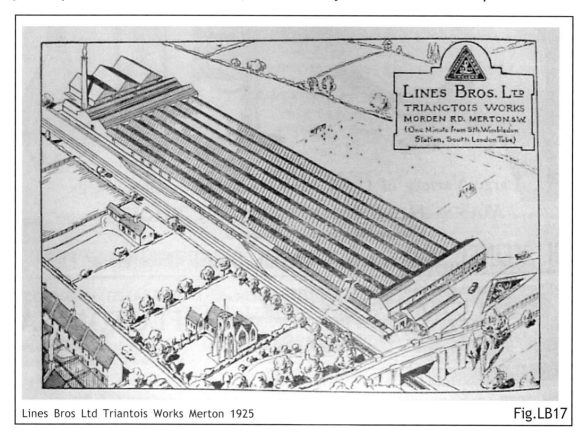

Lines Bros Ltd Triantois Works Merton 1925   Fig.LB17

Building work was started in November 1924 and by the middle of 1925 200,000 square feet of factory floor space was not only built, *Fig.LB17* but also fitted out and fully operational. The factory had its own railway siding with a platform 1,000 feet long. Raw materials were constantly delivered such as all types of timber. This was unloaded onto a 'roller railway' that led to storage sheds and allowed large planks of timber to be moved almost effortlessly. The whole factory was based on ease of work and efficiency, the staff were well cared for with first class sanitary arrangements, canteen facilities and also many 'after hours' recreational facilities, such as football and cricket pitches. With the opening of the new site at Merton, the Hatcham Works and the Old Kent Road site were sold off. The showrooms at Fore Street were kept on. The extra floor space created at Merton was soon filled up and a huge area was further developed as can be seen from the aerial photograph *Fig.LB18* of 1958. The original buildings can be seen on the left, note the steam rising from the railway engines. Inside the new

Aerial View of Lines Bros Ltd Factory Merton 1958   Fig.LB18

works at Merton was the beginning of one of the most sophisticated factories of the day, possibly only rivalled be that of the Motor trade. The following series of pictures *Fig.LB19 - LB33* show the steady increase in automation throughout the factory, from the early days when Lines Bros Ltd had made mainly wooden toys to later when almost all their toys were made from metal. The one exception was the wooden horse, production of this stayed much the same and in a small part of the huge factory was a 'time warp' of toy horses being almost totally hand made. Soon after the move to Merton in 1925, the **'Tri-ang'** trade name was introduced, an abbreviated form of the previous Triangtois trade name. The story goes that the reason for the triangle was the company consisted of three 'lines' (brothers), and three lines go to make a triangle.

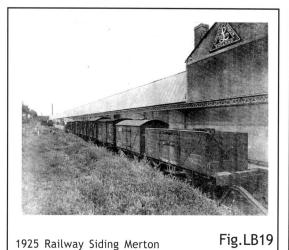

1925 Railway Siding Merton   Fig.LB19

1925 Delivery Vans Merton   Fig.LB20

1925 Saw Mill Merton   Fig.LB21

1925 Carpenters Shop Merton   Fig.LB22

1925 Metal Shop Merton   Fig.LB23

1925 Wheel Production Merton   Fig.LB24

1925 Fairy Kar Assembly Merton   Fig.LB25

1925 Dolls Pram Assembly Merton   Fig.LB26

1925 Shaped Horse Department Merton   Fig.LB27

The shaped horse department *Fig.LB27* although much more 'hands on' than the rest of the factory, still produced a considerable quantity of products. Note at the rear of the picture items stacked almost to the roof, these are the 'bodies' for the rocking horses and also all the 'heads' stacked on the shelves. The workman in the long coat, centre left, is studying a very large horse's head which has an articulated lower jaw and is most likely to be a saddler's display horse.

1929 Nickel Plating Merton   Fig.LB28

1929 Conveyor System Merton   Fig.LB29

1929 Pedal Car Line Merton   Fig.LB30

1929 Pedal Car Line Merton   Fig.LB31

Automation at Lines Bros Ltd. Merton 'Tri-ang' Works 1929

1929 Enamel Conveyor Merton   Fig.LB32

1929 Enamel Conveyor Merton   Fig.LB33

By 1931 Lines Bros Ltd employed over 1,000 staff and had also just purchased the famous London toy store Hamleys. Their subsidiary company that made dolls and prams was registered under the trade name of 'Pedigree'. Another company 'International Model Aircraft Ltd' was also founded. The aircraft firm produced a range of model aircraft that were able to fly and were sold under the 'FROG' trade mark *Fig.LB34* (flies right off the ground).

Lines Bros Ltd Trade Marks   Fig.LB34

In 1933 Lines Bros Ltd became a public company and had an initial issue of 200,000 shares. In 1935 new showrooms were opened in New Union Street London, which allowed Lines Bros Ltd to display their ever growing range of goods, including their rocking horses *Fig.LB35* and related products. The old showrooms at Fore Street were sold off.

Lines Bros Ltd Part of New Showroom 1935   Fig.LB35

Of the three brothers, Walter Lines *Fig.LB36* was the one who spearheaded the company and he also became President of the Toy and Fancy Goods Federation. Besides this he was very well regarded and much liked within the whole of the trade for his views and promotion of the toy trade in general. One of the trade publications of the day ran a series of caricature pictures of all of the leading names within the trade. Walter was no exception and was caricatured driving one of his 'Tri-ang' cars *Fig.LB37*. Ironically a short anecdote about Walter was that in 1945, a time when very few people had access to cars or the precious fuel to power them, he was convicted for 'driving at excessive speed in a built up area'.

He was fined £1 for his trouble.

Walter Lines 1939

Fig.LB36

Walter Lines at 'Speed'.

Fig.LB37

During the war the production of metal toys was stopped and the company turned to the war effort. Their factory was ideally suited to making a huge variety of components, from machine guns to gliders *Fig.LB38*, Lines Bros Ltd worked tirelessly. The staff was now nearing 7000 and their efforts did not go unrewarded. King George VI visited the works in June 1942 and another royal visit from the Duchess of Kent in May 1943. During the hostilities the factory at Merton was bombed on several occasions, but with typical Lines Bros Ltd efficiency their own fire brigade put out the fires and production continued almost totally uninterrupted.

Thankfully no staff were killed during these raids. As soon as the war

Lines Bros Ltd Glider Production 32' Wingspan Merton 1939-1945   Fig.LB38

ended, Lines Bros Ltd quickly returned to the manufacture of toys. As there had been almost no production throughout the war, the demand was now significant and the company continued to expand. A new factory was opened in 1945 at Merthyr Tydfil in Wales and in 1946 another for the manufacture of soft toys in Belfast, Northern Ireland. Interests all round the world were being formed, one in Canada used the old 'Thistle' trade mark *Fig.LB39* of the old G&J Lines company.

In 1957 Lines Bros Ltd purchased the very old firm of Simpson Fawcett, known initially for their prams, but they had also produced an extensive range of rocking horses in their heyday. Lines Bros Ltd became a truly International concern and the Group was associated with names such as Meccano, Hornby, Scalextrics, Minic, Rovex, Dinky and more. However, in 1971 the company collapsed, due mainly to poor exports. £4 million of government money was pumped in and assets sold off. The company managed

1947 Canada Thistle   Fig.LB39

to struggle on for a few years, but finally at the end of 1978 the Merthyr Tydfil plant closed down, the end of 'The Worlds Best Toys'.

As mentioned earlier, the first prototypes were drawn up and made at the bench by Walter and his brothers. Not surprisingly the earliest **Safety Stand Rocking Horses** bore a resemblance to those made by G&J Lines Ltd. Lines Bros Ltd were quick to produce Illustrations of their products and among these was an accurate depiction of their rocking horse *Fig.LB40*. This was published in 1919 and surprisingly the same drawing was used up to the late 1920's, well after the rocking horse had gone through various modifications before being standardised and recognised as one of the products sold under the 'Sportiboy' trade name. From this illustration we see that the first rocking horses were

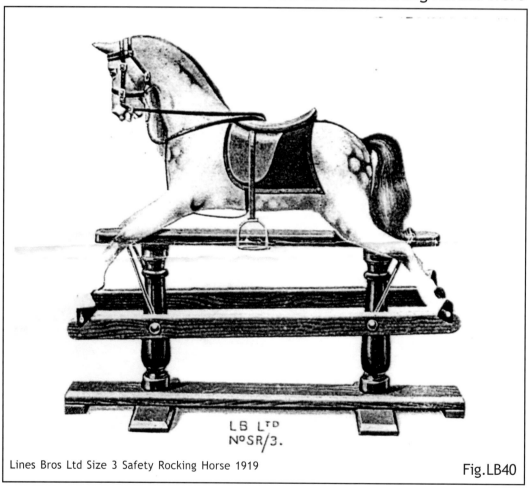

LB LᵀᴰNº SR/3.

Lines Bros Ltd Size 3 Safety Rocking Horse 1919

Fig.LB40

fitted with all detachable tack, this was a quicker method of production, a key to Lines Bros Ltd success. An important point of interest is the shape of the turned posts of the stand as they are very similar to those produced by G&J Lines Ltd, however these were soon to be changed.

A example of an early horse *Fig.LB41* shows all the same details as in the first illustration, There is no harness as this was detachable and now lost. The profile of the horse is a match for the illustration, as are the details of the stand. The horse also has a degree of extra carving, again

Lines Bros Ltd Size 3 Safety Rocking Horse 1919   Fig.LB41

there is a suggestion of this in the illustration. The rocking horses were made in six sizes, these all having the same general profile but this was changed after about a year in 1920. The new shape was then to remain as the standard throughout production, but as with all makers there would always certainly be a few exceptions to this. Subtle changes in the shape of the head have occurred over the years. In October 1920 the first reference to 'Sportiboy' horses was made and a couple of horses from this period *Fig.LB42 & LB43* have the new body shape but still retain the original design of post. Unfortunately neither of these two rocking horses is in an original condition. Despite this the change

Lines Bros Ltd Size 1 Safety
Rocking Horse circa 1920   Fig.LB42

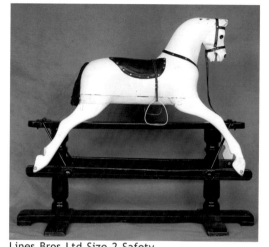

Lines Bros Ltd Size 2 Safety
Rocking Horse circa 1920   Fig.LB43

to the profile is clear, as is the old post design. The smaller horse *Fig.LB42* is a size No.1 and has replacement hoof rails fitted to the stand, been over painted and lost its original harness and hair.

The bigger of the two is a size No.2 and has replacement cross pieces fitted to the stand, been over painted and lost its original harness and hair. The early style of post *Fig.LB44* is clearly very different to the later style *Fig.LB45* that was fitted to the great majority of Lines Bros Ltd rocking horses.

These later posts were all turned to the same design irrespective of the size of horse and were believed to have been introduced in late 1920 or early 1921. Another component that was to become a very good identifying feature was the top plate, or swing iron bracket as it is also referred to.

Early Post
Pre 1921   Fig.LB44

Later Post
after 1921   Fig.LB45

Rocking horses made after the end of 1920, early 1921, had brackets with the companies initials cast into the top surface, therefore being visible at all times. They were typically marked 'LBLTD SP1' *Fig.LB46.* 'LBLTD SP2' *Fig.LB47.* This stands for 'Lines Bros Ltd Sportiboy 1' etc. The number after SP does not necessarily refer to the size of the rocking horse, but to the size of the bracket. The same size brackets were to be used on at least two sizes of rocking horse in the range.

LBLTD SP1   Fig.LB46

LBLTD SP2   Fig.LB47

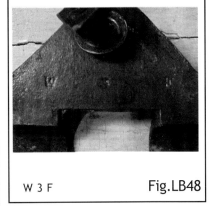

W 3 F   Fig.LB48

Before the type of bracket marked 'LBLTD SP1' etc., the earlier rocking horses have been found fitted with brackets that are plain on the top but marked on the underside, so not visible when assembled. They are often marked with the initials 'W F' in conjunction with a number such as 'W 3 F' *Fig.LB48*. These 'WF' marks are small and can easily be overlooked. Other makes of rocking horse have also been found with brackets marked with the 'WF' initials, one maker was G&J Lines Ltd and another was Ajoy. (See the G&J Lines Ltd chapter for various bracket markings) It is worth noting the the firm Ajoy was only in business for a brief period, circa 1920 and the G&J Lines Ltd examples are also dated to around 1920. It would be fair to assume that these 'WF' brackets, whatever they were fitted to could date the rocking horse to this time. It is not known what the 'WF' refers to, but most likely not produced by either of the separate Lines companies or the Ajoy firm. Lines Bros Ltd were probably the most efficient manufacturer for putting their name on their products and the majority of Lines Bros Ltd rocking horses have one of several applied labels that were used throughout the production of rocking horses. Most, if not all of Lines Bros Ltd products were marked either with the company name or the relevant trade mark. These markings are helpful not only to identify the manufacturer but also they are often a way to help put a date to a product. The labels below *Fig.LB49* are a selection that have been found on Lines Bros Ltd rocking horses. 'Triangtois' was the first trade name

TRIANGTOIS	PEDIGREE PRAMS	TRI-ANG	TRI-ANG
1920 - 1926	circa 1931	1926 - 1939	1945 - 1978

Fig.LB49

to be used from 1920 up to around late 1925, early 1926. After this 'Tri-ang' was used to 1978 when the company closed. The two Tri-ang labels read the same, the first (worn) is a metal label that was nailed on and the second is a transfer. These transfers were probably introduced after World War Two as a cheaper alternative to the metal label. The trade name 'Pedigree' was registered in 1931, basically for Lines Bros Ltd subsidiary doll making company. It is unclear why this was applied to a rocking horse, may be to generally promote the new name. The labels were usually fixed to the base of the stand, one at either end. Some examples have been found where the label is fitted to the top bar of the stand *Fig.LB50* and are usually a triangle shape, depicting the companies earliest trade mark of 1919 *Fig.LB51*.
It is worth noting that the bracket has the 'LBLTD SP1' markings and a date of late 1920 could be that of its manufacture. Also note the 'bowler hat' covering the spigot of the turned post, a quick fix to the otherwise fiddly job of trimming the end of the spigot.

Triangle Label Fixing
Circa 1920

Fig.LB50

Triangle Label Detail	Fig.LB51

A trade advert from October 1920 *Fig.LB52* indicates the available sizes of the 'Sportiboy' Safety Rocking Horse. Note the use of 'Triangle Toys'

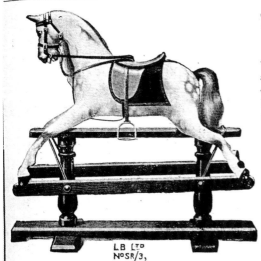

LINES BROS., L^{TD.,}

HATCHAM WORKS, ORMSIDE ST.,
OLD KENT ROAD, LONDON, S.E.

TRIANGLE TOYS
are reliable Toys.

ASK FOR CATALOGUE G.T.

The " Sportiboy " Safety Rocking Horse
has no equal.

These Horses are staunchly constructed of seasoned timber, and guaranteed sound in sight, wind and limb. Saddles detachable. Bells on reins. Stands lined out in colours. Beautifully painted and dappled by experts. The finish sells them.

	Length of Stand.	Height to Saddle.
No. 1	36½ inches	27 inches
,, 2	44 ,,	31½ ,,
,, 3	52 ,,	37 ,,
,, 4	57½ ,,	41 ,,
,, 5	63½ ,,	43 ,,
,, 6	71 ,,	48 ,,

End Seats fitted to Nos. 2, 3, 4, 5 and 6 extra.

Also makers of the finest Pole and Push Horses.

LB LTD
N°SR/3,

1938 Lines Bros Ltd Trade Advert

Fig.LB52

in the advert, a brief but obvious step to 'Triangtois'. The advert has the original 1919 drawing but even now in 1920 is out of date. The rocking horse is described as having a detachable saddle, no mention of the bridle, these were now 'fixed'. The reason for this probably being that it took longer to make a detachable bridle, with all the fitting of buckles and the like, compared to the relatively quick option of pinning leather strap direct to the horse's head. 'Bells on Reins' must have been one of the first thing to be removed or lost. The stands were 'lined out in colours', a faded example *Fig.LB52* shows remnants of red. This stand has

Lined out in Colours circa 1920   Fig.LB53

323

been constructed from a species of pine, most likely Douglas Fir. This material was only used for a short time around 1920 - 1921, after which beech was used for all the timber components of the stand and it was also used for the legs of the rocking horses. A size 2 'Sportiboy' in original condition with a revarnished pine stand *Fig.LB54*, has the later type of post and also has the triangle shaped label on the top bar. It would have had a detachable saddle (now lost), the bridle is fixed.

1920 -1921 Lines Bros Ltd. Sportiboy size No.2   Fig.LB54

Referring back to the 1920 advert, this also mentions the option for 'End Seats', available for Nos.2 - 6 size horses, at extra cost. An example of one can be seen on display in the earlier Fore Street showroom picture, *Fig.LB06*. These 'end seats' are made entirely from timber, whereas most other firms opted for bamboo or wicker. It would certainly be more expensive to make them from timber but Lines Bros Ltd were not involved with bamboo or wicker products. The 'end seat' option was still offered in Lines Bros Ltd 1929 catalogue but was not mentioned in their 1934 edition. Although this option was available for at least ten years, very few examples are known to have survived intact, the 'end seats' were often removed as the children grew up.

The early transitional changes had taken place by early 1921 and an advert for the 'Sportiboy Safety Rocking Horse' was suffixed with the quote '*Ask to see the NEW 1921 shapes*'. Any further changes from now on were purely of a cosmetic nature, such as the introduction in 1924 of the Sportiboy harnessed with **Medieval Tournament Trappings** *Fig.LB55*. Basically this was a Sportiboy with additional harness but only

Kiddies line up for Lines' lines.

The " SPORTIBOY " SAFETY ROCKING HORSE.
Picture reproduced from photo. No. 3 is shown in picture. (Medieval Tournament Trappings.)
This illustration shows the " **Sportiboy** " **Safety Rocking Horse**, harnessed in the Medieval Style.
" When Knights were Bold." This is a new and attractive feature, which is certain to become very popular with the kiddies. This harness is supplied for sizes 3 and 4 only.
For particulars of the " **Sportiboy** " **Safety Rocking Horse** made in six sizes, see page 39.

38

TRIANGTOIS
The World's Best Toys REGD

1924 Lines Bros Ltd Sportiboy with Medieval Tournament Trappings   Fig.LB55

available for size 3 and 4 horses. This new advertisement has a picture that is reproduced from a photograph and now shows the later styling of the Sportiboy. Very few of the Tournament horses have survived

Lines Bros Ltd Sportiboy with Medieval Tournament Trappings circa 1927　　Fig.LB56

intact as the additional harness was rather vulnerable to the attentions of boisterous children. An example *Fig.LD56* is shown above, this has just about survived although it has lost its saddle and other areas of tack. The V shaped rod between the two posts is a later addition that was fitted to alleviate movement in the stand. The stands often became loose around the joints and could fall apart if not attended to. This horse was restored, preserving all of the original tournament harness and making up replacement where necessary. The tournament horse was still being offered in the 1929 catalogue but by the 1934 edition it had been deleted as an option.

Another unusual Sportiboy option that has been found is a version that was **Hide Covered** *Fig.LB57*. No reference to this model has been found in available Lines Bros Ltd catalogues, however some years have not been viewed. This hide covered horse certainly appears to be authentic and has suffered with time. The 'hides' tend to dry out

Lines Bros Ltd Hide Covered Sportiboy circa 1935   Fig.LB57

which makes them split. Repairs to this are difficult and costly, consequently the old hides are often removed and the horse is then either painted or polished. The horse shown above has had the hide removed, this revealed a plain wood finish confirming that it had been originally made as a 'hide covered' model. It has now had all the small fixing nails (for the hide) removed and been wax polished showing the construction layers *Fig.LB58*.

Ex Hide Covered Sportiboy now Wax Polished   Fig.LB58

The overall majority of Sportiboy rocking horses were produced in the standard dapple grey format, this changed little over the years, apart from the very early horses as previously discussed. With the increase in the size of the horse within the range there tended to be more detail to the carving of the horse. The Sportiboy No.1 horse did not have carved teeth, neither did the size No.0 This size (No.0) seems to have been introduced at a much later date. Early lists range from sizes 1-6, even the 1934 list *Fig.LB59* lists only six sizes. It is good to see that the illustration of the Sportiboy has now been updated and a little more true to life. The 1939 Export list *Fig.LB60* clearly shows the size 'O' as

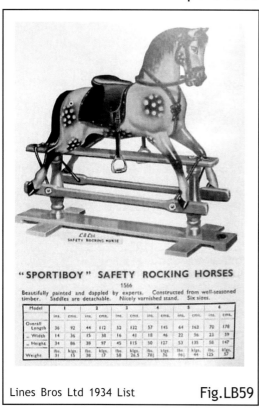

" SPORTIBOY " SAFETY ROCKING HORSES

1566

Beautifully painted and dappled by experts. Constructed from well-seasoned timber. Saddles are detachable. Nicely varnished stand. Six sizes.

Model	1		2		3		4		5		6	
	ins.	cms.	ins.	cms.	ins.	cms.	ins.	cms.	ins.	cms.	ins.	cms.
Overall Length	36	92	44	112	52	132	57	145	64	163	70	178
„ Width	14	36	15	38	16	41	18	46	22	56	23	59
„ Height	34	86	38	97	45	115	50	127	53	135	58	147
Weight	lbs. 31	klgs. 15	lbs. 38	klgs. 17	lbs. 58	klgs. 26.5	lbs. 78½	klgs. 36	lbs. 96½	klgs. 44	lbs. 125	klgs. 57

Lines Bros Ltd 1934 List   Fig.LB59

		ROCKERS AND PUSH HORSES.	1	12	36
3	3889	Swan Rocker	19/8	18/8	
	3890	Royal Jumbo Rocker	15/-	14/-	
	3891	Shaggy Rocker	15/-	14/-	
	3892	Mister Quack Rocker	19/8	18/8	
	3893	Mickey Safety Rocker	15/-	14/9	14/6
	3894	Mickey Old Style Rocker	11/8	11/5	11/2
	3895	Ferdinand Safety Rocker	15/-		
	3896	Tubular Rocker	13/-		
	3897	Old Style Rocking Horse	14/-		
	3898	Cut-out Push Horse	10/-	9/9	9/6
	3899	Double Push Horse	19/8	18/8	
7	3900	1 Push Horse	8/4		
a		2 „ „	13/-		
b		3 „ „	16/8		
c		4 „	21/8		
	3901	A Push Horse	2/8	2/7	2/6
	3902	B „ „	8/4	8/1	7/10
	3903	X Hollow Push Horse	4/8	4/6	4/4
a		Y „ „ „	6/-	5/9	5/6
b		Z „ „ „	7/2	6/11	6/8
	3904	Stool Horse	2/4	2/3	2/2
	3905	Z Combination Rocker & Push Horse	10/-	9/9	9/6
	3906	Z Hollow Rocking Horse	7/-	6/9	6/6
	3907	A Safety Rocker	8/4	8/-	7/6
	3908	O " Sportiboy " Safety Rocker ...	30/-		
a		1 „ „ „ ...	35/-		
b		2 „ „ „ ...	48/4		
c		3 „ „ „ ...	65/-		
d		4 „ „ „ ...	84/-		
e		5 „ „ „ ...	119/8		
f		6 „ „ „ ...	168/-		
	3909	OO Hobby Horse	1/6		
a		O „ „	2/6		
b		1 „ „	3/6		
c		2 „ „	4/6		

Lines Bros Ltd 1939 Export List   Fig.LB60

being available at a cost of 30/- against the largest size 6 at a cost of 168/-. Very few size 0 horses are known to exist, perhaps they were Export only and a few have found their way back to the UK. If they were introduced around the end of the 1930's, production would have been limited due the War and they may well not have been reinstated afterwards. The production of wooden rocking horses after the War was greatly reduced anyway, not only from Lines Bros Ltd but all manufacturers. Initially tin and then plastic were to become the manufacturers choice of material. An example of a size 0 Sportiboy is shown below in a 'before' *Fig.LB61* and 'after' *Fig.LB62* restoration pose. This little horse measured only 26 inches (66cm) from the floor to the top of its head. Despite the small size, this horse was made to the

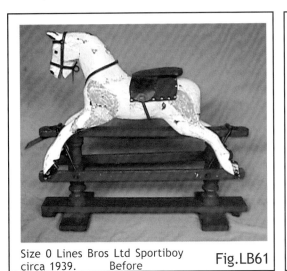

Size 0 Lines Bros Ltd Sportiboy circa 1939.   Before   Fig.LB61

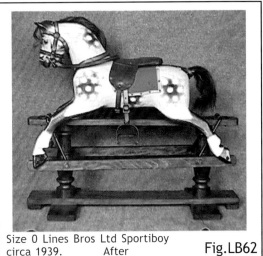

Size 0 Lines Bros Ltd Sportiboy circa 1939.   After   Fig.LB62

Sportiboy 'standard' format although it may have been a bit disproportional in some aspects. A view of four Sportiboys *Fig.LB63* head on, sizes No.1, 2,3,&4, shows their size in relation to each other.

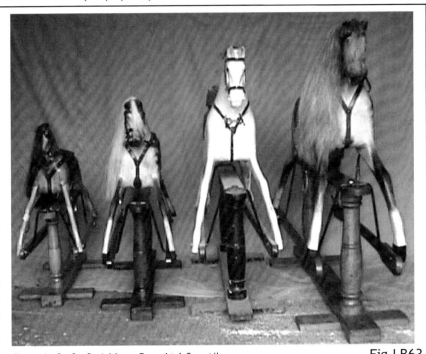

Sizes 1, 2, 3, & 4 Lines Bros Ltd Sportiboys   Fig.LB63

An very good example of a size No.1 Sportiboy *Fig.LB64* in original condition gives an insight into how these rocking horses looked when

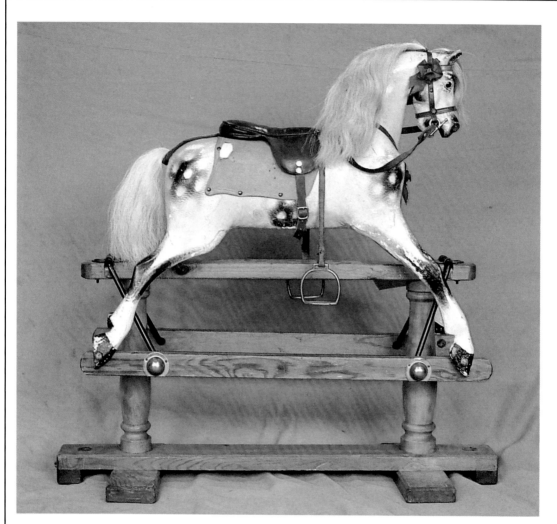

Lines Bros Ltd Size 1 Sportiboy circa 1921

Fig.LB64

they were new. This horse has the round 'Triangtois' label fitted to each end of the base, giving a production date of between 1920 and 1926. The stand is made from pine, so this may mean it was made around the earlier of these dates. The original detachable saddle is still in place as are the nickel plated stirrups and bit. The stand also has its nickel plated bowler hats. All of these metal items would have been nickel plated by Lines Bros Ltd in their own plant. Its not clear if Lines Bros Ltd had the facilities to 'cast' metal. Items such as the stirrups and the bit would have been formed in this method, they may well have out-sourced these items. A close up view of the head *Fig.LB65* shows the nickel plated bit in place. The horse also retains its rosettes, these were made from a cotton weave binding tape and no doubt the staff in the sewing department would have become very adept at producing these in great numbers. As with all Sportiboy Safety rocking horses,

Lines Bros Ltd Size 1 Sportiboy Head Detail   Fig.LB65

glass eyes are fitted, a small item that would have been out-sourced. Another would have been the fancy nails that are fitted to the centre of the rosettes. These fancy nails were only fitted in limited numbers to each horse, certainly to hold the rosettes in place and possibly a couple on the bridle, but they were not generally applied all over the harness as some other manufacturers. They would have been a relatively expensive item, Lines Bros Ltd were always keen to supply their goods at the best possible price so may not have seen these as an essential. There were various different types of these fancy nails used over the years, the earlier horses had the most decorative type and unsurprisingly they were very plain by the time production of the

Sportiboy rocking horse had ended. The early type of fancy nail *Fig.LB66* that was used has in the centre what could be described as a small gothic cross motif. These have been found in two sizes with this design. Most manufacturers used their own style of nail, but as they were 'bought in', it must not be solely used as the only means of identification of a particular make of rocking horse.

Lines Bros Ltd Early Type Fancy Nail   Fig.LB66

The stands of all the different sizes of Sportiboys were made to the same specification with the exception of the runners. On horses size 4,5 & 6 the runners were 'narrowed' between the horses hooves, this gave the stand a more pleasing look as can be seen on the size 4 Sportiboy *Fig.LB67* pictured below. This horse has been restored.

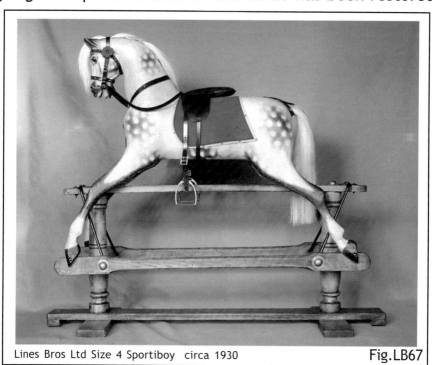

Lines Bros Ltd Size 4 Sportiboy circa 1930   Fig.LB67

An unrestored example of size 5 Sportiboy *Fig.LB68* showing the narrowed runners. This model is 53 inches from the floor to the top of its head. The next size up (6) was 58 inches tall.

Lines Bros Ltd Size 5 Sportiboy circa 1930   Fig.LB68

After the War, although the Sportiboy rocking horse was still produced, it was not as popular and in the 1955 Tri-ang list *Fig.LB69* it was only being offered in the size No.2. It looked very vulnerable surrounded by its contemporary rivals. By 1956 it had been dropped from the list.

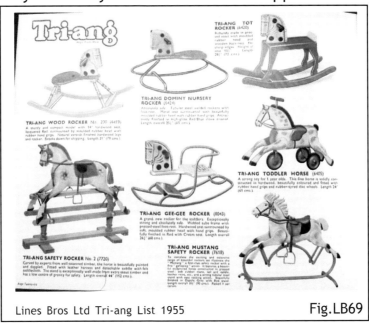

Lines Bros Ltd Tri-ang List 1955   Fig.LB69

A size 2 Sportiboy *Fig.LB70* that is thought to be from the last years of production has a couple of anomalies, bowler hats painted white and G&J Lines cast into the top plates *Fig.LB71*. The stand has an applied Tri-ang transfer. Another anomaly is a size 3 Sportiboy Fig.LB72 that has

Size 2 Lines Bros Ltd Sportiboy
circa 1954
Fig.LB70

Top Plate and
Tri-ang Detail
Fig.LB71

been fitted with a high back saddle that is reminiscent of the Gamages 'Bronko' horse. It is unclear if this was a factory item or a later addition. The horse would have been produced around 1921.

Size 3 Lines Bros Ltd Sportiboy
with High Back Saddle circa 1921
Fig.LB72

The '**Old Style Rocking Horse**' was produced by Lines Bros Ltd from when they started trading in 1919. At this time it was still a reasonably

Lines Bros Ltd Old Style Rocking Horse List 1925

Fig.LB73

popular choice but it had already been superseded by the swing stand rocking horse. In 1925 the Old Style was offered in six sizes *Fig.LB73* and was basically a Sportiboy safety stand horse fitted to a bow rocker. It had an upright stance due to it really being designed to fit a safety stand. A couple of examples can be seen in the Fore Street showroom picture *Fig.LB06* taken in 1921. It continued to be listed in six sizes up to 1927 but in the 1928 catalogue it was only offered it in one size '00'*Fig.LB74* and captioned 'Suitable for a small child'.The last known reference is in the 1939 export list *Fig.LB60* priced at 14/-

Size 00 Old Style Rocking Horse circa 1930

Fig.LB74

A most unusual Old Style rocking horse that has been attributed to Lines Bros Ltd is a **Spotted Polychrome** version *Fig.LB75*. This rocking

Spotted Polychrome Old Style Rocking Horse
Attributed to Lines Bros Ltd. circa 1935

Fig.LB75

horse does not have any maker's label but the dimensions and profile are consistent with Lines Bros Ltd regular dapple grey old style horse. No mention has been found in any of the Lines Bros Ltd catalogues that have been viewed, but a 'commission' certainly would not be listed. At least one more old style horse, the same as the one above, is known to exist. The spots on the other are a little different but with the same theme, also the bow was painted exactly the same. The horse that is illustrated above had some light restoration work carried out in 1991 when this picture was taken. This consisted of new hair and detachable harness being fitted but the paintwork was not touched and is believed to be the factory original. Other manufacturers have painted their rocking horses in this fashion, Baby Carriages produced a number of swing stand horses with a spotted polychrome finish around the mid 1930's. This would also be a reasonable date to apply to the horse pictured above.

The **Hobby Horse** or stick horse as it is also known, was a still a popular item and Lines Bros Ltd produced a range of six sizes as illustrated in their 1922 list *Fig.LB76*. They were fitted with polished wooden wheels

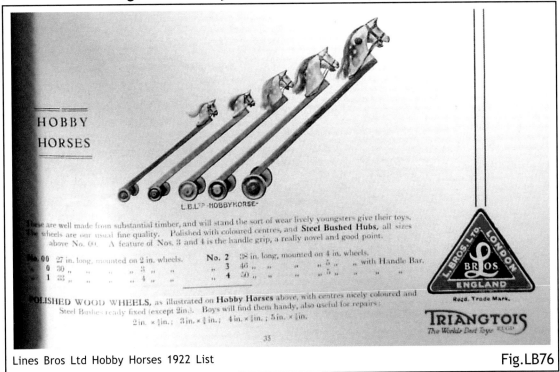

Lines Bros Ltd Hobby Horses 1922 List   Fig.LB76

with 'steel bushed hubs' for longer wear. The illustration also offers to supply the wheels on their own quoting *'Boys will find them handy, also useful for repairs'*. In 1928 the choice was dropped to 5 sizes and by 1934 to four sizes, now fitted with steel wheels. As with some other products the last mention being in the 1939 export list *Fig.LB60*. Due to their obvious vulnerability not many have survived, a battered example fitted with the later steel wheels is shown below *Figs.LB77 & LB78*.

Lines Bros Ltd Hobby Horse circa 1937   Fig.LB77

Head Detail   Fig.LB78

Push Horses were produced in a wide variety of finishes and qualities, the most elaborated being the Sportiboy range of push horse *Fig.LB79.*

"SPORTIBOY" PUSH HORSES.

Made of thoroughly dry timber, beautifully painted and finished. Harness, patent leather. High-class Handle. Stove enamelled Levers. Polished coloured wood Wheels (a speciality) with Steel Bushed Hubs. Very easy running.

No.		On Polished Wheels as illustrated Height to Head	On Rubber-Tyred Disc Wheels with Steel Axle
1	Push Horse ..	17 inches ..	4 ins. dia.
2	Push Horse ..	20½ " ..	4 "
3	Push Horse ..	22½ " ..	6 "
4	Push Horse ..	25½ " ..	8 "
5	Push Horse .. (with steel Axles)	27½ " ..	8 "
6	Push Horse .. (with steel Axles)	31 " ..	8 "

With Nickel-plated Tubular Handle extra.

POLE HORSES same sizes.

1925 Lines Bros Ltd Sportiboy Push Horse List

Fig.LB79

Many different options were available and the Sportiboy push horse could also be had in the **Pole Horse** version. This was the same horse, without the push handles but fitted instead with a single pulling pole attached to the front of the platform. Another derivative of the push horse was the Sportiboy **Combination Rocker & Wheel Horse.** *Fig.LB80.* This was two items in one, a wheeled horse that could easily be removed from the little bow rocker. Not many of these survive intact, most often the rocker is lost and the only indication of its origin are the holes at either end of the platform.

"SPORTIBOY" COMBINATION ROCKER AND WHEEL HORSE.

The horse corresponds in size and finish to our well-known "Sportiboy" Push Horses. The base of the horse is secured to the rocker by means of two strong thumbscrews. When detached from the rocker (which is made of polished elm), the horse is immediately available as a wheel horse.

			Length of Rocker	Height to Saddle
No. 2	..	..	32 in.	18 in.
" 3	..	..	39½ "	20 "
" 4	..	..	43 "	22 "
" 5	..	..	45 "	24 "
" 6	..	..	48 "	27 "

1925 Lines Bros Ltd Sportiboy
Combination Rocker List

Fig.LB80

An example of a pushalong horse fitted with wooden wheels *Fig.LB81.*

Lines Bros Ltd Pushalong Horse circa 1928   Fig.LB81

It is in original condition although a little tatty. This horse also has a Tri-ang label *Fig.LB82* attached to the front of the platform and is fitted with patent leather harness with a red brow and nose band. It was not fitted with glass eyes, but had a basic 'eye' painted on. The levers are stove enamelled black and joined with a wooden handle. This example was made circa 1928, the wood type wheel superseded shortly after by the metal wheel with rubber tyre.

Tri-ang Label detail   Fig.LB82

An alternative to the push horse was the **Pram Horse** *Fig.LB83* that was fitted with spoked wheels and nickel plated handles.

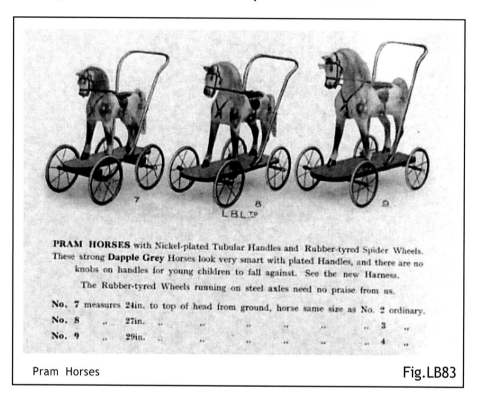

PRAM HORSES with Nickel-plated Tubular Handles and Rubber-tyred Spider Wheels. These strong **Dapple Grey** Horses look very smart with plated Handles, and there are no knobs on handles for young children to fall against. See the new Harness.

The Rubber-tyred Wheels running on steel axles need no praise from us.

No. 7 measures 24in. to top of head from ground, horse same size as No. 2 ordinary.
No. 8   ,,   27in.   ,,   ''   ''   ''   ''   ''   3   ''
No. 9   ,,   29in.   ,,   ''   ''   ''   ''   ''   4   ''

Pram Horses   Fig.LB83

Further models included the **Push/Stool Horse** *Fig.LB84*, the **Push Horse with Carved Head** *Fig.LB85* and the **Hollow Push Horse** *Fig.LB86*.

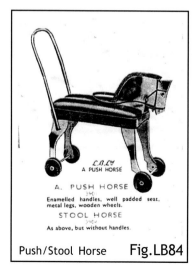

A. PUSH HORSE
Enamelled handles, well padded seat, metal legs, wooden wheels.
STOOL HORSE
As above, but without handles.

Push/Stool Horse   Fig.LB84

B. PUSH HORSE
Chromium-plated handles, carved head. Well upholstered seat, metal legs, 1" solid rubber tyres on die-cast hubs.

Push with Carved Head   Fig.LB85

HOLLOW PUSH HORSES
Strongly made. Hollow wooden body. Nicely painted and dappled. Green base, steel disc wheels with rubber tyres. Three sizes, X, Y and Z. Height to handle: X 20½". Y 24" 7 26".

Hollow Push Horse   Fig.LB86

Derivatives of the hollow push horse were the **Hollow Rocking Horse** *Fig.LB87* and also the **Z Combination Rocker & Push Horse** *Fig.LB88*.

L.B.Ltd
"Z" HOLLOW ROCKING HORSE

Strongly made. Hollow wooden body. Nicely painted and dappled. Green base. Height to seat, 15½".

Z Hollow Rocking Horse   Fig.LB87

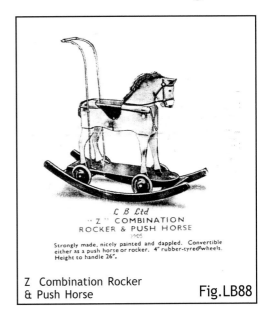

L B Ltd
"Z" COMBINATION
ROCKER & PUSH HORSE

Strongly made, nicely painted and dappled. Convertible either as a push horse or rocker. 4" rubber-tyred wheels. Height to handle 26".

Z Combination Rocker & Push Horse   Fig.LB88

At the cheap end of the rocking horse market, Lines Bros Ltd offered the **Safety Rocker** *Fig.LB89*. This was about as basic as a wooden rocking horse could be. It was still on the 1939 Export list but did not reappear after the War. Cheap metal rocking horses replaced many of these smaller wooden horse-based products after 1945 and became very popular in their own right.

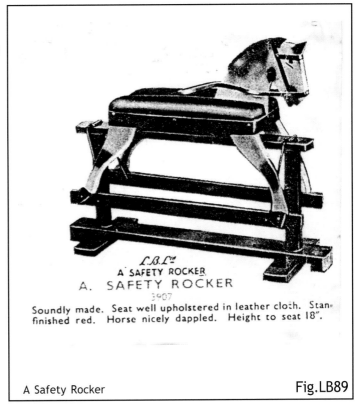

L.B.L⁰
A SAFETY ROCKER
A. SAFETY ROCKER

Soundly made. Seat well upholstered in leather cloth. Stand finished red. Horse nicely dappled. Height to seat 18".

A Safety Rocker   Fig.LB89

Tip Carts & Horses were made by Lines Bros Ltd in two basic formats, the cheaper model had a cart that was made from pine *Fig.LB90* and the other, and more superior, had a cart made from elm *Fig.LB91*. Both of these certainly remained in production up to at least 1939.

BEST LARGE PINE TIP CARTS & HORSES

No. 1   Length overall   ...   ...   24 inches.
„ 2   „   „   26   „
„ 3   „   „   29   „

These Horses and Carts are of very superior quality. The Wheels are much stronger than usual, and the Horses have hard wood legs. All Carts tip.

Pine Tip Cart & Horse   Fig.LB90

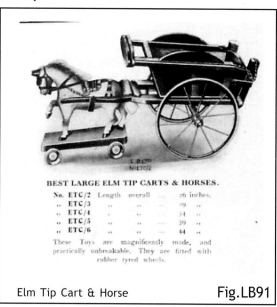

BEST LARGE ELM TIP CARTS & HORSES.

No. ETC/2   Length   overall   ...   26 inches.
„ ETC/3   „   „   ...   29   „
„ ETC/4   „   „   ...   34   „
„ ETC/5   „   „   ...   39   „
„ ETC/6   „   „   ...   44   „

These Toys are magnificently made, and practically unbreakable. They are fitted with rubber tyred wheels.

Elm Tip Cart & Horse   Fig.LB91

A well preserved and original pine version *Fig.LB92* has a Triangtois label fitted to the front of the cart giving a manufacturing date 1920 - 1926.

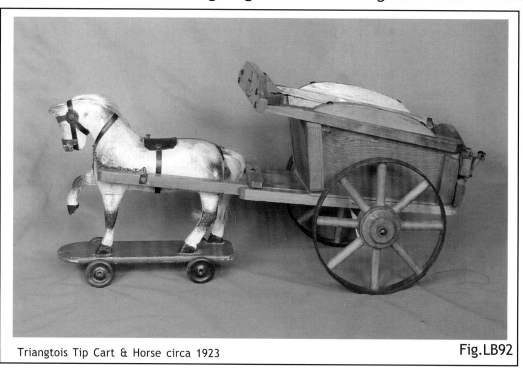

Triangtois Tip Cart & Horse circa 1923   Fig.LB92

Described as being an 'ever popular toy' in the 1925 Lines Bros Ltd catalogue the **Sportiboy Tricycle Horse** *Fig.LB93* was produced in three

"SPORTIBOY" TRICYCLE HORSES.

An ever-popular toy. This one is especially well-made from well-seasoned timber of suitable variety. Beautifully painted and dappled, and harnessed in attractive style. Front wheel with wired-on tyre.

No. 1 Mounted on 12in. Rubber-tyred Wheels.
No. 2 Mounted on 14in. Rubber-tyred Wheels.
No. 3 Mounted on 16in. Rubber-tyred Wheels.

1925 Lines Bros Ltd Sportiboy Tricycle Horse   Fig.LB93

sizes. This had been the case since 1920, but by 1927 only two sizes were being offered. The 1927 catalogue was the last mention of the tricycle horse, the metal tricycle had now taken its place. A survivor is shown below *Fig.LB94*. The metal trike in many different options became one of Lines Bros Ltd most popular lines.

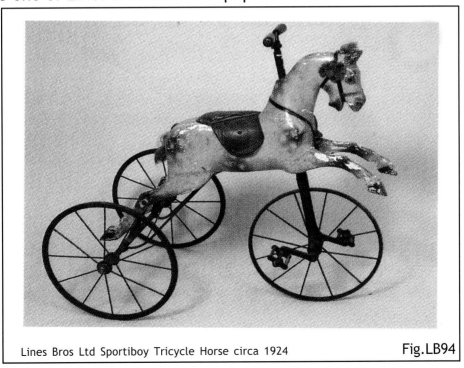

Lines Bros Ltd Sportiboy Tricycle Horse circa 1924   Fig.LB94

A couple of fairly short lived products from Lines Bros Ltd were the **Dandy Dobbin** *Fig.LB95* and the **Pedal Gee** *Fig.LB96*. The former was introduced in 1924 and was based on an American patent and made under licence. This was only manufactured for a couple of years.

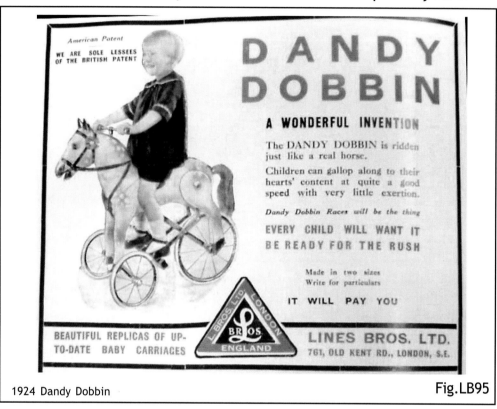

1924 Dandy Dobbin — Fig.LB95

The Pedal Gee was introduced around 1920 initially as the Toddle Gee. It was updated a couple of times but manufacture was ceased after about ten years of production.

1927 Pedal Gee — Fig.LB96

With the advent of the cinema and Walt Disney cartoons, characters such as Mickey Mouse and Snow White were soon to become household names. Lines Bros Ltd launched a series of toys based on these famous faces, two of these were the **Mickey Safety Rocker** and the **Mickey Old Style Rocker** which were illustrated in a 1937 catalogue *Fig.LB97*.

1937 Lines Bros Ltd Mickey Mouse Rockers   Fig.LB97

Despite looking quite fragile, a number of the Mickey safety rockers are known to have survived including the one shown below *Fig.LB98*.

Mickey Safety Rocker circa 1938   Fig.LB98

Liverpool Toy Industry   -1923 - 1925-

Address: 6, Soho Street, Liverpool.

One of the first known references to the Liverpool Toy Industry was when a trade advert appeared in 1923 *Fig.LL01*. From this it certainly read as an industry, with a very comprehensive range of products. The horse related items listed were **Swing Stand Horses, Rocking Horses, Pole Horses, Pram Horses, Combination Horses, Tricycle Horses, Stool Horses, Hobby Horses** and **Horses and Carts.**

LIVERPOOL TOY INDUSTRY,

SHOWROOMS :
99, CHARTERHOUSE CHAMBERS,
18/21, Charterhouse Square,
London, E.C.

6, Soho Street,
LIVERPOOL.

SHOWROOMS :
RAWSON. CHAMBERS,
82, Market Street,
Manchester.

MANUFACTURERS OF

ALL HIGH-CLASS WOOD TOYS, SPORTS GOODS, etc.

SAFETY SWING HORSES,
ROCKING HORSES,
POLE HORSES,
PRAM HORSES,
COMBINATION HORSES,
TRICYCLE HORSES,
STOOL HORSES,
HOBBY HORSES,
HORSE AND CARTS,
PRAMS,
GO-CARTS,
    etc., etc., etc.

ENGINES,
WHEELBARROWS,
SCOOTERS,
WAGGONS,
SEASIDE SPADES,
CRICKET BATS,
CRICKET STUMPS,
TENNIS POLES,
WASHING BOARDS,
TOWEL RAILS,
WOOD SPOONS,
    etc., etc., etc.

We beg to draw special attention to the advantage we have, and can offer our Customers. We have our own Timber also Water-Power to our works, and all our Goods are made under the supervision of experts and men of life-long experience.

SPECIAL TERMS TO EXPORT AND LARGE WHOLESALERS.
WRITE FOR OUR ILLUSTRATED LIST OF PRICES.

1923 Trade Advert   Fig.LL01

The advert also mentions that the firm has showrooms in both London and Manchester. Further adverts appeared through 1924 and 1925, after which time no further information has been found. It does seem a little strange that a firm of this supposed magnitude could have been around for only a few years. It may well have traded for many years either side of these dates.

We do however have a reasonably good picture of a swing stand rocking horse,an enlargement taken from the 1923 advert is shown *Fig.LL02.*

From 1923 Trade Advert   Fig.LL02

Note that the horse is not dappled, just the hooves and knees are painted, as well as some detailing to the head. The stand is of quite a light construction with a chamfered base and cross pieces. The runners are 'thinned' between the swinging irons and it is fitted with delicate turned posts. The saddle looks as if it may be detachable and is fitted with adjustable stirrup leathers and crown shaped stirrups. The mane and tail can only be described as 'lush'.
No actual rocking horses have as yet been attributed to the Liverpool Toy Industry.

Lloyd & Compy.   -1890 - 19ukn.

Address: 1891   131, Borough High Street, London. S.E.
            1893   58, Borough High Street, London. S.E.
            1897   22. Feather Lane, London. E.C.

Lloyd & Co were listed under Perambulator Manufacturers in an 1891 trades directory, and described as 'sole makers of the "Rover" baby carriage'. They also produced **Rocking Horses** and mail carts.

A small bow rocking horse *Fig LD01* was recently found with their manufacturers label *Fig LD02*. The horse was reputedly purchased in 1901 but had been later rubbed down and painted white. The bow had been replaced due to an infestation of wood worm, however, the bow was apparently based on the original. The horse is of typical construction, with mortise and tenon leg fitting, but does have a distinctive 'open' mouth *Fig.LD03*.

It is not known if any different sizes of bow rocking horse were produced, or if the company offered a swing stand option.

Lloyd & Co Bow Rocker circa 1901   Fig.LD01

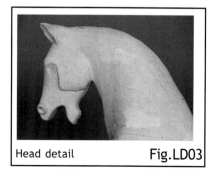

Head detail   Fig.LD03

Makers applied label   Fig.LD02

Lloyd, James.   1878 - 1950-

| Address: | 1878 | 70, Lower Hurst Street, Birmingham. |
| | 1884 | 70 & 71, Lower Hurst Street. |

Lloyd & Hill.   1892

| | 1892 | 69 & 70, Lower Hurst Street. Birmingham. |

Lloyd, James & Co.   1896

| | 1896 | Hurst Street, Birmingham. |

Lloyd, James & Co. Ltd.   1907

	1910	35, Hurst Street, Birmingham.
	1931	153, Bracebridge St. & 2 Hill Street. B'ham.
	1935	111-119, New Town row 6, Birmingham.

James Lloyd was primarily a perambulator manufacturer who as can be seen from above had a variety of trading address's. His business looks to have involved some partnerships over the years although very little is known apart from the information above. The last researched reference was for 1950, but the company may well have traded beyond this date.

One Birmingham directory listing of 1882 has James LLoyd under the heading of **Rocking Horse Maker**, apart from this reference all the others have been in association with perambulators.

Lucas, Henry.   -1841- 1852-

Address: 1841   2, Langley Street, Long Acre, London.

              1851   8, Broad Court, Long Acre, London.

In the official catalogue of the 1851 Great Exhibition, Henry Lucas is listed amongst the 'Miscellaneous Manufacturers and Small Wares' section. His entry states **"Progressive garden rocking-horse"** *Fig LU01*.

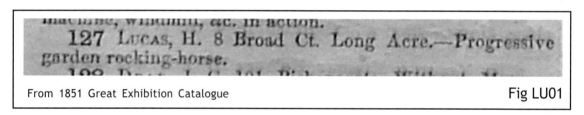

From 1851 Great Exhibition Catalogue   Fig LU01

What 'Progressive garden rocking-horse' refers to is unknown except that the title infers that it is an outdoor product that may well have the capacity to move forwards.

A Henry Lucas is listed as a 'coach joiner' at 8, Broad Court in 1852 and also listed as a 'coach joiner' at 2, Langley Street in 1841. It is assumed that the two listings refer to the same Henry Lucas, Langley Street is only a few minutes walk from Broad Court.

Luckett, T.   1879 - 1929

Address: 1879   109A, (Back of) Bromsgrove Street, B'ham.

                1890   58, Inge Street, Birmingham.

                1895   City Steam Works, Mark Lane, Pershore St.

Incorporated: 1924   **T Luckett & Son Ltd.**   Company No.199,727

The earliest found directory listing for Thomas Luckett is in 1879 as a perambulator maker but later in an 1896 directory , **Rocking Horses** is written after the firm's name. Subsequent listings give other products made by the firm including bamboo furniture and mail carts. From 1896 until 1900 directory entries also listed **Tricycle Horses** among some of the products made by Thomas Luckett.
An advert from 1922 stated that the firm had been making 'Coach-built Toy Perambulators' as far back as 1882 and these were the firm's speciality, an example of this can be seen in Fig.LT01. By 1917 the firm was referred to as *Thomas Luckett & Son* and in 1924 when the firm was incorporated its interests were listed as perambulator, baby car and toy car manufacturers and also manufacturers of household furniture.
In 1929 the company ran into financial difficulties and ceased trading. Unfortunately, very little else is known about the firm of Thomas Luckett which is rather surprising after trading for fifty years.

1923 Luckett & Son Advert   Fig.LT01

Marqua, Philip.   29th Jan 1880

Address: City of Cincinnati. Ohio.   U.S.A.

Patent No. 395. 29th Jan 1880   Improvements in Hobby Horses.

Patent Agent: Herbert Hadden. 67, Strand, Westminster, London.

The firm of P Marqua had been established at Cincinnati in the USA since 1856 and had produced a variety of items including children's carriages, cabs and also basket ware, but became best known for two patents. The first was patented in the USA in 1865, this was a 'rearing' rocking horse, a clever but complicated device.
The second patent was for the **'Safety Swing Stand'**. This was patented in the USA in October 1878 and a provisional specification was filed in the UK on the 29th January 1880.
Philip Marqua's UK patent of 1880 marked a turning point in rocking horse manufacture in the UK. Up to this point almost all rocking horses had been of the bow rocker variety, and while they were thought of as wonderfully romantic play things, in truth many were responsible for a range of mishaps, damage and injuries. They were able to roam around a room under the guidance of a mischievous child.
The new **'Safety Swing Stand'** was an immediate success, benefiting not only the customer by way of entertaining the children in relative safety and without the subsequent destruction of the room. Also from the manufacturing point of view, they were a much easier item to produce, no more worries about cutting the curved bows, which was a very skilled task on its own, just sawing straight pieces of timber. The patent was thought only to be in force for three years, during which time a few makers made swing stand horses under licence, and after its expiration, many more manufactures took up producing the swing stand horse. This was to become the UK's most productive period of rocking horse making, lasting up to the 1930's.
Fig.MA01 & MA02 are technical drawings that accompanied P Marqua's specification of 1880.

P Marqua specification No. 395 Jan 29th 1880.

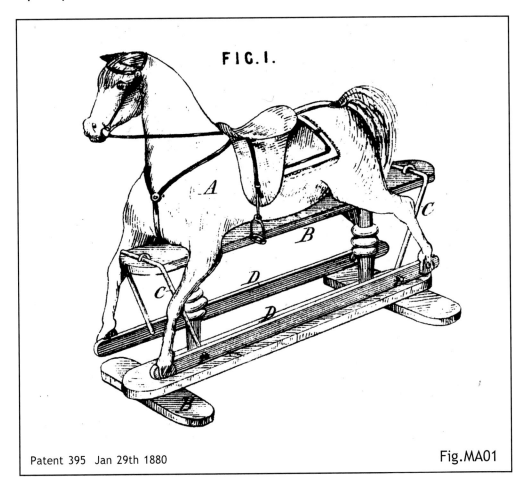

FIC.I.

A

B

C

C

D

D

B

Fig.MA01

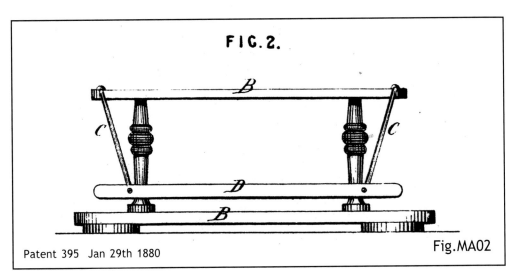

FIC.2.

B

C

C

B

B

Fig.MA02

Mead. Joseph   1871-

Address: 73, Cheapside, London.

Mead. W. F. & Deverell.   -1882-

Address: 73, Cheapside, London.
                        Phoenix Works, Newgate Street, London.

Deverell Bros.   -1891-

Address: 1891   73, Cheapside, London.
            1895   9, Cheapside, London.

Deverell & Sharpe.   -1899-

Address: 9, Cheapside, London.

The earliest known piece of information for Joseph Mead was reported in the London Gazette of February 1874 and reads as follows;
    'Joseph Mead, Manufacturer of Toys and Games, 73, Cheapside, city of London, for an invention of "an improved apparatus for the recreation and amusement of children and invalids, comprising in one article a nursery yacht, see saw, **Rocking Horse**, and swing, with elastic or rigid appliances for muscular exercise" Dated 16th Feb 1871.'
This sounds most curious, but unfortunately it is not known what the apparatus actually was. By 1882 'Mead & Deverell' were trading, but interestingly it was a 'W F' Deverell. In an 1882 trade directory they were listed under a variety of headings including Perambulator Makers, Stove Ornament Makers, Confectioners, Toy Makers(Importers) and also **Rocking Horse Makers,** quite a mix of products. An entry for 1884 was written, 'Importers of Toys, games, fancy goods &c, patentees of improved of improved **rocking horses**, perambulators, gymnastic apparatus &c. Prize medal Paris 1878.' Unfortunately there is no mention of what item the medal was awarded for.

In 1884 further listings under the headings of Christmas Card Manufactures, Fancy Box Makers, Stationers, Wholesale & Manufacturers, and a further listing under the heading of Confectioners read,

'*Mead W F & Deverell manufactures of bonbon and costume cosaques to the wholesale trade & importers of French, German, American & other confectionery Phoenix Works Newgate st and 73 Cheapside*'.

In 1891 Deverell Bros. were recorded at 73, Cheapside as Toy Dealers and in 1895 they were listed at 9, Cheapside. The last known entry in 1899 is for Deverell & Sharpe, Toy makers at 9, Cheapside.

For 28 Years at least, the names of either Mead or Deverell have been associated with toys and more importantly rocking horses. Despite this length of time dealing with rocking horses, no evidence has been found to give any clue as to the actual nature or appearance of their product.

Midland Tent & Strong Toy Co.

-1909 - 1910-

Address: 127, Duddleston Mill Road, Birmingham.

Reported to have made **Rocking Horses** and **Horse and Carts.**

No further information.

Millson, A. C.   -1910-1914-

Address: 303, Oxford Street, London. W.

                124, Southampton Row, London. W.C.

Very little is known about the firm of Arthur Colton Millson except that
he was mainly concerned with the manufacture of baby carriages and
invalids furniture. This is known from an applied label *Fig.MI01* that was
found on a **Horse and Gig** *Fig.MI02*. Its unknown if A C Millson actually
produced the horse or if it was 'bought in'. The Gig section was quite
obviously Millson's work as explained by
the applied label and also the fact that
two Post Office entries of 1910 and
1914 list him as also being a
perambulator maker.

No further information has been found
about A C Millson.

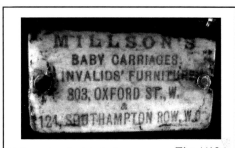

Makers Applied Label   Fig.MI01

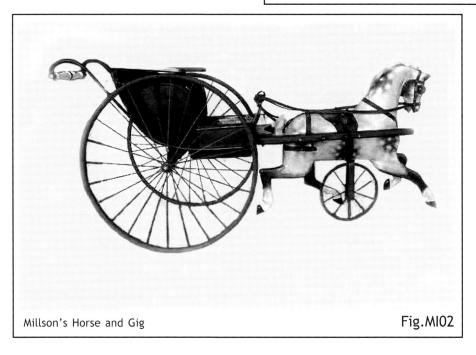

Millson's Horse and Gig   Fig.MI02

357

Montil Mfg. Co. Ltd.   1912 - 1973

Address: 1912   76, Bath Street, Birmingham.
            1914   As above and 29, Shadwell Street. Birmingham.
            1917   3, Gothic Arcade, Snowshill, Birmingham
            1920   65, Lower Trinity Street, Birmingham.
            1926   Britannia Works, Morville Street, Birmingham.

Incorporated: 1912.   Company No. 129,220   Dissolved July 1973

Trade Name: 'Montil'

The Montil Manufacturing Company was mainly concerned with producing metal goods, particularly early on, to do with the manufacture of accessories for the bicycle trade. After several moves around Birmingham, the company finally settled at Morville Street and from around this time produced a range of toys. Among the toys that were made, was a **Spring Horse** that was called 'Bucking Broncho' and also a simple small bow **Rocking Horse** was also produced. Both of these can be seen in the advert *Fig.ML01* from a 1929 trade publication.
The company is recorded as trading up to 1973, but the mainstay of their production had turned to manufacturing folding prams and accessories.

From 1929 Trade Advert   Fig.ML01

Moore, H A & Co. Ltd.   1918 - 1964

Address: 4 & 5, Bridgwater Square, Barbican, London. E.C.1

Incorporated: 1918   Company No.159,105   Dissolved: 8th July 1964

H A Moore & Co.traded for about forty six years, but despite this very little is known about the company. It is not even clear what the their main line of business was. However, in 1946 they advertised *Fig.ME01* a small **Rocking Horse** in the trade press. It's not known if this was a success or not. The company did however continue trading up to 1964.

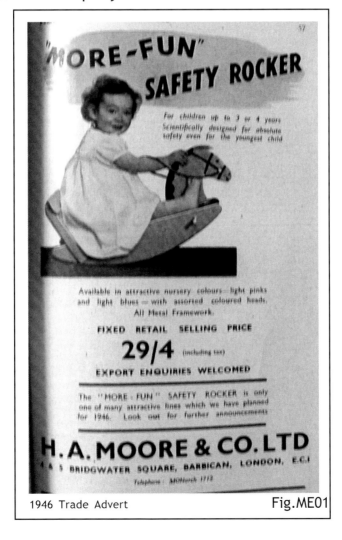

1946 Trade Advert   Fig.ME01

Morgan Nature Toy Co. Ltd. 1917-1922

Address: Not known. Scotland.

Incorporated.   Dec 1917. (Edinburgh)   Company No. 9,713

Formed in 1917, with R. M. Morgan and A. Ogilvie as directors, the
Morgan Nature Toy Company displayed a range of products at the 1917
British Industries Fair in London. It was reported in a trade publication
that they showed a splendid line of **Horses and Carts**.
No other reference to the company has been found except that in 1922
the Edinburgh Gazette reported they had gone into liquidation.

Morris W.   -1863 - 1882-

Address: 1863   25, Princes Street, Birmingham.
                1864   24, Freeman Street, Birmingham.
                1871(Only) 45, Market Hall, Birmingham.

The first known mention for William Morris is in an 1863 Birmingham
trade directory. This lists him as a perambulator maker and numerous
subsequent listings all state the same. However by 1867 he was
advertising *Fig.MS01* a range of goods, many were wicker based items.

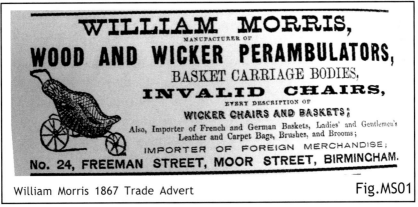

William Morris 1867 Trade Advert   Fig.MS01

This appeared to be a strong theme with his perambulators and invalid
chairs. Many other imported items were also being offered, such as
French and German baskets, Ladies' and Gentlemen's leather and
carpet bags, brushes and brooms. By 1875 an advertisement *Fig.MS02*
also made much of a patent for a wood and or wicker perambulator.

William Morris 1875 Trade Advert   Fig.MS02

Rocking Horses are first mentioned in 1882 and at this time William Morris is listed under a trade directory heading of **Rocking Horse Maker.** Also an advertisement to the same effect *Fig.MS03* was

ROCKING HORSES,
Velocipede Horses, Stool Horses,
AND
Improved Tricycles for Children.

WM. MORRIS,
24, Freeman St., Birmingham,
PATENTEE AND MANUFACTURER OF

PERAMBULATORS.

MORRIS'S
IMPROVED ADJUSTABLE HANDLE
PERAMBULATOR.

May be used either way.

*Much Simpler
and less liable
to get
out of order
than any other
so-called
"Reversible"
Perambulator.*

William Morris 1882 Trade Advert

Fig.MS03

published in 1882. There is a drawing of a **Bow Rocking Horse** and some of the other products that were offered. These included **Stool Horses**, **Velocipede Horses** and improved tricycles for children. From this it would seem that a whole new area of business was taken on. Unfortunately this is the last year that any reference to William Morris has been found. It is not known what became of the firm after 1882.

Motor Necessities Ltd.   1914 - 1942

Address: 47, Streatham Hill, London. S.W.2.

Trade name: 'Joyrida'.

Incorporated: 1914   Company No.138,164

Motor Necessities Ltd was set up in 1914 and an advert of 1915 *Fig.MR01* shows an illustration of a basic **Rocking Horse** which was traded as the 'Joyrida'. It was described as being 'excellently well made' and offered at trade price of 7/6 and retailed at 15/-
A 100% mark up is typical within the toy trade on smaller items. The construction of the main seat and rocker is of simple board construction while the head is illustrated as being well shaped.

It was credited with being *'capable of being carried from room to room and house to house so that children can take their horses with them to their friends' parties.'*

It is not known if the company produced any other items apart from the Joyrida.

In 1931 The London Gazette reported on winding up orders for the company and it was struck off the Companies register in 1942.

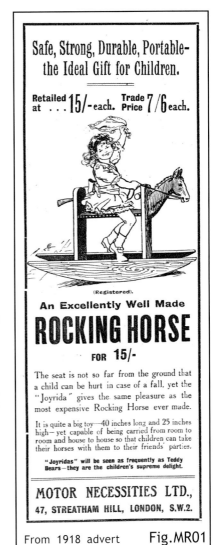

Safe, Strong, Durable, Portable- the Ideal Gift for Children.

Retailed at ... **15/-** each.   Trade Price **7/6** each.

(Registered).

An Excellently Well Made

ROCKING HORSE

FOR 15/-

The seat is not so far from the ground that a child can be hurt in case of a fall, yet the "Joyrida" gives the same pleasure as the most expensive Rocking Horse ever made.

It is quite a big toy—40 inches long and 25 inches high—yet capable of being carried from room to room and house to house so that children can take their horses with them to their friends' parties.

"Joyridas" will be seen as frequently as Teddy Bears—they are the children's supreme delight.

MOTOR NECESSITIES LTD.,
47, STREATHAM HILL, LONDON, S.W.2.

From 1918 advert   Fig.MR01

Norman, W.H. & Co.   1914 - 1916-

Address: 98, Woodhouse Street, Leeds.

W H Norman & Co was an offshoot of an established firm of Norman & Co. who specialised in producing high class office furniture and systems. A general demand for toy forts led to the firm being set up in September 1914 and was immediately successful. This new departure became a permanent feature and subsequently exhibited a range of their forts and other small toys at the 1915 British Industries Fair. Since then the firm increased their range of toys further to include a variety of strong wooden toys which included **Stool Horses, Pole Horses, Pull Horses, Rocking Horses, Tricycle Horses** and **Swing Horses**. Fig.NN01 shows three of their dappled Pull horses and Fig.NN02 shows two views of the item referred to as a rocking horse, this would probably be better described as a 'combination rocker'. These horses are all made to a high standard and were finished as dapple greys with real hair manes and tails. It is not clear from the illustrations if the tack was leather and also whether the horses were fitted with glass eyes.

From 1915 Trade Journal   Fig.NN01

From 1915 Trade Journal   Fig.NN02

In 1916, W H Norman exhibited a fantastic range of his horses *Fig.NN03* at the British Industries Fair. Amongst the display were swing stand horses, tricycle horses, push horses and stool horses, alongside a large range of toy forts. Unfortunately it is not possible to make out any discerning points about the horses so as to be able to make a positive identification.

No further information after 1916 has been found for W H Norman & Co.

W H Norman & Co 1916 Trade Exhibit   Fig.NN03

Norris. Jas.   -1920-

Address: 51, Sherborne Street, Birmingham.

It is not very clear as to what type of **Rocking Horse** is being referred
to in the 1920 advert *Fig.NS01* as all the other items listed may well be
Tin novelties. Certainly most toy manufacturers in the Birmingham area
were occupied in the metal trade, however, it could well be a timber
based item. No further reference to Jas. Norris has been found.

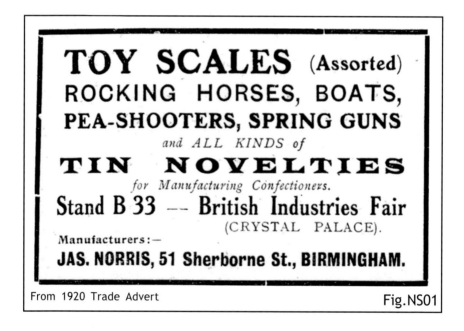

From 1920 Trade Advert   Fig.NS01

Norton & Barker.   -1920 - 1932

Address: Victory Works, 157, Irving Street, Birmingham.

See Also: Barker Wm. (W Barkers & Sons Ltd.)

The earliest found reference to Norton & Barker is in a 1920 trade advert *Fig.NB01*. However, from the range of products that were on offer the firm must have been trading for some time although the earliest trade directory reference for them appears to be from 1921.

1920 Norton & Barker Trade Advert   Fig.NB01

Among the items listed in the advert are **Pole and Plush Horses, Tricycle Horses, Stool Horses, Rocking and Swing Horses.** This is a good range of horse related products, the reference to 'rocking and swing horses' means they are producing the bow rocker type. Despite the range of horse products wheeled items formed a large part of their turnout. In 1928 Norton and Barker took over the Mercury Cycle Co and increased their range of junior cycles, these were now the 'must have' of the day for all boys and girls. Advertisements appeared through the 1920's and a few of these had an illustration of a swing-stand rocking horse *Fig.NB02* is from 1927. Unfortunately it is not possible to use this as means of identification as it is purely a drawing. We do have positive identity of horses that were produced from 1932 onwards when the firm changed to W Barker. It may well be that the horses produced before this date were of the same appearance, but cannot be proved.

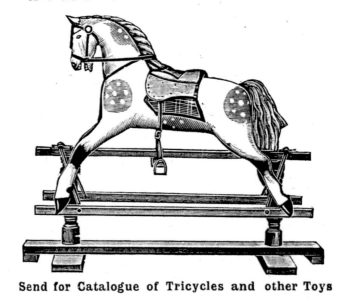

1927 Norton & Barker Trade Advert   Fig.NB02

In 1928 it was reported in a trade journal that the firm were extending their premises so as to allow for an increase in output. The next known reference is for W Barker only, still at 157 Irving Street. It is not known what became of the 'Norton' part of the firm.

Noveltoy Manufacturing Company Ltd.
1920 - 1928

Address: 50a, Birch Lane, Longsight, Manchester.

Trade name: "Jonbul"

Incorporated: 1920   Company No.172,164

Patent: No. 191,954.   Granted: Jan 1923.

Patent spec: Improvements in or in connection with Toy Animals.

In January of 1921 the Noveltoy Manufacturing Company Ltd displayed a range of their products at a London Toy fair. Among the items on show was firm's speciality of Jonbul **Shaped Horses** in three sizes and also a safety **Rocking Horse**, (the patent for which had been applied for). The horse in Fig.NY01 is from an advert of January 1921, in which it states that it was offered in five sizes and was captioned as a **'Jonbul'** shaped horse. Also in January 1921, Marshall Allan Holmes applied for a Patent for what was basically an unbreakable rubber neck and head to fit to a wooden bodied toy animal such as a rocking horse. The specification also detailed the way in which the neck fitted. This was by means of a flange on the neck fitting a groove in the body and also described was the way in which glass eyes were fitted into the head. Fig.NY02 shows the drawings that relate to the specification. The patent was accepted in January 1923. During the 1922 season, the company advertised the 'Jonbul' horse

From 1921 Trade advert   Fig.NY01

with an 'unbreakable head' which was offered in five sizes with the options of either Pull, Push or Rock *Fig.NY03*. The horse that is illustrated appears to be very well finished without any noticeable join between the body and neck. This is not an easy task joining two different materials. The tack looks to be like some type of oilcloth and the horse is finished with a natural hair mane and tail, the platform is also of a good quality and finish.

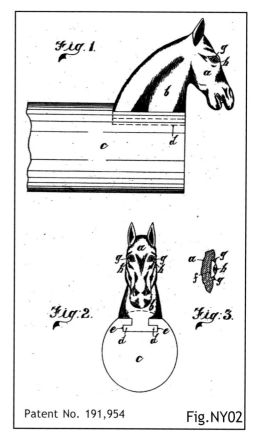

Patent No. 191,954   Fig.NY02

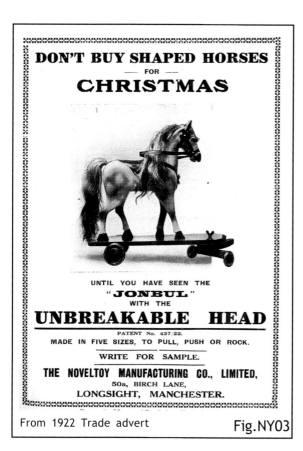

From 1922 Trade advert   Fig.NY03

Despite the best efforts of the company, it was announced by the then Chairman of the company, C. Ratcliffe, in the London Gazette 10th April 1928 that the company could not continue in business due to its liabilities and as a result was voluntarily wound up.

It is not known if any examples of Jonbul horses are still in existence.

Palmer, Stephen.   -1826 - 1845-

Address: 18, London Terrace, Hackney Road, London.

See also: Leach, Paul.

The first account of Stephen Palmer was recorded from Proceedings at
the Old Bailey on 14th September 1826. He and his wife, Isabella, owned
a truck which they 'let out' for so much an hour and a supposed
customer stole their truck. During the trial Stephen Palmer stated that
he was a **Rocking Horse Maker** and also that he had an apprentice,
Paul Leach, who also gave evidence at the trial. From this it would be
reasonable to assume that Stephen Palmer had been involved with
rocking horses for a number of years previously, being experienced
enough to take on an apprentice, thus making him amongst some of the
earliest known makers. Its interesting to note that another rocking
horse maker, John Allen, was working at the same time, just a few
minutes around the corner in Clarence Place, Hackney Road. They surely
must have been aware of each other, but whether there was any
connection or association between the two is unknown.

Astonishingly, Stephen Palmer was recorded again in February 1827 as
giving evidence in another trial, a young lad had allegedly stolen some
soap, and Palmer stated that he was a rocking horse maker in his
witness statement.

The last known recording of Stephen Palmer was in 1845 in a trade
directory, again referred to as a rocking horse maker.

Due to the era that Stephen Palmer was working, the rocking horses
that he made would have been of the 'bow rocker' type. It may be
worth contemplating what form the horses that his apprentice Paul
Leach, took as these would have been influenced by his master and may
well have had a similar look.

Palser, James.   -1845 - 1884

Address: 1845   122, Waterloo Road, Lambeth, London.

            1852   39, Oakley Street, Lambeth, London. S.E.

See also: Palser Samuel.   -1838 30, Webber Row, Lambeth.

Affiliation: Palser & Mansfield. -1878   55, Oakley St. Lambeth.

The first known record of James Palser is in a Post Office directory of 1845 listing him as a **Rocking Horse Maker**. At that time his address was Waterloo Road, Lambeth. This is the same address recorded for Samuel Palser in 1838. Samuel is most likely to have been James' father and James was continuing on in the 'family' business.
In 1852 and 1854 there are two further entries for James Palser in London Post Office Directories, under the heading for **Rocking Horse Makers**. Both of the entries give his address at 39 Oakley Street.

No further references to James Palser alone have been found, but on the 2nd April 1878 a meeting was held in the London Bankruptcy Court. This was instituted by Henry William Mansfield of No.55 Oakley Street Lambeth, **Rocking Horse** and Perambulator Maker, trading as Palser & Mansfield. This was a First General Meeting of creditors of the aforementioned Henry William Mansfield.

The result of this meeting is not known but later in 1882 & 1884, further entries for *Palser and Mansfield* at 55 Oakley Street have been recorded. It would appear that the firm did carry on trading for a while, 1884 being the last entry found.

It would be reasonable to assume that James Palser was the 'Palser' in Palser & Mansfield, this being a somewhat uncommon surname involved in a somewhat uncommon trade. Also the fact that both James Palser and Palser & Mansfield were based at Oakley Street.

Palser, Samuel.   -1835 - 1838-

Address: 30, Webber Row, Waterloo Road, Lambeth, London.

See also: Palser James 1845 122, Waterloo Road, Lambeth.

                     Palser & Mansfield. -1878 55, Oakley Street, Lambeth.

On the 17th July 1835 the London Gazette reported the following;

Samuel Palser, late of Saint Paul's-Place Walworth, Surrey, Toy Manufacturer, and afterwards of No.7, Clarence-Place, Gravesend, then of Peyton-Place, Royal Hill, Greenwich, both in Kent, and lastly of No. 6, Carlton-Terrace, New Peckham, Surrey, out of business.

There is another known directory record of 1838 for a Samuel Palser which reads;

Samuel Palser 30, Webber Row, Waterloo Rd.
*Produced **Rocking Horses**.*

It is not known if this is one and the same Samuel Palser as the first report is one of him going out of business. But this is a relatively uncommon surname and the two references are also linked in so much as they both deal with the toy trade. If not the same person, perhaps they were related.

In 1845 a Post Office directory lists James Palser as a rocking horse maker at 122, Waterloo Road. This is most likely to be the same family, perhaps a son who was to continue the 'family' business. Further entries relating to James Palser are covered in the relevant chapter headed *Palser, James.*

Parker Brothers.

1856 - 1927

Late. W Parker & Son. (W.P & S)

Address: 104 - 108 Curtain Road, Shoreditch, London. E.C.

Incorporated: 1913, Parker Brothers Perambulators Ltd. No.127,329

Initially the firm was known as W. Parker and Son and was set up around 1856. By 1874 the firm was known as Parker Brothers and an advert of that year *Fig.PR01* confirms the original name of the firm and also that **Rocking Horses** were being made, although again from the advert it is clear that the main line of business of the firm is that of the

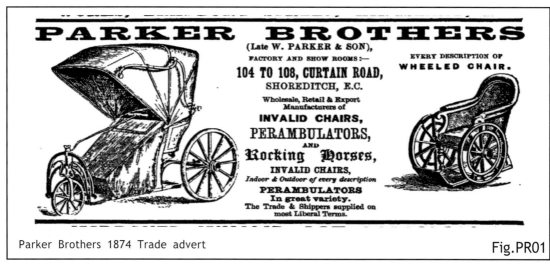

Parker Brothers 1874 Trade advert   Fig.PR01

manufacture of invalid chairs and perambulators. These were offered in a 'great variety' and of 'every description'. The firm dealt with all aspects of the trade, wholesale, retail and export. It would appear that the firm expanded as by 1884, 110 Curtain Road was added to their address. In 1913 Parker Brothers Perambulators Ltd. was incorporated and it is assumed that this new company took over the old firm. However, in 1927 the company went into Voluntary Liquidation. During the period that the firm was known as Parker Brothers, Rocking horses were certainly being made and also later in 1915 the firm is mentioned as producing 'strong wooden toys' a heading under which rocking horses could be listed.

A bow rocking horse from the era of W Parker and Son (pre 1874) is shown *Fig.PR02* in an unrestored condition, but had been over painted brown probably around the 1950's. Its construction is very typical, being a pine box body with hard wood legs tenoned into the body.

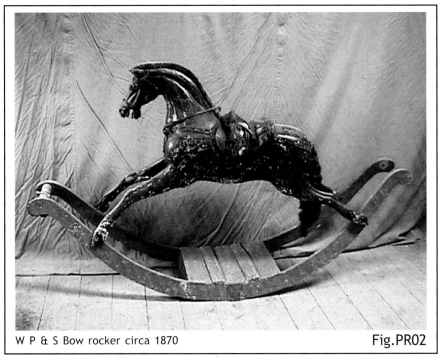

W P & S Bow rocker circa 1870   Fig.PR02

The head and neck are also of made from pine and carved to a high standard as can be seen in Fig.PR03, which also shows the revealed and unusual 'biscuit' coloured base coat as opposed to the more familiar grey.

The dappling of the horse is also unusual in that it is of an elongated design and not the regular circular style found on most other makes. Fig.PR04 shows the horse with the paintwork in restored condition.

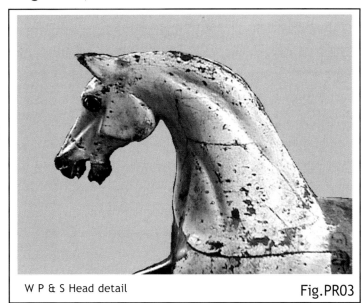

W P & S Head detail   Fig.PR03

W P & S Restored   Fig.PR04

The horse is fitted with large glass eyes which were delicately painted around with very fine eyelashes *Fig.PR05*.
The bow of the horse is typical of the period, being constructed with elm rockers and a pine platform which has three boards and two raised covering strips. The joins of the two halves of the bow are covered with a piece of timber *Fig.PR06* with the same moulding as used in the covering strips. Probably one of the most important features of this rocking horse is the makers mark in the form of a stencil applied to the underside of the platform *Fig.PR07* showing the maker as W. P & S London.

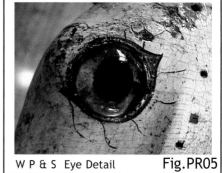

W P & S Eye Detail   Fig.PR05

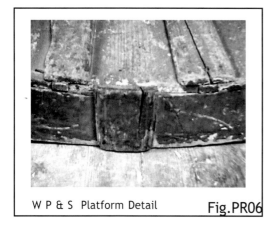

W P & S Platform Detail   Fig.PR06

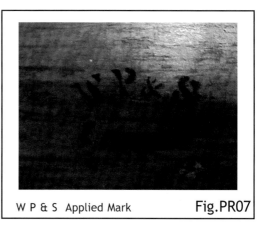

W P & S Applied Mark   Fig.PR07

376

Patterson Edwards.   1892 - 1989

Address: 1892   Small shop in the Old Kent Road, London. S.E.
                        Green Hundred Road, Peckham, London. S.E.
                        152, Old Kent Road, Peckham, London. S.E.
            1911   Culmore Road, Southwark, London. S.E.
            1922   125 - 127, Lee High Road, Lewisham. London. S.E.
            1975   Manor Works, Cray Avenue, St Marys Cray London

Patent: 1918   No.134,344 Improvements in wooden horses etc.

Trade marks: "P.E."   "Leeway" Earliest reference 1926

Incorporated: Patterson Edwards Ltd. 23rd Aug 1926.   No.215,815

In 1892, a 26 year old Henry Stanley Jarvis started up in business for himself in a small shop on the Old Kent Road making barrows and engines. Previously he had been a traveller for a firm that produced prams and similar items, his introduction to the toy trade. He named his firm 'Patterson Edwards', why this name was chosen is a mystery, but there never was an actual person connected with the firm called Patterson Edwards.

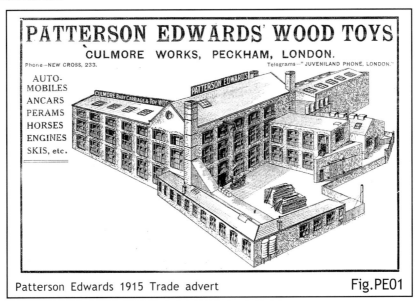

Patterson Edwards 1915 Trade advert   Fig.PE01

His own endeavours paid off, selling all that he could produce, and his small business started to grow to the extent that a couple of subsequent moves were required to find ever bigger premises. In 1911 he moved his then established firm to a huge building known as the Culmore Works *Fig.PE01* with mixed feelings as to if it was a wise decision or not. However, his fears were unfounded and the firm continued to expand. The range of items produced at this time was extensive and is well illustrated in an advert of 1916 *Fig.PE02*. The 54 items illustrated being only a small part of the total range of the firm.

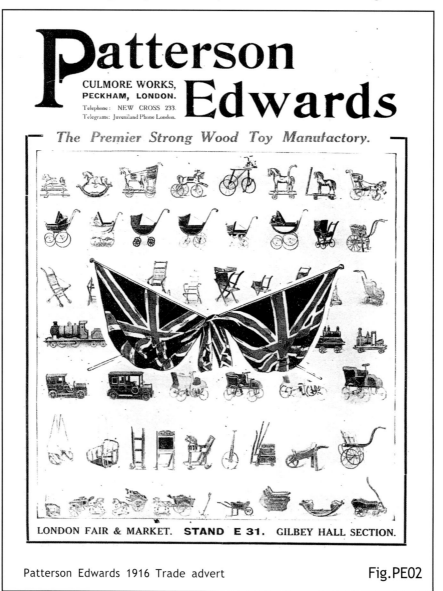

Patterson Edwards 1916 Trade advert

Fig.PE02

The Culmore works was a series of 'shops' for all the different processes that were required for the manufacture of their range of goods. These included saw mills, metal working, painting, assembling and storage rooms through to the showroom *Fig.PE03* where buyers could view the entire range and also see their manufacture if need be. The staff in 1914 numbered around 100 men, women, boys and girls, who were working under Donald Jarvis, general manager, the son of the founder. Fig.PE04 shows five girls working in one of the assembly rooms at the Culmore Works.

Patterson Edwards Culmore Showroom 1914   Fig.PE03

Patterson Edwards Culmore Assembly Room 1914   Fig.PE04

The items produced that concern this directory include, **Bow Rocking Horses, Swing Stand Rocking Horses, Combination Horses, Stick horses, Beech Horses, Tricycle Horses, Horses and Carts** and probably many others. The design of their rocking horses before 1919 was typical of that used in the trade, with mortise and tenon leg joints. A period image of a pre 1919 horse *Fig.PE05* is a type that would have had the mortise and tenon type join.

Pre 1919 Patterson Edwards Swing Stand Rocking Horse   Fig.PE05

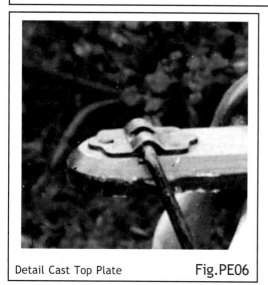

Detail Cast Top Plate   Fig.PE06

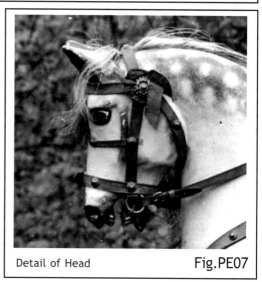

Detail of Head   Fig.PE07

As with all makers, their earlier horses would have been the most elaborate. The stand of the pre 1919 horse has quite detailed turned posts, a heavily chamfered top bar and strong looking cast swing iron brackets *Fig.PE06*. The horse pictured has very little dappling, this is confined to the legs and neck. It is however reasonably well carved, the head is a good early example of the 'look' that came to denote a Patterson Edward horse *Fig.PE07*.

In 1919 Mr Jarvis Snr. took out a patent, No.134,344, which described his invention as an *'improved construction with the legs having extended upper portions that extend to the top of the body section'*. The patent covered a variety of applications and was to become the most notable and unique feature of all subsequent Patterson Edwards rocking horses. Fig,PE08 shows the drawing relating to rocking horses that accompanied the patent.

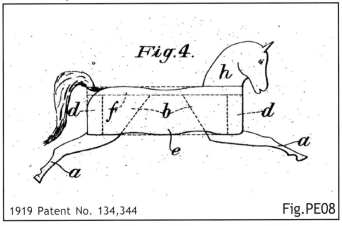

1919 Patent No. 134,344   Fig.PE08

This method of construction allowed for some of the components, legs and head, to be totally shaped before construction. This new method made these horses tremendously strong and very unlikely to suffer 'loose' legs as with all other types of construction. Many other innovative practises were used in the factory which led the firm to become one of the largest at that time. The Culmore Works, once regarded as being far too large, had now reached its full potential. Patterson Edwards now needed more space and in 1922 a five acre site situated at Lee in Lewisham, south east London was purchased. This plot originally consisted of two old country mansions, 'Lee Lodge' and 'Hurst Lodge',set in park land. It is now clear where the trade name of **'LEEWAY'** originated and was first used as a trade name around 1926. The new site, once an area of tranquillity, soon underwent great change. Lee Lodge was demolished and in its place the first of many new purpose-built buildings were erected. Hurst Lodge, a twenty four room Georgian house was to be used as offices and showrooms. By 1924 a staff of around 350 workers were employed between the Culmore works and the new site at Lee which now had 2 acres of floor space. Fig.PE09 is a photograph of the dispatch depot and timber yard at Lee.

Note the enormous stack or timber on the left and under the cover on the right is a large quantity of engines and horses awaiting delivery. The saw mill *Fig.PE10* is a hive of activity with large quantities of components being prepared. In the centre of the picture is what appears to be a pile of logs that are

1924 Dispatch Depot & Timber yard   Fig.PE09

being sawn into blocks on one of four circular saws in the room. The noise must have been tremendous, no ear protection in evidence at all just the obligatory flat hat.

Also note a variety of templates that are hanging up along the wall on the left, these would have been used for marking out some of the many different wooden components that have been made during the course of an average day.

1924 Saw Mill   Fig.PE10

As in the previous pictures, the three pictures on the right also show a great number of workers busy at their tasks. It should be noted that unlike many other photographs taken at other firms these pictures are not posed, just a snapshot of the 'moment' so as not to interrupt production in any way.

Fig.PE11 is a scene in the Smithy where a large number of perambulator chassis are being made, this line was one of the firms major items and had a world wide reputation. In the carpenters shop *Fig.PE12* the bodies for the prams are being made, and on the right of the photograph is a large stack of beech horses lying on their sides, this was still a popular toy as it was seen as a cheaper alternative to a proper rocking horse.

In Fig.PE13, the metal working department, it is difficult to make out exactly what the components are that are being made, certainly in the middle of the floor is a large pile of wheels, the firm must have made tens of thousands over the years. These are just a few views of the many different departments that were operating at the Manor Works in Lee.

1924 Smithy   Fig.PE11

1924 Carpenters Shop   Fig.PE12

1924 Metal Working Department   Fig.PE13

In 1926 the firm took a number of important steps and increased their position in the trade. The expansion at the Manor Works at Lee had progressed to such a degree that all work was carried out at this one address and the old property at Culmore Road was disposed of. It was also the year that Patterson Edwards became a Limited Company. They were now one of the major producers of strong toys and perambulators in the country. The Leeway trade name had been registered and was applied to the majority of their products, usually in the form of a transfer, some examples of which are pictured *Fig.PE14* below. Note the use of the £ symbol in place of the L, indicating the firms 'value for money' policy. These transfers are quite fragile and can easily be

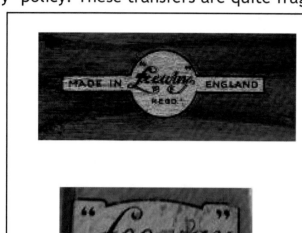

Various 'Leeway' Transfers

Fig.PE14

damaged or removed completely if not treated with due care.
In 1932 Patterson Edwards Ltd. arranged for the selling organisation, L Rees & Co. Ltd. to handle all of their sales so that they could concentrate on production and the development of new items. Up until this time the old firm had attended all the major toy fairs and done all of their own sales and marketing which would have taken an increasing amount of time and effort as the firm expanded. New items that were now being produced included a good range of full size prams along side their toy prams and also an increased range of up-to-date pedal cars, the latter being responsible for the steady decline in rocking horse production as youngsters showed their preference.

By 1934 the once serene parkland at Lee was now all but completely developed, giving nearly five acres of covered workshop. Fig.PE15 is a view of pedal car department and Fig.PE16 is the pram department.

1934 Pedal Car Department   Fig.PE15

1934 Pram Assembly   Fig.PE16

In 1938 the founder of Patterson Edwards, Henry Jarvis *Fig.PE17* sadly passed away, having been ill for some time and not involved with the business for a number of years. This was now under the full and most efficient control of his son Donald Jarvis *Fig.PE18*. Over 500 staff were

Mr H S Jarvis   Fig.PE17

Mr D Jarvis   Fig.PE18

employed just before the outbreak of World War Two but then the toy production had to stop. Only prams and other items for the war effort were made until hostilities ceased and toy production could be resumed.

Postwar production placed more emphasis was being on metal toys, although rocking horses were still being produced. This was probably because so many other rocking horse makers had since ceased trading, Lines Bros. and Collinsons being the only other major producers at this time. Patterson Edwards continued adapting to an ever changing market, the new plastic era had come about and the firm managed to keep pace for many years by introducing a new range of toys. They moved premises again in 1976 but by the 1980's foreign competition undercut their prices and they were unable to compete, so the firm closed down after trading for about 90 years.

It is thought the last rocking horses were produced up until around 1970, still based on the patent from 1918. As mentioned before, their earlier horses were of a different construction and the firm was known to have produced rocking horses from at least 1910. Early illustrations of their **Swing horses** used the same picture as that still being used in the 1926 catalogue *Fig.PE19* alongside which is a similar type of drawing for the **Cycle Horse**. The cycle horse was described in an article of 1914 as

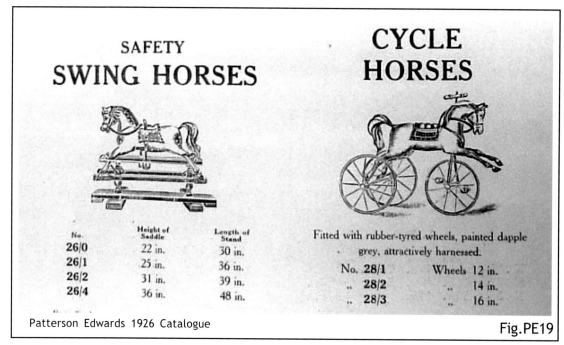

SAFETY
SWING HORSES

CYCLE
HORSES

No.	Height of Saddle	Length of Stand
26/0	22 in.	30 in.
26/1	25 in.	36 in.
26/2	31 in.	39 in.
26/4	36 in.	48 in.

Fitted with rubber-tyred wheels, painted dapple grey, attractively harnessed.

No. 28/1	Wheels 12 in.
„ 28/2	„ 14 in.
„ 28/3	„ 16 in.

Patterson Edwards 1926 Catalogue

Fig.PE19

'the rubber-tyred, carved cycle horse, painted dapple grey, fitted with reins, bridle, saddle, and glass eyes'.

Other items in the 1926 catalogue were depicted with images based on actual photographs and gave a much clearer indication of what the item looked like.

Fig.PE20 is a catalogue illustration of their **Hobby Horse** range and
Fig.PE21 shows a size 3 Hobby horse. Fig.PE22 shows illustrations of the

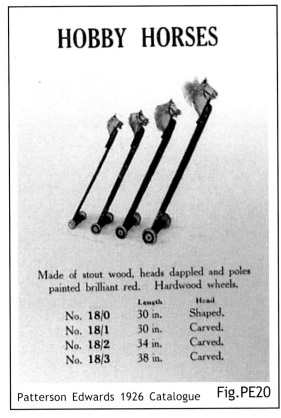

HOBBY HORSES

Made of stout wood, heads dappled and poles
painted brilliant red.   Hardwood wheels.

	Length	Head
No. 18/0	30 in.	Shaped.
No. 18/1	30 in.	Carved.
No. 18/2	34 in.	Carved.
No. 18/3	38 in.	Carved.

Patterson Edwards 1926 Catalogue   **Fig.PE20**

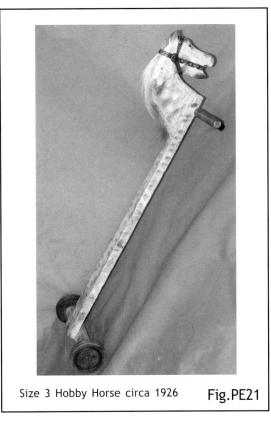

Size 3 Hobby Horse circa 1926   **Fig.PE21**

Gig Horse, Beech Horse, and **Stool Horses,** all with the sizes available.

Patterson Edwards 1926 Catalogue   Fig.PE22

Other **Carved Wood Horses** that were manufactured are shown *Fig.PE23* in the list, these were available with either a hand carved or machine carved finish. A machine carved horse was basically a hollow box with rounded edges, a hand carved horse would have had a solid body and been carved by hand to a much higher standard of finish throughout.

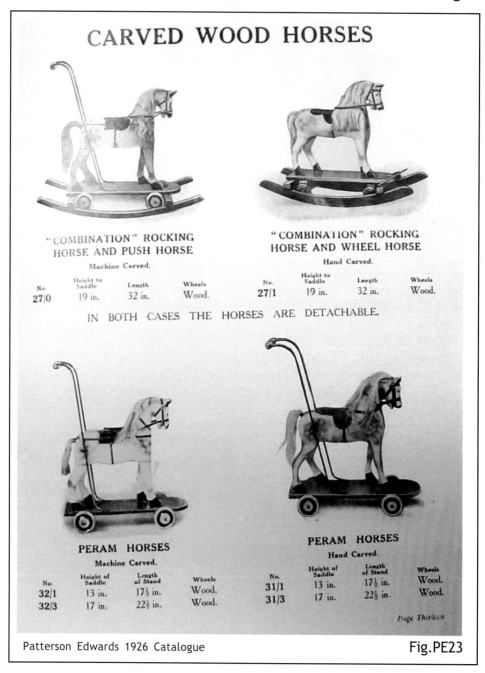

CARVED WOOD HORSES

"COMBINATION" ROCKING
HORSE AND PUSH HORSE
Machine Carved.

No.	Height to Saddle	Length	Wheels
27/0	19 in.	32 in.	Wood.

"COMBINATION" ROCKING
HORSE AND WHEEL HORSE
Hand Carved.

No.	Height to Saddle	Length	Wheels
27/1	19 in.	32 in.	Wood.

IN BOTH CASES THE HORSES ARE DETACHABLE.

PERAM HORSES
Machine Carved.

No.	Height of Saddle	Length of Stand	Wheels
32/1	13 in.	17½ in.	Wood.
32/3	17 in.	22½ in.	Wood.

PERAM HORSES
Hand Carved.

No.	Height of Saddle	Length of Stand	Wheels
31/1	13 in.	17½ in.	Wood.
31/3	17 in.	22½ in.	Wood.

Page Thirteen

Patterson Edwards 1926 Catalogue   Fig.PE23

1934 New Illustration   Fig.PE24

By 1934 a new illustration of a rocking horse was printed *Fig.PE24* and this was a true representation of the article. At this time turned posts were fitted to the stands and the way the saddle and blanket are cut and fitted is typical of Leeway horses. Fig.PE25 is of a horse dated to 1936 and is in its original condition. Both the illustration and picture are of model size 26/5 this was the middle of the 3 sizes available at the time.

1936 Rocking Horse Model 26/5   Fig.PE25

It would be worth noting that the catalogue of 1926 offered four sizes of swing horses, none of these tally in size with the later catalogues. By 1936 the smaller size 26/2 *Fig.PE26* no longer had turned posts, instead they were a sawn octagonal shape, a quicker and cheaper alternative. Note the lack of saddle blanket, another cost saving, but one that did

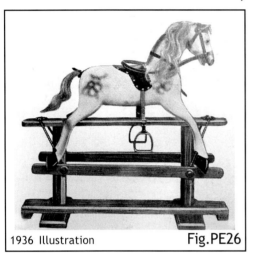

not really detract from the overall appearance. The larger sizes of horse retained the turned post up until at least 1950, after which they were also replaced with square posts. Fig.PE27 is from a 1948/9 catalogue and the largest size horse, 26/7, is illustrated. Note the same saddle and blanket arrangement as on the 1930's model. In fact, the design is hardly changed at all since the 1918 patent.

1936 Illustration   Fig.PE26

Leeway PE

Model 26/2

Hand carved horse with upholstered saddle, leather harness and reins, enamelled stirrups. Length of stand, 32", width 13½", height to saddle, 23".

Model 26/5

Exceptional value in "Leeway" hand carved safety Rocking Horses. Beautifully painted "dappled" horse mounted on stout varnished stand. Leather harness and reins and well-upholstered saddle with enamelled stirrups. Metal swing rods. Length of stand, 36", width, 13½", height to saddle, 26½".

Model 26/7

(Illustrated), as Model 26/5, but improved shape and larger. Chromium-plated swing rods. Horse painted Cream and "dappled" Brown. Length of stand, 52", width of stand, 16", height to saddle, 33".

ROCKING HORSE MODEL 26/7

Patterson Edwards 1948/49 Catalogue   Fig.PE27

Fig.PE28 is from a 1950 Patterson Edwards catalogue

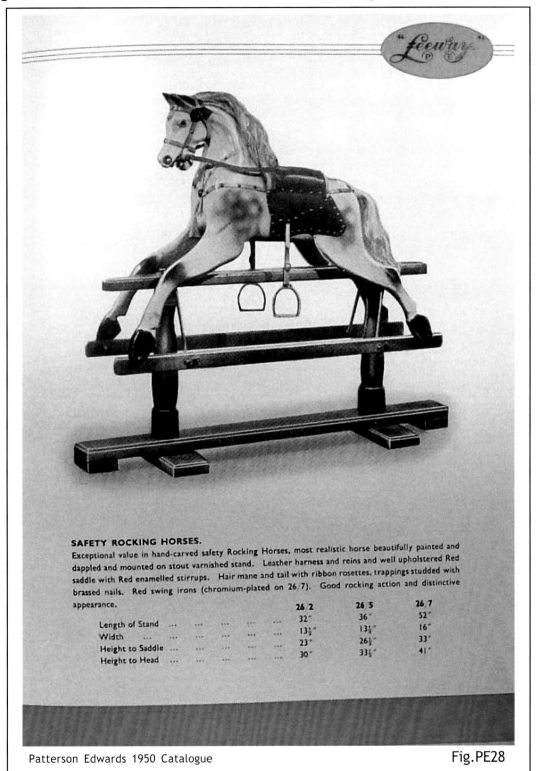

SAFETY ROCKING HORSES.
Exceptional value in hand-carved safety Rocking Horses, most realistic horse beautifully painted and dappled and mounted on stout varnished stand. Leather harness and reins and well upholstered Red saddle with Red enamelled stirrups. Hair mane and tail with ribbon rosettes, trappings studded with brassed nails. Red swing irons (chromium-plated on 26/7). Good rocking action and distinctive appearance.

	26/2	26/5	26/7
Length of Stand	32"	36"	52"
Width	13½"	13½"	16"
Height to Saddle	23"	26½"	33"
Height to Head	30"	33½"	41"

Patterson Edwards 1950 Catalogue

Fig.PE28

Two horses that are both size 26/7 have their original factory finish and harness. The first *Fig.PE29* is dated to 1953 and the latter *Fig.PE30* to 1963. Both horses have 'sprayed' paint work, which was the method of finish used since before the War. The tack was leather for the straps with saddles made from a type of oil cloth, though later, vinyl was used.

1953 Leeway Horse

Fig.PE29

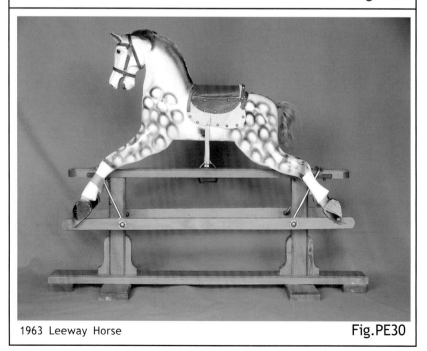

1963 Leeway Horse

Fig.PE30

From after 1950 the larger horses were fitted with square posts and had small buttress pieces at the bottom for extra strength, subsequently they very rarely gave any problem. From about 1960 the only carved horse that was available was the large size, 26/7, the other available option was the small simple box or 'machine carved' horse, model 26/0 *Fig.PE31*, this was constructed from plywood, crudely painted and mounted on a simple pine stand. Although these horses were constructed on the principle of the 1918 patent, they did not stand up to rough treatment and so became more of a disposable item. Other items that were also produced at the cheaper end of the market was the **Push Horse** *Fig.PE33* for toddlers and for older older and hopefully more children was the **Horse and Cart** *Fig.PE32*.

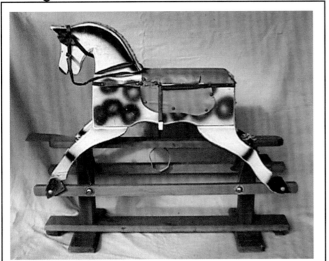

1960's Leeway Model 26/0   Fig.PE31

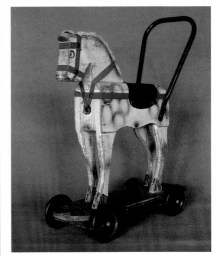

1960's Push Horse   Fig.PE33

Below is a letter-head showing the Leeway logo *Fig.PE34* circa 1960.

1950's Horse & Cart   Fig.PE32

Leeway Letter-head Logo   Fig.PE34

MANUFACTURERS OF THE   CHILDREN'S CARRIAGES

METAL AND WOOD TOYS

Pegram Henry.   -1882-1895-

Address: 320 & 332, Euston Road, London. N.W.
                  103, New Oxford Street, London. W.C.
                  187, Gt Portland Street, London. W.

See also: Bonner, G. & Co.   1884
                  Abbott, Bonner & Co.   1899

Various trade listings appear for Henry Pegram in London directories
including **Rocking Horse Maker** and are as follows;

*1882   Pegram Henry,   320 & 332 Euston Rd. Rocking horse maker.

*1882 Pegram, Bonner & Co. 187 Gt Portland St. Life size model horses
                                               (roundabouts.)
* The above two listings are from the same directory entry.

1884   Pegram Henry,   320 & 332 Euston Rd. Rocking horse maker.

1891   Pegram Henry,   320 & 332 Euston Rd. 103 New Oxford St. W
                                            (Perambulator makers)

1895 Pegram Henry,   332 Euston Rd. 103 New Oxford St. W
                                            (Perambulator makers)

1895 Pegram Henry,   320 Euston Rd. Rocking horse maker

During the approximate period of 1880 to 1900 Henry Pegram and
George Bonner seem to have had some sort of business ties. Various
directory entries list them as individuals and also together, both names
are associated with rocking horse making, perambulators and also life
size horses and roundabouts. Henry Pegram also seemed to have had
business dealings with 'Matthew & Co.' in 1884, listed as '*Pegram,
Matthew & Co. 187 Gt Portland St & 103 New Oxford St*' under the
heading of perambulator maker.

In 1884 Henry Pegram was also noted to be a bicycle manufacturer and advertised that

'*Old rocking horses and perambulators repaired; carts of every description of superior toys made to order*'

Products were also available for wholesale, retail, and for exportation.

The last directory entry regarding the name Pegram was in 1899 is as follows;

'*Abbott, Bonner & Co (late H Pegram) estd. 50 years*'

However it is not clear who was established for 50 years, whether it was George Bonner or Henry Pegram, or both.

Despite his various business associates and also being listed for at least thirteen years, and possibly in business for fifty years, no known products have been attributed to Henry Pegram either as an individual or as part of any known company. His output and variety of items are certainly most intriguing

Henry Pegram had a son, Henry Alfred Pegram 1862-1937, who was a 'Sculptor of portraits and ideal groups'. His work was of some note, having some exhibitions at the Royal Academy and he also had some statues displayed publicly.

Perambulator & Manufacturing Co. Ltd.
-1900 - 1952

Registered office: Crown Works, Spring Hill, Halesowen, Birmingham.

It is unsure when this company began trading, but most likely it was in the late 19th century. For in their catalogue of 1902 it states that
'All Previous Lists are hereby Cancelled',
implying they had produced a number of yearly catalogues beforehand, certainly a catalogue from 1900 is known to exist.
Under the management of Mr Samuel Williams, they were primarily a manufacturer of perambulators and mail carts, but in their catalogue of 1902, they offered the **'Prince' Tricycle Horse** in three different sizes *Fig.PM01* and showing their prices.

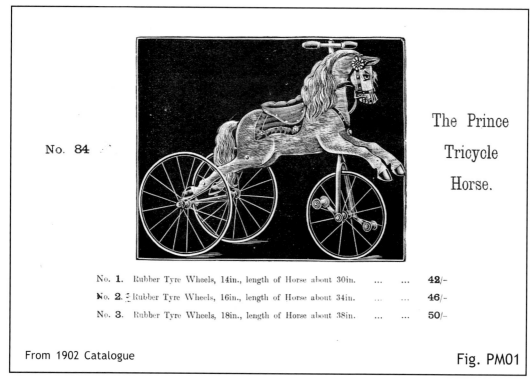

No. 84

The Prince

Tricycle

Horse.

No. **1**. Rubber Tyre Wheels, 14in., length of Horse about 30in.	**42**/-
No. **2**. Rubber Tyre Wheels, 16in., length of Horse about 34in.	**46**/-
No. **3**. Rubber Tyre Wheels, 18in., length of Horse about 38in.	**50**/-

From 1902 Catalogue

Fig. PM01

In May 1952 the company went into liquidation.

Pope, James & Sons Ltd.   1916 - 1927-

Address: Brockenhurst, New Forest, Hampshire.

Trade name: 'Stag Brand'.

Incorporated: 1916   Company No.142,990

James Pope and Sons were manufacturers of a variety of wooden toys which included blackboards and easels, barrows, engines and a good range of both **Beech Horses** and also **Push Horses.** Their advert of 1921 *Fig.PS01* shows the sizes and relevant trade prices per dozen.
The known trading dates for the firm are certainly from 1916 to 1927 but it is unclear for how long the company traded after their last known advert that appeared in February 1927.

Pope's Famous Beech Horses

BEECH HORSES.

Height of Saddle..	5"	6"	8"	9"		
Length of Platform	5"	6"	8"	10½"		
No..	01	02	03	04		
Price per dozen ..	5/3	7/6	10/6	14/2		

PUSH HORSES.

Height of Saddle..	10½"	12"	13"	14½"	16½"	17"
Length of Platform	9"	11"	12"	13"	14"	15"
No..	1	2	3	4	5	6
Price per dozen ..	17/3	20/9	27/8	36/8	42/7	54/-

Height of Saddle..	17"	18"	20"	20"	22"	24"
Length of Platform	15"	17"	19"	21"	24"	25"
No..	7	8	9	10	11	12
Price per dozen ..	58/8	76/-	96/9	126/-	159/-	186/-

To be obtained from all the principal Merchants or direct from—

JAMES POPE & SONS, Limited,
BROCKENHURST, NEW FOREST, HANTS.

Pope's 1921 Trade advert   Fig.PS01

Randall, John.   c.1930

Address: Fishponds, Bristol.

From an undated catalogue of circa 1930, we know that John Randall traded as an *'English and Foreign Timber Merchant, Toy and Domestic Wood-Work Manufacturer'*. Within the catalogue were offered the following items, Engines, **Stool Horses, Stool Horse & Rocker**, Wheel Barrows, **White Horses**, Scooters Blackboards & Easels. Stools, Prams, Parlour Hoops, and a variety of domestic woodwork. Fig.RL01 & Fig.RL02 show the Stool Horses and White Horses respectively. All the items produced were advertised as being 'well and strongly made' but were quite obviously of a fairly basic nature. The most elaborate item made was the **'Combination' Stool Horse & Rocker** *Fig.RL03*.

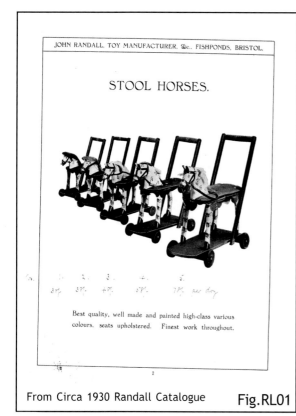

From Circa 1930 Randall Catalogue   **Fig.RL01**

From Circa 1930 Randall Catalogue   **Fig.RL02**

It should be noted that all the pages of the catalogue have been over written with prices, in shillings, most probably the wholesale ex-works prices of the company. It is not known how long the company traded for as no other information has yet come to light.

JOHN RANDALL, TOY MANUFACTURER. &c., FISHPONDS, BRISTOL.

STOOL HORSE & ROCKER.

This combination (Stool, Horse and Rocker) makes an excellent toy for the nursery. The horse which can be detached from the rocker in a few seconds by a simple screw attachment, is suitable for outdoors.

3

From Circa 1930 Randall Catalogue

Fig.RL03

Raper, Joseph. (& Mrs. S, & Thos.)
-1882 - 1899-

Address: 54, Werrington Street, Oakley Square, London. N.W.

Joseph Raper was born in 1824 and aged 24 in 1848 he married Sarah Mackay.

Joseph was involved with printing, working for a firm in Alms Houses on or near Farringdon Road.

In 1882 Joseph was listed as a Toy Maker at 54 Werrington Street and there are also several other entries, for 54 Werrington Street, detailing various other members of the Raper family, all of whom are listed under the heading of **Rocking Horse Makers**.

1884	Raper, Joseph.	Rocking, pole and shaped-horse maker Wholesale retail & for exportation.
1891	Raper Mrs. S.	54 Werrington St. Somers tn. NW
1895	Raper Mrs. S.	54 Werrington St. Somers tn. NW
1899	Raper Thos,	54 Werrington St. Oakley Sq. NW

Joseph Raper died in 1886 at the age of 62. Sarah appeared to carry on with running the business for at least another nine years and then was succeeded by one of their six children, Thomas who was born in 1850. It is not known how long Thomas Raper was involved with the business but only one directory reference from 1899 has been found.

R. H. Manufacturing Co. 1922 - 1923-

Address: 1922:   26, Wellington Street, Strand, London. W.C.2
              1923:   Waterside Works, Lower Kings Road. Berkhampstead.

Incorporated: 1923.   Company No. 188,014

Patent: 1924   Patent No.206,679 *'Improvements in Animal Toys'*

The R.H. Manufacturing Company was set up by two gentlemen, a Mr Laurence Norman Reader and a Mr Charles Arthur Haynes, sometime in 1922 through an advert of 1923 referred to the firm by the alternative name of Reader Haynes Manufacturing Company Limited. They offered a range of indoor games, one of which was called Buzz-Ball and by all accounts proved to be quite popular and was protected by a patent.

They also produced the 'Roc-O-Long', which was also protected by a patent. This was a very unusual type of **Wooden Horse** that was described as being the latest development in Rocking Horses, it was not a horse on wheels or propelled by pedals, but a wooden horse that actually walked, taking a child about 15 - 20 minutes to master. The technical drawing below *Fig.RH01* accompanied the patent description.

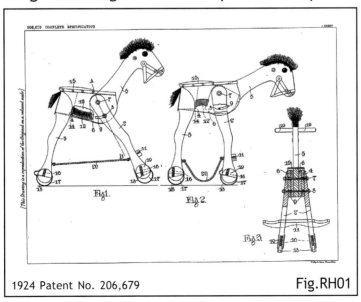

1924 Patent No. 206,679   Fig.RH01

A picture from a 1923 advert *Fig.RH02* shows two actual 'Roc-O-Long' horses with their young jockeys.

From 1923 Trade advert   Fig.RH02

Reader Haynes attended the 1923 London Fair and displayed a variety of his products including the 'Roc-O-Long'. Since then there has been no further information found about the firm, probably indicating that the 'Roc-O-Long' was not a commercial success.

It is not known if any examples of the 'Roc-O-Long' have survived.

Ridingbery & Co. Ltd.   1914 - 1958

Address: 30-38, Gloucester Lane, St. Philip's, Bristol.

Agents: G. Greiner & Co. 10-12 Milton Street, London. E.C.

Incorporated: 1914   Company No.136,430   Dissolved Nov 1958.

A trade report from 1925 stated that Messrs. Ridingbery & Co. Ltd were
one of the oldest manufacturers of wooden toys in the country and
have been specialising in the production of **Beech horses** and **Stool
horses** and the like for many years. An advert from 1925 *Fig.RY01* also
refers to **Painted Horses.** Unfortunately no illustrations have been
found to give a clue as to the appearance of the company's products.
No other information about Ridingburys has been found except that the
company was dissolved in 1958.

From 1925 Trade Advert   Fig.RY01

Rivett Campbell & Co. Ltd. 1906 -1928-

Address:	Richardson Street, Rochdale Road, Manchester.
Incorporated:	1906. Company No. 90,239
Trade Name:	'Rivco'.

An advert from 1928 *Fig.RT01* takes much pride in telling the reader about the high quality of the items that are produced by Manchester firms. Amongst the toys produced by Rivett Campbell were **Pole Horses, Push Horses** and **Swing Horses** as well as many other items such as prams and barrows. Fig.RT02 is an illustration of a Pole Horse which was made in five sizes and all fitted with steel bushes in the wheels. Although the advert mentions other horse items, there is little indication as to what sort of range there was.

We specialise in the manufacture of Pole, Push and Swing Horses. All Pole Horses (excepting No. 1) fitted with swivelled Poles.

No. 1, 17in. No. 2, 19in. No. 3, 22in. No. 4, 25in. No. 5, 28in.

Fitted with steel bushed hardwood wheels

From 1928 Trade Advert   Fig.RT02

MANCHESTER MADE !

FOR centuries Manchester Goods have gone all over the world and the term "Manchester Made" is a guarantee of quality. "Rivco" Toys are made in Manchester, they differ from the Mass Production machine made toys as every "Rivco" Toy bears the stamp and individualism of the skilled craftsman, withal they are produced at prices which are competitive, while the quality and finish is true to the traditional standard of "Manchester Made" Goods.

RIVETT CAMPBELL
& CO., LTD.,
Richardson Street,
Rochdale Road,
MANCHESTER

From 1928 Trade Advert   Fig.RT01

Roebuck, John.   -1854-

Address: 28, Endell Street, Long Acre, London.

                          2, Bath Place, New Road, London.

Only one Post Office trade directory listing for John Roebuck has been found. This was from 1854 and it lists him as a **Rocking Horse Maker.** This sole listing did however give two addresses for him, suggesting that he may well have been in charge of a reasonable sized concern.

The only other consideration is that a *Frederick Roebuck* migrated from England around 1880 and settled in Australia. Subsequently he set up a business making rocking horses. This was the beginning of a long running and successful Antipodean company that traded for three generations right up until 1972.

Rothschild & Baker.   -1896 - 1958

Address: 70 - 72, Summer Row Works, Birmingham.

                         97, Curtain Road, London. E.C. (from circa 1910)

Trade Name: 'Rab'

Incorporated: Circa 1941   Rothschild & Baker Ltd.

The partnership between George Louis Rothschild and Henry Vincent
Baker was thought to have been formed in the 1890's. One of the firms
earliest known records is a trade directory listing of 1896. They were
primarily involved with the manufacture of perambulators and mail carts
and originally based in Birmingham.
Around 1910 they had expanded and acquired premises at Curtain Road,
London. Curiously another perambulator manufacturer, Parker Bros,
were based only a few doors away at 104, Curtain Road. Around this
time they were listed as makers of "Rab" baby carriages, folding carts,
invalid chairs, toys and furniture.
In October 1933 the partnership was dissolved and Henry Baker carried
on trading on his own but still under the firm's old established name.
A trade publication of 1939 described the contents of Rothschild and
Baker's latest catalogue as having a great variety of items on offer, it
then went on to state;
      *'Boy's cycles and tricycles have a page of their own and horses
are shown in the form of **Combined Rocker and Push Horses** and **Pull
Horses**. In this connection we are informed that Rothschild and Baker
are the only firm outside London producing **Wood Rocking** and other
Horses in the traditional London style of these goods'*.

Sadly there is no accompanying illustration so it is not known what the
range of horses were like.
Around 1941 the firm became incorporated and continued trading upto
1958 when it was announced in the London Gazette that they had
ceased trading and the company had been dissolved.

Ryland. F.   1906 - 1928

Address: 165, Sherlock Street, Birmingham.

Frank Ryland is thought to have set up business around 1906 although it may have been earlier as a directory entry of 1903 mentions a Frank Ryland as a cycle maker. The name Ryland was not uncommon at the time and it not clear if this is one and the same person. However later directory entries for Frank Ryland all give 165 Sherlock Street as his address. Trade publications also mentioned the products he made.

Frank Ryland soon became known as a producer of strong and well made toys. The range of these toys included juvenile tricycles, wood engines, wheel barrows, pole carts *Fig.RD01* and also a good variety of horse based products.
These included **Velocipede Horses, Shaped Horses, Stool Horses, Improved Rocking Horses, Old Style Rocking Horses, Combination Horses** and **Beech Horses** and very likely many other similar lines.

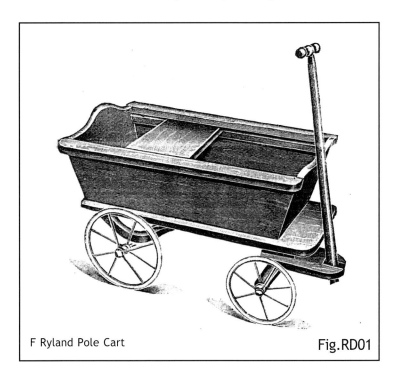

F Ryland Pole Cart   Fig.RD01

An article relating to a 1917 trade fair included the following description of Mr Ryland's stand;

Mr Ryland had a nice show of strong toys, horses representing a very fine line. The velocipede horses were of an improved pattern and well finished, with rubber tyred wheels and padded saddles. With bodies made out of the best seasoned pine and and birch legs these were distinctive. The "flat back" horses had strong hardwood seats that were upholstered in various colours, and rubber tyred wheels. There were many patterns of rocking horses from the old style, with or without end chair seats and straps, to the well known safety pattern. The stool horses with leather cloth backs, stuffed and buttoned, and provided with iron wheels, were two other good lines. Then we inspected combination rocker and pole or pram horses, stool horses on rockers and gig horses, with basket to sit in. Beech horses were another strong series.

The description gives us only a clue as to the appearance of some of the products, regrettably there were no illustrations of any of the horse products with the article. However it would appear that with regard to the rocking horses a series of different size bow rocker were available, with the option of end chairs. Also a series of different size swing stand horses were being produced as well.

It is thought that Frank Ryland continued trading up to around 1928. These were difficult times for many businesses and no further mention or information has been found for after this date.

Scott & Walker Ltd.　　1914 - 1935

Address:　　　　　　　65-68, Princip Street, Birmingham.

Incorporated:　　　　1914　　　Company No.137,916

Dissolved:　　　　　　12th March 1935

Scott and Walker Ltd. was set up in 1914 as an offshoot of an old established company F.C.Scott, gun makers. The premises were near the heart of Birmingham in a most imposing building known as the Defiance Works *Fig.SC01*. This building was still standing as of January 2008, but it was in a rather run down state as can be seen in Fig.SC05. The reason behind the formation of the company was that with the onset of World War One and the lack of imported toys, they decided on the new enterprise. They began by producing indoor and outdoor games and toys, cardboard boxes and general stationers' sundries. Before long the company produced a range of horse based items, which included **Horses & Carts, Double Horse Chariot, Rocking Horses** etc.

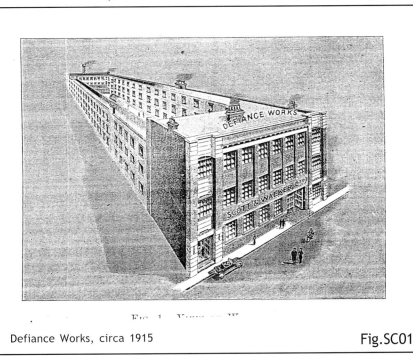

Defiance Works, circa 1915　　　　　　　　　　　　Fig.SC01

These were made in the woodworking department *Fig.SC02* where the finished articles *Fig.SC03* can also be seen. These items were destined for display at the 1915 London Toy Fair at the Agricultural Hall, Islington.

Woodworking Department Circa 1915   Fig.SC02

Woodworking Department Circa 1915   Fig.SC03

The items listed and shown in the previous illustrations were produced as samples and its not known what sort of response they received at the Toy Fair or if they were ever put into full time manufacture.

TIPCART.

Scott & Walker Tip Cart 1915

Fig.SC04

Above is an illustration of a **Tip Cart and Horse** *Fig.SC04* made by the company in 1915.

In March of 1926, it was reported in the London Gazette that a meeting of Creditors was to take place, the immediate result of this is not known but in early 1935, Scott & Walker Ltd were struck off the companies register.

The photograph below *Fig.SC05* shows a view of the building referred to as the 'Defiance Works' at Princip Street, Birmingham. This photograph was taken in January 2008. Compare this to the old illustrated drawing *Fig.SC01*. The drawing exaggerates the length of the property, in reality it is probably only half as long as the drawing suggests. However, it may well be that the property will soon disappear, being located in a part of the city where much new development is taking place. Note the metal framed windows on the top story and compare these to the windows in

Defiance Works, January 2008   Fig.SC05

the woodworking department *Figs.SC02 & SC03*. As far as working conditions generally went in the early 20th century, the staff in the woodworking department at least had a reasonable view.

Shaw, Edward & Co.   -1876 - 1936

Address: 1876   79, Stretford Road, & 11a, Piccadilly, Manchester.
           Works: 4, Booth Street East, Chorlton-on-Medlock.

           1895   143, Stretford Road, & 13, Piccadilly, Hulme.
           Works: Booth Street East.   Oxford Street,   C-on-M.

Incorporated: 1912   E.Shaw & Co. Ltd.   Company No.124,181

Edward Shaw has been found listed in various Manchester trade directories, mainly under the heading of Perambulator maker, trading as a wholesaler and retailer. In 1879 he advertised as the manufacturer of the;
> *'New Slide Handle Reversible Perambulator, patented 1877'.*

In a trade listing of 1886 the firm was described as being;
> *'Patentees of the American hickory bassinette'.*

It would seem that the firm was always looking for new ideas and again in 1923 they applied for and were granted a patent, No 196,705 for the *'Improvements in Suspension Springs for Baby Cars, Invalid Carriages & the like.* This patent was registered as being the invention of Frederick Stevenson, who was also recorded as being the Managing Director of the firm at the time.

All the ideas that have been mentioned show that Shaw's main line of business was the manufacturing of perambulators and no trade listing for any other items have been found. However we do know that the firm was responsible for the manufacture of **Rocking Horses** as they were prudent enough to apply their makers label to some models which allows us to make a positive identification of the brand. When the production of rocking horses started is not known, but they would not have been produced after 1936 as this is when the company went into receivership and ceased trading.

A few **Rocking Horses** have turned up with a makers label *Fig.SW01*. It is unknown for how long Shaw made rocking horses for, but the picture

E Shaw & Co Makers Label   Fig.SW01

Small Shaw Horse C.1909   Fig.SW02

of the young girl on the horse *Fig.SW02* is thought to date from around 1909. As we can see this is quite a small horse and is the same size as a very dilapidated horse *Fig.SW04* that had the makers label. This was eventually restored and put back into use. The horse in Fig.SW03 is also a small size horse and does have some slight differences to the other two

horses previously mentioned. This would suggest that they were in production over a reasonable period of time and had 'evolved' as the firm got to grips with the manufacturing of this new line of goods, outside their normal production of perambulators and the like. A much larger example of a Shaw horse has also been identified *Fig.SW06*.

Small Shaw Horse   Fig.SW03

It would be reasonable to assume that an intermediate size was also produced as was typical of other makers. Fig.SW05 shows detail of the

Small Dilapidated Shaw Horse   Fig.SW04

turned post, all the horses that have been found have had this same design that is quite unique to Shaw horses.

It will also be noted that the small horse has no hoof notches but these were cut on the larger model, *Fig.SW07*.

The picture Fig.SW08 is a more detailed view of the head of the larger horse that has been over painted brown at some time and has now lost its glass eyes.

Construction of their horses was quite standard, box body with tenoned leg joins and generally well shaped.

All known examples appear to have been originally painted as dapple greys and fitted with glass eyes.

Shaw Small Post Detail   Fig.SW05

Large size Shaw horse *Fig.SW06*, post and hoof detail *Fig.SW07* and head detail *Fig.SW08*.

Large Shaw Horse

Fig.SW06

Large Shaw Horse
Post Detail

Fig.SW07

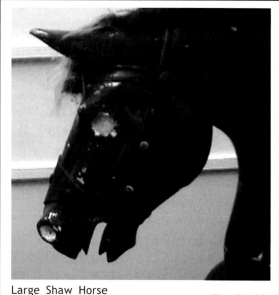

Large Shaw Horse
Head Detail

Fig.SW08

Shillelagh Wood Industry   1916 - 1920-

Address: Shillelagh, Co. Wicklow. Ireland.

See also: Galway Toy Industry.

Although not a British firm, it is important to record the Shillelagh Wood Industry as its products were commonly sold throughout the UK and were also similar too those produced by British makers.

The Shillelagh Wood Industry was borne out of nothing more than a series of tutorial classes, of around forty pupils, formed for the purpose of educating workers in the art of toy making. The classes were initially set up to create work for the inhabitants of Shillelagh, most of whom were tenants of the Fitzwilliam Family, the family having sponsored the early formation of these classes.

The classes were carried out under the tutelage of Mr Hunter, who had a good knowledge of all the various aspects of toy making, having run his own business some years earlier. The classes went well to such an extent that by the end of 1916 it was possible to set up a firm on a proper commercial basis, under the management of Mr Hunter.

One important fact to note is that geographically Shillelagh is in the centre of one of the finest oak growing districts in the country and this resource was used in many of their products, which by 1918 was quite extensive. The firm enjoyed early successes at both the 1918 and 1919 British Industries Fairs. Not only did they produce toys but also a large range of domestic furniture, these items certainly being made from the local oak resource. Their range of toys included motor cars and vans, dolls' swing cots, scooters, engines, barrows and a comprehensive list of different types of horses;

          Safety Rocking Horses in at least six sizes
          Combination Rocking Horses
          Cycle Horses
          Combination Pole Horses in four sizes.
          Push Horses
          Pole Horses
          Stool horses from 1919 in 2 new shades, brown and cream.
          Horses and Carts

The illustration of their 1918 **Push and Pole Horses** *Fig.SH01* shows they

Push & Pole Horses 1918   Fig.SH01

have quite a distinctive look, with their slightly elongated bodies and large side facing, almost 'Bat like' ears. Both these features appear to be common to all of their horses, although not as pronounced, the small horse and cart *Fig.SH02* shares these traits as well.

The range of **Swing Stand Horses** was offered in at least six sizes and the illustration *Fig.SH03* is one of their larger horses. Although the illustration is not too clear, some interesting points can be seen and allow positive identification of the Make. The general shape of the

horse, with the elongated body and unusual ear make it quite discernible. The basic elements of the swing stand are also clear enough to see, the style of turned post and its general proportion and finish.

Horse & Cart 1918   Fig.SH02

The dappling on the horse illustrated *Fig.SH03* is fairly crude compared with some of the more refined makers, this could be a helpful point for identification. Fig.SH04 is an example of a Shillelagh horse that has been

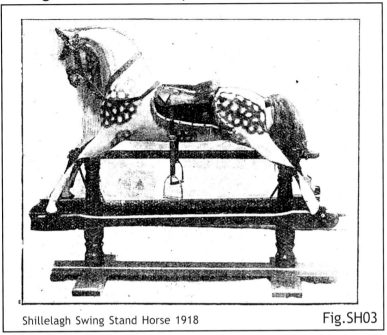

Shillelagh Swing Stand Horse 1918   Fig.SH03

painted over at some time in the past and may also have had 'new' runners fitted as they appear a little out of scale. It may well be that

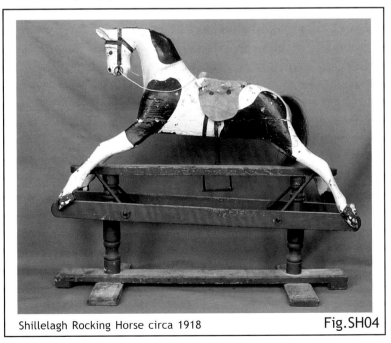

Shillelagh Rocking Horse circa 1918   Fig.SH04

they are original, being a relatively new firm with not too much experience, specifications were very likely to have been changed. The same horse is illustrated below *Fig.SH05* with the original factory coat of paint now revealed and showing it to have crude and irregular dappling. It is possible to see the lines around the leg joins, this shows

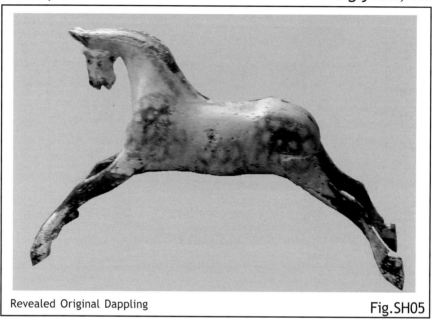

Revealed Original Dappling   Fig.SH05

the method of how the legs were fitted into notches cut in the body of the horse. They legs would have been glued and nailed into position, for this was the quickest method of fixing legs. Despite this, in other areas more time was taken during manufacture, the hooves have been notched onto the runners and also turned posts are fitted to the stand, both these features are quite time consuming and can be seen in detail in Fig.SH06

In 1919 Mr Hunter resigned from the firm and accepted the position of manager of the toy industry in Galway for the Congested District Board of Ireland who were to embark on producing a range of products very similar to those produced by the Shillelagh Wood Industry. No subsequent information has been found about the Shillelagh firm since Mr Hunter left and it is not known for how much longer they continued trading.

Post Detail   Fig.SH06

Simkinson, Samuel.   -1853-

Address: 37, Broughton Street, Salford, Manchester.

From a directory for Manchester & Salford of 1853, Samuel Simkinson was listed as a **'Rocking Horse Manufacturer'**. No further listings have been found. If Simkinson was a manufacturer of large rocking horses, they would have been of the 'bow' rocking type as the swing stand had not yet been invented.

Simpson, Fawcett & Co.   1847-1957

Address: Black Bull Street, Hunslet Road, Leeds.

Affiliation: Star Manufacturing Co. Cubitt Town, London.

Trade mark: 'Swan' toys.   See also: Gamages 'Bronko'

The firm Simpson Fawcett had its origins in 1847 when James Simpson set up business as J Simpson & Co. In 1866 James Simpson went into partnership with Samuel Thomas Fawcett and formed Simpson Fawcett & Co. At that time the partners bought up all the pail machinery in the country and this was also used in the construction of the round ends of perambulators, one of their main products. In 1866 they were listed as coopers and as producing pails, tubs, washing machines etc. from the Whitehouse pail works. In 1869 the Baby Carriage trade developed rapidly which allowed the firm to expand, helped by various patents that stopped competitors taking away business from them and 'Simcett' prams were to be seen on every London and other city street corner.

In 1908 the business was incorporated into a Limited company and at the same time was joined by a number of other firms, one of these being the 'Star Manufacturing Co.' of Cubitt Town, London. The firm continued expanding and by 1914 had branch showrooms and agencies in Leeds, Manchester, Birmingham, London, Bombay, Calcutta, Lahore, Cape Town, Johannesburg and Buenos Aires. By 1921, the firm employed over 1000 work people in its Leeds and allied factories. The work force was well cared for, with its own sports ground for football, cricket, tennis and the like. The firm had its own Industrial Theatre where workers put on plays.

"The first 'Industrial Theatre' in this county caters for the masses in the same way as the 'Old Vic' in London, but it really goes farther, and aspires to produce plays for working men, performed by working men, and even in some cases written by working men."

                               "TIMES," London, Nov 19th 1921.

Fig.SF01 shows the front view of the Leeds factory circa 1915 with some members of staff in attendance. Note the 'flat hats' and not a single

Simpson Fawcett Works 1915

Fig.SF01

motor car in view. The Industrial Theatre Fig.SF03 is were the workers staged plays and held weekly dances.
Fig SF02 shows a view of part of the sports facilities with the football team beside one of the pavilions.

S F Sports Facilities 1915

Fig.SF02

S F Theatre 1915

Fig.SF03

Toy production was probably started at the Leeds factory around 1908, with the amalgamation of other firms under the heading Simpson Fawcett & Co. and were marketed as **'Swan Toys'**. A catalogue from the Star Manufacturing Co. of 1916 states;

" By mutual agreement, the designs shown in this catalogue are also manufactured in Leeds by Messrs Simpson Fawcett & Co. Ltd."

Simpson Fawcett Stock Room 1915   Fig.SF04

Fig.SF04 shows the partly empty stockroom at the Leeds factory, the picture having been taken in December during the firm's busy time when most of the stock had been sold.

The 1914 range of 'Swan Toys' included many lines, some of which the name of 'toy' almost seems a misnomer. Magnificent miniature motor cars listed at up to £18, while at the other end of the range were listed 'foot cycles'. Fifty six pages of toys that included doll carriages, cycling novelties, engines, motor cars, jointed animals, wheel barrows etc., and also a comprehensive range of wooden horse toys, including **Rocking Horses, Horses and Carts, Pole and Push Horses, Tricycle Horses,** etc. In the photograph of the 'Toy Paint Shop' *Fig. SF05* a variety of the firm's products can be seen along with some members of staff as well.

Simpson Fawcett Paint Shop 1915

Fig.SF05

An interesting line from the 1914 catalogue is a **Trotting Sulky** *Fig.SF06*, the description mentions that 'a good speed can be obtained'.

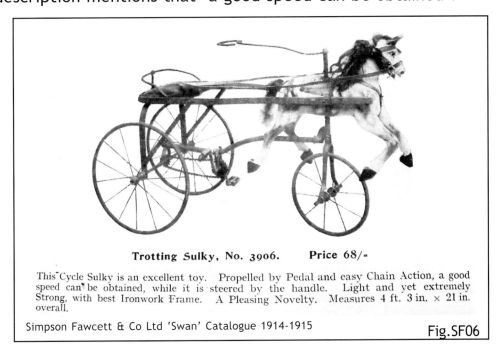

Trotting Sulky, No. 3906.   Price 68/-

This Cycle Sulky is an excellent toy. Propelled by Pedal and easy Chain Action, a good speed can be obtained, while it is steered by the handle. Light and yet extremely Strong, with best Ironwork Frame. A Pleasing Novelty. Measures 4 ft. 3 in. × 21 in. overall.

Simpson Fawcett & Co Ltd 'Swan' Catalogue 1914-1915

Fig.SF06

Simpson Fawcett exhibited their 'Swan' brand toys at various trade fairs over the years, but with changing times and tastes, the old firm was taken over by Lines Bros Ltd in 1957 mainly for the pram side of the business. Rocking horses were probably only produced up to the beginning of the Second World War.

While the company was in its heyday the quality of the firm's products were no doubt of a high standard and this is well illustrated throughout the 1914 catalogue *Fig.SFO7*. Each product was available in a variety of qualities, as illustrated by the selection of **Tricycle Horses** priced from 22/6 for the flat seated version up to 48/- for the largest 'best finish' *Fig.SF08*. With the various size and colour options, it would appear that there were 32 different models available to choose from.

There was an equally impressive choice with their range of **Rocking Horses** *Fig.SF09*. These were available in either the 'Old Style' or more commonly known as a bow rockers. There were four sizes and two qualities to choose from, but only painted in grey.
The 'Safety' or swing-stand rocking horse was available in seven sizes in the 'best' finish and in four of the smaller sizes with the ordinary finish. They were all listed with a choice of either the grey or roan colouring. Twenty two different variations in all.

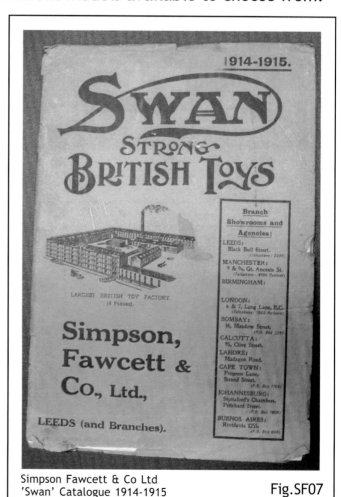

Simpson Fawcett & Co Ltd
'Swan' Catalogue 1914-1915   Fig.SF07

Swan Tricycle Horses.

No. 4052.

Tricycle Horse with Flat Seat, Leather Cloth Saddle, Rubber-tyred Wheels.

A Diam. of Wheels, 12 in., **22/6** each
B   ,,   14 in., **26/-**   ,,

No. 4050. Tricycle Horses.

The Strongest and Smartest Tricycle Horse on the market. Realistically Hand Carved from Well-seasoned Timber, Handsomely Painted in Grey, Roan, or Bay Colourings. Complete with Trappings, Glass Eyes, and Rubber-tyred Wheels. Strong Ironwork.

	To suit ages	Diam. of Wheels.	Ordinary Finish Price.	Best Finish Price.		To suit ages	Diam. of Wheels.	Ordinary Finish Price.	Best Finish Price.
O	3 to 4	12 in.	**27/6**	**31/6**	B	6 to 8	16 in.	**38/-**	**42/-**
Small A	3 to 4	12 in.	**31/-**	**34/-**	C	8 to 10	16 in.	—	**46/-**
A	4 to 6	14 in.	**34/-**	**37/6**	D	10 to 12	18 in.	—	**48/-**

31

Simpson Fawcett & Co Ltd 'Swan' Catalogue 1914-1915

Fig.SF08

Swan Rocking Horses.

No. 4054.
Old Style Rocking Horses.

Hand Carved from Well-seasoned Timber, Hand-somely Painted in Grey Colouring. Complete with Saddle, Stirrups, Reins, and Bit, and all Trappings. Rockers of ample length to prevent tipping.

	Length overall.	Height to Saddle.	Ordinary .. Finish. Price.	Best Finish Price.
O	.. 4 ft. 4½ in. ..	21½ in. ..	**23/-** ..	.. **28/-**
Small A	.. 4 ft. 6 in. ..	23 in. ..	**28/-** ..	.. **33/-**
A	.. 4 ft. 9 in. ..	24 in. ..	**33/6** ..	.. **38/6**
B	.. 5 ft. 4½ in. ..	25 in. ..	**41/-** ..	.. **49/-**

No. 4060.
Safety Rocking Horses.

Hand Carved from Well-seasoned Timber, Hand-somely Painted in Grey or Roan Colourings, and complete with Saddle, Stirrups, Reins, and Bit, and all Trappings. This pattern has the advantage of being both absolutely safe and absolutely silent, while rocking more easily and saving furniture through its position never altering.

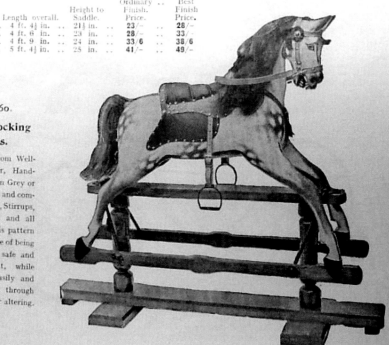

				Height to Saddle.		Length of Stand.		Ordinary Finish. Price.		Best Finish, with Padded Saddle, Extra Carving. Price.
O	..	..	..	23 in.	..	31 in.	..	**24/6**	..	**28/6**
Small A	..	..	..	27 in.	..	34 in.	..	**30/6**	..	**33/6**
A	..	..	..	27 in.	..	36 in.	..	**34/-**	..	**37/-**
B	..	..	..	29 in.	..	38½ in.	..	**40/6**	..	**43/6**
C	..	..	..	32 in.	..	46 in.	..	—	..	**62/6**
D	..	..	..	36 in.	..	54 in.	..	—	..	**87/6**
E	..	..	..	39 in.	..	58 in.	..	—	..	**120/-**

32

Simpson Fawcett & Co Ltd 'Swan' Catalogue 1914-1915

Fig.SF09

The horses were well carved and had some unique features that helps to identify this make. Horses have long ears and were made from separate pieces of timber as can be seen *Fig.SF10* below. This horse has lost all its gesso and shows how the ears were joined to the main part of the head. The bodies of the horses were made in the usual way consisting of a hollow box construction with legs being fitted with a mortise and tenon joint. Rear legs were fitted square to the body, front legs were fitted at an angle. On some models, the size letter has been found stamped onto the belly of the horse *Fig.SF11*. This letter size is also often found on the underside of the runners as well. Most horses also

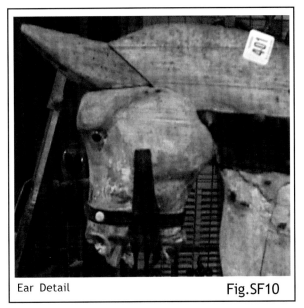

Ear Detail   Fig.SF10

have a small metal plate *Fig.SF12* which has a serial number stamped on it. The position of this metal plate varies, on some horses it is pinned on the belly while on other horses, notably the 'Bronko' version, it is fixed under the saddle.

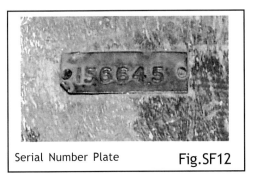

Serial Number Plate   Fig.SF12

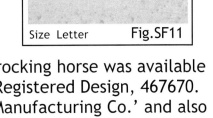

Size Letter   Fig.SF11

The **'Bronko'** version of the 'Swan' safety rocking horse was available only from A W Gamage, London and was a Registered Design, 467670. This is described in detail under the 'Star Manufacturing Co.' and also under 'A W Gamage'.

The stands of the safety rocker have a few notable identifying features, the posts are of a particular design, although there are variations according to size and quality, see Fig.SF13 and Fig.SF14 for two slightly different styles of turned post. Another feature is that the swinging irons tend to have a 'crank' bent into them near the top bar, again this can be seen in Fig.SF13.

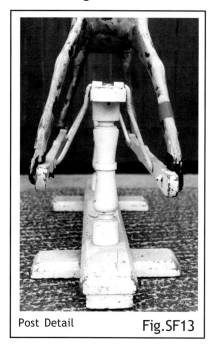

Post Detail   Fig.SF13

Post Detail   Fig.SF14

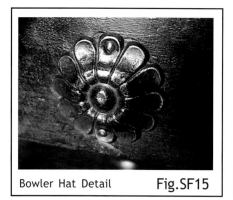

Bowler Hat Detail   Fig.SF15

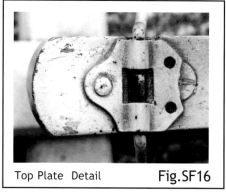

Top Plate Detail   Fig.SF16

A unique style of 'bowler hat' is fitted to most 'Swan' brand horses and is of a petal or flower design, an example is shown in Fig.SF15, however not all horses have been found with these, some horses, as in Fig.SF17 have no bowler hats at all and the swinging iron is just riveted over a washer. Top plates are usually of a three point fixing, Fig.SF16, one bolt and two screws and have not been found with any cast markings. The runners are cut to a specific shape as can be seen the catalogue illustration and also the horse shown in Fig.SF17.

The horse illustrated below in Fig.SF17 is marked with a 'C' on its belly and corresponds to the dimensions given in the 1914 catalogue, and as

'Swan' size C swing stand   Fig.SF17

such would have only been available in 'best finish' at a price of 62/6.

The small horse *Fig.SF18* is a size 'A' and an judging by the relatively plain style of carving is most likely to be an 'ordinary finish' horse. This has been over painted at some time and has lost all of its original tack.

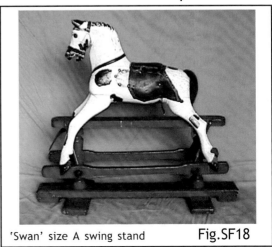

'Swan' size A swing stand   Fig.SF18

An unusual Simpson Fawcett rocking horse *Fig.SF19* is of a 'spring' type. This is based on an American patented design, taken out in 1862 by Jesse Crandall . The rear legs of the horse are attached to two large

Simpson Fawcett & Co Spring Rocking Horse circa 1890   Fig.SF19

coil springs that are in turn fixed to a cross shaft that is housed between the cast iron sides of the base. When a child sits on the horse it is with very little effort that the horse can be made to 'bounce'. This example has been restored and the horse has lost all traces of original paintwork and harness. The main frame has the firms name cast into the iron sides and reads '*Simpson Fawcett & Co Makers Leeds*'. This is very helpful in dating the horse as the firm was incorporated in 1908 and almost certainly any display of the company name after this time would include 'Ltd'. No mention of the 'spring' rocking horse has been found in any researched Simpson Fawcett documents. However, these documents did not cover the early years of the firm. It is thought that the spring horse was made around 1890 and would have been produced in reasonable numbers as to justify the casting and tooling costs.

Smeeton, Arthur.   1884 - 1899

Address: London.   See below.

Trade directory entries for Arthur Smeeton, some of which list him as a
Rocking Horse Maker are reproduced below;

  1884   Perambulator maker, 367 Bethnal Green Rd,

  1891   Perambulator maker, 367 Bethnal Green Rd, E

  1891   Rocking horse maker, 11 Hollybush Pl. Bthnl.gn.rd. E

  1895   Rocking horse maker, 469 Bethnal Green Rd. E

  1899   Rocking horse maker, 469 Bethnal Green Rd. E

Apart from the above listings nothing is known about Arthur Smeeton
except that like so many other small firms the manufacture of
perambulators seem to go hand in hand with rocking horse making. It is
also worth noting that three different addresses are recorded over a
period of fifteen years.

An uncommon surname, see also 'Smeeton, George'.

Smeeton, George.   1882 - 1910

Address: 72, Hackney Road, London.

Various London Post Office listings have been found under the heading **'Rocking Horse Makers'** for Smeeton, 72 Hackney Road and are as follows;

1882	Smeeton, George.	72 Hackney Road.
1891	Smeeton, George.	72 Hackney Road.
1895	Smeeton, George.	72 Hackney Road.
1899	Smeeton, Mrs. Mary	72 Hackney Road.
1910	Smeeton, Samuel.	72 Hackney Road.

In 1884, George Smeeton was also listed in a directory as a Perambulator maker, also at 72 Hackney Road.

Nothing further has been found out about George Smeeton, but it may be fair to assume that Mary could have been his wife, and Samuel was possibly his son?

An unusual surname, see also Smeeton, Arthur.

Smith, Jas.   -1895 - 1899-

Address: 22, Compton Street, Goswell Road, London. E.C.

Jas (James?) Smith was listed in the London Post office directories of 1895 and 1899 under the heading of **'Rocking Horse Makers'**. No other entries have been found so it is unknown if he was in business before or after these dates. No other information has been found about him or his products.

Smith, J. R.

1881 - 1916

Address: 1895   284, Kingsland Road, London. N.E.
                 1913   96,   Downham Road, London. N.E.
                 1913   397, Lockner Road, Dalston, London. N.E.
                 1913   528, Kingsland Road, London. N.E.

See Also: J R Smith Ltd. 1916-1932   J R Smith(Toys) Ltd. 1932-1938

In 1881 the firm of J R Smith was founded by Mr J R Smith senior, but around 1910 he retired and handed the business over to his two sons, Thomas and John Richard junior. In 1916 a trade publication reported that John Richard Jnr. and Thomas were the third generation in that family of wooden toy makers, but no record of their grandfather has yet come to light. In 1895 J R Smith was listed as a **'Toy Horse Maker'** at 284 Kingsland Road but it is unclear when they moved to 96 Downham Road, but this was probably around 1910. In an advert of 1913 the firm was advertising 'Strong Wooden Toys' and was illustrated with an elegant **Tricycle Horse** *Fig.SJ01*. By 1914 the firm seemed to have made rapid progress and was producing a variety of toys in some quantity.

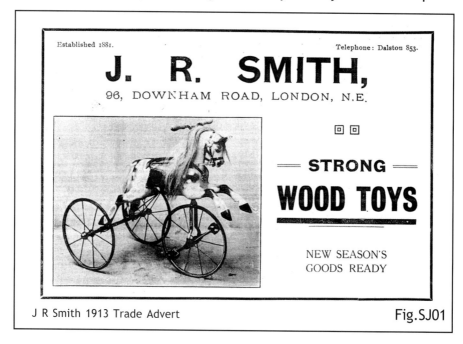

J R Smith 1913 Trade Advert   Fig.SJ01

It was reported that timber used in the manufacture of goods had been in stock at the least for two years and that there was always enough to make over one thousand **Rocking Horses**, **Cycle Horses** and similar items. They also produced **Beech Horses** and wooden engines, both in a variety of sizes as well as many other items. The Beech horses were to become one of the firms most popular lines, being one item that was manufactured throughout the existence of the company. Fig.SJ02 is a view of the beech horse department where the young ladies are working, surrounded by an enormous quantity of beech horses of all different sizes. They all appear to be in a line, and quite probably all carrying out a different task in the finishing of the horses.

Beech Horse Department 1914   Fig.SJ02

Fig.SJ03 is in the rocking horse department and what can only be described as organised chaos. Unlike the orderly scene in the 'beech horse department', there seems to be no real system at all with part-made horses all over the place and very little room for the men to actually do any work. The lad in the foreground is holding a large carving axe!

Rocking Horse Department 1914   Fig.SJ03

Whilst the growth of the firm and the busy workshops were a success story the brothers management was a completely different matter. The arrangement was that Thomas supervised the Works and John looked after the books, sales and the dispatch of goods. In 1913 they had borrowed money from their father and increased their turnover from about £800 up to around £7000 but were in three years arrears of rent to him. In 1913 they took up making baby carriages at 528 Kingsland Road, this production was supposed to occupy the slack period from Christmas to August, but unfortunately this enterprise lost money. They did however make some repayment of their debts but with the outbreak of the War things took a turn for the worse. The majority of their staff, they employed 45 men, went to The Front, and the cost of raw materials increased dramatically. There were disagreements between the two brothers and John was not giving the business his full attention. By 1916 things had come to a head, and the brothers agreed that something had to be done as they were being pursued by a great number of creditors.

So, the brothers registered J R Smith Ltd. on June 13th 1916, this company acquired the former firm of J R Smith but did not take over any of the old firms debts, they didn't even inform their creditors of the intention to form the company. Shortly after this John walked out of the business and joined the army.

It is not known what became of him or if he survived the War. Meanwhile Thomas continued running the new company of J R Smith Ltd. This period is covered in a separate chapter.

J R Smith 1914 Trade Advert   Fig.SJ04

The actual products that were produced by the old firm, some of them are listed in an 1914 advert *Fig.SJ04* were generally of good quality.

An illustration from circa 1914 *Fig.SJ05* shows a medium size dapple grey swing-stand **Rocking Horse**. These were made in at least four different sizes and also available in other colours, such as *Fig SJ06* a chestnut variation. These were also offered by other rocking horse makers at the same time but were nowhere near as popular as the dapple grey. The chestnut horse pictured has a pommel hole on the left hand side of the saddle, but none on the right hand side. This feature has been found on other J R Smith horses, while some have no pommel holes at all, others have been found with one each side.

J R Smith 1914 Trade Advert   Fig.SJ05

J R Smith Chestnut Rocking Horse Circa 1912   Fig SJ06

Other variations included a swing stand horse fitted with end chairs *Fig.SJ07* often referred to as **Nursery Rockers,** the chairs were made from bent bamboo, this was a popular material of the day. Some swing stand horses had an unusual arrangement for the swing irons. These were fitted in a vertical position, making the rider have to put in a far greater effort as opposed to horses fitted with swing irons set at an angle. A horse with the 'vertical' swing irons is pictured below *Fig.SJ08.*

J R Smith Nursery Rocker Circa 1914   Fig.SJ07

J R Smith With Vertical Swinging Irons   Fig.SJ08

There seemed to be constant changes with J R Smith horses as another unusual feature on some horses was the way that the top brackets were aligned. Typically they were the same one bolt and two screw design as G&J Lines, some have even been found with Lines casting marks. Others were fitted with the bolt end facing inwards as shown in Fig.SJ09. Posts were generally turned to a standard pattern and the hooves of the horse were not notched on to the runners. See also Fig.SJ09. Again some horses were fitted with bowler hats over the ends of the swinging irons while others were left with the cotter pin fixing exposed.

Post & Swing Iron & Bracket Detail   Fig.SJ09

Bow Rocking Horses were also produced for a while, an example can be seen in Fig.SJ10.

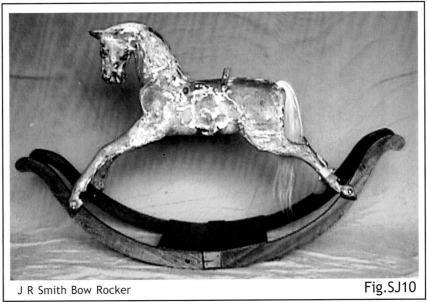

J R Smith Bow Rocker   Fig.SJ10

Push Horses and Pull Horses were produced by J R Smith up to 1916. A trade advert of 1914 *Fig.SJ11* shows an example of each type. They are painted dapple grey and fitted with real hair mane and tails.

J R Smith 1914 Trade Advert   Fig.SJ11

Fig.SJ12 is a **Tricycle Horse** made around 1912. It was supplied by the retail store of A W Gamage as can be seen by the brass applied label in Fig.SJ13. The horse had replacement wheels fitted in the 1990's.

J R Smith Tricycle Horse circa 1912   Fig.SJ12

A W Gamage applied label

Fig.SJ13

A 'tinted' period photograph *Fig.SJ14* that was postmarked in 1911 shows a horse was used as a studio prop, the rear swinging iron has been tied to the post so as to stop the rider 'rocking' about while their picture was being taken. The horse appears to be in a new condition and as it would have been on leaving J R Smith's workshop around 1910.

J R Smith Swing Stand Rocking Horse circa 1910   Fig.SJ14

Smith Ltd., J. R.   1916 - 1932

Smith(Toys) Ltd. J.R.   1932 - 1938

Address: 1916   96, Downham Road, London.

              1921   329, Hoxton Street, London.

Incorporated: J R Smith Ltd.   June 1916.   Company No.144,675

Incorporated: J R Smith(Toys) Ltd. June 1932. Company No. 265,844

See Also: J R Smith 1881-1916

1916 was a significant time when J R Smith Ltd. was formed from the old and recently declared bankrupt firm of J R Smith. The two Smith brothers who ran the old firm had fallen out and the finances were in a mess. So the new firm was created leaving their debts behind. Almost immediately John walked out and joined the army and left Thomas running the new company. It would seem that he was better off on his own because before long the order books were full and business was on the up. The range of items that were produced had also changed. **Beech Horses** *Fig.SL01* continued to be produced in a variety of sizes as well as the old favourites like engines and barrows. With the increase in business, a new and much larger premises was acquired at 329 Hoxton Street in North London.

J R Smith Ltd 1924 Trade Advert   Fig.SL01

The new factory was equipped with the latest machinery and over the main entrance was hung a large sign *"J R Smith Ltd. Wood Toy Makers"*. Since the new limited company was formed no mention of rocking or tricycle horses has been found, so its almost certain that they were not produced after 1916. However, other new lines were introduced over the years and in 1926 an ingenious novelty for very young children was exhibited at the British Industries Fair in London. This new invention was called **"Ride-a-Cock-Horse"** and it took the form of a stool horse, only it was made to fit over the knee of an adult. The base fitted comfortably on the knee and strong springs were attached to the horse so that when the knee was moved up and down, it gave the child the notion it was riding a real horse. It was made in two sizes but unfortunately we have no illustration. Other new items subsequently produced were toy forts in 1931 and dolls houses in 1932. Cricket bats and cricket sets were also popular lines that were made from around 1916. The firm did have a setback in 1928 when a fire broke out in an adjoining factory, some 150 firemen were needed and the principle damage to Smith's was water related.

Mr Tom Smith   Fig.SL02

In 1932 the firm's title changed again to J R Smith(Toys) Ltd., the reason for this is not clear but may have been financial. In 1934 Mr Tom Smith *Fig.SL02* became very ill and died aged just 47 under tragic circumstances. An autopsy revealed his cause of death as asphyxia from coal gas poisoning. He had previously mentioned to his wife that the pain and troubles were getting too much. Though the driving force of the firm had gone, his wife and son Eric took over and continued running things. Sadly during the next four years things had not gone well and in 1938 the company went into receivership, subsequently ceasing trading after 57 eventful years.

Smith & Son's. W.H. -1916-

Address: Factory: Toyland, Norfolk Street, Shelton, Stoke-on-Trent.

            Office: 9 & 11, Lovatt St. Stoke-on-Trent, Staffordshire.

A trade magazine of 1916 reported that on the initiative of George Henry Buckmaster, manager of the local (Shelton) branch of W.H.Smith & Son, a 'new enterprise' was to be set up. This 'new enterprise' was also mentioned in a trade advert *Fig.SA01* and worded:

'New enterprise'. To keep out German Toys and have established a large Toy Factory in Staffordshire with pleasing address.

A description worded like this today would probably cause some objection, but during the Great War things were a little different.

The firm listed many items within their range including dolls in various styles, teddy bears, a large selection of cloth toys and a wide selection of wooden toys, including engines, wheelbarrows, scooters, mail carts and **Beech horses.**

No further reference has been found in relation to the 'new enterprise'.

From 1916 Trade advert   Fig.SA01

Spooner. C.J.   1892 - 1930

Address: 1892   Swan Works, Burton-on-Trent, Staffordshire.

                     1900   Meadow Road, Burton-on-Trent, Staffordshire.

Charles Spooner was primarily a maker of fairground horses, he was regarded as one of the most inventive of the showman's carver, producing some of the finest menagerie figures of the day.

His career started when he was apprenticed to the carver Walter Hilton where he learnt the rudiments of the trade. After three years he left and set up his own business at his late fathers premises at the Swan Hotel. He changed the name to the Swan Works and commenced producing carved work of all kinds, especially for showmen. His business went well and by 1900 he had moved to a larger site at Meadow Road. He married into the Orton family and after some years, in 1925, the two firms officially merged.

Certainly while Spooner was at the Swan Works, two sizes of swing stand **Rocking Horses** were produced, most likely as a sideline. They were reasonably conventional with the exception of the heads. These were carved with a tendency to resemble the fairground gallopers that were produced at the time. The rocking horses were painted as dapple greys and fitted with fixed leather saddles. The leather bridles were also fixed. Real hair, probably cow, was used for the manes and tails. The stands for the horses had turned posts, but the swinging irons were quite short. Due to this the runners were proportionally quite high up which gave the impression of the horse looking a little top heavy. With the short swinging irons, the 'rock' would have been quite poor, a long iron gives a much better swing.
Spooner is also recorded as producing **Push Horses**, these were dappled and had real hair manes and tails.

It is not known for how long or how many rocking horses were produced by Spooner.

Sports & Hobbies -1913 - 1917-

Address: Daybrook, Nottingham.

Little is known about Messrs. Sports & Hobbies apart from two entries in Nottingham trade directories of 1913 and 1915 where they are listed as sports manufacturers. Their full address is not even known, Daybrook is on the northern outskirts of Nottingham.

The only other known reference was in a toy trade publication states;

Rocking Horses, wheel horses and *Hobby Horse Cycles* were included in the range from Messrs. Sports & Hobbies.

This reference was part of a report about Toy Horses that were exhibited at a 1917 trade fair in London. No further record has been found in connection with Messrs. Sports & Hobbies.

Star Manufacturing Co.   1887 - 1957

Address: Factory,   Davies Street, Cubitt Town, London. E.
            Show room,   6&7, Long Lane, Aldersgate, London, EC.

Affiliation: Simpson, Fawcett & Co. Leeds

Trade Name: 'Swan' Toys.   See also: Gamages 'Bronko'.

The Star Manufacturing Co. originally started at Goodinge Road, London in 1887 by making baby carriages and from this easily progressed to producing dolls prams. By doing this, it introduced the firm to the toy trade with the result that they were asked to make other items for toy buyers. Gradually the manufacture was extended to include practically a full range of strong toys that included a variety of shaped horses in the style of **Tricycle Horses**, **Rocking Horses and Pole Horses**, other items also made were **Push Horses**, **Horses and Carts**, **Stool Horses** etc. With the introduction of motoring, there was a demand for toy cars and the firm very soon produced some very elaborate models of juvenile motors and these represented some of the best finished in the country. Below is an illustration of the cover *Fig.SM01* of their catalogue c.1890 and a Post Office trade directory entry from 1910 *Fig.SM02*.

Star Catalogue c.1890   Fig.SM01

Star Directory Entry 1910   Fig.SM02

The premises at Cubitt Town, (now Tower Hamlets on the Isle of Dogs), appear to have been spacious and with various departments for the different tasks involved in toy making. Below is a general view *Fig.SM03* of the factory and a view of the 'shaped horses department' *Fig.SM04*.

Star Manufacturing Co. General view of Factory circa 1919   Fig.SM03

The department appears to be a well lit, very busy and productive area with quantities of part-made horse bodies stacked on the left of the shot and a pile of heads to the right. Different workmen can be seen shaping some of the various components prior to the horses being assembled. Obviously this was the most cost effective means of production and in all there were fourteen people in this picture, note the ladies up in the loft area. Tricycle, push, cart and safety are some of the different horses included in the picture.

From about 1908 the Star Manufacturing Company was affiliated with the firm Simpson Fawcett & Co Ltd. They produced toys under the trade name of '**Swan Toys**' and in their 1916 catalogue it states,

" *By mutual agreement, the designs shown in this catalogue are also manufactured in Leeds by Messrs Simpson Fawcett & Co. Ltd.* " .

Shaped Horse Department circa 1919   Fig.SM04

'Swan' toys were displayed at many of the leading trade fairs and became recognised for their craftsmanship and quality. One of the

earliest 'horses' to be illustrated was the **'Star' Tricycle Horse** *Fig.SM05* in their 1890 catalogue. Interestingly, the same illustration appears in the 1902 catalogue of the Perambulator & Manufacturing Co. It is not known if there were any business links between the two firms. Figs.SM06-09 are illustrations from the Swan brochure of 1915 and show some of the range of toys produced. Other examples can be seen under the 'Simpson Fawcett' chapter including illustrations of the swing stand rocking horse and some contemporary pictures.

Tricycle Horse 1890   Fig.SM05

1915 - 1916 Swan Catalogue   **Fig.SM06**

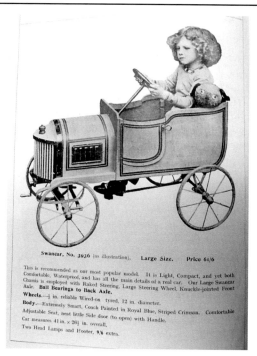

Swancar, No. 3936 (as illustration).   **Large Size.**   **Price 61/6**

This is recommended as our most popular model. It is Light, Compact, and yet both Comfortable, Waterproof, and has all the main details of a real car. Our Large Swancar Chassis is employed with Raked Steering, Large Steering Wheel, Knuckle-jointed Front Axle. **Ball Bearings to Back Axle.**

Wheels.—½ in. reliable Wired-on tyred, 12 in. diameter.

Body.—Extremely Smart, Coach Painted in Royal Blue, Striped Crimson. Comfortable Adjustable Seat, neat little Side door (to open) with Handle. Car measures 41 in. × 26½ in. overall.

Two Head Lamps and Hooter, **9/6** extra.

1915 - 1916   Swan Catalogue   **Fig.SM07**

1915 - 1916   Swan Catalogue   **Fig.SM08**

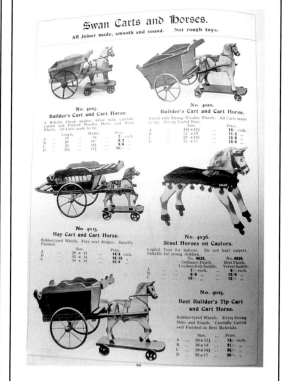

1915 - 1916   Swan Catalogue   **Fig.SM09**

The **'Bronko'** rocking horse was based on the 'Swan' safety stand horse but with various modifications based on A W Gamages specification. The Registered Design No. 467,670 was dated 23rd October 1905 and was extended on the 1st October 1910 for probably another five years. Below is Gamages 1913 catalogue illustration *Fig.SM10* that shows the 'Bronko' registered design is still in force.

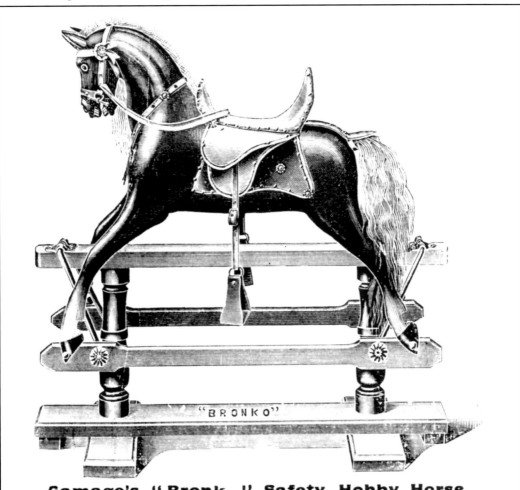

Gamage's " Bronk " Safety Hobby Horse.

Registered No. Ty. 467,670. This horse is specially constructed our **own** designs. Fitted with cowboy saddle and stirrups, which not only give it an elegant appearance, but render it a much safer horse for a child than the old style. Made in four sizes.

No. B .. **34/6** No. C, **42/6** No. D, **63**/- No. E, **75**/-
Hei. to saddle, 27½ in.   31½ in.   36½ in.   40½ in.
Len. of stand, 36½ in.   44 in.   52 in.   57½ in.

1913 Catalogue Gamages Bronko

Fig.SM10

However by 1924 the description had dropped the 467,670 registration number and was shown as being available in only two sizes *Fig.SM11*. The main difference between the standard horse and a 'Bronko' was the addition of a high back cowboy saddle and leather type cowboy stirrups. Examples of 'Bronko' horses turn up quite rarely, presumably it must not have been a very popular model. These horses have all had a small metal plate, stamped with a serial number, pinned underneath the saddle. The registered number has also been found marked on the leather saddle flaps of the horse. As with the standard model of horse, the Bronko stand also has the same distinguishing features which are fully described in the

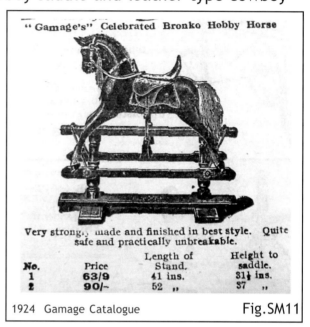

"Gamage's" Celebrated Bronko Hobby Horse

Very strong, made and finished in best style. Quite safe and practically unbreakable.

No.	Price	Length of Stand.	Height to saddle.
1	63/9	41 ins.	31¼ ins.
2	90/-	52 ,,	37 ,,

1924 Gamage Catalogue | Fig.SM11

Simpson Fawcett chapter. An illustration from a 1912 Star Manufacturing Co catalogue *Fig.SM12* shows the standard 'Safety Rocking Horse'

A restored example of a 'Bronko' size 'D' horse *Fig.SM13* has a small A W Gamage label affixed to the stand. A common practice that allowed the supplier or retailer to put their name in front of the buying public. Other pictures show details of the leather 'cowboy' stirrup and the type of decorative nail

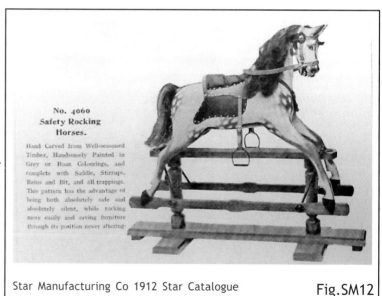

No. 4060
Safety Rocking Horses.

Hand Carved from Well-seasoned Timber, Handsomely Painted in Grey or Roan Colourings, and complete with Saddle, Stirrups, Reins and Bit, and all trappings. This pattern has the advantage of being both absolutely safe and absolutely silent, while rocking more easily and saving furniture through its position never altering.

Star Manufacturing Co 1912 Star Catalogue | Fig.SM12

often found on 'Bronko' horses *Fig.SM14*.

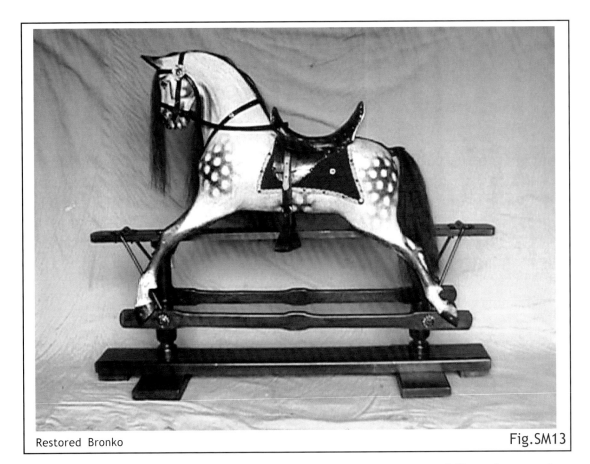

Restored Bronko   Fig.SM13

Below, details of A W Gamage label, leather stirrup and fine decorative nail *Fig.SM14* as found on the restored 'Bronko' in Fig.SM13 above.

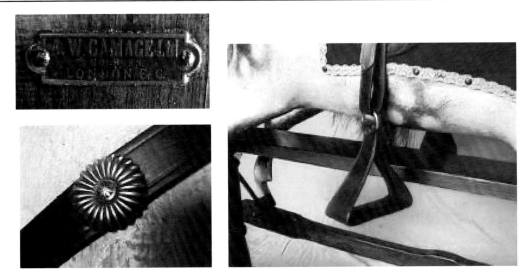

Detail of A W Gamage Label, Decorative Nail and Stirrup   Fig.SM14

Star Yacht Works.   -1931 - 1941-

Address: Marion Street, Birkenhead, Wirral.

Thought to have been set up around 1931, the Star Yacht Works was owned by a Mr F Deyne who was mainly interested in the production of model yachts and model speed boats, for which he had gained a good reputation. However, the firm did produce a variety of other goods, and in 1934 introduced the **"Star" Spring Horse** *Fig.ST01.*

From 1934 Trade Catalogue   Fig.ST01

The 'spring' horse was available in two sizes, these retailed at 10/6 and 14/6. The smaller was suitable for a child of up to three years, the larger up to about seven years. They were described as *'being able to be rocked with confidence and a minimum of effort due to the easy spring motion'*. They appeared to be well produced and advertised as *'daintily enamelled in white and finished with pale blue or orange'*.

Steam Rocking Hobby-Horse Co. Ltd.
1886 - 1891

Registered Office: 1886. 1, Green Street East, Over Darwen, Lancs.

1887. Bank Chambers, Market Square, Over Darwen.

Incorporated: 21st May 1886.   Company No.22,659

Although not a manufacturer of rocking horses, but with the name 'The Steam Rocking Hobby Horse Company Limited', the firm had to be listed.
The Company was set up for the purpose;

' to bring before and introduce to the public the latest improvements in "**Hobby Horses**" or "**Roundabouts**",

and was established with a capital sum of £1,600. The notion was to build roundabouts and hire them out as a money making venture. Messrs. Ambrose Porter and Walter Wilkinson being the two main inventors of, and having the sole Patent right to the Steam Rocking Hobby Horse, must be permanent Directors of the Company.
Below is a letter head for the company *Fig.SR01* dated March 7th 1887.

1887 Letter Head   Fig.SR01

Unfortunately the Company was wound up in April of 1891.

Sykes, William & Co. Ltd   1875 - 1950

Address: Horbury, Yorkshire.

Trade Name: 'Trojan'

See also: F H Ayres Ltd.   Ayres Sports Goods Ltd.

William Sykes started his career as an apprentice saddler, this completed he became a journeyman saddler for his master. Not satisfied with this and at the age of 23 took a gamble on buying the saddler's business for £19. After only a few successful months of trading he was in profit of exactly £1, in four crown pieces, which he decided to keep safe so that he would always be worth at least a £1. They were found amongst his personal effects after his death in 1910.

William Sykes' business was initially based on leather goods, some of the very first footballs originated from his workshops, but many other sporting lines were added over time and the company grew to become one of the principle sports goods manufacturers, along side other leading firms such as Ayres, Slazengers and Gradidges.

Toys were to become part of Sykes' ever growing business around 1937, with the introduction of their own brand of wooden toys under the trade name 'Trojan Toys'. This was further enhanced by the acquisition of the toy manufacturer Dunham White & Co Ltd. London, who were manufacturers of metal toys. Both the wood and metal toys would be marketed through Dunham White and sales were to be handled through London agents, J K Farnell & Co. for the wooden 'Trojan' toys and Alec Cohen & Randall handled the sales of the metal toys. In 1938 the range of Trojan toys was described as being comprehensive, and special mention was made of **Swing Horses**. The report stated;

These are very strongly made and will bear the weight of an adult. The woodwork is well finished and the upholstery is of bright washable American cloth in various colours. There is a small size for children under five, and what is particularly noticeable is that the upholstery is chosen to harmonise with the colour of the stand. An important point is the fact that the head can be detached for packing.

Accompanying this description is an illustration *Fig.SY01* of what is
thought to be the swing stand
described. Unfortunately the
illustration is black and white
so we are unable to see if the
upholstery does harmonise with
the colour of the stand. Also in
the range of Trojan toys are
small **Stool horses** which have
an American cloth body top and
were to retail from 3s 11d.
Many other toys were also being
produced, such as wagons,
lorries, vans etc.

From 1938 Trade Advert   Fig.SY01

The article also goes on to mention that **Shaped Rocking Horses** of the
old familiar type are to be made and would be available by the time the
article was published (May 1938). These were to be new models
available in a variety of sizes. It is probable that Sykes are intimating
that the soon to be acquired Ayres concern is to be the source of these
horses, the actual takeover was not until early 1940, Ayres Sports Goods
Ltd, the newly formed Sykes subsidiary, was incorporated in April 1940.
The shaped horses mentioned above are those which have applied
'F H Ayres' transfers *Fig.SY02* on the top of the stands as the horse in
Fig.SY03. Horses were initially produced in three sizes and a skin
covered option was also available. Sykes had acquired amongst other

Post War Trade Mark   Fig.SY02

Post War Rocking Horse   Fig.SY03

things, the trademarks of F H Ayres Ltd., so it made perfect sense to
label the item with the most appropriate trade name. A merger of this
size would have taken some time to organise, and talks would have
begun months if not years in advance.

In 1942, the Sykes and Ayres merger was in turn taken over by Slazengers who previously in 1902 had taken the supply of tennis balls for Wimbledon away from Ayres. Despite these mergers, the different trade names were still applied to the relative products up to around 1950 so as to maximise sales of a known brand. Sykes had paid £100 for the trademarks and patents of F H Ayres.

During the war the old Ayres factory at 111 Aldersgate Street was destroyed in the Blitz so production was moved up to Horbury in Yorkshire, this was left in peace away from the attention of Hitler's bombers. The main reason behind the mergers between Ayres, Sykes, Slazengers and their subsidiaries was for the ever growing market in sporting goods for tennis, golf, cricket etc. The production of rocking horses and a few other oddities like billiard tables were purely a sideline in a now multi million pound business for in 1952 Slazengers had annual sales of £2.5 million. In 1950 Sykes' Horbury workshops stopped the production of billiard tables and rocking horses but continued to expand the production of sports goods. It is thought that the production of their Trojan range of toys also ceased at around this time as well, allowing the company to concentrate on the production of sports goods. Ayres Sports Goods Ltd continued trading to the mid 1980's. Some of the last produced rocking horses, still bearing the *F H Ayres* name, were sold through the prestigious London firm of Harrods. Needless to say, it is pretty sure Harrods sports department was also full of sports goods with the Ayres name.

The 1949 export list *Fig.SY04* had all four of names of the 'group' and still listed rocking horses *Fig.SY05*.

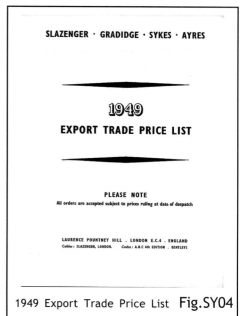

ROCKING HORSES

29003 Beautifully finished hand carved models mounted on firm wooden stands and suitable for children between the ages of 5 and 12. Approximate sizes : Floor to saddle, 30 in. ; Length of body excluding head, 21½ in.
PAINTED WOODEN ..   ..   .. 130/- ea.

29014 SKIN COVERED ..   ..   .. 180/- ea.

1949 Rocking Horse List   Fig.SY05

SLAZENGER · GRADIDGE · SYKES · AYRES

1949

EXPORT TRADE PRICE LIST

PLEASE NOTE
All orders are accepted subject to prices ruling at date of despatch

LAURENCE POUNTNEY HILL . LONDON E.C.4 . ENGLAND
Cables : SLAZENGER, LONDON.   Codes : A.B.C 6th EDITION . BENTLEYS

1949 Export Trade Price List Fig.SY04

460

Tan-Sad Ltd.   1921 - 1983

Address: 1, Albert Street, Birmingham.

                  9, Phoenix Place, Mount Pleasant, London. W.C.1.

Trade Mark: 'TAN-SAD'.

Incorporated: 1921 Tan-Sad Ltd.   Company No.179,354
Changed name: 1969 Tan-Sad Allwin Ltd.   Dissolved April 1983.

Tan-Sad Ltd. were primarily manufacturers of wheeled toys such as
scooters, prams, bicycles, pedal cars and many other items. They did
however also make some horse related items, **'Tishy'** *Fig.TS01* was a
pedal trike introduced in 1926.

From 1926 Trade Advert   Fig.TS01

"TIPPERARY TIM"

A new and wonderful toy with realistic action.
This is no ordinary pedal-driven horse but
one that runs with realistic galloping movement, the rider posting in the saddle exactly
as a horseman would on a real live horse.
This is a toy which will irresistibly appeal to
the imagination of children, and sell at sight.
PRICE 52/6.

From 1928 Trade Advert   Fig.TS02

A couple of years later,
'Tipperary Tim' *Fig.TS02*
was introduced. This was also
a wheel based toy but was
reported as having a 'realistic
galloping movement' and it was
noted in the trade press that a
couple of these had been
supplied to the Royal Family.

461

Tan-Sad also made a range of **Stool Horses** *Fig.TS03*. They were available in three sizes, 13", 15", and 17.5" in length. They had wheels fitted to the legs and the seats were covered in leather cloth.

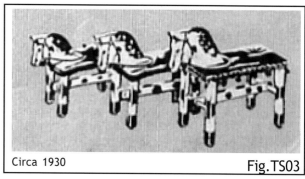

Circa 1930

Fig.TS03

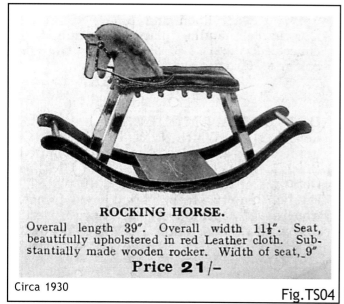

ROCKING HORSE.
Overall length 39". Overall width 11½". Seat, beautifully upholstered in red Leather cloth. Substantially made wooden rocker. Width of seat, 9"

Price 21/-

Circa 1930

Fig.TS04

A regular type of simple **Bow Rocking Horse** was also produced, but in one size only *Fig.TS04*. This would appear to share many components with the stool horse above.

In 1933 the **'Galloper' Rocking Horse** was introduced *Fig.TS05* , patent No.380,611 it was described as;
'An entirely new type of rocking horse which moves forward with a natural realistic action. No mechanical parts to break or get out of order.'
In 1948, a member of Tan-Sad's staff, Mr Joseph Bennett was awarded the 'British Empire Medal' (Civil Division).

In 1983 Tan-Sad Allwin Ltd were struck off the Companies register.

"GALLOPER"

From 1933 Trade Advert

Fig.TS05

Taylor, John & James.   -1807 - 1844-

Address: 2, Shoemaker Row, Black Fryers, London.

See also: Thomas Taylor.

Following on from a reference in 1807 to 'Taylor and Son', it is
presumed that either John or James was the 'Son' referred to.
The address at Shoemakers Row is constant throughout all of the Taylor
references.
In 1821,a Sun Assurance document read as follows;

> *19th November 1821 James TAYLOR   Policy 985569*
> *"James Taylor of N 2 Wellington*
>   *Place Albany road Camberwell Gent*
>   *On a house only N 2 Shoemaker row Blackfriars*
>   *in tenure of a rockinghorse maker. Brick*
>   *& timber Six hundred pounds ----------------------"*

This is a little curious as James Taylor is not resident at Shoemaker
Row, but at Wellington Place. Further directory listings for J & J Taylor,
'Rocking Horse Makers' have been found for 1839 and 1841. John Taylor
died in 1844 and no further mention of Taylors has been found.
Fig.TR01 shows a trade card for J & J Taylor c.1822.

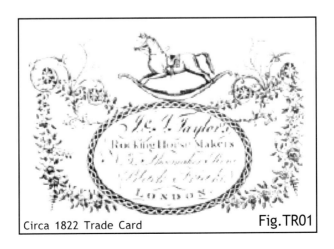

Circa 1822 Trade Card   Fig.TR01

Taylor, Thomas.   -1798 - 1807-

Address: 2, Shoemaker Row, Black Fryers, London

See also: John & James Taylor.   William Dungate.

One of the earliest records of a **Rocking Horse Maker** is that of Thomas Taylor, when on April 29th 1798, it was recorded in the Chislehurst Parish Records, 'Order of Vestry Book 1796-1819' that;

> *'And whereas William Dungate is to be bound apprentice to Thomas Taylor of Shoemaker Row Black Fryers, Rocking Horse Maker'.*

In essence this was a record that William Dungate who was resident in the parish was to serve an apprenticeship under the tutelage of Thomas Taylor. A payment of £5 was made by the parish from a charity set up by Sir Philip Warwick to Thomas Taylor. Apprenticeships at this time were not uncommon and helped ease what may have been a local employment problem by relocating parish residents to areas of gainful employment.

It would be reasonable to assume that Thomas Taylor had been trading for some time before 1798, as he was noted and skilled enough to take on an apprentice.

A later mention of Thomas Taylor was from around 1806;

'Taylor and Son, rocking-horse-makers, 2, Shoemaker Row, Blackfriars.'

Other subsequent mentions of the name Taylor at Shoemaker Row are in the names of John & James, one of which is being referred to in the reference to 'Son'.

The type of rocking horse that was being made by Thomas Taylor would have been the 'bow rocker' as the swing-stand was not introduced until 1880.

Technigraphic (Bristol) Ltd.　　　c.1950

Address:　　　　　　Hampton Lane, Bristol. 6.

The **Rocking Horse 'Winner'** was a small self assembly kit that was available for 24/6. Figs.TT01 & TT02 show a small coupon that was probably handed out at a trade show, this being coupon 513. It is thought to date from around 1950. No other record of the firm has been found.

Circa 1950 Trade Coupon　　　　　　　　　　　　　　　　Fig.TT01

Circa 1950 Trade Coupon　　　　　　　　　　　　　　　　Fig.TT02

Thorp, J & T.   1865 - 1915-

Address: Radium Street, (Late German Street.!) Manchester.

This long running firm was originally founded by a Mr John Thorp who subsequently went into partnership with his brother Thomas. John died in 1887 and the firm passed in its entirety to Thomas. He was subsequently succeeded upon his death in 1914 by his three sons, Thomas jnr, Henry, and Walter. It was noted that Thomas Senior had been a city magistrate for some six years prior to his death. A wonderful illustration *Fig.TP01* shows the extent of the premises, although initially only a part of one 'mill' was occupied, but over time the adjoining mills were incorporated for use by the firm.
In the foreground of the illustration is a horse and cart carrying two **Bow Rocking Horses** *Fig.TP02*, off to some lucky children.

J. & T. THORP, MANCHESTER: EXTERIOR VIEW OF PREMISES.

J & T Thorpe. Manchester. circa 1900   Fig.TP01

Detail of Two Bow Rockers on Cart   Fig.TP02

Within these buildings all the various processes of toy making were
carried out. The ground floor of the main building housed the saw mill
where timber was reduced to size for all the various toys that the firm
produced. Many items, including rocking horse bodies and beech horses
were made by skilled men, but some of the other departments were
staffed by women and children. Fig TP03 shows a view of the painting

J & T Thorpe. Paint Shop 1915   Fig.TP03

shop and in the background a line of **Beech Horses** can be seen. This and subsequent pictures were taken in 1915 and up till then the firm had employed up to 70 hands, but with the recent onset of the war many of the staff had enlisted in the armed services. It is not known if women and children usually made up part of the work force or if this was because of the shortage of workmen during the war. The firm produced a wide variety of toys, some of these being barrows, engines, dolls prams, bassinettes, mail carts, and many more.

J & T Thorpe. Fitting Shop 1915   Fig.TP04

A line, two dozen in fact, of small shaped horses that would probably have been either **Push** or **Pull Horses** can be seen *Fig.TP04* in the picture above. This picture was taken in one of the 'fitting' rooms where any ironwork would have been applied to the relative item. The firm had its own 'smithy' where all of the necessary iron components would have been made for their entire range of products. Thorps produced a very comprehensive range of horse based products of all sizes and these are listed as follows:-

The simple **Victoria Horse and Cart** in three sizes.
The **Alexandra Horse and Hay Cart** in two sizes.
A **Swivel Cart and Horse.**
A **Victoria Pole Cart and Horse.**
A **London Tip-Cart and Horse** *Fig. TP05* in three sizes.

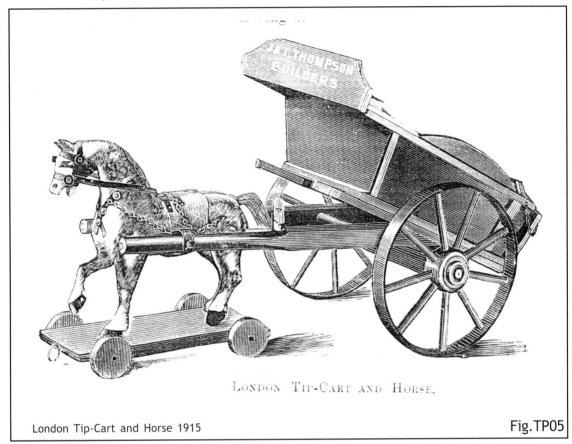

LONDON TIP-CART AND HORSE.

London Tip-Cart and Horse 1915   Fig. TP05

A **Rail cart and Horse** in three sizes.
An **Extra Large Cart and Horse** in three sizes.
A **Toy Hurry and Horse.**
Plain Varnished Horses in two popular sizes.
Plain Varnished Horses in three large sizes.
Shaped Horses through a series of sizes, also available with a superior finish and fitted with rubber-tyred wheels in four sizes.
Stepping Horses in three sizes.
Hobby Horses, Stool Horses, Perambulator Horses, Perambulator Chair and Horse. Tricycle Horses available either shaped or flatback.
Safety Swing Horses and **Rocking Horses** *Fig. TP06*. These being the old fashioned style of 'bow' rocking horses.

The illustration below of the old style bow rocking horse shows that they were made to a good standard with attention to detail, such as

Bow Rocker 1915

Fig.TP06

adjustable stirrup leathers and buckled reins and a generally neat appearance. None of the many and varied items that have been produced by Thorps have been formally identified and it is not known how long Thorps continued in business after 1915, this being the last known record of the firm.

Trebeck, T. F.   -1851 - 1852-

Address: 3, Sun Street, Bishopsgate, London.

Thomas Fred Trebeck was listed under the heading 'Miscellaneous Manufactures and Small Wares' at the 1851 Great Exhibition and his entry *Fig.TK01* mentions 'A variety of **Rocking Horses**, dolls and miscellaneous toys.

200 TREBECK, T. F. 3 Sun St. Bishopsgate.—A variety of rocking-horses, dolls, and miscellaneous toys.

From 1851 Great Exhibition Catalogue   Fig.TK01

Only one directory entry has been found for T F Trebeck and that was in a Post Office directory of 1852, which states;

Trebeck Thos Fred. toy & fancy goods importer. 3 Sun St Bishopsgate

It is unknown whether he was a manufacturer at all, or if he just dealt as an agent for other manufacturers goods.

Troy Toy Mfg. Co. Ltd.   1934 - 1936

Address: 165/167, Moorgate Street, London. E.C.2.

Introduced in early 1934 with much fanfare was the **"Troy" Toy Horse**
Fig TY01 that was claimed could do everything that a real horse can do
except bite. With no mechanism or pedals it was still able to move
forward, also to the left and the right. However, despite the claims and
the advertising, the company went into receivership in March 1936.

From 1934 Trade Advert   Fig.TY01

One of the company's last adverts *Fig TY02* mentions 'new models'. Sadly it does not say exactly what the new models are although it is most likely that they are updated versions of the Troy Toy Horse. The Troy Toy Horse was also advertised with being protected by a patent, No.949-34. However despite various searches it has not been traced.

The

"TROY" ▬ • •

TOY HORSE

goes globe-trotting!

We have received orders and enquiries from every corner of the world for The "Troy" Toy Horse. It is the kind of toy that sells well anywhere and at any time—because it is "alive." It does everything that a real horse can do—yet has no mechanism to get out of order and no pedals to strain young legs. Moves forward, to the right or to the left, at a pull of the corresponding rein.

Have you seen our *NEW MODELS?*

EARLY ORDERING is ESSENTIAL TO ENSURE PROMPT DELIVERY

Send for further particulars to

THE TROY TOY MFG. CO. LTD.

167 MOORGATE ST., LONDON, E.C.2

Telephone: Metropolitan 3291

From 1934 Trade Advert

Fig TY02

Turnbull & Co., C. E.　　　1875 - 1982

Address:　　　1884　　5, Charterhouse Buildings, London. E.C.
　　　　　　　　1921　　St John's House, Clerkenwell, London. E.C.
　　　　　　　　1945　　4, Bevis Marks, Bishopsgate, London. E.C.

Incorporated: 1921. C.E.Turnbull & Co. Ltd. Company No. 175,498.

Little is known of the firm C E Turnbull, but it was reported that by the early 1890's they were the largest specialised toy wholesalers in the country. This may however, have been the result of the changing ways in which Business Directories attempted to define their categories.

In the 'Athletic Sports and Pastimes' of 1896, it was reported that;
　　　　　'a very attractive line of toy horses and donkeys has been prepared by Messrs. C E Turnbull & Co. These are well and strongly made, and finished in first class style. The **Pegasus Rocking Horses** with American rockers are supplied in two qualities and are remarkably well turned out at the price, brightly but not gaudily printed and caparisoned in first class style.　　Then there are the old fashion **English Rocking Horses** in various sizes, **Skin Push Horses, Pole Horses Bicycle Horses** etc. The **Donkeys** to push and rock will prove very popular with the youngsters. These are shapely of form and nicely harnessed, and covered with vicuna which gives them a natural appearance. The **Charterhouse Skin Gig Horse** is a strong and useful toy, made of the best materials, and with a chain handle to push. This can also be had fitted with large vicuna donkey in place of the skin horse, at the same price.'

Two illustrations accompanied the article, the first *Fig.TB01* is an illustration of a **Push Donkey**, as referred to above, and it should be noted that this illustration has 'C.E.T & Co' on it. This would suggest that the artwork was commissioned by the firm and would have been a reasonable depiction of the article. The same does not apply to the second illustration, *Fig.TB02* this is actually a G &J Lines drawing. It was used just to show the style of the 'Pegasus Rocking Horse' with American rockers, as per P Marqua's 1880 safety stand patent No.395.

From 1896 Trade Journal Fig.TB01

The illustration below *Fig.TB02* has 'C E T & Co' written just under the base of the stand, however the dark mark above it is covering the authors initials, these were 'G & J L.'. It was quite common at the turn of the 19th century for pictures to be repeated as they would

have originated from engraved printing blocks. These were not the cheapest or quickest items to produce which is why the same one would be used over and over. It would be used to indicate the 'style' of a product rather than to show an exact likeness.

From 1896 Trade Journal Fig.TB02

It is not known how long the firm produced its range of rocking horses, certainly the firm traded for many years and was confirmed in their advert Fig.TB03 of 1945. The 'limited' company remained on the register until 1982, after then it was removed.

In 1997, The Rocking Horse Workshop restored an unusual swing stand rocking horse that

had the remnants of a paper label, which had been painted over years before. After removing some of this paint, it was just possible to make out an illustration of a 'winged horse' in the centre and around the lower edge the letters 'PEGA___' *Fig.TB04*. This really could only be Pegasus. At this time only C E Turnbull had used the name 'Pegasus' in association with a swing-stand horse. The horse the label came from, which has been attributed to Turnbull, was of a good quality, although in a poor state, and had a couple of very distinctive features about the stand. The swinging iron arrangement *Fig.TB05* is made up of three components, a central bar with 'spigot' ends, onto which the two drop rods are fitted by means of the end of the rod being formed into an 'eyelet' . The ends of the spigot are in turn peened over so as to retain the drop irons. The lower end of the drop iron passes through the runner and is held in place by means of a washer and peened over. Looking at a general side view of the horse *Fig.TB06* another unusual feature, that of the half moon shaped pieces of timber that are fitted to either side of the top bar, behind the swinging iron drop rods. These may well have been to stop sideways movement which would have been inevitable due to the swinging iron arrangement. The posts of the stand are turned *Fig.TB07* and are of a large diameter and distinctive pattern.

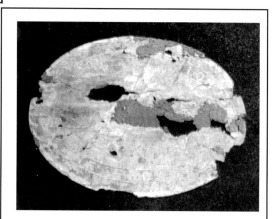

Remnants of Label   Fig.TB04

Fig.TB05 shows the unusual swing iron arrangement, the manufacture

Swinging Iron Detail   Fig.TB05

of which would have been awkward and very labour intensive to produce, with all the forming and peening over of the ends, to create a serviceable item.

Pegasus Rocking Horse attributed to C E Turnbull   Fig.TB06

Fig. TB08 is a detailed view of the head which shows that it was once fitted with glass eyes and was carved to a reasonable standard. In the text of 1896, it refers to two qualities of the 'Pegasus rocking horse' on offer but it is not known which of these would apply to the horse pictured here. Another example of this make of horse has been found, though smaller in size than the horse shown here It was also fitted with the same unusual swinging irons and half moon arrangement on the top bar and all other details were of a very similar nature, giving support to the notion that these features were standard items on a range of rocking horses.

Post Detail   Fig. TB07

However it should be observed that some of the early references to C E Turnbull are that of a wholesaler, and one trade listing from 1884 refers to the firm as 'fancy goods importers'. All of this does question if the firm were actual manufacturers or just suppliers of other firms products but the 1945 advert *Fig. TB03* does indeed state that they are manufacturers. Having received all of the evidence available it was decided that this rocking horse be 'attributed' to C E Turnbull.

In 1928, it was reported in the trade press that Mr E Turnbull, Governing Director, had sadly passed away at the age of 88.

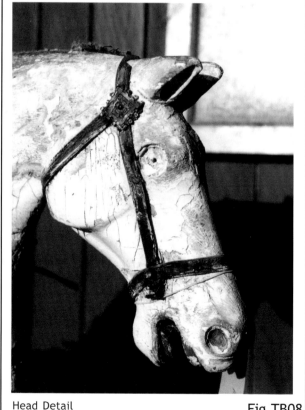

Head Detail   Fig. TB08

Tweed, H. C. & Co.   -1920 - 1925-

Address: Lexden, Colchester, Essex.

H C Tweed were manufactures of engines, barrows, scooters, trucks
and **Beech horses** that they produced in a wide variety of sizes, as can
be seen in their advert of 1923 *Fig.TD01*. No further reference for
Tweed's has been found after 1925 and it is not known how long they
continued trading for.

From 1923 Trade Advert   Fig.TD01

Usher, J & Co. Ltd.   1909 - 1918-

Address: 4, Back Guildford Street, Everton Road, Liverpool.

Patent: No.118,553   Accepted: Sept 5th 1918

 Very little is known of John Usher's company except for a Patent of
1918 and a small paragraph in a trade publication of 1917 which reads;

          'From Messrs. J. Usher & Co. we saw many fine horses.
They included **rocking horses, safety swing horses, tricycle horses,
pole horses** and one and all proved sound value for the money'

This description implies that Usher & Co were a reasonably sized firm
being able to produce a relatively wide range of products.
Unfortunately the only illustrations that are known to exist are those
which apply to Patent No. 118,553 *Fig.UR01*. This was a device which
allowed a wheeled toy/horse to be converted into a rocking toy/horse
by means of hinged longitudinal side members.

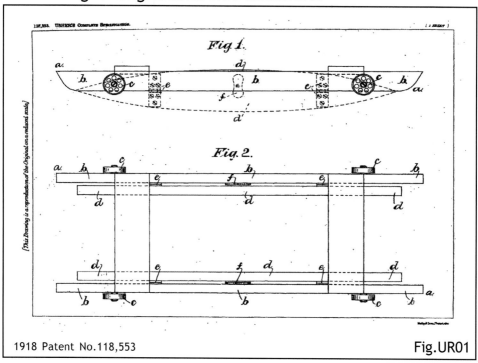

1918 Patent No.118,553   Fig.UR01

Victor Aviation & Toy Co.   - 1922 -

Address: Type Street, Old Ford, London. E.

Only one reference to **Rocking Horse** has been found for the Victor Aviation & Toy Co., this was in an advert from 1922 *Fig.VR01*.

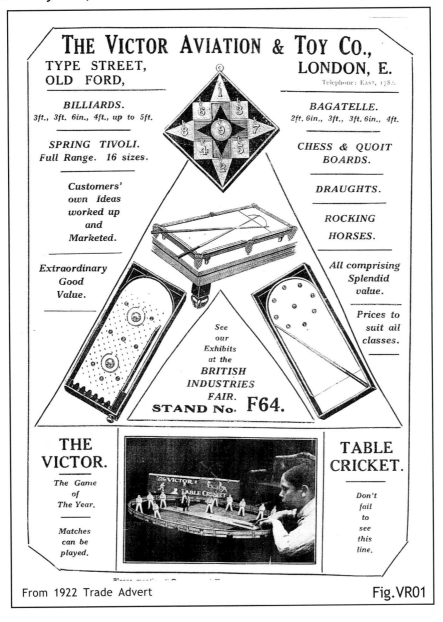

From 1922 Trade Advert   Fig.VR01

Wallington, G.

Address: 58, Bull Street, Birmingham.

The first mention for G Wallington describes him as 'perfumer and hair cutter' and 'toy merchants'. Further directory entries over the years always refer to him as a perfumer and hairdresser, but other listings include him as a 'manufacturer of writing desks, work boxes and dressing cases'. In 1852 an advert *Fig.WA01* makes a reference to **Rocking Horses** but it is not clear if he is a manufacturer or just an agent for either British or imported rocking horses.

NOAH'S ARK TOY WAREHOUSE.

Rocking Horses, Dolls,

G. WALLINGTON

Magic Lanthorns, &c.

G. WALLINGTON,
(Late of New Street,)
Perfumer, Hair Cutter, Hair Brush and Comb Manufacturer, and Importer of Toys and Fancy Articles, 58, Bull Street, 4 Doors from Snowhill, BIRMINGHAM.

G Wallinton 1852 Trade Advert   Fig.WA01

Wanklyn. H. A. 1895 - 1933

Address: 17, Manchester Avenue, Aldersgate Street, London. E.C.

Early trade directory listings for Herbert Alexander Wanklyn give him as a general merchant. Other listings over the years also give him as a perfume wholesaler, whip maker and Indian rubber eraser maker. In 1915 he is listed as a 'Government Contractor' and also the proprietor of the 'Velvey' company which manufactured Indian Rubber Sponges.

An advert from 1915 *Fig.WN01* illustrates **White Wood Horses** with special terms for quantities.

Wanklyn is believed to have been incorporated as late as 1930 but went into liquidation shortly afterwards in 1933.

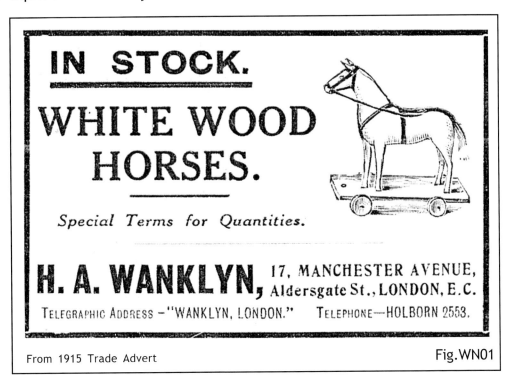

From 1915 Trade Advert   Fig.WN01

483

Welsh Toy Industries.   - 1919 -

Address: Crwys Bridge, Cardiff. Wales.

Brand Name: "We-To" Toys.

Proprietors: Messrs. W. Gibbons & Sons Ltd.

Welsh Toy Industries made a variety of toys that ranged from soft toys, like teddy bears, to china dolls and included a wide range of wooden toys. Some of these are shown in their 1919 advertisement *Fig.WT01*. Stating that the Firm had showrooms not only in London but also in five other major cities around the U.K., the firm had the capacity to supply bulk orders and deliver them with pre-war promptitude.

The firm announced that they had a special range of horses made from well seasoned timber, moulded and shaped from life, and excellently finished. They listed **Hobby Horses, Horses and Carts** and **Rocking Horses,** the latter was described as;

   'a combined toy, being a rocking horse and a push horse.It can be converted in a minute. The rockers, or "base," are screwed throughout, and made with well seasoned timber. The length of the rockers is thirty six inches, and the price of this excellent number is one hundred and sixty-eight shillings per dozen'.

This combination rocking horse is illustrated *Fig.WT01* along with two different models of **Pole Horse** and a **Horse and Cart**.

Despite the many showrooms and large workshop capacity, no further mention of the Welsh Toy Industries has been found after 1919.

Toys that create and hold new business.

"WE-TO" TOYS

THE BRAND THAT THE YOUNGSTERS LOVE.

You have only to show "WE-TO" Toys and their attractibility and excellent value commend ready appreciation.

We would like YOU to see "WE-TO" Toys and let them convince you of this fact.

They are made in a widely-varied range of models at all the popular prices.

Why not get into touch with us to-day and include some "WE-TO" numbers in your Autumn and Winter Samples?

"WE-TO" SPECIALITIES

DOLLS	SOFT TOYS	WOOD TOYS
A wide range of Composition and China Dolls, at all prices from the dozen	In TEDDY BEARS, ELEPHANTS, DOGS, etc., at all prices from the dozen	Soundly made in HORSES, FORTS, ENGINES, AEROPLANES, etc., at all prices from the dozen
15 9 *to* 250 -	18 - *to* 132 -	14 - *to* 1000 -

¶ We are in a position to take bulk orders for any of our numbers and deliver them with pre-war promptitude.

WELSH TOY INDUSTRIES,
CRWYS BRIDGE, CARDIFF.
Proprietors:
Messrs. W. Gibbon & Sons, Ltd.

LONDON SHOWROOMS: BUCHANAN BUILDINGS, 24 HOLBORN, E.C.1

OTHER SHOWROOMS:
LEEDS, 20, Kings Street.
LIVERPOOL, Eagle Stock Rooms, 6, Paradise Street.
MANCHESTER, 19, Marsden Square.
GLASGOW, 70, Brunswick Street.
BIRMINGHAM, 113, Gillet Road.

From 1919 Trade Advert

Fig.WT01

Wheatley, George & Jane. - 1883 -

Address: 104, Hyde Road, West Gorton, Manchester.

In 1883 there are two separate directory listings for George Wheatley and Jane Wheatley, both as **Rocking Horse Makers**, both at the same address. No previous or later reference to either of them has been found.

Whiley Bros.

1854 - 1948

Address: Jubilee Grove, Woodhouse Street, Leeds.

Trade Mark: Fanfare (1930's)

Incorporated: 23rd Aug 1933 Whiley Bros (Leeds) Ltd. No.273,320

The firm was established in 1854 by the father of the two brothers H.W. and J.T. Whiley and was gradually developed to the point of employing around forty people by 1915. Wooden toys, such as barrows, engines, mail carts, foot cycles etc. were the original products of the firm. Around 1907 they started to produce horse related toys and by 1915 their range included;
Swing-stand Rocking Horses in five sizes. **Combination horses** in three sizes. **Rocking Horses (Bow)** in four sizes. **Bicycle Horses** with glass eyes in three sizes. **Shaped Pull and Push Horses.** *Fig.WY02*
Horses & Carts and **Stool Horses,** both in a variety of sizes.

Fanfare Trade Mark Fig.WY01

From 1936 Trade Advert Fig.WY02

During the 1930's the firm adopted the trademark *'Fanfare' Fig.WY01*. From then on all products were marketed under this name. A Fanfare label was applied, as a transfer, to the firm's larger products but it was rather fragile and was often damaged or removed.

In 1915 the firm appeared to be quite busy , a view of the main toy making shop Fig.WY03 shows four workmen involved in producing shaped horses and numerous barrows.

Whiley Bros Toy Making Shop 1915   Fig.WY03

In 1935 the firm still proudly displayed a swing stand horse that it had made in 1909 as proof to the long lasting quality of their products. Also in 1935, one member of staff commented that he had completed 1,247 shaped horses within the last year. Two years later it was reported that their large swing stand rocking horse was made up of 35 blocks of wood and that they were made under the supervision of one member of staff who had been continually making them for forty years. 1938 saw the introduction of an unusual rocking horse that was finished in black, which Mr Milton, the managing director, said had been very successful. In 1936 '167 lines' were being offered, and by 1937 this had increased to nearly 200. Production of all lines increased in the run up to the War, and rocking horses were still being produced at this time. During the War toy manufacturers were prohibited from producing their standard range of toys and most firms changed over to help with the war effort. It would seem that Whiley Bros never really recovered from this and in 1948, after trading for 94 years, the firm was forced into bankruptcy by its creditors. Despite the long running production of rocking horses, no relevant illustrated catalogue or trade publication has been found.

However, a couple of Fanfare products have turned up. One is a small item that can be positively identified is a 'Fanfare' pull along horse *Fig.WY04* which has the makers applied label. This would date from around 1937 and would have been one of the smallest 'carved' horses they made. The horse is gessoed, painted dapple grey and is fitted with red leather cloth tack, and real hair mane and tail. The platform is made of timber, painted green, and fitted with red metal disc wheels. The Fanfare label is applied to the centre of the platform. For a small horse it is of good quality and has survived well.

Fanfare Pull Along Horse Circa 1937   Fig.WY04

The other product with a Fanfare label fitted to the base is a swing stand rocking horse *Fig.WY05* that is in an original condition, apart from the saddle being covered. The horse appears to be quite conventional in its construction with mortise and tenon leg joints. It does have a little extra carving to the neck and the head is generally well defined.

Whiley Bros Fanfare Swing Stand Rocking Horse circa 1935

The overall proportions of the horse could be described as 'chunky' or 'stocky', as opposed to other makers of very 'fine' horses. The horse is gessoed and has then been dappled in a traditional manner. It is fitted with glass eyes and has delicately painted eyelashes which can be seen clearly in the detailed picture of the head *Fig.WY06*. The strap work is leather but unfortunately the original saddle is obscured so it is unclear what form it takes.

The harness is decorated with two different types of fancy nail and the regular domed nails have been applied in 'groups', as can be seen on the martingale and the bridle. The remnants of the mane and tail

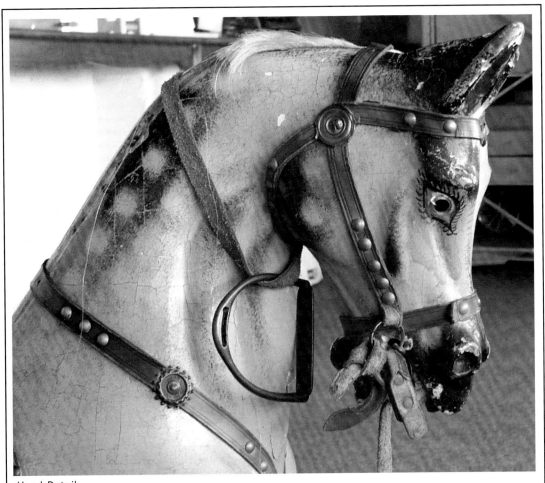

Head Detail
Whiley Bros Fanfare Swing Stand Rocking Horse circa 1935

Fig.WY06

appear to be real hair but it is unclear if this is cow or horse hair. The horse is not mounted on its stand *Fig.WY07* in any of the pictures, it was taken off while the rocking horse was being moved. The stand is of the regular design but does have an unusual and easily recognisable design of turned post *Fig.WY08*. The top bar also has a slightly unusual feature in that just the round ends have been chamfered. The base bar and cross pieces also have a small chamfer around the top edges. The runners are plain with rounded ends and the horse has notched hooves to stand on the runner. The bowler hats are of a decorative design *Fig.WY09* but it is not clear if they are original or later replacements.

The swinging irons and the brackets are painted a maroon colour. The brackets *Fig.WY10* are cast and of a three point fixing design that is not a known casting, so they are most likely to be unique to Whiley Bros.

Whiley Bros Fanfare Swing Stand circa 1935

Fig.WY07

Bowler Hat Detail

Fig.WY09

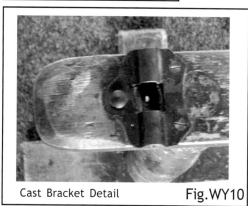

Cast Bracket Detail

Fig.WY10

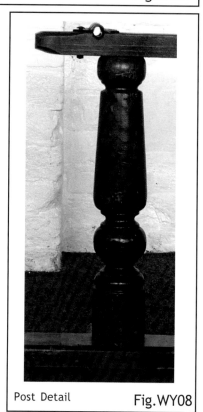

Post Detail

Fig.WY08

Wild, George Lewis. 1882 - 1927 -

Address: 1882   2, Devonshire Square, London. E.

               1891   13, Edmund Place, Aldersgate Street, London

               1910   12 - 14, Barbican, London. E.C.1.

The earliest known directory entry for (George) Lewis Wild is from 1882 in which he was listed under various headings, implying that he was an Agent rather than a manufacturer. Early listings included hardwaremen, clocks, fancy goods, china & glass, fancy stationery, foreign lamps, etc.

In 1910 he was listed under games and sports, *Lawn and parlour games a speciality* and in 1915 listed under Toymakers, *harmless pistols and rifles, water pistols, building blocks, puzzles games and novelties*. The advert from 1920 *Fig.WD01* shows that a variety of **Rocking Horses** were available, including wooden shaped horses. It is still unclear if these were actually made by Wild's or if he was purely an agent as he was when first listed in around 1882. Lewis Wild died in 1922 but the firm Lewis Wild Ltd. was still exhibiting in 1927.
By 1930 the firm had gone into voluntary liquidation.

FOR
ROCKING HORSES
(PLUSH)

PAINTED   WOOD   HORSES
(SHAPED)

PAPIER   MACHÉ   HORSES
AND

HORSES and CARTS
CALL AT
LEWIS   WILD
(George Lewis Wild)
12-14, BARBICAN, E.C.1

Lewis Wild 1920 Trade Advert   Fig. WD01

Wilkinson, C. & Co.   1824 - 1915 -

Address: 41 - 47, Portugal Street, Poland Street, Manchester.

The long established firm of C Wilkinson & Co. were based in the heart of Manchester and they produced a wide variety of large and small horse related items as well as other wooden toys. Some of their smaller principal items in 1915 were **Whitewood & Varnished Horses** (plain, shaped, stool or stepping), **Horses and Carts, Hay Carts, Sand Carts, Tip Carts and Horses**, priced from 4d upwards.

A product identity number system was used by the firm, some of them are known and have been listed below indicating the product.

No. 41, Wheelbarrow, London pattern. No.42 & 43, Manchester barrows.

No. 17, **Pull Shaped Horse** on wheels with draw pole.

No. 18, **Pull Shaped Horse** on wheels with connecting ring.

No. 20, **Perambulator Horse** in five sizes.

No. 23, **Perambulator Chair and Horse** in three varieties, with iron wheels, iron spider wheels and rubber wheels.

No. 24, **Rocking Horse** in seven sizes.

No. 25, **Safety swing horse**, in six sizes.

Tricycle horses, flatback or with shaped horse, were available in various sizes with either 12in., 14in., 16in., or 18in., wheels, either iron or rubber tyred.
In 1915 it was noted that Tricycle horses were still in strong demand despite the advent of the toy motor car that was being produced by many other rocking horse and toy manufactures.

Unfortunately no illustrations of a Wilkinson rocking horse have been found. One of the two pictures discovered shows a horse and tip cart *Fig.WK01* but this is thought to have been 'borrowed' from another source and does not depict one of Wilkinsons' own. The illustration has the name 'WHITLOW' on it, but no further information about Whitlow has been found.

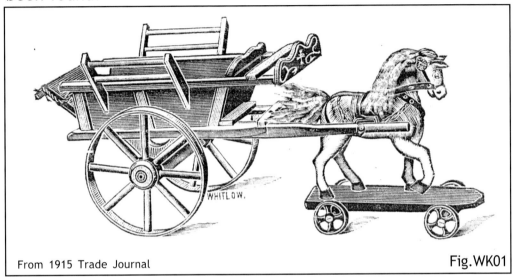

From 1915 Trade Journal   Fig.WK01

The other illustration is of a wheelbarrow *Fig WK02*, again it is not known if this an actual Wilkinson product. Wilkinson & Co. were obviously quite a large concern but despite this no other information has been found, and it is not known how long the company continued trading for after 1915.

From 1915 Trade Journal   Fig.WK02

Wilson, W. & Sons.   1877 - Present day.

Address: Silver Cross Works, Whitehouse Street, Leeds.

Trade Mark: "Silver Cross"

Mr William Wilson *Fig.WW01* started his business as a perambulator manufacturer at Hunslet, Leeds. He started working at the age of eight in a saw mill in Sunderland and later served his time in an engineering works. When he was 21 he moved to Leeds, working first as a perambulator spring smith, before starting his own business. With the help of Mrs Wilson the business rapidly grew and resulted in moving a couple of times to ever larger premises . In 1897 a new factory was built in Whitehouse Street but was destroyed by fire a year later. Undaunted by this disaster and without wasting any time, another larger factory was built on the same site and was known as the 'Silver Cross Works'. In 1913 Mr William Wilson died, but during his life time he had been one of the most prolific inventors in the pram trade and had been granted

over 30 patents. After his death, the business was carried on by his three sons, James W Wilson, W Irwin Wilson, and Alfred Wilson. In 1926 the business was incorporated and continued to expand. During the Second War much of the factory was requisitioned by the Air Ministry, with over 16,000,000 air-craft parts being produced, along with wartime baby carriages and rickshaws.

William Wilson Snr.   Fig.WW01

Undoubtedly the main production of the firm from the outset was that of perambulators, however many other items were produced over the years. These included wood toys, dolls prams, juvenile cycles, tricycles, pedal cars, engines and also **Push, Pole, Stool** and

Rocking Horses. It is not sure when rocking horses were first produced, but certainly in 1918 there were adverts offering 'shaped horses'. This was a common reference to a rocking horse. Confusingly, adverts from around this time used a 'G&J Lines Ltd' illustration of a swing stand rocking horse, but by 1921 this had been replaced with an illustration of Wilsons own rocking horse illustration *Fig.WW02*. As can be seen in the

Wilsons 1921 Trade Advert.

Fig.WW02

advert, the horse was adapted so as to possibly accommodate a disabled or very young child by means of the chair and harness arrangement. The horses were well made and of good appearance, with glass eyes, leather harness, and real hair manes and tails. The stands had turned posts and again were finished to a high standard.

The above advert is aimed at pointing out that the firm will be exhibiting at a forth coming trade fair. These were most important events for the manufacturers as a great deal of business was done with buyers from all the department stores from around the country. Another up and coming method of marketing, with the advent of motor vehicle, was the travelling showroom *Fig WW03*. By forwarding your address, the van could be 'in attendance' on the day you so wished.

LOOK OUT FOR THE SILVER CROSS VAN

The travelling showroom of Messrs. Wm. Wilson & Sons, Manufacturers and Patentees of The Silver Cross Strong Toys and Baby Carriages, Whitehouse Street, LEEDS, will be touring SCOTLAND during the month of AUGUST with a complete range of the latest and most up-to-date models of the celebrated Silver Cross Strong Toys, comprising Perambulators, Motor Cars, Rocking, Push and Pole Horses, etc. These toys are famous throughout the world for their fine finish.

It will also contain 9 models of the latest and most up-to-date models in Baby Carriages, including the famous WILSON-LITEX.

This affords a unique opportunity of the retailer inspecting the actual goods before purchasing, and the fine finish of these Toys and Baby Carriages will be brought clearly to view.

Our Scottish Representative, Mr. J. Lamberton, 49, Athenaeum, GLASGOW, will be in attendance with the van, and to ensure him calling upon you, would you forward to his address a P.C. stating the day on which you wish him to call, or write to our address ?

WM. WILSON & SONS, Manufacturers and Patentees,
Silver Cross Works, Whitehouse Street, LEEDS.

1921 Trade Advert   Fig. WW03

A ramp at the rear of the van may have been more appropriate than the rather steep steps. especially for wheeled items such as prams. It is thought that rocking horses were only produced for a relatively short period during the firm's long running existence. The last reference to rocking horses that has been found is from 1924, but a list of Silver Cross Toys on show at a trade fair in 1935 does mention amongst its exhibits, **'Horses and Carts'.** It would be unlikely that such a large item as a rocking horse would not have been mentioned if they were still available at this time. However, no further mention has been found despite the fact that 'Silver Cross' continued to advertise their prams on a regular basis in various trade publications. A wonderful period photograph *Fig.WW03* is of a Wilson Silver Cross rocking horse, this corresponds entirely to the horse illustrated in the 1921 advert *Fig WW02*.

The firm is still in existence today as Silver Cross(UK) Ltd. having gone through many changes, but its core business is still in the production of prams. But interestingly they also produces a range of 'plush' rocking horses.

A Wilson Silver Cross Rocking Horse Made Circa 1921   Fig. WW04

Attributed to Wilson, circa 1921   Fig.WW05

Not very many Wilson Silver Cross horses have turned up but the horse pictured above *Fig.WW05*, although in a rather poor condition, is attributed to Wilson. The similarities between this and the the horse in the 1921 illustration *Fig.WW02* are quite distinctive. The stands share many common elements, a short top bar and a long base, runners are the same with a narrowing between the swinging irons, and also the base and cross pieces are chamfered. The posts *Fig.WW06* are also distinctive. Note the horses hooves are notched to stand on the runners.

Post Detail   Fig.WW06

Wilson, J. & Co.   - 1919 -

Address: 88, Hackney Road, London. E.2.

Only one small advert in a trade publication has been found for J Wilson & Co. *Fig.WJ01.* From this it would appear that one of the main items produced by the firm was **Beech horses,** although other items were

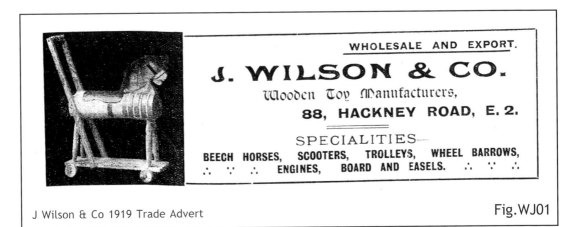

WHOLESALE AND EXPORT.

J. WILSON & CO.

Wooden Toy Manufacturers,

88, HACKNEY ROAD, E. 2.

SPECIALITIES—

BEECH HORSES, SCOOTERS, TROLLEYS, WHEEL BARROWS, ∴ ∵ ∴ ENGINES, BOARD AND EASELS. ∴ ∵ ∴

J Wilson & Co 1919 Trade Advert   Fig.WJ01

also manufactured. Some of these included scooters, trolleys, wheel barrows engines and board and easels. As with most manufactures, they were wholesalers and exporters as well. It is not known how long the firm continued trading for after 1919.

Woodrow, G & Co. Ltd.   1932 - 1963

Address: Works   638, High Road, Tottenham, London. N.17.
            Showroom   3, Aldermanbury Avenue, London. E.C.2.

Incorporated: 31st. March 1932.   Company No. 263,989

Trade Mark: "Swallow".

Association: G&J Lines Ltd.

Mr George Woodrow was for many years a director and secretary of the well known firm of 'G&J Lines Ltd.', London. On the death of Joseph Lines in December 1931. Mr Woodrow very quickly set up his own firm in a large and spacious factory, some 15,000 sq ft, where he manufactured a range of goods not dissimilar to that of his previous employ. It should be noted that he did not succeed G&J Lines Ltd., the trade names, good will and patents of G&J Lines Ltd. were secured by Lines Bros. Ltd., a point that Lines Bros Ltd were at pains to point out within the trade press.

However, practically all of the staff of Woodrow & Co. were ex-employees of G&J Lines Ltd. and the new firm was up and running in only a few months. The sales representative from Lines also joined Woodrow, so the new firm was able to secure orders without to much problem. From the outset, all of their goods were sold under the 'Swallow' trade mark *Fig.WR03* which became a well known and respected brand.

The range of 'Swallow' toys was very extensive and of good quality, amongst some of the items they produced were, barrows,engines, dolls' prams, motor cars, cranes, garden toys, desks, blackboard, cycles, scooters, pedal cars, and horses of every description, and not surprisingly a great number of Swallow products were very similar to those previously made by the old Lines firm.

Within the range of horses that they produced, were **Beech Horses**, **Horses and Carts** in many types and styles and also a range of swing-stand **Rocking Horses**. Figs.WR01 & WR02 show some items from 1935.

SWALLOW TOYS

A FEW SPECIALITIES FROM OUR TOY CATALOGUE.
WE CAN ONLY GUARANTEE DELIVERY OF ORDERS PLACED
AT ONCE.   CATALOGUE ON REQUEST, PER RETURN.

CARAVAN AND HORSE. No. 1825.

An appealing novelty completed by miniature cleaning set and
fitted with fireplace. The young owner will find many hours
of pleasure with this fascinating model. Measures 33 in.
overall.

THE DOBBIN. No. 1821.

A strong folding horse, well made and living up to
the "Swallow" reputation for finish. Mounted on
rubber-tyred disc wheels. Ironwork stove enamelled
blue and seat upholstered bright colour. Measures
12 in. high to seat. 21½ in. high to handle.

UNITED DAIRY CART. No. 1824.

All kiddies will find a special attraction in this
realistic model of the London Milk Van. Even the
grown-ups will be intrigued by the successful effort
to reproduce a miniature model at a reasonable
price. Measures 31 in. overall. Hand-carved horse.
Two crates of bottles. Extra crates can be supplied.
Van highly finished in correct colours.

BAKER'S BARROW. No. 1806.
(Measures 32 in. overall).

Our ever popular Baker's Barrow has been brought
right up-to-date by the inclusion of most realistic
Model Loaves (8) and Pastries (6), and a Baker's
Basket. The barrow is nicely painted in blue with
yellow and red lettering and lining. Two sliding
trays are fitted inside and a drawer beneath.
Mounted on large rubber-tyred wheels, painted in
bright red. Two Hovis loaves now included.

MANUFACTURED BY
Showrooms :—
3 ALDERMANBURY AVENUE
LONDON, E.C.2

Phone: MET. 6341/2
Works: TOT. 3405/6

G. WOODROW & CO. LTD.
SWALLOW WORKS, TOTTENHAM, N.17

Please mention "GAMES AND TOYS"

G Woodrow & Co Ltd 1935 Swallow Toys   Fig.WR01

G Woodrow & Co Ltd 1935 Swallow Toys

Fig WR02

The Mark of Quality

Swallow Trade Mark Fig.WR03

One simple type of rocking horse offered was the **'Prentice Rocker'** *Fig.WR04* below which dates from 1936. Despite being of a plain and therefore cheaper design, the pillars of the stand were turned. This was normally reserved for more 'up market' products. Over the years, many different types of the simpler swing stand rocking horse were produced. In November 1946 a patent application for a swing stand horse with a novel **Moving Head and Tail** action was submitted.

Swallow Toys 1936 Prentice Rocker   Fig.WR04

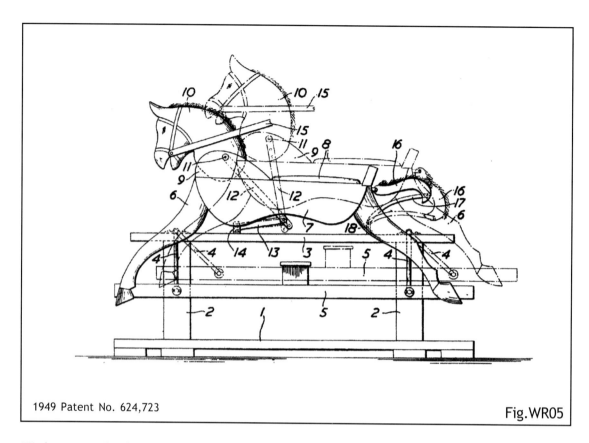

Fig.WR05

Eight months later a full patent, No.624,723, was granted. Above is the technical drawing *Fig.WR05* and below *Fig.WR06* is an actual horse.

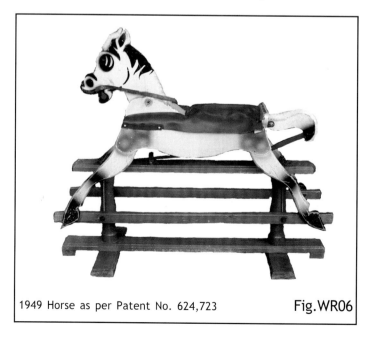

1949 Horse as per Patent No. 624,723

Fig.WR06

G Woodrow & Co Ltd also produced a range of traditional carved wooden horses *Fig.WR07*. They were sold under the Swallow brand and were listed as 'Model No.21' in their 1935 catalogue. They were available in three sizes and produced from around late 1932 up until around or just after the Second World War. After this time it appears that only the simpler styles of rocking horse were produced.

1936 Swallow Toys Advert No.21 Swing Stand Rocking Horse   Fig.WR07

The No.21 range of horses were well made, being of a standard yellow pine box body construction with tenoned beech legs. The carving was of a high standard, with good definition to the head and some 'extra' carving to the neck and legs. Extra pieces of wood were glued to the body of the horse on the front shoulders and rear quarters so as when the horse was carved it was a little more 'life like'.

Swallow Toys No.21 Swing stand horse, circa 1936   Fig.WR08

Horses were fitted with glass eyes and leather harness. Note the horse illustrated in Fig.WR07 has a detachable saddle and no saddle cloth. It was more time consuming to make a fixed saddle as opposed to a detachable one. Fig.WR08 is a 38" tall 'Swallow' No.21 that has been restored, the original coat of paint has been revealed and retouched. It now looks very much like it would have been when it was first made. Woodrow's use of 'No.21' to describe the swing stand range is directly from G&J Lines who used the same number to list their swing stand horses. This would make sense as most of the work force from the old Lines factory would be familiar with this and not be confused by using a different number or letter system. The stands were advertised as being made from Oregon pine, the name used for timber from the Douglas Fir tree and they were fitted with turned posts which are of a similar style to those of G&J Lines. The turned posts have a plain spigot fitting to the base bar and top bar and held tight in place with wedges.

The swing iron brackets are of the same design as Lines, those on the horse in Fig.WR08 having the G&J Lines Ltd castings *Fig.WR11* but this was not always the case, as other brackets have been found without any markings at all. It is unwise to identify any rocking horse by the brackets alone as these were often copied by subsequent makers. The brackets and swinging irons were often painted red on Swallow rocking horses. This is apparent from the picture *Fig.WR11*. The brackets have been painted over in black at a later

Mr G Woodrow   Fig.WR09

date *Fig.WR10*. They can be seen in position and just to the front of the bracket is a vestige of the 'Swallow' brand label, compare this to the trade mark in Fig WR03.

The founder, Mr Woodrow *Fig.WR09* sadly died in 1939 at the young age of 45. However, the company continued, changing its name in 1963 to 'Skylark Properties' and traded under this name until 1982.

Swallow label and Bracket   Fig.WR10

Underside of Bracket   Fig.WR11

Some of the wide range of 'Swallow' toys dating from 1935.

G Woodrow & Co Ltd
1935 Swallow Toys

Fig.WR12

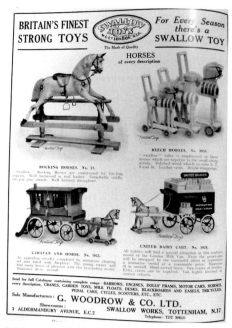

G Woodrow & Co Ltd
1935 Swallow Toys

Fig.WR13

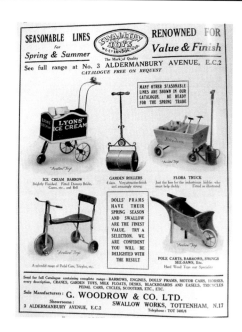

G Woodrow & Co Ltd
1935 Swallow Toys

Fig.WR14

G Woodrow & Co Ltd
1935 Swallow Toys

Fig.WR15

Woods, William & Son.   - 1903 - 1915 -

Address: 57, High Street, Maidstone, Kent.

A listing in a 1903 directory gives William Woods & Son as a 'toy dealer' and in 1904 they are listed as a 'fancy repository'.

A brief paragraph in a trade publication of 1915 describes the firms activities as;

'now engaged manufacturing toys for the trade of the district. The articles turned out include R.N. motor lorries, Red Cross and Royal Mail cars, **Rocking Horses**, engines, ski cycles, and armoured cars.

From this description it would appear that the firm of William Woods was of a reasonable size being able to produce a variety of toys. Also the fact that they had premises in a sought after commercial address on the High Street.

Despite this, no further records or information about William Woods & Son has been found.

Wychwood Toy Co. Ltd.   1915 - 1918

Address: Shipton-under-Wychwood, Oxford.

Incorporated: 1915   Company No.138,920

The Wychwood Toy Company was incorporated in 1915. They specialised in the production of **Beech Horses,** to the extent that it was reported in 1916 the company had ceased to produce any of their other lines, concentrating solely on beech horses *Fig.WB01*.

However it was only three years later, in 1918, that it was reported in the London Gazette that the company had gone into liquidation.

BEECH HORSES.

A line of which the trade have not been able to obtain enough has been beech horses, and it is gratifying to know that at least one firm specialises in these ever-wanted toys. The Wychwood Toy Co., Ltd., of Shipton-under-Wychwood, Oxford, have cut out all their other lines, and are now devoting the whole of their energy to the production of beech horses. This firm are making a point of keeping stocks to enable them to give prompt deliveries, and are offering free carriage terms on orders of £3 and upwards. By concentrating on this single line, the Wychwood Toy Co. should be in a position to quote exceptional prices for these goods.

From 1916 Trade Journal   Fig.WB01

Ye Olde Yorkshire Toy Co.   - 1916 -

Address: Farsley, Near Leeds, Yorkshire.

An article published in a trade magazine of 1916 states that Ye Olde Yorkshire Toy Co has taken over from a previous firm that had been in existence for a 'long time'. The new firm is now under the direction and management of a Mr John Gott, who it was reported had had 40 years experience in the business. The firm's premises *Fig.YT01* were of a modest size on the outskirts of Leeds in the village of Farsley.

From 1916 Trade Journal   Fig.YT01

Items produced seem to have been of the larger variety. Barrows made up a great deal of production, but engines were also produced. Fig.YT02 shows children 'helping to make toys' and also in the picture some of the previously mention items can be seen.

On the bench is a small horse that by its look, is designed to be fitted onto a platform to become either a **Pull or Push horse**. Also in the picture on the floor to the rear is a **Stool Horse**. Both of these horse based items were popular at this time and it is quite possible that the firm made other small horse based toys.

CHILDREN HELPING TO MAKE TOYS.

From 1916 Trade Journal   Fig.YT02

The use of child labour is quite unacceptable today, but in the early 20th century it was still common practice especially during the First World War with so many of the country's skilled men having gone off to the 'Front'.

No further mention of this provincial firm has been found and it is not known how long they continued trading after 1916.

Acknowledgments

I would like to express my most grateful thanks to all of the following, without whose assistance and help this publication would not have been possible. To Stuart Ayres for providing valuable information about the family and company history of F H Ayres. To Philip and Christopher Bashall for their time and information about Betty Bashall. John Raper for his help and information regarding Joseph Raper. Margaret Russell for sharing her family history of the Allen's. Ron & Gladys Narcott for sharing their fond memories of working at Crossley Brothers. To Peter Crossley for the information and the insight of his family's firm Crossley Brothers. To Esther Lutman and all the staff at the Bethnal Green Museum of Childhood. Brian Simpson for his help with research into the firms of W Sykes and F H Ayres. Tony Dew and Jane Cook for all of their help and advice and allowing me access to their collection of rocking horses. Fiona Miller for sharing her research of the firm of Lloyd & Co. Judith Hoyle for her guidance and assistance with my research. The staff of Pollock's Toy Museum for allowing me access to Marguerite Fawdry's archive. To the staff at Company House for all their ongoing assistance. To Debbie Walsh for allowing me to photograph her collection and her assistance with my research. To Jane Hooker, Jan Rusling, Patricia Mullins and Tony Jackson, all of whom have shared their observations and findings with me.

Photographic Acknowledgments

I would especially like to thank the following for supplying me with their own photographs and allowing me to publish them herein.
Dawn Cummings, Mervin Thompson, Sue Castle, Jane Hooker, Louis Spartin, Cynthia Noakes, Tony Dew.

Bibliography:-

Places:-

Bethnal Green Museum of Childhood	Cambridge Heath Road, London, E2 9PA
Birmingham Central Library	Chamberlain Square, Birmingham, B3 3HQ
British Library	96 Euston Road, London, NW1 2DB
British Library Newspapers	Colindale Avenue, London, NW9 5HE
Bromley Public Library	High Street, Bromley, Kent, BR1 1EX
Companies House	Crown Way, Cardiff, CF14 3UZ
Guildhall Library	Aldermanbury, London, EC2P 2EJ
Liverpool Central Library	William Brown Street, Liverpool, L3 8EW
London Metropolitan Archives	40 Northampton Road, London, EC1 0HB
National Archives	Kew, Richmond, Surrey, TW9 4DU
Nuneaton Public Library	Church Street, Nuneaton, CV11 4DR
Patent Office	Cardiff Road, Newport, South Wales, NP10 8QQ
Pollock's Toy Museum	1 Scala Street, London, W1
University of Reading	Redlands Road, Reading, Berkshire, RG1 5EX

Books:-

Bottemley, Ruth.	Rocking Horses.	Shire Publications	1994
Brown, Kenneth D.	The British Toy Business.	The Hambledon Press	1996
Fawdry, Marguerite.	International Survey of RH.Survey	New Cavendish Books	1992
Fawdry, Marguerite.	Rocking Horses	Pollock's Toy Theatres.	1986
Green & Dew	Restoring Rocking Horses	Guild of Master Craftsman Pub.	1992
Jones, Barbara.	The Unsophisticated Arts	Architectural Press	1951
Lines, Walter.	Looking Backwards & Looking Forwards		1958
Marsden & Stevenson	Rocking Horses	The Apple Press	1993
Mullins, Patricia.	The Rocking Horse	New Cavendish Books	1992
Simpson, Brian.	Winners in Action	JJG Publishing.	2005
Weedon & Ward.	Fairground Art	Abbeyville Press Inc.	1981

Bibliography:-

Trade Catalogues, Journals & Periodicals:-

Army & Navy (store catalogues)
Ayres FH (manufacturers catalogues)
Ayres Sports Goods (manufacturers catalogues)
Athletic Sports, Games and Toys.
Bashall (manufacturers catalogues)
British Toymaker
Childrens Pictorial
Crossley Brothers (manufacturers catalogues)
Edinburgh Gazette
Fancy Goods Journal and Toy Trade Review
Gamages (store catalogues)
Games and Toys
Games Gazette and Athletic, Toys and Fancy Goods Record
Hamleys (store catalogues)
Harrods (store catalogues)
Indoor Games and Amusements
Ironmonger Diary and Text Book
Lines Bros (manufacturers catalogues)
Lines, G&J (manufacturers catalogues)
London Gazette
Morning Chronicle (Meyhew)
Randall (manufacturers catalogues)
Simpson Fawcett (manufacturers catalogues)
Star Manufacturing Co. (manufacturers catalogues)
Sports, Games and Toy Trades Journal
Sports Trader
Strand Magazine
Times
Toy and Fancy Goods Trader
Toy Trader
Trade Directories